Applied Business Ethics

Custom Edition for Regis University

Dean A. Bredeson

Australia • Brazil • Japan • Korea • Mexico • Singapore • Spain • United Kingdom • United States

CENGAGE
Learning·

Applied Business Ethics: Custom Edition for Regis University

Dean A. Bredeson

Senior Project Development Manager:
 Linda deStefano

Market Development Manager:
 Heather Kramer

Senior Production/Manufacturing Manager:
 Donna M. Brown

Production Editorial Manager:
 Kim Fry

Sr. Rights Acquisition Account Manager:
 Todd Osborne

Applied Business Ethics: A Skills-Based Approach, 1st Edition
Dean A. Bredeson
© 2012 Cengage Learning. All rights reserved.

For product information and technology assistance, contact us at
Cengage Learning Customer & Sales Support, 1-800-354-9706

For permission to use material from this text or product,
submit all requests online at **cengage.com/permissions**
Further permissions questions can be emailed to
permissionrequest@cengage.com

This book contains select works from existing Cengage Learning resources and
was produced by Cengage Learning Custom Solutions for collegiate use. As such,
those adopting and/or contributing to this work are responsible for editorial
content accuracy, continuity and completeness.

Compilation © 2013 Cengage Learning

ISBN-13: 978-1-305-03130-2

ISBN-10: 1-305-03130-X

Cengage Learning
5191 Natorp Boulevard
Mason, Ohio 45040
USA
Cengage Learning is a leading provider of customized learning solutions with
office locations around the globe, including Singapore, the United Kingdom,
Australia, Mexico, Brazil, and Japan. Locate your local office at:
international.cengage.com/region.

Cengage Learning products are represented in Canada by Nelson Education, Ltd.
For your lifelong learning solutions, visit **www.cengage.com/custom.**
Visit our corporate website at **www.cengage.com.**

Printed in the United States of America

About the Author

Currently in his fifteenth year on the faculty at the University of Texas at Austin, **Dean Bredeson** specializes in business ethics, business law, and discrimination law. He has received several teaching awards, including the Lockheed Martin Excellence Award, which is awarded annually to the faculty member at the McCombs School with the highest student course evaluations. He is also among the youngest recipients of the Board of Regents Teaching Award, and he was UT's nominee for the Carnegie Foundation's United States Professor of the Year Award in 2010.

He has recently published *Student Guide to the Sarbanes-Oxley Act* with Robert Prentice, and he is the new co-author of *Business Law and the Legal Environment* by Jeffrey Beatty and Susan Samuelson. He earned his undergraduate degree from the McCombs School of Business and a J.D. from the School of Law at the University of Texas.

Dean Bredeson lives with his family in Austin.

Brief Contents

Contents

UNIT 2 Purpose of the Corporation

3   UNIT   Selling, Marketing, and Advertising

UNIT   Workplace Ethics: Treatment of Employees

U N I T   Responding to Employee Behavior

UNIT Workplace Privacy

UNIT 8   Special Obligations to Customers

UNIT Environmental Ethics

UNIT 10   International Ethics

U N I T 12 Government Actions and Corporate Influence

Preface

Introduction for Instructors

Greetings, and thank you for choosing my textbook. I welcome your feedback, questions, or comments at any time.

It has been a decade since my department chair asked me to design and teach an ethics course. I have a background in law, and I had been exclusively teaching business law courses. For several weeks, I was unsure how to proceed.

In the end, I decided to follow three ideas in designing my course. I have stuck to them for ten years now, and they have served me well.

Idea #1: Ethics dilemmas arise beyond the edges of legal requirements.

Businesses operate in a dense regulatory environment. Leaders must be familiar with any number of statutes, regulations, and common-law principles to avoid losing hard-won gains to lawsuits. The study of law, at least for business students, is centered on actions in which businesspeople either must or cannot engage if they are to avoid negative consequences for themselves and their companies.

If the question "What should I do?" has a clear legal answer, then the question is not within the realm of ethics. When a person complies with clear legal directives, his actions do not speak to whether he is an ethical decision maker.

Ethical dilemmas arise when the law neither requires nor prohibits any particular action. A person "behaves well" (or fails to behave well) when he or she is left to do what is right, and not what is required.

Idea #2: Every business course should teach students a skill.

I often overhear students talking among themselves about their classes. I'm not nosy, but when 90 percent of the people in the building are students, one can't avoid hearing various kinds of gossip.

When students complain about classes, the third most common complaint boils down to, "This professor is unreliable. He doesn't do what he says he'll do, and I have no idea how to get an A in his class." The second most common is, "She's a hard grader," or, "Her tests are impossible." But, by far, the most common complaint is, "This class is useless. We're not learning anything from this guy."

When they enroll in a course, business students expect to learn how to *do* something. In other classes, my students learn to analyze financial statements, position products, and keep their future companies out of legal trouble.

I have come to think of the skill I teach in my ethics class as this: the ability to comfortably make business decisions when a) neither action is legally required or prohibited, *and* b) it is not a win-win situation.

To elaborate on item "b," no one lies awake at night when she has benefitted all sides. If a company gives money to a worthy cause, and if customers then take favorable notice and the company's profits increase by triple the amount of the charitable donation, everyone is better off. Such opportunities certainly constitute ethical behavior, and they should be actively sought out.

But, often, managers, owners, and executives must resolve issues that pit stakeholders against each other. Should I give Ann a double raise to reward excellence and no raise to Bill, or should I split the raise pool more evenly? Should I lay off workers or operate in a way that will likely lead to a smaller return for the shareholders? Should I give the green light to an ad campaign that is not fraudulent or illegal but that might mislead some of our customers?

These are the kinds of decisions that arise regularly. Often, leaders must make decisions that may harm one group in order to benefit another, and they must be able to live with the consequences.

Idea #3: The key to sharpening this skill is participation in lively class discussions about dilemmas that businesspeople often encounter.

Ethics courses can't make someone who is intent on lying, cheating, and stealing through a career into a well-behaved person. But most people want to do the right thing. And, for them, having a context in which to process ethical issues will be useful. Opinions of peers help to create this context.

Diversity programs have worked quite nicely, and there are *lots* of points of view in any given section. Everyone has an ethical context from their family and inner circle of friends, but many people lack a natural tendency to seek out other points of view. Vigorous debate in diverse sections is, I believe, the best way to expose students to as many ideas as possible.

For ten years, I have generated ethics discussions largely through presenting hypothetical situations. I usually lecture on the law that surrounds an issue for a few minutes to identify the point at which a decision enters the realm of ethics. I then present a hypothetical situation that I hope will be "50–50" in the sense that about half the class will take one side, and half will take the other side. Too many textbook cases seem to me to have a clear "moral answer," and I find them unhelpful because they don't generate any debate.

If care is taken to raise issues that managers commonly face, and if classroom discussions are lively, students will take with them new tools in their toolbox. When they face the same issues as professionals, they will be better equipped to anticipate both the ways in which people are impacted by decisions and also the ways in which people will perceive the decisions that they make.

My students respond very favorably to this approach. Of the 200 or so full-time instructors at my business school, I have won the award for having the highest course evaluations in the college for two years running, and I have won every major teaching award for which I am eligible at least once. My students like my class, and they email me from the "real world" to tell me that it has been useful.

Introduction for Students

When I was a student 15 years ago, and I started a course, I wanted to know:
1. How can I get an A in this class? and,
2. How can I get something useful out of this class? or, occasionally,
3. How soon can I drop this class?

If you are interested, I'm going to spend the next couple of pages discussing these three items and this text and also making educated guesses about your professor. If you aren't interested, then by all means skip ahead to the first reading assignment you have.

1. How can I get an A in this class?

I, of course, have nothing to do with assigning your grade in any direct sense, but I can make a guess or two. This book is fundamentally different from every other ethics textbook on the market in that it contains fictional scenarios that are intended to spark lively classroom debate. I strongly suspect that your professor values participation in class discussions, because, otherwise, it is likely that you would have one of the many other business ethics textbooks in your hands right now.

In college and graduate school, I found some textbooks most useful as a way to reinforce lectures after they were given. For your ethics class, though, I would recommend reading each of the scenarios that you are assigned before class. You ought to take a few notes, perhaps, on the points of law in the background information that begins each module, but there is probably little need to take notes on the scenarios themselves, as it is difficult to write an exam over fiction.

After you've read through a scenario a time or two, spend some time going through the five questions at the end. Sketch out answers, even if you are not directly assigned to do so. The five questions are often the exact prompts I use in my classes at the University of Texas, and even if your instructor does not use all of them, I suspect that he or she will use many of them.

There will obviously be specific "keys to the game" that are different for each of you as you pursue an A, but if you are consistently prepared to engage in classroom debate, and to passionately state opinions that you've spent some time thinking about and applying to the scenarios, then you should be in a good position to impress the kind of professor who would adopt this book.

2. How can I get something useful out of this class?

I often overhear students talking among themselves about their classes. I'm not nosy, but when 90 percent of the people in the building are students, one can't avoid hearing various kinds of gossip.

When students complain about classes, the third most common complaint boils down to, "This professor is unreliable. He doesn't do what he says he'll do, and I have no idea how to get an A in his class." The second most common is, "She's a hard grader," or, "Her tests are impossible." But by far, the most common complaint is, "This class is useless. We're not learning anything."

You are a business student, and business students expect to learn how to *do* something. In other classes, my students learn to analyze financial statements, position products, and keep their future companies out of legal trouble.

I have come to think of the skill I teach in my ethics class as this: the ability to comfortably make business decisions when a) neither action is legally required or prohibited *and* b) it is not a win-win situation.

To elaborate on item "b," no one lies awake at night when she has benefitted all sides. If a company gives money to a worthy cause, and if customers then take favorable notice and the company's profits increase by triple the amount of the charitable donation, everyone is better off. Such opportunities certainly constitute ethical behavior, and they should be actively sought out.

But often, managers, owners, and executives must resolve issues that pit stakeholders against each other. Should I give Ann a double raise to reward excellence and no raise to Bill, or should I split the raise pool more evenly? Should I lay off workers or operate in a way that will likely lead to a smaller profit for the shareholders? Should I give the green light to an ad campaign that is not fraudulent or illegal but that might mislead some of our customers?

These are the kinds of decisions that arise regularly. Often, leaders must make decisions that may harm one group in order to benefit another, and then they must be able to live with the consequences.

The key to sharpening this skill is participation in animated class discussions about dilemmas that businesspeople often encounter. Ethics courses can't make someone who is intent on lying, cheating, and stealing through a career into a well-behaved person. But, most people want to do the right thing. And for them, having a context in which to process ethical issues will prove useful. Opinions of peers create a context.

There are *lots* of points of view in any given section. Everyone has an ethical context from family and an inner circle of friends, but many people lack a natural tendency to seek out other points of view. Vigorous debate in diverse sections is, I believe, the best way to expose students to as many ideas as possible.

I've taken care to raise issues in this book that are commonly faced by managers. If you work through them, and engage in lively, interesting discussions, you will have new tools to carry in your professional toolbox. When you face the same issues as a businessperson, you will be better equipped to anticipate both the ways in which people are impacted by decisions, and also the ways in which people will perceive the decisions that they make.

3. *Should I drop this class?*

I've won a lot of teaching awards at UT, but my way of teaching is not necessarily for everybody. Unlike any other textbook you've had in college outside of an English Lit. course, this one is roughly 60 percent fiction. Each of the 64 units has a factual and legal background, followed by a longer fictional scenario. I like using hypothetical scenarios because they can be fine-tuned to make specific points and generate debate.

If you have any doubts about whether you want to stay in the class or add another one, I suggest spending ten minutes flipping through the first module. Module 1 is typical of many of the lessons in the book. If it seems at least reasonably interesting, then you will likely enjoy the course. If it seems unbearable, then you might be in the wrong place, and no hard feelings.

This is a first edition, and it is difficult to overstate the amount of time it takes to write a new text from scratch. I have spent many nights here at my laptop wearing my Cardinals cap, which tends to begin the evening forward but generally gets turned around backward at some point. I hope you find it to be a useful book, and one that is relatively painless to read.

Comprehensive Learning Solutions

Instructor's Manual

Written by the author, the Instructor Manual contains the author's background and perspective on each Unit, associated issues to consider, Module Teaching Notes, Discussion Points for the Scenario Questions, and Suggested Writing Assignments.

Microsoft® PowerPoint™ Slides:

The PowerPoint™ slides are available to instructors to enhance their lectures and contain outlines of each module's background information and concepts and the module discussion questions for ease-of-use during class.

The Instructor Manual and PowerPoint™ lecture slides are available on the textbook companion site. To access them, go to **login.cengage.com**, create or sign in to your faculty account, and search for this text by ISBN, title, or author last name. Select this text from the available options and then select "Add only the Instructor and Student companion site resources" to add the resources to your Bookshelf. Access to the instructor assets is available under "Additional Resources," located on the "My Dashboard" page.

Additional resources available with adoption of any South-West Legal Studies in Business textbook include:

Business Law Digital Video Library

Featuring more than 60 video clips that spark class discussion and clarify core legal principles, the Business Law Digital Video Library is organized into four series: Legal Conflicts in Business (includes specific modern business and e-commerce scenarios); Ask the Instructor (presents straightforward explanations of concepts for student review); Drama of the Law (features classic business scenarios that spark classroom participation); and Law-Flix (contains clips from many popular films). Access for students is free when bundled with a new textbook or can be purchased separately at **www.cengagebrain.com**. For more information about the Digital Video Library, visit **www.cengage.com/blaw/dvl**.

Student Guide to the Sarbanes-Oxley Act (ISBN 0-324-82719-9)

Co-written by the author, this brief overview for undergraduate business students explains the Sarbanes-Oxley Act, describes its requirements, and shows how it potentially affects students in their business life. The guide is available as an optional package with the text.

Cengage Learning Custom Solutions

Whether you need print, digital, or hybrid course materials, Cengage Learning Custom Solutions can help you create your perfect learning solution. Draw from Cengage Learning's extensive library of texts and collections, add or create your own original work, and create customized media and technology to match your learning and course objectives. Our editorial team will work with you through each step, allowing you to concentrate on the most important thing—your students. Learn more about all our services at **www.cengage.com/custom.**

Cengage Learning's Global Economic Watch

Make the current global economic downturn a teachable moment with Cengage Learning's Global Economic Watch—a powerful online portal that brings these pivotal current events into the classroom. The watch includes:

- A content-rich blog of breaking news, expert analysis, and commentary—updated multiple times daily—plus links to many other blogs
- A powerful real-time database of hundreds of relevant and vetted journal, newspaper, and periodical articles, videos, and podcasts—updated four times every day
- A thorough overview and timeline of events leading up to the global economic crisis
- Discussion and testing content, PowerPoint® slides on key topics, sample syllabi, and other teaching resources
- Social Networking tools: Instructor and student forums encourage students

Visit **www.cengage.com/thewatch** for more information.

Acknowledgments

This book would not be possible without the invaluable feedback from instructors who reviewed early versions of the manuscript or who tested the content in their courses, including:

Vincent Agnello, Niagara University
Brian Bartel, Mid-State Technical College–Steven's Point
Randy Beck, University of Wisconsin
Barry Bennett, Marylhurst University
Carolyn Berrett, Mid-State Technical College–Wisconsin Rapids
Norman D. Bishara, University of Michigan
Andrea Boggio, Bryant University
Cynthia A. Brown, University of Central Florida
Joan E. Camara, Bryant University
Wade M. Chumney, Georgia Institute of Technology
Mark Clark, Collin College
Cheri A. Dragoo, Southeast Community College–Milford
Jim Edmonds, Freed-Hardeman University
Stewart W. Edwards, Northern Virginia Community College–Annandale
Brian Elzweig, Texas A&M University–Corpus Christi
Nancy Fallon, Albertus Magnus College
Rosemary Hartigan, University of Maryland
Dr. Linda C. Isenhour, Eastern Michigan University
Frederick D. Jones, Kennesaw State University
Johndavid Kerr, Harris-Stowe State University
Toni Knechtges, SPHR, Eastern Michigan University
Vonda Laughlin, Carson Newman College
Linda Pall, Washington State University–Pullman
Susanne Polley, SUNY–Cortland
Tony Quinn, Colby-Sawyer College
Lydia Segal, Suffolk University
Mark R. Solomon, Walsh College
Shane Spiller, Western Kentucky University
Marion R. Tuttle, New Jersey Institute of Technology
John Waltman, Eastern Michigan University
Lorrie Willey, Western Carolina University
LeVon Wilson, Georgia Southern University
Steven Zitnick, Augsburg College

My thanks also to Kendra Brown, Scott Dillon, Laura-Aurora Stopa, Kristen Meere, Michelle Kunkler, Nicole Parsons, and the entire Cengage team. It has been a pleasure working with everyone.

Special thanks to Vicky True-Baker, who bought the idea for an unconventional book in the first place, and to Robert Prentice and John Allison, colleagues at UT who gave wise counsel, as always.

Dean A. Bredeson

Challenge to Students

As the author of this textbook, I issue you this challenge: Keep this book and the comments you write in it, and refer back to it as your career unfolds.

The goal of this course is to provide you with tools that will be useful in thinking through the countless ethical dilemmas you will face while working in a typical business. Tremendous care has been given to present realistic scenarios that get at the real and difficult decisions that come up in actual companies. Whatever you do for a living, you will have to face many of these scenarios in your career.

That being the case, this book can be a valuable reference to have on your office bookshelf. It can serve as a reminder of what you once thought, and can, thereby, give you added confidence in navigating the dilemmas you will face. It can also help you to recall what your professor and peers had to say about business problems, and it can give you insight into how others perceive ethical dilemmas.

I have a 20-year-old course packet from a class I took as an undergraduate called "Leadership Issues." Its binding is weak and worn out, and its pages are yellowing, but I still review parts of it every semester. In the same way, I believe that this book will be a useful thing for you to have in the future.

Ethical Dilemmas

Unit Background

When, if ever, is lying acceptable? What is an ethical dilemma? How do people respond to ethical dilemmas? Many have weighed in on the factors that motivate decisions when tough choices are at hand. This unit presents some leading ideas.

Module 1

Intentional Misrepresentations: Are Some Lies Better than Others? [When is deception justified? Does it matter whether the deception violates the law? Are the outcomes generated by lies a relevant consideration?]

Module 2

Utilitarian vs. Deontological Ethics. [Do most people look out for themselves whenever possible, or do they tend to look out for others? Is an ethical action one that generates favorable outcomes, or is it one that is made for a "moral" reason in the first place?]

Module 3

Scope of Utility: Selecting Relevant Groups. [If a businessperson wishes to "maximize the good," should she focus on generating positive outcomes for her subordinates? Her entire company? Her society? The whole world?]

Module 4

Kant and "Unique Human Dignity". [Does utilitarianism miss the boat by focusing on results? Are there some situations that maximize the good that are nonetheless unacceptable because they exploit people or treat people as commodities?]

Module 5

Kant's Duty Ethics. [Is there a difference in quality when decisions that produce the same outcomes are made for different reasons? Is it preferable to act from a sense of obligation rather than from a simple desire to "do good"?]

Ethical Dilemmas

Many decisions in a career or in a life are driven by the fear of negative consequences. A person often thinks, at least subconsciously, "I can't do that because _____." The blank might be "it's against the law, and I'll get in trouble," or, "I'll get fired," or, "people won't like me," or any number of other things.

But what about situations in which a person has a free choice? What if someone can do one of two things (or one of many things), and none of the paths has any particular negative consequence attached to it? These are the true ethical dilemmas: when a person is left to do what he or she feels is right.

How do people behave in such situations? Are they egoists who pursue personal benefits whenever a free choice presents itself? Or are people more utilitarian? Do they try to maximize the benefits to groups of people with their decisions?

And whether a person tends to focus on himself or on a group of people, can he really be called "ethical" if he is constantly focused on the results his decisions are likely to generate? Do the ends justify the means? Can an ethical person lie if his deception will generate favorable results? Or do ethical decision makers take actions based on noble principles, regardless of the outcomes that are most probable?

These are questions that have been subjects of debate among ethicists for centuries, and they are the focus of this first unit in the text.

In this unit, we will look at deception. We will examine utilitarian thought and whether it presents a system of ethics that is preferable to other models. We will also examine some of the ideas of Immanuel Kant, who is on the all-time list of important thinkers in ethics. His ideas surrounding "unique human dignity" and "duty ethics" will be applied to various business situations. We will ask the question, "If a company does a good deed, does the motivation for doing the good deed matter?"

After completing this first unit, you will be equipped with basic analytical tools that will help you analyze many of the specific business issues in the remaining units.

Intentional Misrepresentations: Are Some Lies Better than Others?

The question presented in this module is simple: When, if ever, is lying *good*?

We are taught from an early age that we must tell the truth to our parents, teachers, and others. And, usually, honesty is clearly the best policy. The consequences of lying can be severe: Children are grounded, students are suspended, employees are fired, and witnesses are convicted of perjury. Sometimes the problems are more subtle but still significant: a loss of trust, a loss of opportunities.

But in some specific circumstances, intentional deception is tolerated and even admired. In sports, for example, athletes spend countless hours perfecting techniques designed to trick opponents. If Peyton Manning looks one way and throws the other, no one is upset, even though his intention is to deceive the defensive backs. Lionel Messi is short and slow by the standards of professional strikers, but he is among the greatest goal-scorers in soccer because he is better than anyone in the world at turning sharply in unexpected directions and leaving perplexed opponents behind.

In other settings, lying is equally acceptable. When poker players bluff their way through lousy hands, we call them "skilled." When people are asked, "How are you?" and always answer, "Great," even if they feel terrible, we call them "cheerful" and "easy to work with."

What about in business? Does the presence of *competition* make a difference? Can the ends ever justify the means if deception is necessary to generate good outcomes?

The first scenario in this module begins with what may be the greatest misdirection of the twentieth century, and the story requires some background.

D-Day Background

Everyone has at least a nodding acquaintance with D-Day. Every June 6, news stations show black-and-white footage of landing craft approaching the beaches of Normandy and interview aging veterans of the invasion. Countless movies reenact the landing, as does *Medal of Honor: Frontline*, perhaps the best-reviewed war-based video game of the last decade.

D-Day was, quite simply, the turning point of World War II. Until the 1944 invasion, the Nazis had imposed their will on much of Europe. After the Allies gained a foothold at Normandy, they efficiently drove the German army backward. Ten months after D-Day, Adolf Hitler committed suicide as the Allies closed in on Berlin. Eleven months after D-Day, the Nazis offered their unconditional surrender, and the war in Europe was effectively over.

What if the D-Day invasion had failed? What if the Allied forces had been killed, captured, or driven back, and the Allies had remained "bottled up" in England? World War II might well have gone differently. At the least, millions more would have died in battle and in concentration camps.

Fortunately, D-Day was an immense success. A large part of the success was due to the fact that the Nazis were fooled about where the invasion would take place.

Allied Deception

Every year, a handful of gifted swimmers seek to swim the English Channel. It is possible for a few super athletes to swim from England to France. At the closest, the two nations are separated by only about 20 miles of ocean.

In 1944, this short trip from Dover to Pas-de-Calais seemed a logical route for an invasion force. Hitler knew that Allied forces were massing in England, and he knew that an invasion would soon happen somewhere in France.

Hitler's mistake was in keeping 19 of his Panzer divisions in and around Pas-de-Calais. An enormous number of tanks were far from Normandy where the invasion actually took place, and thus were useless to the Nazis. But Hitler didn't simply blunder on his own. He was *led to believe* that the invasion would come at Pas-de-Calais by an elaborate hoax called Operation Fortitude.

SCENARIOS

Dover, England—February, 1944

The corporal opened the tent's flap. "The new man is here, Major."

Major Cole looked up from a stack of papers. "Excellent. Send him in, Corporal."

"Yes, sir." The corporal disappeared and was soon replaced by an officer.

The officer offered Major Cole a crisp salute. "Lieutenant Thatcher, 55th Infantry, Lancashire, reporting, sir."

"At ease, Lieutenant," Major Cole said, returning the salute. "Have a seat," he said, extending his hand to a folding chair.

"Thank you, sir."

Major Cole smiled. "I imagine you are full of questions, Lieutenant."

"Yes, sir. I, ah, was not briefed on the, ah ..."

"Nature of this operation?" Cole's grin widened.

"Correct. Sir. I was told only to bring my men here to rendezvous with the 58th Infantry and await further instructions."

Now Cole laughed out loud. "Hmm, yes (snort)—the 58th."

"Sir?"

Cole got his chuckling under control, but a gleam remained in his eye. "There's no such thing as the 58th, Lieutenant," he said.

"I, ah ... I'm not surprised, sir. After what I've seen around the camp so far."

"Yes. And I apologize for laughing—not very sporting of me. Everyone who comes here reacts the same way in the beginning. Shall I fill you in on Operation Fortitude?"

"Yes, sir. Please."

"You've probably seen the tanks."

"Yes, sir. Are they ... inflatable? Like ... giant children's toys?"

"Indeed, they are. We have about 500 blown up now, but some of your boys will be helping us inflate another 10,000 over the next few months."

"Ten thousand rubber tanks?"

"Just so. And you'll also be building thousands of artillery pieces from plywood."

"Plywood?"

"Yes. Life-sized and painted to look like the real thing. But the people we need most are your communication specialists. We're going to set up several radio tents around the perimeter of this base, and we're going to broadcast false orders around the clock. We'll encrypt them, but we'll be using an easy-to-break code. So, Lieutenant ... can you guess what we're up to here?"

"We're ..." Lieutenant Thatcher trailed off. Then his eyes sharpened and he said tentatively, "We're, ah, we're creating a fake invasion force ... to ... mask a real invasion force somewhere else?"

"Excellent, Lieutenant! Spot on!" Lieutenant Thatcher smiled at the praise. Major Cole continued. "Our orders are to make it look like 150,000 men are massing for an invasion. When German spy planes fly high overhead, we want them to see and report back on a growing number of barracks, tanks, artillery, landing vessels, and the like. And when they listen to the airwaves, we want them to get the amount of radio traffic you'd expect with a force of that size."

"Outstanding."

"Indeed. And word is that next month General Patton will be joining us on a regular basis for photo ops. He's been deemed the 'most recognizable allied commander.' So we'll be staging a lot of photos in front of a few of the real tanks and so forth that we'll have scattered around, so that the newspapers can run stories like, 'General Patton Inspects Troops at Dover,' that kind of thing. Meanwhile, Eisenhower will be gearing up for the real thing—'somewhere else', as you say."

"But that's brilliant."

"Just so. While the Nazis are cooling their heels and waiting for us at Calais, we'll land somewhere else. And once we have secure supply lines open, we can beat Adolf back to Berlin and bloody well go home. Be nice to get back to my wife."

"Yes, sir."

"And to get the football league going again. I bloody miss football. I'd give a week's pay to listen to an Arsenal match on the wireless. And a month's pay to see a game at Highbury. Who are you for, Lieutenant?"

"Blackburn, sir."

"Ah, the Rovers. Good club, that. Well, one day soon if we all do our jobs, then, what?"

"Yes, sir. One day soon."

Greentown, Illinois—Present Day

Harold finished his explanation to his brother. "There's just no other way to do it," he said, tapping a folder in front of him.

"You can't be serious," replied Harold's brother, Tom. "You're just going to walk in there."

"Yes."

"And hand off a file of fake documents? And walk out of there with a $100,000 loan you can't get without lying?"

"I am."

"You're nuts."

"Like I said, it's the only way."

"Harold," Tom paused and rubbed his eyes. "Man, you've done some dumb things in your life, but this is just ... what if you get caught?"

"I won't get caught. I'm only exaggerating the numbers a little, and I've never fudged a single thing in 20 years of banking with them. They won't look too closely."

"You're nuts."

"I won't miss payroll, Tom. I have 20 employees with families to support who are counting on me to make it work. I'm going to make it work."

"Harold ..."

"And it's not like the bank is going to lose its money. Orders are already picking up, and they'll come all the way back, just like they did in the last two recessions. I'll pay the bank every penny back—with interest—this time next year. Who gets hurt?"

"You get hurt if you're wrong about anything you just told me."

"I'm a big boy, Tom. It might go badly, but I don't think so. And besides, I'm willing to chance it."

"I wish you wouldn't."

"I know you do. But you've always worked for somebody else, Tom. You don't know what it's like to be on the other side, to have good people depending on you. It'll be fine, you'll see."

DISCUSSION QUESTIONS

1. Rate Harold's plan to lie to his bank to secure the $100,000 loan so that he is able to pay his employees.

Completely Wrongful ← → Completely Justified
1 --- 2 --- 3 --- 4 --- 5 --- 6 --- 7

2. Now assume that a year passes and that business does in fact pick up for Harold's company. He is able to repay the loan in full, with interest. No one is laid off from Harold's company, no one misses a paycheck, and Harold's lie is never caught. Is the rating the same with the benefit of hindsight? Do the ends at least partially justify the means?

Completely Wrongful ← → Completely Justified
1 --- 2 --- 3 --- 4 --- 5 --- 6 --- 7

3. What, specifically, makes Operation Fortitude a "better lie" than Harold's planned course of action?

_____

_____

_____

_____

4. Now speaking generally, when is making a misrepresentation acceptable? (Check all that apply.)

_____ To protect life or the physical safety of people

_____ To protect a job

_____ To protect another person's feelings

_____ To gain an advantage

_____ To get out of trouble

_____ When others expect it and may do the same (war, poker, football)

5. Rate the degree to which you believe different groups of people to be trustworthy. Fill in, as appropriate, "all," "most," "some," "few," or "none" in the blanks.

_____ of my closest family members and friends can be counted on to be truthful.

_____ of my peers can be counted on to be truthful.

_____ people in general can be counted on to be truthful.

Utilitarianism vs. Deontological Ethics

Questions of ethics arise when there is a choice to be made, and no law or specific negative consequence requires or prohibits any particular action. If a man chooses to file an honest tax return because he fears going to jail for cheating on his taxes, for example, he has not processed an ethical dilemma. True ethics problems can be framed as "how *should* I act," not "how *must* I act."

Philosophers have debated the nature of right and wrong throughout recorded history. Most ideas have faded from modern consciousness, but a few have held up well under the weight of passing centuries. This module will focus on two of these long-standing theories: utilitarian ethics and deontological ethics.

Every person makes countless choices every day. Most are done almost automatically and without a great deal of internal debate. And there is, of course, no reason to make one's life overly complicated—no reason to make easy decisions difficult.

But occasionally, everyone encounters tough calls. In making difficult decisions, it is sometimes helpful to have a framework for making a decision. Utilitarian ethics and deontological ethics each provide such frameworks. Neither is "better" than the other, but at least one of the two makes intuitive sense to most people.

Utilitarian Ethics

In 1863, Englishman John Stuart Mill wrote *Utilitarianism*. He was not the first to write on utilitarian ethics, but his book has best stood the test of time. To Mill, a correct decision was one that tended to maximize overall happiness and minimize overall pain. In cases of happiness of various types, he scored happiness of the mind higher than that of the body; he would have ranked a sense of achievement above a beer buzz. "Better to be a man dissatisfied than a pig satisfied," he wrote.

Many writers have added their own ideas to Mill's over the years. In the end, most utilitarian thinkers agree that one acts ethically if one's decisions tend to benefit the greatest possible number of people or harm the fewest possible number. Risk management and cost-benefit analyses are examples of utilitarian business practices.

The best Hollywood line that reflects utilitarian thinking comes from *Star Trek II: The Wrath of Khan*. Toward the end, Mr. Spock saves the *Enterprise* but in doing so takes a lethal dose of radiation. Captain Kirk cradles the dying Spock and says, "Spock! WHY?" Spock replies, "Because *(ug)* Captain, the needs of the many outweigh the needs of the few *(cough)* or one."

Oddly, the best movie line for the opposite view comes from *Star Trek III: The Search for Spock*. In that film, the crew of the *Enterprise* goes to extraordinary lengths to bring Spock back to life. When he regains consciousness, he asks Kirk, "Why?" Kirk replies, "Because sometimes the needs of the one outweigh the needs of the many." Trademark Captain Kirk cocky grin, and … end scene.

Critics of utilitarianism often argue that it is too mechanical, and that ethics cannot be a mathematical concept. They will cite the countless times in history that a minority group has been oppressed, and will ask, "Is discrimination ethical so long as the majority of people approve of such an arrangement?" Critics also sometimes argue that ethical decision making cannot be judged on the basis of results or outcomes.

Deontological Ethics

Many ethicists believe that utilitarians have it all wrong, and that it is incorrect to look at the results decisions produce when evaluating whether or not decisions are ethically made. These critics generally prefer deontological models, which focus on the reasons for which decisions are made in the first place. To a deontological thinker, the ends do not justify the means.

The best-known thinker who followed a deontological model was eighteenth-century German philosopher Immanuel Kant. Kant thought that human beings possessed a unique dignity, and that no decision that treated people as commodities could be considered just, even if the decision tended to maximize overall happiness, profit, or any other quantifiable thing. He also wrote that the highest justification for an action was to act out of a sense of duty or obligation.

Although not all followers of deontological ethics agree with Kant's specific ideas, most agree that utilitarianism is lacking, and that winning in the end does not automatically make right. Ethical decisions, deontologists argue, are those made for good and moral reasons in the first place, regardless of the outcome that they end up producing.

Read the following scenario and justify or condemn the actions of the characters using whatever combination of utilitarian and deontological thinking makes sense to you.

SCENARIOS

Ed the Entrepreneur

Ed the Entrepreneur buys a cheap piece of California land in the middle of the Mojave Desert. It is located a mile back from a major highway, and it is exactly between the two closest gas stations, which are 85 miles distant in either direction. In the summertime, average high temperatures are above 110 degrees.

Ed then builds a shack and paints it bright orange so that it is easily visible from the highway. He installs a phone, a large refrigerator, and the strongest air conditioner available. He adds a giant HDTV, a couch, and a PlayStation 3. Usually, weeks or months pass without anyone dropping in. From time to time, however, desperate people knock on his door. When they do, Ed offers to let them have a gallon of cold water, the use of his phone, and a chance to wait for their ride inside the air conditioning. His price is $50,000.

If his customers don't have the money handy, Ed makes them sign a contract promising to pay him later, out of future wages if necessary. If they refuse to pay or sign, Ed throws them out, locks the door, and goes back to playing PlayStation 3 inside after telling his surprised visitors to "say hello to the vultures." In the end, everyone signs the contract.

No one has ever walked away and met with harm in the heat. In his heart, Ed knows he would not allow someone to remain outside, even if they refused to sign his contract.

Ed makes a profit of about $300,000 per year.

Ignore the fact that a court would probably invalidate the contracts. Assume the contracts would stand up in court, and answer the relevant questions at the end of this module strictly from an ethical perspective. Remember to support your answer with at least one of the two theories introduced in this unit.

Alpha Company

Alpha Company has had a major breakthrough: They have developed a new drug that is an effective treatment for HIV. It is not a cure, but it appears to be able to postpone the onset of AIDS indefinitely.

Before this breakthrough, HIV-positive patients were treated with a "cocktail" of medications. Although effective, the combination of drugs required patients to take several pills at a time several times per day. Alpha Company's drug is a single pill that must be taken only twice per day.

Alpha spent tens of millions of dollars developing the drug, but now that it has been developed, each pill only costs a few dollars to manufacture. Alpha charges $4,150 for a 30-day supply, or about $50,000 per year. The pills are generally not covered by insurance plans. The older "cocktail" of drugs is still available from other drug companies and is about half the cost of Alpha's drug. In addition, the company does have a program that makes its drug available at no cost in extreme circumstances, and about 1 percent of the people taking the drug receive it directly from Alpha at no charge.

Alpha has several successful drugs, and had earnings of nearly three billion dollars last year.

Some activists have called on Alpha to do the following:

- Reduce the price of its drugs for all patients to $35,000. This would be a premium of $10,000 above the cost of the older treatment.
- Expand its free drug program to cover 10 percent of the drug's current users.

DISCUSSION QUESTIONS

1. Overall, is Ed's operation ethically justifiable as it is currently run? Why or why not?

_____

_____

_____

_____

2. Everyone would presumably be in favor of a convenience store at Ed's location that charged $5 for water and let customers use a phone and rest inside for free. Let's change the price points for Ed's services. Following is a string of prices that increase each time by an order of magnitude. Label each as "acceptable" or "excessive," and be prepared to defend the point at which you think Ed would be charging too much (or why you find his services fair at any price).

   $50 _____

   $500 _____

   $5,000 _____

   $50,000 _____

   $500,000 _____

   $5,000,000 _____

3. In the second scenario, should Alpha meet the first demand and reduce its prices across the board? Why or why not, using the ideas raised in the background section?

   _____

   _____

   _____

   _____

4. Should Alpha meet the second demand and expand its free drug program?

   _____

   _____

   _____

   _____

5. Directly compare Alpha's practices to Ed's desert shack business in the first scenario. Are they reasonably equivalent, or is one more ethically justifiable than the other?

   _____

   _____

   _____

   _____

Scope of Utility: Selecting Relevant Groups

BACKGROUND

Jeremy Bentham, John Stuart Mill, and many other thinkers have weighed in on utilitarianism. Broadly stated, it is the principle that actions are moral if they have the tendency to create "the greatest good for the greatest number."

Utilitarianism is, in some ways, an almost mathematical approach to ethics. Consider this classic example. If you have two extra candy bars and two friends, and if you decide to share the candy bars, you might be naturally inclined to give one to each friend. But what if one of your friends likes candy bars and the other does not? The transaction might look something like this:

Friend 1: (1 candy bar) x (1 unit of happiness per candy bar) = 1 unit of happiness produced

Friend 2: (1 candy bar) x (0 unit of happiness per candy bar) = 0 units of happiness produced

Overall happiness generated by the gifts = 1 unit of happiness

A utilitarian might suggest giving both candy bars to the friend who likes them. The transaction might then look like this:

Friend 1: (2 candy bars) x (1 unit of happiness per candy bar) = 2 units of happiness produced

Friend 2: (0 candy bars) x (0 unit of happiness per candy bar) = 0 units of happiness produced

Overall happiness generated by the gifts = 2 unit of happiness

The idea is straightforward. A decision is "right" if it generates more happiness, money, or opportunity than its alternative.

Criticisms

The critics of utilitarian thought are many. Some argue that it is simply not possible to "measure" ethics in the way that one would measure distance or the passage of time. Others say that utilitarians simply let the ends justify the means, and they allow for bad behavior as long as the bad behavior generates good in the end. A third group argues that utilitarian and other hedonistic philosophies err in equating pleasure with ethical behavior, and pain with wrongful behavior. Caring for an elderly relative with Alzheimer's disease, for example, might generate little pleasure and much pain, but it is still a worthwhile and good endeavor.

Other modules in this series examine deontological ethics theories. These theories focus on the reasons for which decisions are made, not on the results that are ultimately generated. But we will return to and remain focused on utilitarian thought for the remainder of this module.

Key Issues

One interesting question is: *Do many people, and perhaps most people, make a quick utilitarian calculation when they have decisions to make?* Is it natural for people to seek to compare anticipated results from different actions, and to make choices to create the greatest perceived benefit? Some argue that, whatever its faults, the principle of utility is a practical tool for making difficult decisions that human beings are "programmed" to use.

A second interesting question is: *To whatever extent people make utilitarian calculations,* should *they do so?* Is it right to make ethics decisions based on perceived outcomes, or must a moral person make choices for more "pure" reasons?

And perhaps the most interesting question of all is: *When people make utilitarian calculations, what kinds of people do they tend to consider?* Who is relevant? Who makes it into the equation? If someone is trying to "maximize the good," for whom is she trying to maximize the good? Everyone in the world? Everyone in her nation? Perhaps everyone in her company, division, or working group. Maybe only the people in her family. Or maybe she is actually an egoist, only seeking to benefit herself. What kinds of people does a typical decision maker hope to help?

The following scenarios present several dilemmas that explore these questions.

SCENARIOS

At the University

"So it turns out I'm eligible to retire at the end of next year," said Professor Harrison.

"You're kidding," his colleague said, expressing genuine surprise.

"No."

"How old are you? Fifty?"

"Fifty-one, actually. I always graduated early—high school, college, graduate school. I started young. And next year, I'll have enough credits to get the pension."

"Wow. But, I mean, you're not really going to do it, are you?"

"I haven't decided yet. I might."

"What about your students? You're the most popular teacher around here. And your research is influential. You aren't going to just walk away, are you?"

Harrison smiled. "Not sure yet. It would be nice to be home more. My family has made a lot of sacrifices because of the hours I've put in. It might be good to start paying them back."

"I can't imagine this department without you."

"Well, like I said, I haven't decided anything yet."

After exchanging a few more niceties, Harrison's colleague returned to his own office.

Decision 1: Should Harrison retire next year at age 52?

Good for: Harrison and his family

Bad for: Harrison's future students and his university. Perhaps for society

Harrison turned his attention to the spreadsheet on his screen. Because of his seniority in the college, he had the first crack at reserving time slots and classrooms for courses his department offered. He looked at the blanks that filled his screen and thought of his colleagues. Like almost everyone, the faculty members in his department preferred to teach between 11:00 and 2:00.

Harrison considered reserving every classroom in the building from 11:00 to 2:00 for his department's use. He had the power to reserve whatever time slots he wished, and the action would certainly make his closest colleagues happy. But it would make professors in the college's other three departments irritated at having to teach early-morning or late-afternoon classes.

Decision 2: Should Harrison grab all or most of the preferred time slots for use by his own department?

Good for: Faculty in his department

Bad for: Faculty in other departments

Harrison's last task of the morning was to decide on what kind of paper to order for his department for the coming year. Last year, he switched his department to 100 percent recycled paper. Several of his colleagues have complained that the recycled paper "feels cheap" and jams the copiers more often than the old brand. There is no significant price difference between the recycled paper and the type that was used before.

Decision 3: Should Harrison order the recycled paper?

Good for: The environment

Bad for: Some of Harrison's colleagues

At a Car Company

CEO Bridget Allen sat at the monthly meeting and listened as her division chiefs made proposals.

"So, anyway, Ms. Allen, the Kaflor technology really is a big deal. We estimate that it could *prevent* 3 percent of the total annual fatalities in car accidents. It's that much better. Drivers and passengers can take a much harder hit and survive because of the way the Kaflor is designed. We're working past the prototype stage now, and it should be ready for the production line in 12–18 months."

"That's terrific," Bridget answered. "Have we patented it yet?"

"Ah, not yet. The team actually wanted for me to ask if you ... thought we should consider making this design available to everyone."

"As in, not seek a patent?"

"Yes. Some on the team feel like this technology is too important for us to lock up for ourselves for the next 20 years. If we really can reduce fatality accidents by 3 percent, that's about 1,200 American lives a year that could be saved, *if* everybody uses the technology. But if the Kaflor is only on our vehicles, then maybe only 200 people a year can be saved."

"Yes, but we could patent the Kaflor and let others use the technology if they pay us licensing fees."

"That's true. But some of our competitors won't do it. But I'm just presenting the idea. Volvo didn't patent the first seat belt. Some of the designers want us to think about doing the same thing. Others disagree. We invented the Kaflor, after all. Maybe we *should* own it. It would certainly be a selling point."

Decision 4: Should Allen patent the Kaflor seatbelt and not give the technology away?

Good for: Her shareholders

Bad for: Drivers of vehicles made by other car companies

Later in the meeting, Bridget's CFO gave a lengthy presentation on one of the company's several manufacturing plants.

"So the reality of it is, the Ohio plant shows no signs of getting any closer to profitability, and we do not expect any new developments," the CFO said. "We're not losing a ton of money by keeping it open, but we're losing some now, and we expect to lose more going forward. It is my recommendation that the plant be closed and that some production activities be transferred to other facilities."

"And how many jobs are at that plant?" Bridget asked.

"Twelve hundred full-time, another 300 or so part-time."

"I see."

Decision 5: Should the CEO close the Ohio plant?

Good for: The company's shareholders

Bad for: Fifteen hundred total workers who will be laid off, the community in which the factory operates

Toward the end of the meeting, the CEO listened to another lengthy presentation on proposed vehicle prices for the upcoming model year.

"And so, while some of our models should retain the same price, we believe that an increase of 5 percent on our premium sedans, sports cars, and larger SUVs would not hurt market share. We are recommending the 5 percent increase on those models."

"It's a recession. People won't like it," Bridget said.

"Maybe. But cost-conscious customers can still buy many of our models at the same price as last year. They have options. The customers in the market for our more expensive vehicles can afford the increase, and we can still be competitive with other brands with the higher prices—we'll just go from being substantially less expensive than our competitors to being about the same price."

Decision 6: Should Allen approve raising the prices on some models by 5%?

Good for: The company's shareholders

Bad for: Consumers

DISCUSSION QUESTIONS

1. What would you do in the three university examples (Decisions 1 through 3)? Why?

   Decision 1: _____

   Decision 2: _____

   Decision 3: _____

2. What would you expect an average person to do in the three university examples? Why?

   Decision 1: _____

   Decision 2: _____

   Decision 3: _____

3. What would you do in the three car company examples (Decisions 4 through 6)? Why?

   Decision 4: _____

   Decision 5: _____

   Decision 6: _____

4. What would you expect an average person to do in the three car company examples? Why?

   Decision 4: _____

   Decision 5: _____

   Decision 6: _____

5. Thinking generally now, which of the following groups do you seek to benefit when you make decisions? Which of them do you think average people regularly take into account? Circle as appropriate below.

Group	Yourself	Average People
Family and close friends	Yes // No	Yes // No
Close coworkers	Yes // No	Yes // No
Everyone in a company	Yes // No	Yes // No
Everyone in a community	Yes // No	Yes // No
Society in general	Yes // No	Yes // No
The environment	Yes // No	Yes // No

_____

_____

_____

_____

Kant and "Unique Human Dignity"

Eighteenth-century German philosopher Immanuel Kant certainly left his mark. His many contributions have helped to frame legal and ethical debates for more than two hundred years.

The fundamental question in ethics is, "How should I behave?" Kant presented an alternative way to think through this question. He argued that the answer lay in following *categorical imperatives*. He believed that, with proper thought, universal rules of conduct could be divined. This module will focus on one such idea: unique human dignity.

The cornerstone of Kantian (or deontological) ethics is that decisions are only morally correct if they are made for the right reasons.

Many thinkers disagree and subscribe to a *consequentialist* model instead. Consequentialists weigh the results of decisions, or the consequences that they will have. Many consequentialists are *utilitarians*, who focus on doing the greatest good for the greatest number of people. To them, a decision that causes more good than harm may be deemed morally correct, even if it was not made for "pure" reasons in the first place.

Categorical Imperative: Unique Human Dignity

Kant believed that there was an essential worth in all human beings based on their ability to create and follow a system of ethics. He believed that all people were special, especially when compared with animals. Kant believed that others must respect the unique dignity possessed by all people, and that it should be an absolute moral rule that people not be exploited or treated as a means to an end.

Consider the CEO of a clothing company who is thinking of opening a new plant in Indonesia. Workers in Indonesia who make clothing for the American market earn an average of $0.26 per hour. Those who earn below the average are considered "subsistence workers," which means that they can afford to buy enough white rice and other basic food items to maintain body weight, but very little else. The proposal before the CEO outlines opening a plant and paying workers $0.20 per hour. It indicates that the company would find no shortage of workers willing to work for that wage.

If the CEO follows Kantian thinking, he might decide, "We can't do it. We have to either pay these people more than subsistence wages or, if that would make us unprofitable, we shouldn't operate in Indonesia at all. We can't treat them as a means to an end, and we can't exploit them."

But if the CEO takes a more utilitarian approach, he might reason, "On balance, this new plant would create more good than harm. Our shareholders will make more money, and our customers will enjoy lower prices if I can reduce our labor costs. And, the jobs may not pay much, but at least I would be creating jobs in an area that needs them. Earning $0.20 per hour is better than earning nothing."

In the end, utilitarians focus on the impact that decisions are likely to have, and Kantian thinkers focus on the reasons for which decisions are made in the first place.

Criticisms

Many critics argue that Kant has created an ethical system of absolutes that cannot be applied in real-world situations. For example, a follower of Kant's ideas might well determine that he has a categorical imperative to always tell the truth. But what if he has a lighter in his pocket and a stranger says to him, "Hey, I want to burn that duplex down. Do you have a light?" Is it then morally acceptable to say, "No, I don't"? If his girlfriend buys a pair of "mom jeans," tries them on, and asks, "How do they look?" is he ethically required to say, "They look awful ... but I ... still love you anyway"?

Critics of consequential thinking argue that it is a backward approach to ethics, and that a person should not be considered to have acted correctly merely because things turned out well.

Do the ends always justify the means? In the following scenarios, various people engage in ventures that seem to have a "net gain" in the sense that the good outweighs the harm. But are there some things so exploitative, so blind to Kant's idea of unique dignity, that they just shouldn't be done?

SCENARIOS

Leslie

Leslie is a kindergarten teacher. In 2007, she joined the bone marrow registry. In 2011, she received a call from a doctor in Florida who told her that she was a match for one of his patients, who was in desperate need of a marrow transplant. Leslie never thought she would get such a call, and in the end, she decided to not go through with the donation.

A week later, Leslie got another call. Although it broke hospital rules, the patient in need of Leslie's bone marrow was able to bribe a desk clerk and get Leslie's contact information. The key part of the conversation went like this:

"Listen, Leslie, I know you're afraid of side effects, but there really aren't any. I have to have a marrow transplant, and I'm in a position to make it very worth your while," the patient said.

"I was told that I can't be paid for the donation," Leslie answered.

"In the United States, maybe, but we can fly somewhere without those kinds of restrictions."

"Look, I just don't want to do it."

"I'll pay you a million dollars."

"You're kidding."

"Not at all. I've made a fortune in business, and I can afford to part with a million dollars. I don't need money, I need bone marrow. Specifically, I need yours. What do you say?"

If Leslie changes her mind and agrees to the plan, a utilitarian might argue: "Everybody wins here. The wealthy patient is better off, because she has a new chance to live. Leslie is better off, because in exchange for undergoing a fairly minor surgical procedure with an extremely low risk of side effects, she gets a million dollars, which might amount to 25 years' salary for a schoolteacher. The positives outweigh the negatives, and this is an entirely reasonable transaction."

Lou

Lou owns and operates a strip club. He hires young women to dance nude, and most of them earn exceptional wages. Lou was recently asked how he sleeps at night, and he answered (in a utilitarian fashion), "Look, it's a legal business. And, besides, I take good care of my dancers—anybody who touches them gets roughed up by my bouncers and kicked out. They're safe here. And they make a ton of money, much more than they could make anywhere else. A lot of my girls make over $100,000 per year. And they're all adults. I never, ever hire anyone under 18. It's just good clean fun! Why wouldn't I sleep well at night?

"You see that nice respectable hotel across the street? You know what they pay their maids? Eight dollars an hour. You know what kind of filth they have to clean up sometimes? For $8 an hour? Now who's exploiting workers?"

Glen

Glen goes to a homeless camp on the outskirts of town every morning. He fills up the bed of his truck with a dozen homeless people and drops them off at 12 busy intersections around the city. He gives each of them a cardboard sign that he has prepared at home. The signs have messages like "Lost my Job" and "HELP—HUNGRY—ANYTHING HELPS." At the end of the day, he picks everyone up and returns them to the homeless camp, and he demands 50 percent of the money that they have earned panhandling throughout the day. If he suspects anyone of shorting him, he never allows them back on his truck.

One day, one of the homeless men complains that he is being exploited. Glen replies, "HEY! No one is forcing you to get on my truck. If it wasn't for me, you wouldn't have made a penny today. If you don't like me taking my cut, don't come back tomorrow. You think I like coming down here every day? You think you're entitled for a ride for nothing? I'm helping you, I'm getting paid for it, and we're both better off. That's the American way."

A strict utilitarian might argue: "Where's the harm? The people who give money to the panhandlers feel good about helping people in need. The homeless people get to keep half of the money and are better off. And Glen gets a cut for setting everything up. More good than harm is done all around."

DISCUSSION QUESTIONS

1. Do you agree with Kant's fundamental proposition that human beings are all in possession of a unique dignity? Does a person automatically act unethically if he violates another person's dignity?

_____

_____

_____

_____

2. What do you think of Kant's idea of the categorical imperative? Is it possible to arrive at universal principles or rules that always apply to every situation? Or, in the real world, are absolute rules with no exceptions unrealistic?

_____

_____

_____

_____

3. Rate the characters in the four hypothetical scenarios on the following scale:

	Wrongfully Exploited Others ←	→ Did Nothing Wrong
Leslie (bone marrow donor)	1 --- 2 --- 3 --- 4 --- 5 --- 6 --- 7	
Lou (club owner)	1 --- 2 --- 3 --- 4 --- 5 --- 6 --- 7	
Glen (panhandling profiteer)	1 --- 2 --- 3 --- 4 --- 5 --- 6 --- 7	

4. Consider the CEO in the background information example who is considering creating subsistence-level jobs. Do American corporations have a moral duty to pay reasonable "living wages" to workers outside the United States? In the United States, we have a legally required minimum wage of $7.25 per hour. Do corporations have a duty to pay "living wages" above the minimum wage to employees inside the United States?

_____

_____

_____

_____

5. Do you find yourself making decisions more often based on whether they seem like the right thing to do, or because they will be likely to produce the best results? What percentage of the time do you make decisions for each reason?

_____

_____

_____

_____

Kant's Duty Ethics

BACKGROUND

Let's recap a few points from the previous module. Philosopher Immanuel Kant (1724–1804) has greatly influenced ethical debates for more than two hundred years. The fundamental question in ethics is, "How should I behave?" Kant posited that decisions are only morally correct if they are made for the right reasons. Many "consequentialist" thinkers disagree; they believe that the results of decisions, or the consequences that they will have, are critical in assessing whether decisions are properly made.

The previous module examined Kant's idea of unique human dignity. This module looks at his notion of duty ethics.

Duty Ethics

Kant believed that the best reason for acting was a sense of pure moral obligation or duty. He rejected the notion that an ethical decision maker would act on feelings of compassion, sympathy, love, or instincts of right and wrong. He certainly believed that one should not act out of fear. Emotion is not relevant to Kantian thinkers.

Consider a student who passes a homeless man who asks, "Spare change?" If the student tosses 50 cents into the man's upturned hat because she is afraid that the homeless man will become angry if she does not, she has not acted "well" if her actions are evaluated on Kant's scorecard. Similarly, she receives no credit if she gives him 50 cents because she feels sorry for him, or if she cares about people in general. She scores points only if she gives money because she feels that she has a duty to do so.

Criticisms of Duty Ethics

Utilitarian thinkers would address the previous example by saying, "What does it matter *why* she gives the man 50 cents? Whatever the motivation, he receives the same amount of money and the same amount of good is rendered to him."

Other critics argue that if a sense of obligation is the only acceptable motivation for doing good deeds, many good deeds will remain undone. Many people will act out of fear, sympathy, or other emotions, but comparatively few will act out of a sense of duty alone.

Some critics argue that acting out of a sense of duty alone makes people "feel bad," and that good deeds tend to be less sustainable. If the student in our example gives the panhandler money today only because she feels she must, she may well take another route to class tomorrow. But if she feels compassion for the man today, she may give him 50 cents a day for many days to come.

Kant also provides little guidance for conflicting duties. What if a man feels an obligation to his company, but also to his family, and what if he must make a decision that will benefit either his family or his company?

Kant and Corporate Decision Making

For all the criticisms, Kant at the very least presents an interesting way of thinking through ethical dilemmas.

Companies often attempt to be good "corporate citizens." Frequently, part of their efforts centers on whether or not corporate dollars should be spent in support of good causes. In the next unit, we will examine whether such expenditures are justified in the first place. But in this module, assume that all four of the companies described in the next section decide to give money to Youth Meals, an organization that provides nutritious food to low-income elementary school students who are in after-school care.

Each of the companies decides to give the same amount of money: $100,000. Thus, each ends up buying the same amount of food for the same number of children. Only the motivation for making the gifts differs from one company to the next. After reading through the scenarios, answer the questions that follow and assess the relative merits of the companies' actions.

SCENARIOS

For all four examples, imagine a well-appointed executive meeting room. An employee of each firm is making a presentation to the corporation's officers and favors making a $100,000 donation to the Youth Meals program.

Alpha Company

"And so it is imperative that we improve our image. The lawsuit is taking its toll. We've been taking a beating in the newspapers for weeks, and things will get substantially worse if the jury sides against us.

"Although it is inconvenient for customers to switch cable providers, we cannot rely on the fact that people will stick with us if they have the impression that we are a crooked company. Our prices and service remain competitive, but those things will not necessarily be helpful if people don't like or trust us.

"We must rebuild our image. The Youth Meals program is highly visible and highly relied on in this community. Sponsors that donate $100,000 or more and become 'Platinum Level' donors are featured on all Youth Meals promotional materials, including the in-school posters. If we pledge that amount, every parent at every school meeting in town will have a chance to see our logo next to a good cause. Even with the negative publicity surrounding the lawsuit, I believe we can avoid losing market share if we make heavy contributions to this kind of program. We should write the check."

Beta Company

"This next slide, ah ..." the presenter paused as he clicked his remote, "there it is. This next slide shows how other Youth Meals Platinum Level donors have fared in recent years. As you can see, 12 companies have made the large pledges. On average, their local sales have jumped 44 percent during the year following the Platinum Level gift.

And even if they don't remain Platinum Level sponsors, their increased sales sometimes remained for many years. People care about this program."

He clicked again. "I've analyzed here what the likely effects would be on our own sales. Of the 12 previous Platinum Level sponsors, the smallest jump in sales over the next year was 14 percent. For us, that would translate into an additional profit of $110,000. So, even in a worst-case scenario, I would expect that if we 'spend' $100,000 on making this donation, we'll make back $110,000 in increased profits over the next year and come out ahead.

"The average Platinum sponsor saw, like I said earlier, a 44 percent jump in sales. For us, that would mean about $350,000 in additional profits for us. The best sponsor saw a 90 percent jump in profits, which would be a bit over $700,000 for us.

"This is a good program, and people know it. Looking at these numbers, we would be crazy not to support it. We will likely make a substantial return by associating ourselves with the program.

Gamma Company

"One of the best things we've done in the ten years I've been here is hosting the field trips this fall. I know a lot of you feel the same way." Several heads nodded in agreement around the conference table. "I can't tell you how much I came to look forward to Thursday afternoons. Walking around with those kids and answering their questions, and seeing their faces light up when they got to see how candy is actually *made* … it was a fine thing. Fine. I've received thank-you cards from several of the classes, and I have them tacked up in my office. I hope we can get all eight of those schools back next year.

"So, anyway, schoolkids are on my mind.

"I saw a piece on the late news last month about Youth Meals, and I've been looking into the company ever since. A lot of low-income kids get hungry. The government sees that they get a discounted or free breakfast and lunch at school, but a lot of kids are in after-school programs until 5, 6, or 7 o'clock every day. There aren't school meals at those times, and for a lot of kids, dinner at home is not necessarily a sure thing.

"Youth Meals provides, as far as its budget allows, a hot meal for kids in the late afternoon or early evening. I believe that the program is 100 percent legitimate, and that almost all the money that comes in its door goes to food preparation and delivery.

"This has been a record year for us. We are flush with cash. Our shareholders are going to be thrilled whether our profit is $4.7 million or $4.6 million.

"I liked those kids who came through here. I can't stand thinking of any of them being hungry. I want to help them, and I think, or … at least I hope, that you'll agree with me. We should give $100,000 to Youth Meals and help out. I'd sure feel good about it if we did."

Delta Company ("Kant's Favorite")

"We've been in this community for many years, and there has always been a good labor pool. We have never had to recruit factory workers from out-of-town; there are always plenty of qualified applicants right here for any open positions we have. We owe a lot to the city.

"We should give something back. It is our duty to support this community that we could not do without.

"I have been charged with researching local charities, and it is my considered opinion that Youth Meals is most worthy. The program improves the lives of many children, some of whom may end up working for us one day.

"I am recommending that we give $100,000 to the program. We are fortunate to be as successful as we are, and as a successful operation, we have an obligation to help when we can. Making this donation is the right thing to do."

DISCUSSION QUESTIONS

1. Rank the four donations from most admirable to least admirable. You may assess that some or all of them are "tied," or are of equal value.

   1. _____

   2. _____

   3. _____

   4. _____

2. If you assessed some as "better" than others, which were better, and why? If you ranked all of the gifts as the same, why are all of the same quality?

   _____
   _____
   _____
   _____

3. Do any of the gifts seem more sustainable? In other words, would you expect that some of the companies would be more likely than others to make the same gift next year and the year after? If so, which motivations seem more likely to lead to continuous support?

   _____
   _____
   _____
   _____

4. Consider Beta Company. What percentage of corporate gifts do you imagine are made for this kind of reason? Nearly all? Half? Just a few? Assume that you heard about Beta Company's gift to Youth Meals. Now, assume that later, you learned that they only made the gift because they thought they would make more money than the amount of the gift. Would this bother you? Would you be less likely to buy the company's products?

   _____
   _____
   _____
   _____

5. Do you tend to view companies more favorably if they make charitable donations and support "good causes"? Have you ever switched brands or remained loyal to a company because of that kind of thing, or is that not something that has ever influenced your own decision to buy or not buy a product?

   _____
   _____
   _____
   _____

UNIT 2

Purpose of the Corporation

Unit Background

What is the purpose of a corporation? Is it simply a money-making entity for its owners? Can it be expected to do "good deeds" or care for employees, customers, and society?

Module 6

Stakeholder Ethics. [Is a company obligated to protect the interests of stakeholders? If so, are some stakeholders more important than others?]

Module 7

Milton Friedman and Shareholder Ethics. [If owners (shareholders) and stakeholders collide, which side should take priority? Are owners obligated to listen to stakeholders? What if *every* stakeholder wants the same thing?]

Module 8

Stakeholder Focus: Employees. [Does a corporation have an obligation to care for its employees? What if the company can make a lot more money if it lays everyone off and "outsources" jobs? What if the company has a "golden opportunity" to make such a change?]

Module 9

Stakeholder Focus: Plant Closing. [Does a corporation owe more to its employees if it lacks the kind of "golden opportunity" presented in Module 8? At what point do profits become more important than protecting jobs?]

Module 10

Stakeholder Focus: Communities. [Do organizations have obligations to the communities in which they operate? Are some kinds of companies "special," and if so, do they have a greater responsibility than "regular" businesses?]

Module 11

Stakeholder Focus: Customers and Dangerous Products. [Are customers owed particular obligations by the companies they patronize? What if their safety is involved?]

Purpose of the Corporation

Unit 1 examined general ethical issues. This unit looks at the first of many questions that are central to *business* ethics, "What is the purpose of a corporation?" For much of our nation's history, the answer to this question was both simple and legally required, "To make money for the shareholders." And, although no longer required by law, many companies continue to operate with an eye exclusively on the bottom line.

Many other companies, though, follow some form of the *stakeholder* model. Stakeholders are groups that have a stake in a firm's success. They include employees, customers, suppliers, the communities in which businesses operate, and other groups. Owners of a corporation (shareholders) are also stakeholders, but they are not the only group worthy of consideration under the stakeholder model.

In many circumstances, what is good for shareholders is good for stakeholders. A company with happy employees who are well treated tends to be more profitable. The same applies for a company with satisfied and loyal customers, and a company that operates in stable communities with strong labor pools and healthy local economies.

But some decisions pit shareholders against other stakeholders, and these are the difficult ethical questions. In such cases, should the shareholders "win," or be given top priority, due to the fact that they put up their own money to make the company run? Or is it sometimes appropriate to give preference to other stakeholders, even if, in the end, the company makes a lower profit?

In this unit, we will identify various stakeholders. Then, we will evaluate a variety of situations that pit shareholders head-to-head with other stakeholders. Should employees be taken care of even if a company will lose money? Should a plant be kept open to protect a community if the company would make more money relocating the operation? Does a corporation have an obligation to give to charity and support projects that will benefit society? Does a company have an obligation to protect customers, even if it is not cost-effective? These and other questions will be examined.

MODULE 6

Stakeholder Ethics

A fundamental question in business ethics is, *What is the purpose of a corporation supposed to be?* The way in which this question is analyzed has changed over time. To start at the beginning . . .

In a famous 1919 lawsuit, Henry Ford was sued by the Dodge brothers and other major shareholders of Ford Motor Company. The shareholders were upset because, despite fabulous profits, Ford paid essentially no dividends. The shareholders complained, especially about Ford's use of corporate profits to support humanitarian and charitable works. The Michigan Supreme Court found in favor of the shareholders because corporation laws at the time required corporate boards to put shareholders first. The Dodge brothers won enough money to start their own car company, which still exists as part of Chrysler.

Companies were legally required to follow the "shareholder model" until the decade after the close of World War II. In the late 1940s and early 1950s, the attitude of many powerful politicians toward corporations changed. There existed a powerful belief that American companies had contributed mightily to stopping the Nazis. Many believed that, but for the ability of American corporations to turn out a massive volume of planes, bombs, ammunition, and other items essential to the Allies fighting in Europe, Hitler might well have been victorious. There was a feeling that maybe corporations weren't mere things, but instead were perhaps an essential part of society.

Many politicians wanted corporations to be able to participate more fully in society. They softened restrictive language in incorporation laws, and in the end it became legally acceptable for companies to "do good deeds." Such action was not and is still not required, but it is allowed.

Many make the case that corporations should take care of more than shareholders alone. They argue that, to be ethical, executives must seek to take care of a range of "stakeholders." Stakeholder model advocates certainly do not argue that the owners of a corporation should be ignored—shareholders are included as one of the several stakeholders in a firm. But, they argue, a company must also look out for (among other groups) its employees, its customers, and the communities in which it operates. Some take a very broad view and argue that "society" or "the environment" ought to be considered stakeholders.

The basic notion of stakeholder ethics is that even if a company will make less profit for shareholders, it should nonetheless pay decent wages, support charitable causes, and the like. A great many Fortune 500 companies put the stakeholder model into practice.

Milton Friedman is one of the best-known economists in recent times. He disagreed strongly with the stakeholder model and was a leading advocate of the shareholder model. Friedman argued that corporations have two primary responsibilities. First, they must comply with the law. Second, once they have complied with the law, they must make as much money as possible for shareholders. If shareholders compete head-to-head with any other stakeholder, Friedman argued that the company should act in the best interests of the shareholders. He argued that only shareholders have put their own money on the line, and that they should therefore be given preference over others. He characterized acting in any other way as "imposing a tax" on the shareholders.

Every executive will treat employees well if he or she believes that doing so will lead to increased productivity and increased profits. Every executive is in favor of donating money to charity if the donation improves the company's image and leads to increased sales that exceed the amount of the donation. But such win-win cases are not ethical dilemmas.

In a true dilemma, a company considers an action that would not increase the shareholders' return in any certain or measureable way. In such cases, the shareholder model advises, "Don't spend the shareholders' money." The stakeholder model counsels, "It is often acceptable to consider the interests of stakeholders other than the owners."

As with most all ethics questions, neither side is "right" in the sense that everyone agrees or that the law requires following either set of ideas. Countless companies follow each of the models.

In the next hypothetical scenario, a corporation has an unexpectedly large surplus and considers different things that might be done with it.

SCENARIO

Kensington Reiss

Kensington Reiss, an American drug company, has had a record year. In recent years, it has made an average profit of $1 billion. This year, it launched a wildly successful new antidepressant and an equally successful drug to treat high blood pressure. Profits doubled to $2 billion.

Shareholders will receive a significant dividend increase, but its leaders are debating its exact size. Some members of the board of directors favor returning the entire "extra" billion dollars to shareholders. Others favor setting some portion aside for other stakeholders. Specifically, seven items are under consideration.

Assume that, in each case, no compelling evidence exists to show that the action would necessarily lead to a higher profit for the company. Many corporate good deeds do in fact improve public perception, customer loyalty, and the like, but in each of these cases the evidence suggests that the company will most likely not improve profit if it chooses to take care of the "stakeholders."

1. Kensington Reiss makes a drug that is a highly effective therapeutic treatment for patients with HIV. When it is taken in conjunction with several other drugs, it can help delay the onset of AIDS for years, in some cases for decades. Two companies that make other parts of a "cocktail" of HIV drugs have recently contacted

Kensington Reiss to discuss starting a program that would make medicine available to HIV patients in Africa at extreme discounts.

Stakeholders impacted: Global society
Expected cost: $40,000,000 (4 percent of the unexpected surplus)

2. One of Kensington Reiss's over-the-counter cold drugs can be used as an ingredient in manufacturing "midnight," an illegal street drug that has gained immense popularity in recent years. The company has quietly paid for a study that shows that as much as 15 percent of this drug's sales are made for the purpose of making midnight. Although few deaths have been linked to midnight, there has been an increase in crime in the neighborhoods in which midnight is most commonly abused. Kensington Reiss does not operate a plant in any of the 20 metro areas in which midnight is most commonly abused.

   The company's research and development leaders have studied ways in which the drug could be reformulated. They believe that it can be made in such a way that it would remain effective as a cold remedy but would no longer be useful to illegal drug manufacturers. The reformulation would, of course, come with a price.

   Stakeholders impacted: U.S. society
   Expected cost: $20,000,000 (2 percent of the surplus)

3. Kensington Reiss has manufacturing plants in Detroit, St. Louis, and Philadelphia. The corporation relies on having a reasonably educated workforce available in these areas. Usually, the company does not have problems filling positions, but occasionally there is a shortage of qualified applicants for some manufacturing jobs.

   The company's leaders are considering making three donations of one million dollars each to adult literacy programs in Detroit, St. Louis, and Philadelphia. Students enrolled in the programs would have absolutely no obligations to Kensington Reiss, but some of them might eventually work for the company.

   Stakeholders impacted: Local community
   Expected cost: $3,000,000 (3/10 of 1 percent of the surplus)

4. The leaders of Kensington Reiss are also considering making three gifts of one million dollars each to fund expanded parks programs in Detroit, St. Louis, and Philadelphia. The new open spaces would likely be used frequently by some employees, but they would be public parks open to everyone.

   Stakeholders impacted: Local community
   Expected cost: $3,000,000 (3/10 of 1 percent of the surplus)

5. Kensington Reiss is in a highly competitive industry, and top executives in the field are paid very well. The board is concerned that several top executives will leave the company because Kensington Reiss's salaries for officers have not kept pace with industry averages. The board is considering significant raises, particularly for the CEO and CFO.

   Data suggests that pharmaceutical companies of Kensington Reiss's size with first-class leadership earn 40–250 percent more in profits over time. The board estimates that key strategic decisions this year directly led to fully half of the billion dollar unexpected surplus.

   Stakeholders impacted: Management/top employees
   Expected cost: $20,000,000 (2 percent of the surplus)

6. The board has long been aware that the wages of clerical staff and "line workers" at the manufacturing plants lag behind industry averages. It is considering rewarding loyal employees by giving an across-the-board 10 percent raise to lower-paid workers who have been with the company for at least two years.

   Stakeholders impacted: Most employees
   Expected cost: $10,000,000 (1 percent of the surplus)

DISCUSSION QUESTIONS

1. Of the actions previously listed, which two are the *most* justifiable? Why?

_____

_____

_____

_____

2. Of the actions listed above, which two are the *least* justifiable? Why?

_____

_____

_____

_____

3. If you were a decision maker at Kensington Reiss, which of the actions would you actually vote to approve?

_____

_____

_____

_____

4. Would you vote to approve any additional items if the unexpected surplus were $3 billion instead of $1 billion?

_____

_____

_____

_____

5. Assume that you are a shareholder of Kensington Reiss, and that you received a dividend check for $1,000. Assume further that you learned later that Kensington Reiss had adopted many of the programs in this module, and that if they had not done so, your dividend check would have been $1,100. With $100 of your own money in the equation, would you be less supportive of any of the actions?

_____

_____

_____

_____

Milton Friedman and Shareholder Ethics

Let's continue the debate between the shareholder and stakeholder models of business ethics. In case you are working on this module by itself, and not as part of a series, following is a brief recap of the two sets of ideas that surround the basic question: *What is the purpose of a corporation supposed to be?*

Milton Friedman and the Shareholder Model

The shareholder model's answer to the key question is that the purpose of a corporation is to make money for the shareholders. The shareholders (owners) risk their own money by investing in a company, and therefore corporate leaders have an ethical obligation to protect shareholder wealth and generate a return for shareholders.Many followers of the model scoff at the notion that corporations have any degree of social responsibility, and that likening a business to a human being is folly.

Economist Milton Friedman, a champion of the shareholder model, has been a particularly harsh critic of using corporations to advance environmental goals, end discrimination, and achieve other social ends. In a *New York Times* interview, he once said that such practices were "pure and unadulterated socialism," and that "businessmen who talk this way are the unwitting puppets of the intellectual forces that have been undermining the basis of a free society these past decades." To Friedman, the only goals for corporate leaders were to:

1. Comply with the "rules of the game" (law); and,

2. After complying with the law, make as much money for shareholders as possible.

Stakeholder Model

Advocates of the stakeholder model believe that corporate leaders are under an obligation to evaluate the impact decisions will have on many groups with special relationships to the firm. The company's shareholders are only one of several stakeholders worthy of consideration. Even if the owners receive a somewhat smaller return on their investments, it is acceptable, and even ethically required for corporate leaders to, on occasion, first take care of employees, or customers, or the cities in which a business operates. Some stakeholder model followers will identify very broad entities such as "the environment" or "all mankind" as stakeholders.

Sometimes, the shareholder and stakeholder models compel the same decision. For example, if a company can donate $100,000 to charity, but in the process attract favorable publicity, new customers, and earn an extra $200,000, then the models agree that the donation should be made.

But sometimes "doing the right thing" seems likely to cost money and not generate new revenue over the long run. In such cases, the models diverge.

The Debate

Most academic papers that debate the two models focus on profits. This is a perfectly legitimate way to frame the issue, and it is how the other modules in this unit have been set up. When dealing with a large group of shareholders, the desire to make money is the most obvious common denominator.

But at the heart of the debate is a tension between protecting the interests of owners and looking out for everyone else. Sometimes, strategies can be devised that benefit shareholders and other stakeholders, but when such a path does not open up, who should win? Should shareholders receive a larger dividend, or should workers receive larger raises? Should some profits be sacrificed to spend more money on environmental research, or should the bottom line be maximized as much as possible?

The real fundamental questions are these: *Are the owners the only game in town? Ought their wishes be followed to the exclusion of everyone else that has an interest in the organization?*

Athletes in Trouble

Many owners of NFL franchises have had to deal with a wide range of off-the-field problems in recent years. Some players have committed illegal acts. Plaxico Burress served jail time on an illegal weapons charge after a gun in his waistband discharged and wounded his leg. Michael Vick served a sentence related to his dog-fighting operation.

Others have not been charged with crimes but have become entangled in ugly situations. Ben Roethlisberger faced a four-game suspension over allegedly having sex in a nightclub restroom.

When players behave badly, owners must decide how to react, and many stakeholders come into the equation. Sometimes players stay, and sometimes they are traded. Generally, though, when players are cut loose, it is true that most or all stakeholders are in favor of the trade. But what if the ultimate decision maker stands alone in wanting to trade a troubled player? What if the other stakeholders are against the move? Is an owner under an *obligation* to consider the wishes of other stake-holders, or is it all about the owner?

SCENARIO

For this example, assume that the Los Angeles Goliaths are owned by the Jones family. Lenny Jones, the largest shareholder, owns 52 percent of the team, and his younger brother, Sam, and younger sister, Sarah, own 24 percent each.

At a Sprawling Mansion in Beverly Hills

"Will there be anything else, Mr. Jones?" the butler asked.

"No, no," Lenny answered, waving his hand. Without a word, the butler exited the room, closing the door behind him. Lenny took a Cuban cigar from a cedar box, snipped the end off, and struck a match. He turned to his siblings.

"So . . . so, so, so. Mr. Walters." His brother and sister nodded but said nothing. "What shall we do with our preposterous knucklehead of a quarterback?" He let the question hang.

His brother, Sam, was the first to speak up. "We have to keep him. We're too invested in him. We won't be competitive for five years if we get rid of him."

"So?"

"So that's what a football team is for—winning."

"Says who?"

"Said Dad, for one."

"Dad would never have put up with Mr. Walter's shenanigans."

"Dad ran the team in a simpler time."

"Perhaps. And what do you think, dear sister?"

Sarah looked up. "Everybody wants him to stay."

"Everyone who?"

"Everyone involved. I actually speak to the people involved in the team on occasion."

"Tsk. Such a temper. But go on, what does 'everyone' have to say?"

"The season ticket holders want him to stay. I had the staff quietly run a phone survey over the weekend. Eighty percent of them said 'keep him.'"

"Mmm hmm. Go on."

"And it's not just them. The people of Los Angeles want to keep him, too. Channel 4's poll ran about the same as ours, 3-to-1 in favor of not trading him."

"And I should care about them because . . . ?"

"Because they're our fans, Lenny. They buy our merchandise and drive TV ratings. Not to mention the fact that they're the voters who approved chipping in $200 million toward our new stadium."

"I don't remember signing anything giving them a stake in running the team. But go on."

"Well . . . the coaching staff is passionate about keeping him. They've built their careers . . . to a large extent their lives . . . around creating an offense and a team for him. He's taken us from 2–14 when we drafted him to a field goal away from the Super Bowl last year. They can smell a title, and they'll be crushed if they have to start over. I think a lot of them will leave."

"That's certainly their right."

"Our sponsors want to keep him. He's the face of this franchise."

"Yes, and he's also now the bare bottom of the franchise, running away from the TMZ cameras through a strip club parking lot."

"Come on, Lenny, he's 24 years old."

"Yes . . . only 24. Old enough to go to war, have children, do most anything. But not old enough to stay clothed and sober for $8,000,000 a year? What say you, brother?"

"Boys will be boys," Sam said. When Lenny didn't reply, Sam added, "It's a new world. The paparazzi follow famous people everywhere, and they capture everything on film. People understand that. Are you telling me that none of Dad's sainted players cut loose from time to time and did something unflattering? But back then, nobody was recording."

"Hmm . . ."

"It's embarrassing, but other players have done worse. There are no criminal charges here, and there won't be any civil lawsuits either because nobody got hurt. He didn't punch anyone. He didn't sexually assault anyone. He didn't get caught with a gun or cocaine or steroids or anything else. He got really drunk with his friends and he, ah, he, you know, lost a bet."

"And that makes it OK? Putting us in the headlines? Making us look like classless fools?"

"It's not OK. But we shouldn't cut him loose over this . . . escapade." Despite himself, Sam found himself fighting to stifle a laugh.

"Are you actually smiling now?" Sam's grin widened. "For heaven's sake, why are you smiling?"

Sam started chuckling. "Come on, Lenny, be human. A giant man with no pants running away and hopping a chain-link fence?" His chuckle became a laugh.

"And that TMZ reporter running after him," Sarah added, laughing herself. "With the 'Mr. Walters! John! What do you think of the Goliaths' chances for the Super Bowl next year, John?'"

"'NO COMMENT!'" Sam said, mimicking the reply Walters had made in the infamous tape. Sam was laughing quite hard now. "I mean," he spread his hands, "that's . . . just funny." He nearly fell from his chair.

"STOP LAUGHING!" Lenny shouted, raising his voice for the first time. The laughs quieted, and Lenny regained his composure. "Funny, you say? Not to me, it isn't," he said with a clenched jaw.

"Look, Lenny," Sarah said. "We're both in favor of giving him another chance."

Sam nodded his agreement and added, "And so is everyone else who matters. The coaches, the fans, everybody. By the time the commish hands you the Lombardi Trophy next year, no one will even remember this."

"Well," Lenny said quietly, "that's 48 percent of the votes that matter." He paused and took a long draw on his cigar. He kept it in his teeth and talked around it. "I don't want the Lombardi Trophy so much as I don't want to be disgraced." He smoked for a while longer. Eventually he said, "Here's what we're going to do. We will not trade Mr. Walters."

"Oh, Lenny, good," Sarah said.

"We will cut him," Lenny said.

"What?" Sarah said, and at the same time, Sam said, "You'll ruin the team!"

"I will fire him myself. We will not pay him another penny. If he sues us, we shall defend ourselves. If we lose in court, we shall pay. Any other team that wishes to hire him, may." Lenny was on a roll now, and his speech quickened. "You may not see now that this is for the best, but no matter. Father left me in control of the team and the rest of the businesses for a reason: He knew that, no matter what, I would protect the family's honor. And that . . . is . . . that."

Sam rose from his chair and treated the door roughly as he left. Sarah said, "Father would be disappointed," and followed. Lenny sat alone and finished his cigar.

DISCUSSION QUESTIONS

1. If you were Lenny, to what degree would you consider the other stakeholders described in this scenario? If you were the president of a football team owned by shareholders in the same situation, to what degree would you consider the other stakeholders described in this scenario?

_____

_____

_____

_____

2. Was it "wrong" for Lenny to ignore the other stakeholders' wishes?

_____

_____

_____

_____

3. Lenny, as majority owner, can't be fired for his decision. If the CEO of a "normal" corporation goes against the wishes of his stakeholders, should he or she be fired? Or is part of leadership making tough decisions, even if they are widely unpopular?

_____

_____

_____

_____

If a corporate leader chooses to follow the stakeholder model, accurately gauging the wishes of various stakeholders is of critical importance. The last two questions apply that idea to this module.

4. Of the three real players in the introduction and the fictional quarterback in the scenario, which ones would you have *wanted* to be cut or traded from *your* favorite team?

_____ Michael Vick (conviction related to dog fighting)

_____ Plaxico Burress (convicted on a weapons charge)

_____ Ben Roethlisberger (allegations of sexual assault but no criminal charges)

_____ John Walters (drunk and caught on tape streaking in a strip club parking lot)

5. Assume that after Walters is cut, the Goliaths miss the playoffs next year. If you had season tickets, would you renew them? As a voting taxpayer, would you be more or less likely to vote in favor of taxpayer dollars being used to support the team in the future? As an assistant coach, would you look for a position with another team?

_____

_____

_____

_____

Stakeholder Focus: Employees

Business leaders must comply with the law. When a choice involves a legal action and an illegal action, the decision is easy to make. Once all legal requirements have been met, and choices involve multiple legal alternatives, decisions often become more difficult.

An often useful way of choosing between legal alternatives is to answer the question, *What is the purpose of a corporation supposed to be?*

Followers of the **shareholder model** answer that question by asserting that corporations are supposed to maximize the wealth of the owners.

Those who adhere to the **stakeholder model** argue that corporate leaders should consider many groups alongside the shareholders when they have decisions to make. They believe that the interests of employees, customers, or communities should sometimes be placed ahead of some portion of shareholder profits.

This module will look at a scenario in which interests of shareholders and employees seem to compete. It is loosely based on an actual business case from the 1990s.

In 1995, the Malden Mills factory in Lawrence, Massachusetts, burned to the ground. The company is the maker of the fabric Polartec, which is used to make jackets and other winter clothing. The company's CEO, Aaron Feuerstein, gained a measure of fame from two decisions he made in the fire's aftermath.

First, he decided to rebuild the factory in Lawrence. Most textile manufacturers had moved their factories outside the United States, where labor costs are lower; it is relatively unusual today to find a shirt or any article of clothing with a "Made in the USA" label. Despite a golden opportunity to make an overseas move, Feuerstein directed that his factory be rebuilt in its traditional home.

Second, he paid his workers their full wages during the period of rebuilding. For months, Malden Mills employees picked up paychecks, although there was no fabric to be made.

Feuerstein received a slew of honorary degrees and positive press. He was recognized by President Clinton at a State of the Union address; he was the feel-good story of the year in business.

But Feuerstein was more than the CEO of Malden Mills. He was the owner. Shareholders did not own the company. Feuerstein certainly made decisions that were easy to cheer for, but then again, he was playing with his own money.

Leaders of corporations and other types of companies are often playing with other people's money. The next hypothetical scenario examines what ought to be done in such cases.

SCENARIO

PART 1

Friday Afternoon

Alan Dawson sat in his office and watched the local weather forecast.

A reporter spoke with some difficulty from South Beach. "The winds are starting to noticeably pick up out here, and with landfall of this strong Category 3 storm less than 24 hours away, this is only the beginning," she said. The camera swung around and focused on an unsettled ocean beyond. Alan sighed.

"Mr. Dawson," said a man as he knocked softly. Alan didn't look up, and the man knocked louder. "Sir? Mr. Dawson?"

"Huh? Oh, Reggie," Alan eventually replied. "I'm sorry . . . I was woolgathering."

"Yes, sir, and I don't blame you. How's the storm?"

"Still Category 3, still headed straight for us. Sometime tomorrow, they say."

"Ah," Reggie replied softly. "Well, I came up to say that we've done what we can do. The windows are boarded, and everything that can be tied down is tied down. The last of the inventory went out this morning. We're as ready as we can be."

"I appreciate your efforts, Reggie. Give my thanks to everyone, will you?"

"Yes, sir."

"And send everyone who hasn't left already home. Get somewhere safe, Reggie."

"Yes, sir. I'll be back as soon as it's over to start cleaning up."

"I know you will, Reggie."

"Goodnight, Mr. Dawson."

"Goodnight."

Dawson sat watching TV for a long while. Eventually, he turned it off and stepped through his side office door to a platform that overlooked his factory below. Gold DAWSON COMPUTERS logos boldly stood out on the light gray floor and the darker gray workstations. Silver conveyor belt rollers gleamed dully in the auxiliary lights and snaked endlessly from one assembly area to the next. Alan Dawson surveyed the plant he had created. He smiled as he thought of starting the company by assembling computers in his parent's garage 15 years earlier.

A strong gust of wind rattled the factory's metal roof. Frowning, Alan collected his things, locked up his office, and left.

Monday Morning

A blue BMW 750iL with a license plate that read DAWSON 1 slowly navigated tree limbs and other debris at the edge of the factory parking lot. It came to a stop in a relatively clear parking spot, and Alan Dawson emerged from it.

"Crap," he said, to no one in particular.

One wall was partially collapsed. Another had a hole in it the size of a school bus. And the roof was just . . . gone. Broken glass, insulation, and harder-to-identify chunks of metal were everywhere.

The parking lot was nearly empty of cars, but Dawson did see a familiar green Celica. He smiled and thumbed "Bldg. Super." on his phone's touch screen.

His call was answered on the first ring. "Hello?"

"Reggie."

"Mr. Dawson. Where are you, sir?"

"I'm out in the parking lot; I saw your car. How does it look in there?"

There was a long pause. "It's bad, Mr. Dawson. Real bad."

"I'm coming in. Can you meet me at the back loading dock in five minutes?"

"Yes, sir. Be careful coming in."

Dawson grunted an acknowledgement and ended the call. He started to put his phone in his pocket, then hesitated and thumbed, "COO."

"Alan?" a voice answered.

"Hey, Carol. Look, don't bother coming down here."

"That bad?"

"Yeah. Yeah, it is. I think we're looking at a total loss."

"Oh, Alan."

"I'm going to look around for awhile, but, ah . . . " he trailed off. "Any word from Coral Gables?"

"Yes. The call center is fine. No flooding, no major damage—they even have power."

"Wow. OK, well, let's use that for our base of operations. Email the manufacturing folks and tell them they have two paid weeks off, and that we'll follow up with them soon about what happens next."

"Will do. Alan?"

"Yeah?"

"What does happen next?"

"Not sure yet. I want to take a couple of days to think about it and take care of my house—we lost a couple of the big palms out back. Let's meet at the call center on Wednesday. Noon?"

"Noon it is."

Wednesday Afternoon

An assistant brought in two grande Starbucks lattes in a cardboard cup holder.

"Ah, terrific," Dawson said. "Thanks a lot."

"No problem, Mr. Dawson."

"Close the door on the way out, will you?"

"Sure thing." The assistant left Dawson and his Chief Operating Officer alone in the call center's main conference room.

"So," Dawson began.

"So," she replied.

"I want to start putting together our basic strategy for what we're going to do about our factory. That's really it for today."

"OK."

"I talked to our insurance guy yesterday, and we're fully covered. He's been by the plant, and he agrees that it's a total loss. We'll get the full $100,000,000 sometime this month."

"That's good."

Dawson sipped his coffee and stared out a window for a moment. "I want to rebuild here in Miami," he said.

"I thought you'd say that," Carol said.

"The insurance money will pay for a new top-of-the-line facility. We can be running again in six months—nine months, tops—and our output will be better than before."

"Right . . . or we could build a facility in China for 30 percent less and operate it for half the labor costs we've had here," Carol replied. "This is a golden opportunity to do what all of our competitors have done already."

"Some of these people have been with me for fourteen years. They built this company. What about them? They can't relocate to China."

"They'll find other jobs."

"But not equivalent other jobs. Where is Reggie going to earn a six-figure salary? And the assembly-line workers, most of them have a high school education. Some of them less than that. Where are they going to earn $20 an hour? They have families to support."

"They can retrain, start again somewhere else."

"I don't accept that."

"The shareholders won't like it. They're getting a 4 percent return from us, and they want the 8 percent that most of our competitors are returning."

"I don't care."

"We've gone public, Alan. This isn't your company anymore."

"I'm the CEO, and I'm the Chairman of the Board!"

"You won't be either for long if this company doesn't make more money. The shareholders will replace you."

"I started this company!"

"They won't care. At least not for long."

Dawson sat in silence for awhile. "Are you playing devil's advocate or is that what you really think?"

"Does it matter?"

Dawson thought about that. "No. No, I guess it doesn't. And I'm sorry, Carol. I'm not myself . . . "

"I know, boss. All of this is awful."

"Yeah. Yeah, it is." Dawson finished his coffee. "It's just that . . . I mean, personal feelings aside, unemployment is bad. The country needs to stop losing jobs. Where does it stop? Somebody has to protect the jobs."

"It's the government's job to set the rules of the game to protect American jobs . . . "

"I disagree. I disagree with that."

"Fine. But it is absolutely your job to look out for the shareholders."

"Maybe. Maybe so," Dawson said quietly. "I need to think about this."

"I know."

"Let's talk about it again on Friday morning."

"OK, Alan."

DISCUSSION QUESTIONS

PART 1

1. Should Dawson push to rebuild the plant in Miami? Why or why not?

2. If you were in Dawson's position, and if your organization were a private company that you owned yourself (as opposed to a corporation owned by shareholders), would you rebuild the plant in Miami or relocate to China?

3. To what degree do you agree with Carol's idea that it is the government's job to create and protect American jobs, and that it is a CEO's job to create wealth for shareholders?

Strongly Disagree ◄——————————————► Strongly Agree

1 --- 2 --- 3 --- 4 --- 5 -- 6 --- 7

SCENARIO

PART 2

Friday Morning

"I'm firmly decided. We're rebuilding here."

"I'm glad, Alan," Carol said.

"So you were playing devil's advocate," Dawson smiled.

"That's what I get paid for. Part of it, anyway."

"True enough. I think with expanded capacity, and with tax incentives for a new, environmentally friendly plant, we can be very competitive right here."

"I'm 100 percent behind you, boss."

"And I want to pay our workers their wages while the plant is being rebuilt."

Carol paused, surprised. "You're kidding."

"No."

"OK, I'm not playing devil's advocate now. We can't do that."

"We have to do that. The majority of them live paycheck-to-paycheck, and unemployment benefits won't cover half of what they earn."

"Alan! There's no work for them to do, and there won't be for months."

"Even so. These are loyal workers."

"And these are grownups who need to save money for emergencies."

"Most people don't do that."

"Well . . . they certainly should."

"Maybe so, but they don't. If we don't pay them, they'll fall behind on their mortgages. They'll lose their homes."

"I admire your concern, but we can't ask the shareholders to foot the bill for wages when no value is being added to the company."

"We pay pensions to retirees—they're not working for us anymore."

"That's different!"

"In some ways," Dawson said. "I'll be giving up all of my pay for the rest of the year to help foot the bill."

"That will only cover 10 percent of the costs."

"It's a start."

"The shareholders won't stand for it. They'll oust you, Alan."

"Maybe. Maybe not. I'm betting a lot of them will trust me and appreciate that we're taking care of the people that make money for them."

"I urge you to reconsider. I mean, if you want to pay a handful of irreplaceable people, I can see a benefit. But most of the assembly line workers' positions could be filled by any number of people who could be trained in a few weeks."

"We pay everybody. We have the lowest turnover in the industry, and our customers have the fewest problems in the industry because of it. Having a happy and stable workforce matters."

"And we also have the lowest profit margins in the industry. And we're going to lose market share during our manufacturing downtime. We need to be more careful than ever with the money we have."

"There's more to business than profits."

"Not to the shareholders."

"They put me in charge of this company. I'm the coach, and I call the plays until they say otherwise. This is the right thing to do, and we're going to do it."

PART 2

4. Should Dawson Computers' factory employees be paid during the several months of rebuilding? Would it be any more or less justifiable to pay only a handful of high-level difficult-to-replace workers?

_____

_____

_____

_____

5. Imagine that you personally own $1,000 worth of shares in Dawson Computers. Would you be upset with the decision to rebuild the factory in the United States?

Not Upset ◄————————————————————► Highly Upset
       1 --- 2 --- 3 --- 4 --- 5 --- 6 --- 7

What about the decision to pay all workers while the factory is rebuilt?

Not Upset ◄————————————————————► Highly Upset
       1 --- 2 --- 3 --- 4 --- 5 --- 6 --- 7

Stakeholder Focus:
Plant Closing

BACKGROUND

Usually, contract law is fairly clear as far as bodies of law go. Law students who have a talent for memorizing rules and who like order in their thinking often prefer contracts to all other first-year law school courses. Mr. Spock would like contracts; Captain Kirk would prefer torts.

That said, "promissory estoppel" is an interesting legal doctrine that allows for contract law to be stretched beyond clear standards and almost into the realm of ethics. To illustrate, let's look at the case *Ypsilanti* v. *General Motors Corporation* from 1993.

General Motors (GM) had a pair of manufacturing plants in Ypsilanti, and the company received a series of substantial tax breaks from the town over a period of many years. It is not uncommon for cities to give special tax treatment to large employers. GM saved millions.

In the early 1990s, demand for some GM cars dropped significantly, and the company's leaders decided to shut the Ypsilanti plant and move its operations to Texas. The town sued to try to stop the plant closure, arguing that they had an "implied contract" and that GM had agreed to stay in town in exchange for the tax incentives. They cited statements that GM had made such as "we're partners" and "we look forward to growing together."

Although it was presented much more grandly than this, the town essentially argued, "No fair! GM made millions here, and if they just leave, we'll be ruined. Don't let them, judge!"

The lower court judge did not find any contract—implied or otherwise—between Ypsilanti and GM. But he did block the proposed move to Texas, citing the doctrine of promissory estoppel, which is a fuzzy equitable (fairness) standard. If a judge believes that a plaintiff like Ypsilanti "relied" on statements a defendant made, and that it should have been "reasonably foreseeable" that it would do so, and if a "substantial injustice" would be done, then a judge can essentially rule that there is a contract even though there is no contract. The "substantial injustice" part of the standard, in particular, varies depending on what a particular judge thinks is fair.

In the end, GM won the case on appeal. A higher court found that the lower court judge had improperly applied promissory estoppel.

The Ypsilanti case aside, plant closures present a variety of issues that are good subject matter for a discussion of shareholder and stakeholder ethics.

When plants are relocated, the company's leaders have strong reason to believe that the company will be more profitable in its new location, and that the shareholder will benefit over the long run. And, unless there are unusual facts surrounding such a move, the law allows companies to make such changes.

But the law also does not require such changes. Companies are legally free to make less money and stay put. This is no longer the era of the *Dodge* v. *Ford* case, in which a judge in 1919 told Henry Ford, "Mr. Ford, make no mistake: the purpose of a corporation is to make money for the shareholder, and none other."

Corporate leaders can take groups other than a corporation's owners into account when making decisions. If they go too far, they may find themselves out of a job, but the law does not compel a single-minded drive for maximized profits.

Many have made the case that corporations should take care of more than shareholders alone. They argue that, to be ethical, executives must seek to take care of a range of "stakeholders" who have special relationships with corporations, such as its employees, its customers, and the communities in which it operates.

In the following scenario, a company's leaders debate a plant relocation like the one in the Ypsilanti case.

SCENARIO

At a Starbucks in Kentucky

"They're not really thinking of closing the plant, are they?" Lauren sipped her tea and looked at her brother, Roger, a manager at WoodWorks Company.

"I don't know. Maybe. The furniture business is different now, and it's not going back. We don't sell much to independent furniture stores anymore because fewer and fewer of them exist every year. We used to be able to get a good markup from them, but now we have to sell through Rooms To Go and IKEA, and they aren't willing to pay us as much."

"But WoodWorks has always made really good stuff. Some of Grandma's furniture is, what, 40 years old?"

"That's true, but it only goes so far. We're getting squeezed, and it's getting almost impossible to make any more money off of what we make. If we're going to stay in business, we have to make it cheaper, and a lot of our costs are out of our control."

"Can't you be more efficient? Does it have to be moving the plant?"

"There are a lot of things that might save a few dollars here and there. We can eliminate waste a little, maybe save a little on energy. But the thing is, we're just barely breaking even. We have to save big."

Roger sipped his coffee and continued.

"The cost of the wood, and of the fabric, and the other stuff we make furniture out of isn't going to go down by much. We could switch to cheaper, flimsier raw materials, but I don't think making cheap furniture is going to work for us. We've survived to this point because people know we make sturdy furniture that lasts a long time."

He took another sip of coffee.

And the union won't accept deep cuts in wages or benefits. And nobody wants to move overseas, thank goodness. So, anyway, that leaves out reducing labor costs by much.

"If we're going to make furniture for a lot less, we have to get big breaks on taxes. The Feds won't do that kind of thing for our kind of company, so that means we have to get breaks on local taxes."

"Can't you ask the city council for tax breaks? Explain everything to them?"

"We have, and they said no."

"Really?"

"Really."

"They'd rather lose 500 jobs?"

"Apparently."

"Wow."

"I agree. But, anyway, we've been looking around. We've found a town in Tennessee that's desperate to create jobs. If we move there, we'll cut our tax payments in half for 25 years."

"But won't it cost millions to move the plant?"

"Yes. But we have cash on-hand, and we can finance the new facility if we decide to go. Our problem is profits. If we move and get the tax incentives, we expect to be able to generate a 5 percent, maybe a 10 percent, return for a long time. If we don't move, we expect to continue to make a 2 or 3 percent return, maybe less."

"But is that so bad? If you're still making money, why not stay here? This town would never have been founded, I mean, it wouldn't exist without WoodWorks. It's been here for, what, 75 years?"

"Eighty-two. No one wants to leave. But we're a corporation. A lot of the shares are owned by people around here, but a majority of them aren't. We owe it to our shareholders to make higher profits."

"Maybe. But what about your workers?"

"We want to keep as many of our people as possible. We think a lot of them will be willing to relocate to Tennessee. It's only about 150 miles we'd be asking them to move. We're not considering moving overseas."

"What about the town?"

"What about it?"

"If you leave and the town loses the tax revenue from WoodWorks . . . "

"They're going to lose it one way or another. If they cut us a deal and we stay, they might keep some of it, and the ball is in their court to make us a proposal. We just can't afford . . . "

"You just said you were still profitable. Even paying full taxes."

"Not very profitable."

"Fine. Look, I'm just saying that the town can't handle losing the plant. If you leave, then unemployment will go from 10 percent to, what . . . 18 percent right away if those 500 jobs are lost."

"I just said we expect a lot of people will come with us."

"Some will, some won't. But OK, say unemployment only goes up to 14 percent. I volunteered at the food pantry last weekend, and they're out of everything even as it is. It can't feed another two or three hundred families. And the potholes on Main Street haven't been patched for two years. The schools haven't fixed the hole in the room over the gym. We're out of money, and we can't handle any more."

"Which is why the town should give us a partial abatement on our taxes so that we'll stay."

"You grew up here, Roger."

"Look, it's not my decision. I'm just telling you how the winds are blowing."

"But you're a part of the decision."

"Maybe. Maybe so. But we have to do what the shareholders want over what helps the town."

"Is a few cents more on the dollar at any cost what the shareholders really want?"

DISCUSSION QUESTIONS

1. Assess the next-to-last sentence in the scenario: "But we have to do what the shareholders want over what helps the town." Rate the degree to which you agree with it.

   Strongly Agree ⟵————————————⟶ Strongly Disagree
   1 --- 2 --- 3 --- 4 --- 5 --- 6 --- 7

2. In this scenario, the town in Kentucky will lose 500 jobs. But a town in Tennessee stands to gain 500 jobs. Does the benefit cancel the harm, or does leaving the first town create more harm than operating in the new town will create?

   _____

   _____

   _____

   _____

3. The current town has refused WoodWorks' request for tax incentives. Does the company have an ethical obligation to give the town a "last clear chance" to make a deal, or is the company ethically free to negotiate a deal with the new town?

   _____

   _____

   _____

   _____

4. If the town in Tennessee offers tax abatements, and the town in Kentucky does not, where should the plant ultimately be located?

   _____

   _____

   _____

   _____

5. Assess the overall fairness of companies that engage in this type of "location shopping" for lower manufacturing costs. First, rate a company that, like WoodWorks, decides to relocate to another town in the United States.

   Fair ⟵————————————⟶ Unfair
   1 --- 2 --- 3 --- 4 --- 5 --- 6 --- 7

   Now, rate a company that decides to close an American plant and relocate outside the United States.

   Fair ⟵————————————⟶ Unfair
   1 --- 2 --- 3 --- 4 --- 5 --- 6 --- 7

   If your second rating differs from your first, elaborate on the reason.

   _____

   _____

   _____

   _____

Stakeholder Focus: Communities

A special relationship often exists between businesses and the communities in which they operate. A company is sometimes the very reason that a town exists in the first place. In days gone by, countless U.S. cities grew around mills and manufacturing plants as workers flocked to new jobs, homes were built to house them, and retailers and service companies emerged to take care of the needs of the new workers. In modern times, many cities still expand dramatically when a major new employer opens its doors. For example, Round Rock, Texas, became the home of Dell in the 1980s. In the 1970s, Round Rock was home to fewer than 3,000 people. Today, it is home to 100,000.

Companies do more than provide jobs. They are often a source of civic pride. The taxes they pay support local schools, police and fire departments, and public utilities. They can give a community a sense of identity.

Businesses often also benefit from communities. Cities provide a labor pool from which many of a firm's employees are drawn. Well-managed cities with low crime rates make it less expensive for a company to operate and make it easier for a company to recruit and retain workers. Well-planned zoning laws and street construction can help a company operate more efficiently.

The special relationship between companies and the communities in which they operate can be one of society's great win-win propositions. But if the relationship sours, both sides can be harmed.

Cities can throw up many roadblocks to smooth operations if such things are desired. Poorly executed road construction projects can make it nearly impossible for customers to access retailers and restaurants. Tax exemptions can be allowed to expire, and new taxes can be levied. The courts can be used in a variety of interesting ways.

When companies decide to shut their doors, communities can be devastated. If a company was a major employer, unemployment rates can skyrocket at the same time that local tax revenue falls off. Many communities in Michigan, for example, have been hammered by losses in manufacturing jobs in the auto industry. Over

400,000 positions have been lost over the last decade, and several more General Motors plants are currently scheduled to be closed as that company seeks to restructure.

Different Categories of Business Closings

Corporate leaders who must make decisions about store and plant closings usually face one of the following basic situations:

1. *A location is profitable, but it is likely that the company could generate a larger profit with a similar location somewhere else.* A restaurant chain, for example, might make an 8 percent overall return but decide to close all locations that are generating less than a 3 percent return to free up money for expanding into areas that look more promising.

2. *A location is breaking even but shows no signs that indicate a likelihood of improvement.* Many businesses reach an equilibrium in which they can meet expenses and keep people on the job, but they no longer generate any significant profits for shareholders.

3. *A location is losing a small amount of money.* Even if the number of dollars is fairly small, many corporate leaders will think differently about a store that is generating a 0.2 percent return than they will about a store that is generating a –0.2 percent return. The negative sign often signals the end of the road.

4. *A location is losing a large amount of money.* Such locations are rarely maintained, even if a corporation is very wealthy and could "afford" to subsidize the money-losing part of the operation.

Strict adherents to the shareholder model would argue that companies have no obligation to the communities in which they operate if a greater return can be generated for the shareholders elsewhere. In all four of the cases previously discussed, they would agree with decisions to close locations.

Stakeholder model advocates would likely reason that at least some duty exists, but they might disagree about the degree to which it exists. They would draw the line in different places if asked to weigh in on the four cases.

"Special" Types of Businesses

Some subscribers to the stakeholder model will also make the case that certain types of businesses have enhanced duties to keep locations open and serve the communities in which they operate. Businesses that support public safety, education, the media, and meeting basic needs such as food or housing are sometimes cited as examples.

The occurrence that inspired this scenario will seem underwhelming: in January of 2010, a mall bookstore closed in Laredo, Texas. (In the real case, the store was a part of the B. Dalton Bookseller chain, and the store's parent corporation—Barnes & Noble—pledged to open a standalone bookstore in 2011.) The facts about Laredo itself, and the nearest bookstore, are accurate.

SCENARIO   **Laredo Bookstore**

"Mr. Donovan?"

"Yes?" The bookstore chain executive looked up from his laptop screen.

"Frank is here."

"Ah, good. Send him in." The assistant opened the door wide. "Hello, Frank!"

"Hello, Mr. Donovan."

"Have a seat, have a seat." Donovan gestured vaguely to a pair of chairs and closed his laptop.

"Thank you."

"What did you want to see me about, again? Something with the closings, was it?"

"Yes, sir," Frank said.

"OK."

"I want to . . . plead the case for one of them."

"Oho! An advocate today!"

"Yes, sir."

"Alright, I'll be sporting. You have five minutes to convince me why we shouldn't close the, ah . . . "

"Laredo store," Frank finished.

"The Laredo store! That's Texas, right?"

"Yes, sir."

"OK, Frank. Clock's running." Donovan spread his hands, smiled, and waited.

"OK, well. The Laredo location is slated to be closed because it's in a mall, correct?"

"Correct. Look, I hate layoffs too, but you know as well as I do that there's no future for us with shopping mall bookstores."

"I completely agree."

"You do? OK, so then . . . "

"I've, ah, marked up a map here of the 30 locations we're closing." Frank slid the map across Donovan's desk, and Donovan studied it. "The red circles around each city are drawn to touch the nearest town with a bookstore."

Donovan peered over the top of his glasses. "A lot of them are red dots."

"Those are cities that will still have another bookstore after ours closes."

"Ah, I see. So then small circles show a town left with no bookstore, but with one in a town nearby. And so forth."

"Yes, sir."

"And the only really big circle is around Laredo."

"Yes. If we close that location, there won't be a bookstore closer than San Antonio. That's about 150 miles away."

"Huh. Nothing closer?"

"No, sir. That part of Texas is largely rural."

"Huh. Well, that's interesting enough. But, Frank, the decision's been made. All the mall bookstores have to go."

"Two hundred and fifty thousand people live in Laredo."

"Yes. And . . . ?"

"And they'll be left without a reasonably accessible bookstore."

"OK, but, Frank, that location made, what, about a 3 percent return last year?"

"About 3 percent, yes."

"OK, and if we close everything in Texas except for the big box stores in Houston and Dallas, our supply chain is different and it would be more expensive to run the Laredo location. It would probably lose money."

"Actually," Frank pulled a file out of his briefcase, "I ran the numbers, and it would break even."

"Ah, a thorough advocate! I appreciate the extra effort, Frank, and I appreciate what you're trying to do, but it's not our responsibility to make sure that everybody has a neighborhood bookstore if we can't make a profit in the neighborhood."

"Maybe."

"Maybe?"

"Laredo has a big problem with illiteracy. If we can help them get kids reading . . . "

"Frank," Donovan took off his glasses and rubbed his eyes. "A, we're not a nonprofit, and B, they'll still have a library."

"Did you learn to read from library books, Mr. Donovan?"

"I checked out a lot of library books when I was a kid."

"Yes, but did you learn to read from them?"

"I certainly . . . well . . . I guess I . . . well, no. No, I learned to read with a kid's dictionary I had in my room."

"That's how most people learn to read."

"OK, so the parents of Laredo will have to order books online. Amazon is killing us, but as long as we're just talking about the good people of Laredo, if they want books for their kids, they can join everybody else in the free world and order them from Amazon."

"Some can, some can't. There's a 30 percent poverty rate in Laredo. Internet access isn't a given."

"Come on, Frank." Donovan opened his hands. "Are you worried about bad press, here? A boycott, that kind of thing?"

"Not particularly, no. I think we could skip town quietly with no consequences like that."

Donovan squinted. "So you're telling me that you're pitching this change purely because ... "

"It's the right thing to do. We serve a large town in a way no one else will."

"My obligation is to the shareholders, Frank."

"And the shareholders will have the same return whether or not we close the Laredo store. We are currently eking out a small profit there, and we should be able to at least break even for the foreseeable future."

Donovan sighed. "If I rethink the Laredo store, are you going to be back in here next week talking about another one?"

"No. The others are losing money, or they are located near other bookstores, or both. The Laredo store is different, Mr. Donovan."

DISCUSSION QUESTIONS

1. Do you agree with the general proposition that companies owe a duty to the communities in which they operate? Rate it below.

   No Duty at All ←——————————————→ Significant Duty

   1 --- 2 --- 3 --- 4 --- 5 --- 6 --- 7

2. Rank the following stakeholders. Place a #1 by the stakeholder that you think corporate leaders should give the most consideration when making decisions, a #2 by the second most important group, etc.

   _____ Shareholders/owners
   _____ Communities in which the company operates
   _____ Employees
   _____ Customers

3. Is there a shorter-term "substitute" action that would be easier than continuing to operate the Laredo bookstore that would be acceptable? Would making a sizeable donation, say $50,000 or $100,000, to local libraries be a reasonable alternative?

   _____

   _____

   _____

   _____

4. In your opinion, would the moral obligation to keep the Laredo location open be any different if it would likely lose money if it were kept open? Would it be any different if the location would still be profitable if it were kept open—perhaps just less profitable than other locations?

_____

_____

_____

_____

5. Are there other kinds of "last-in-town" companies that have an obligation to remain open if the location is no longer profitable but the corporation that owns the location is very profitable? What if the company is the last grocery store? Cable TV provider? Fast food restaurant? Bank?

_____

_____

_____

_____

Stakeholder Focus: Customers and Dangerous Products

BACKGROUND

Toyota had great success for most of the first decade of the twenty-first century. By decade's end, two of the big three American automakers needed sizeable government bailouts, but Toyota had become the largest automaker in the world. In 2009, however, problems began to surface.

"Unintended acceleration" problems became a top news story. Many Toyota customers complained that their gas pedals became "sticky," and that their cars accelerated out of control. Dozens of deaths had been attributed to the problem. The chairman of Toyota was grilled by Congress, and Toyota recalled millions of vehicles and offered to install a new part designed to prevent the sticky accelerator problem.

The impact on Toyota has been substantial. Although the number of serious crashes was very small when compared with the millions of Toyota vehicles sold, political cartoonists, comedians, and *Saturday Night Live* had a field day with "out-of-control Toyotas" routines. While the recall was rolled out, Toyota dealers were ordered to stop selling several models. January 2010 sales were down 16 percent, and Edmunds.com, as well as others who track the auto industry, dropped their forecast market share for Toyota for all of 2010. Toyota was currently offering costly incentives in an attempt to win back buyers.

Another danger lurks for Toyota in addition to problems related to lost consumer confidence. Many attorneys are, shall we say, rather excited. Large corporate defendants with deep pockets can often generate handsome fees for tort lawyers, particularly in the case of defectively designed or defectively manufactured products. The legal standards are easier to meet in many such cases than in ordinary tort cases, and damages can often exceed the value of actual losses.

In lawsuits to come, plaintiffs' lawyers will try to show that Toyota knew about the sticky accelerators for years and did not adequately address the problem, and that they blamed the unintended acceleration cases on floor mats when they knew that there might be other causes. It remains to be seen what evidence will be produced and what juries will think of it, but the courtroom losses for Toyota could potentially be jaw-dropping.

Many companies large and small face similar issues every year. Most manufacturers act in good faith when they make whatever it is they make, but sometimes products have unintended problems. And, in many cases, corporate leaders must consider complicated trade-offs.

Some cases have an obvious answer, but in others, risks are small or perhaps unproven, and the cost of fixing problems is high. In this module's scenario, a manager is introduced to such a dilemma.

SCENARIO

Cooper Fan Company

"OK, this all looks good," Mark talked loudly over the substantial noise inside manufacturing building #2. "If we get that big account as hoped, we should be able to add a third shift sometime this summer."

"If we add 75 jobs, we can double our tax credit with the city," Ernie said.

"That should be doable—if we get that contract."

"I'll keep my fingers crossed," Ernie said as a heavy machine gronked loudly and spit out several dozen newly cut ceiling fan blades.

"What?"

"I say I'll keep my fingers crossed!"

"Yeah. We should know something in the next month. Now, what was that other thing you wanted to talk about?"

Ernie paused. "One of our testers says there's a problem with the CPRF-300 model."

"What kind of a problem?"

"Let's go ask her."

"Lead on."

Ernie led the plant manager to a side door marked with a sign reading "Quality and Design" above it. He hung his hardhat on a peg beside the door before he went through it, and Mark did the same.

Quality and Design Lab

"OK," Ann said, "so this is the standard remote control for the CPRF-300." She handed Mark a small rectangle with buttons marked "Lo," "Hi," "Off," and "Reverse." Mark hit "Lo," and a ceiling fan just above his head started to rotate lazily. He pushed "Off," and the blades slowed to a stop.

"So what's the problem?" Mark asked.

"It's the reverse button. All of our models except the CPRF-300 have a switch on top of the fan itself that allows for the fan to be set to spin clockwise or counterclockwise. People who use it at all set their fans to blow air downward in the summer to make it feel cooler in a room, and reverse the fan's motion to draw air upward in the winter to make rooms feel warmer."

"And the CPRF-300 has it on the remote because . . ."

"Because the design team didn't want our customers with high ceilings to have to drag a ladder out twice a year to use the feature."

"Makes sense. What's the problem?"

"The problem is that, with the old design, the fan had to be stopped for an owner to be able to reach up and flip the switch. But the remote allows for the reverse feature to be engaged while the fan is running."

"What does that do?"

"Press 'Hi,' and wait for the blades to cycle up to speed." Mark did so. When the blades were a blur, Ann said, "Now push 'Reverse.'" When Mark did, there were several rapid clicks and a soft grinding sound as the blades lost speed. The noises stopped after a few seconds, and the blades slowed, came to a stop, changed direction, and began to speed up again.

"Huh. Well, that's a pretty annoying sound, all right," Mark said, somewhat dismissively.

"True," Ann said. "It's what happens after doing that a lot of times that concerns me."

"Oh, come on, no one's going to do that a lot of times. If it makes that sound, they'll remember to stop the blades before they hit reverse."

"Maybe. But these buttons are close together. What if someone hits the reverse button by mistake?"

Mark grunted. "Just for the sake of argument, how many times would someone have to make a 'mistake' before he started to have problems beyond the noises?"

"At least fifty, maybe a hundred or more."

"So come on, now, nobody's going to hit the wrong button a hundred times by mistake."

"What if it's somebody's kid, and the kid wants to make a game of it?"

Mark thought that over for a moment. "OK, so go ahead. What happens if a kid makes a game of it?"

Ann pulled a file from a cabinet drawer and began to recite her findings. "We tested 50 CPRF-300s last week. All of them eventually failed after they were reversed from the high setting repeatedly. The first failed after 55 rounds, the average was 112, and the last one failed at 193 rounds."

Ann continued. "Forty-five of them simply ceased to operate without further incident. Three of them emitted sparks but did not start a fire. One of them started a fire. And the last one threw out a half-inch piece of metal from the inner casing with considerable velocity."

"Define 'considerable velocity,'" Mark said.

"Well, not lethal velocity. But I was there—it hit the wall pretty hard. It was traveling fast enough to put an eye out, certainly."

"OK. And the one that caught on fire, it was a big fire?"

"Not at the point we extinguished it, but it would have spread, yes."

"Ugh," Mark said. "This is terrible timing. We're gunning hard for that new big account. That could double our business."

"Yes," Ann agreed.

Mark pursed his lips and thought for a moment. "What do you recommend?" he asked Ann.

"Well, the first thing has already been done. I've talked to the designers about redesigning our future models to automatically kill the power until the blades are stopped anytime the reverse button is engaged."

"Yeah. That's good."

"As for the CPRF-300s, they're not safe. We could recall them, but because of the way they're put together, there isn't a cheap fix for the mechanical problem. I'm not really sure what to say about how to handle them."

"OK. Thanks, Ann," Mark said. Then, to Ernie, "Get all the numbers and meet me in my office at 3 o'clock."

"Sure thing, boss," Ernie said.

Manager's Office

"Here are the numbers," Ernie said. "We've sold 50,000 CPRF-300s to date. We have had no reports of malfunctions, fires, anything from our customers, retailers, or from the government. I mean, seeing is believing; there is a potential problem with the CPRF-300, but nobody has reported an actual problem, at least so far."

"Yeah. You talk to Lawyer Dave and Jimbo?"

"I did. Lawyer Dave estimated legal costs at probably $20,000 to $200,000 per incident, with no upper limit on a worst-case scenario in which someone dies in a fire or is disabled by flying debris. 'Manufacturers usually get hammered in those kinds of cases no matter what happened,' he told me."

"Jimbo told me that it would be cheaper to just replace the fans than to try to repair them, especially with shipping costs factored in."

"OK." Mark scribbled some notes. "What about that recall we did in 2005 over the sliplock screws? How many people took us up on that?"

"About 15 percent of them. We'd probably have fewer take us up on this one because a lot of them won't want to take down and remount a fan if the problem is not something that they see as an issue. If we send everybody a warning not to reverse while running at high speed, and offer to replace the fan for free, I'd estimate that about 10 percent of them will actually make us send them a new fan. And most of them would be parents with small kids. If we offer to replace their remotes with new ones that don't have a reverse button, maybe we can get down to only replacing 5 percent of the fans."

Mark scribbled some numbers. "Still," he said, "That's maybe a million, million-and-a-half bucks."

"True enough."

"So, just talking dollars and cents, we'd have to have a lot of real-world problems to add up to the cost of a recall."

"Unless someone is killed in a fire, and then all bets are off."

"And then there's the whole matter of, ah, timing. The contract we're up for could set the company up for years. I hear it's a five-year deal. Even if we decide to recommend a recall, I don't want to saddle the executives with this now."

"I know."

"I mean, that deal will probably be done in a month. Six weeks, tops."

"Yeah."

Mark tapped his pen on his paper. "What's your gut tell you, Ernie?"

DISCUSSION QUESTIONS

1. If you were in Mark's position, would you recommend a recall today? Why or why not?

   _____

   _____

   _____

   _____

2. If you were in Mark's position, would you recommend a recall in two months, after the deal has been completed?

   _____

   _____

   _____

   _____

3. Ann's testing showed 6 percent "bad" results (sparks) and 4 percent "really bad" results (fire and thrown metal). Would your answers to questions 1 and 2 change if Ann's testing had shown 18 percent "bad" and 12 percent "really bad" results? What if it had shown the same number of "bad" results but zero "really bad" results?

   _____

   _____

   _____

   _____

   For questions 4 and 5, assume that no recall is done. Assume further that a fan started a fire and burned a home in your town to the ground, and that a local newspaper identified the ceiling fan as the cause. The newspaper later reported that the Cooper Fan Company knew about the potential problem and did nothing about it. Finally, assume that no one was badly injured in the fire.

4. If you had read the newspaper article and later that year went shopping for ceiling fans, would you consider Cooper fans, or would you pass them by even if they were competitive in pricing, appearance, and features?

_____

_____

_____

_____

5. Assume that you are a juror in a lawsuit filed by the family with the burned-down house. If you were convinced that the Cooper fan caused the fire and that Cooper knew about the potential problems, would you award the family more than the value of its lost home and possessions, if you had the chance? Would you award substantially more?

_____

_____

_____

_____

Selling, Marketing, and Advertising

Unit Background

Advertising is often highly effective. Most forms of marketing that do not involve fraud are legally allowed. Should a company ever decide to stop selling its products in a way that is legal and effective for ethical reasons?

Module 12

"Best-Case Scenario Ads". [Many companies adopt an "all-time champion" as their spokesperson. A gym customer who lost 300 pounds might be featured, for example. Is this an ethically sound practice if typical results are dramatically different from those presented in the ad?]

Module 13

Quickly Flashed Fine Print. [It is common for blocks of small text to flash across the screen during commercials. In many cases, viewers would have to pause the broadcast to be able to read everything. Is this a reasonable way to make disclaimers?]

Module 14

Using Fear to Sell. [Fear is a powerful tool. But is it an appropriate device for motivating buyers? Is the answer different for different kinds of products and services?]

Module 15

Celebrity Endorsements: What If the Celebrity Does Not Use the Product? [Famous people often cash in by endorsing products. Is there anything wrong with a celebrity pitching a product that she does not use herself?]

Module 16

Marketing Unhealthy Food to Children. [Obesity is a significant problem. The number of overweight children has skyrocketed in recent years. Do the makers of junk food bear some responsibility for making unhealthy products seem "fun"? Or does the blame lie elsewhere?]

Module 17

Children and Violent Video Games. [M-rated games, on average, outsell milder games. Do game makers have any obligation to keep violent games out of the hands of younger players? Do they have any responsibility to produce more games that are appropriate for younger players?]

Module 18

Ethical Selling: Labeling Sleight-of-Hand. [Laws require several types of accurate information on food product labels. But many misleading tricks are completely legal. Are such tricks ethically acceptable?]

Module 19

Marketing in the Public Schools. [Marketers frequently seek opportunities to sell, or at least advertise, products in public schools. Cash-strapped school districts often jump at the chance to bring in extra funds. When, if ever, do such arrangements cross the line?]

Selling, Marketing, and Advertising

Most businesses play to win, at least most of the time. They seek to sell as many products and services as possible. And marketing is an essential part of the game. The best product in the world won't sell if no one has heard of it.

Companies enjoy a healthy (but not unlimited) amount of First Amendment protection when they seek to communicate with customers. One might argue that the Founding Fathers did not have corporations in mind when they created the right to free speech, but the courts disagree. Although human beings have "more" speech right than organizations, companies are covered (at least in this way) by the Constitution.

The right to free speech allows companies to be fairly aggressive in advertising their wares. Because the Constitution is above everything else in the legal system, the government often *can't* pass laws that would place significant new restrictions on marketing campaigns. Businesses are therefore often left to decide for themselves how to sell, because the law often fails to set any particular requirements.

So when does a company cross a line and act unethically? What is the difference between an acceptable ad campaign and one that is manipulative? Companies always try to paint their products in a favorable light, but can this go too far?

This unit examines disclaimers, fine print, and "best-case scenario" ads. One module asks whether it is "right" to use a celebrity to endorse a product that the celebrity does not use. Two modules examine ads targeted at children. Another looks at deceptive product labels. The last module in the unit looks at marketing in public schools. If you think that it stops with soda machines, then you don't have a child between the ages of 5 and 17.

The central issue in the unit is this: If a marketing campaign is the *most profitable* option, is it necessarily a "good" option for selling products?

"Best-Case Scenario" Ads

BACKGROUND   Advertising is a make-or-break endeavor for countless products. Consider sugary breakfast cereal. There are dozens of varieties on the market that are similar to one another. Sure, maybe one has artificial flavor that is supposed to taste like chocolate and another has artificial flavor that (primarily because the cereal is pink) is supposed to taste like strawberries. Perhaps some varieties contain tiny marshmallows that are of a slightly different shape. But, there is no substantial difference in taste, nutritional value, or price. So who wins? Which gains market share? Usually, it is the brand with the most appealing advertising.

What is true for breakfast cereal is true for soft drinks, sliced cheese, shaving cream, and most of the items in a grocery store. To a lesser but still significant degree, advertising influences the purchases of big-ticket items like appliances, computers, and cars.

The Constitution, Free Speech, and Corporations

The right to free speech is perhaps the best-known of all constitutionally guaranteed liberties. People have the right to say almost anything, and express themselves in almost any way, as long as such expressions do not result in direct harm to others. You can't say, "Hey, kill that guy." You can't lie about people in hurtful ways, such as telling your boss that a coworker is stealing from the company when there has been no theft. But, you are certainly free to express unpopular opinions, criticize the government, create offensive artwork, and the like.

Many people fail to appreciate that free speech rights are not limited to human beings. The Supreme Court has found that, to an extent, speech rights apply to organizations. Corporations have weaker First Amendment rights than people do, to be sure. The government can restrict corporate advertising, for example, if restrictions are directly related to a "substantial" government interest and go no further than necessary to protect the substantial interest. Cigarette ads are heavily regulated on the grounds that they pose a threat to the substantial government interest of enhancing the public's health. In addition, the government can ban ads that are deemed false and misleading altogether.

Some argue that the Founding Fathers intended for constitutional liberties to apply only to people and not to companies. But, in the end, the Supreme Court decides what the Constitution means and the circumstances to which it applies. And, if anything, the current Supreme Court is trending toward expanding free speech rights for corporations.

Citizens United v. *Federal Election Commission* is likely the most important Supreme Court decision of 2010. In it, the Court struck down portions of a law that restricted the ability of corporations to give money to political campaigns on the grounds that the law violated the First Amendment. The five-justice majority reasoned that companies were merely collections of people, and that the groups of people enjoyed free speech rights.

It is true that the *Citizens United* case does not directly deal with commercial messages, but nevertheless it strongly hints that the current justices will not be inclined to restrict corporate First Amendment rights.

In the end, it is reasonable to characterize corporate free speech rights for nonhazardous products in this way: If ads present truthful information, they are probably protected by the First Amendment; if ads present factually false information, they can be regulated.

There exists a common type of ad that presents truthful but perhaps misleading information. This author refers to them as "best-case scenario" ads. In them, a company presents a truthful story featuring an actual customer who had an exceptional experience involving a product or service. Jared from Subway is probably the best known of them. The story, although entirely true, presents a very rare, sometimes unique, case. The companies running best-case scenario ads often feature the all-time grand champion customer, but they say little or nothing about typical results. Some argue that these messages are exploitative. They are not illegal, but some argue that they should nevertheless not be on the air.

In the following scenario, four fictional ads are presented. They parallel real best-case scenario television commercials that have run recently. Does any of them cross a line, or are all perfectly reasonable attempts to entice customers?

SCENARIO

Jane sat on her couch with her eyes wide after watching *Dancing with the Stars*, trying to shake off a genuinely disturbing attempt at a salsa dance by the guy in the ShamWow! commercials. Speaking of commercials, Jane watched four ads right after the show ended.

Ad 1—Mr. Burger

A spokeswoman in a small black dress walked confidently across the screen. "This used to be me," she said as she passed an image projected on the wall behind her. The image showed her three years earlier. "I used to weigh 250 pounds. But I lost half my weight eating Mr. Burger cheeseburgers."

The next scene showed the woman at a cash register in a Mr. Burger restaurant. She smiled, pointed to a menu, and held up two fingers. The cashier laughed and made entries on his cash register. The woman turned her face toward the camera. "For three years, I've been coming to Mr. Burger every day for lunch. I always order two regular cheeseburgers. And the pounds have just melted away!"

Across the bottom of the screen, the words "results not typical" flashed for one second.

"Mr. Burger was part of my diet plan. It was my reward for my morning workouts, and it kept me motivated. Maybe Mr. Burger can work for you!"

The spokeswoman's statements were truthful. She did in fact eat two cheeseburgers at Mr. Burger nearly every day, and, while doing so, she did lose 125 pounds. But, she said nothing about the fact that she ran up to 50 miles per week during the same time, and that she ate healthier food at every meal other than lunch.

Mr. Burger's food is typical of fast food—high in fat, high in calories, and low in nutritional value.

Ad 2—Ever Link

A man sat on his porch swing and patted an old golden retriever on the head. "I love my truck, and so does old Jake here," he said, nodding toward the dog. "*Woof!*" Jake the dog said. The man laughed, looked at the camera again, and said, "I never thought it would save my life."

The screen went black, and the words "Actual recording of Ever Link call, 1/15/11" appeared. The audio clip featured the voice of an Ever Link operator and the panicked voice of the man in the porch swing. A transcription of the conversation appeared on the screen as it unfolded.

Operator: Ever Link, how may I help you?

Customer: Help me, help me, the water's rising!

Operator: Sir?

Customer: I'm cut off! The water's rising fast!

Operator: Stay calm, sir. I've pinpointed your location, and I'm calling for emergency assistance right now.

Customer: Hurry! Hurry!

Operator: Stay on the line, sir.

Operator: I have an Ever Link customer in need of an immediate water rescue at the 22 hundred block of Elm Street. Yes. Correct. Thank you.

Operator: Sir, help is on the way. I'll stay on the line with you until emergency services respond.

Customer: Thank you! That water's still coming up!

[*minutes later*]

Customer: They're here! They're here! Thank goodness!

The screen returned to the image of the man on the porch swing. "That was pretty scary," he said, smiling. "And wouldn't you know, I'd left my cell phone at home. If it hadn't been for the Ever Link button in my truck, I wouldn't be here today."

"*Woof!*" said Jake the dog.

"Ha, ha, ha," the man laughed.

"Ever Link is standard equipment in all new models," a voice-over proclaimed. A car company logo briefly filled the screen, and the commercial ended.

The recording was an actual recording, and the man would likely have been swept away by rising flash flood waters if he had not received prompt rescue.

But of the 77,000 calls made to Ever Link operators over the program's first year of operation, it is the only one that directly led to rescuing a customer from a life-threatening situation.

Ad 3—Super Lotto

A grandmother leaned out the window of a Rolls-Royce. "Super Lotto changed my life!" she said. She put the Rolls in gear and drove away from the camera, revealing a license plate that read "BLING."

In the next scene, a little girl asked her, "What time is it, Grandma?" She held her wrists up toward the camera one at a time, a diamond-studded Rolex on each. "East Coast or West, dear? Ha Haaa!"

The next scene was inside a church. A collection plate made its way down a pew. A woman put in a dollar and passed it to a boy, who put in two quarters. When the plate got to the grandmother, she put in a thick stack of $100 bills, and the congregation burst out in an excited hymn. The grandmother looked at the camera, smiling and nodding.

The last scene showed the grandmother in an enormous first class seat on an airplane. A handsome flight attendant handed her a drink. "Super Lotto!" she said as the commercial ended. "Be in it to win it!"

The grandmother did win $40,000,000 in the Super Lottery. She does own the Rolls and the Rolexes and does donate large sums to her church.

The odds of winning the Super Lottery are 1 in 80,000,000. No statistics about the odds of winning are shown in the commercial. Almost everyone who plays receives either $0 or $5 for matching some but not all numbers. Even with the enormous jackpots, the state takes in twice as much in revenue as it pays out in winnings.

Ad 4—Sonomour College

A man sat at a large, well-polished desk. He looked up from his computer screen and said, "I've come a long way." He looked around his well-appointed office. He turned back to the camera and said, "Thanks to Sonomour College, I got my degree online, on my schedule. It only took two years to get my bachelor's degree in business administration, and my instructors taught me everything I needed to know to run this office. And, most important, I learned how to show the owner of this company that I had the skills he needed. My starting salary was $110,000, and my future is unlimited. Thanks, Sonomour College."

For the remainder of the ad, a voice-over actor gave instructions for enrolling or requesting additional information.

Sonomour College does not have a physical campus; all courses are taught online. The man in the ad is an actual graduate of Sonomour College, and he took actual courses for two years as described. His starting salary was in fact $110,000.

Of the several thousand graduates of Sonomour College, his was the highest starting salary. The second-best starting salary among the several thousand graduates was much lower, starting at $64,000. The average starting pay was $30,000, and 25 percent of graduates were unemployed for a year or longer after earning their online degrees. No statistics were given in the ad other than the $110,000 that the star of the ad earned.

DISCUSSION QUESTIONS

1. To what degree are you influenced by best-case scenario ads? Do you feel "immune" to them?

_____

_____

_____

_____

2. To what degree do you think other people are influenced by best-case scenario ads? Are the ads "fair," or do they manipulate some people? Should the government do more to protect viewers?

_____

_____

_____

_____

3. Should there at least be a requirement that additional information be shown about things like overall odds of winning the lottery, average starting salaries for Sonomour College graduates, and so forth?

_____

_____

_____

_____

4. Which of the four ads is the most acceptable? Which is least acceptable?

_____

_____

_____

_____

5. Should businesses have constitutional free speech rights in the first place, or should constitutional liberties apply only to individuals?

_____

_____

_____

_____

MODULE **13**

Quickly Flashed Fine Print

Everyone is familiar with fine print. Many contracts contain dense blocks of type that create or dissolve any number of rights. Even for a lawyer, reading the fine print thoroughly can be a time-consuming chore.

Of course, fine print shows up in many places other than formal contracts. The backs of baseball tickets usually contain fine print to the effect that you cannot sue the team if you are hit by a foul ball. Fine print often takes the form of an interactive "I Agree" box that must be consented to before digital content will download. And, on many kinds of television ads, text is flashed on the screen for a brief time at some point during the commercial. This last kind of fine print is the subject of this module

The First Amendment and Commercial Speech

To repeat an important point from the last module: The Supreme Court has found that, to an extent, speech rights apply to organizations. Corporations have weaker First Amendment rights than people do, to be sure. The government can restrict corporate advertising, for example, if restrictions are directly related to a "substantial" government interest and if they go no further than necessary to protect the substantial interest. Cigarette ads are heavily regulated on the grounds that they pose a threat to the substantial government interest of enhancing the public's health. The government can ban ads that are deemed false and misleading altogether.

But, generally speaking, *truthful* ads are acceptable and unrestricted, even if they are arguably misleading. The "game" with quickly flashed fine print is often to try to provide enough facts so that an ad is just barely on the right side of the line, and that it is just barely factually accurate.

Of course, sometimes flashers of fine print seek to accomplish other goals.

Where Is the Line?

The scenarios that follow describe four fictional ads. In each, a message appears for fewer than two seconds on the screen. After reading through the four examples, answer the questions that follow. Are the ads unethical, or are they perfectly reasonable attempts to get customers interested in products and services?

SCENARIOS

Ad 1—Unrealistic Car Deal

The owner of a car dealership starts talking loudly in his showroom.

"Come on down to Big State Chevrolet and get the Big Deal from me, Big Mike! Lemme show you what I mean. Here's the best-selling, 300 horsepower, Chevy Camaro. New car, zero miles, ONE-EIGHTY-NINE a month! This is not a lease!" As he proudly gestures to the numbers 1-8-9 on the windshield of the red Camaro, a large block of fine print briefly flashes on the bottom third of the screen.

The fine print indicates that, to get the $189 per month deal, you have to be a consumer with nearly perfect credit, who is willing to finance the car over seven years instead of the usual five, and who has a trade-in worth $10,000. This example is described with more words than necessary, and it would be impossible to read without pausing the commercial.

A typical consumer with average credit, who wants to finance over five years, and who has an average-value trade-in, would pay about $380 per month, or twice the advertised rate.

Ad 2—Sneaky Caffeine Claim

A very well-dressed businesswoman sits at an outdoor table at a coffee shop. She sips coffee from a paper cup with a large "Smith Bros." logo and smiles at the camera.

"Stopping at Smith Brothers Coffee Traders is the best part of my day," she says. "After the rush of early-morning meetings, it's the perfect getaway, and with 24 downtown locations, there's probably one near your office." She sips from the cup again, and then turns to another camera.

"Nothing's better than perking up and planning for the rest of the day with a warm cup of Smith Brothers, and with less caffeine than a bottle of soda, I know I'll be calm enough to handle anything that comes up."

At this point, for one second, the tiny words (5 oz. serving size Smith Bros. original roast vs. Super Turbo Cola 20 oz. size) flash by. Although Smith Brothers does technically have a 5-ounce cup, that size is not on the menu, and almost no one in the history of Smith Brothers has ever ordered a 5-ounce coffee. Also, "original roast" is the blend with the lowest level of caffeine served at Smith Brothers. Several more-popular blends have as much as double the caffeine of original roast. In addition, Super Turbo Cola is one of the most-caffeinated soft drinks, and the 20-ounce bottle is the largest personal serving size of the beverage.

The bottom line is that an average can of an average soft drink contains 40 milligrams of caffeine, and an average cup of an average Smith Brothers coffee contains 250 milligrams of caffeine.

Ad 3—Wireless Service

"Why pay $59, $69, or even $89 a month for cell phone service?" asks the actor in a reasonable voice. "Almost no one really benefits from 'unlimited' voice and texting. If you talk on your cell phone for less than three hours per day, and if you send less than 300 text messages per day, then Super Wireless has you covered for $39 per month. That's right. Nationwide coverage, 100 hours of voice, and 10,000 text messages per month—39 bucks. Why pay more?"

When he says "39 bucks," the bottom of the screen briefly reads: "$39 rate applicable with enrollment in three-year plan. Early termination fee $475." The line is in an *extremely* small font size. A person with 20/20 vision sitting 8 feet from a television would need to be watching a 52-inch screen to be able to read the message.

And so the $39 rate is real, but anyone wanting to cancel service in fewer than 36 months will be hit with a $475 penalty, which is essentially the cost of one year of service.

Ad 4—Weight Loss Program

Aside: A gun firing makes a sound of about 150 decibels. The space shuttle, at launch, is closer to 175 decibels. The meteor impact at Tunguska, Russia, in 1908 weighed in at a world record of 315 decibels and is considered to be the loudest event in recorded history.

The character featured in this ad might be even louder.

As familiar guitar licks from a 1980s-era hair band play loudly, the camera zooms in on an unbelievably ripped spokeswoman. She is standing opposite a life-sized cardboard cutout of herself when she weighed twice her current weight.

"THIS USED TO BE ME!" she shouts, gesturing at the cutout while flexing tremendous biceps. After nodding to the camera, she rears back and punches the cardboard hard enough to send the head flying a dozen feet into the background. "THEN I HEARD ABOUT 'THIN NOW'!"

She picks up a quart-size bottle of an orangeish drink with a distinctive 'THIN NOW' label, upends it, and chugs it down. "AAAHH…THAT'S GOOD!" She crushes the bottle and throws it near the cardboard head.

"'THIN NOW' GAVE ME THE ENERGY I NEEDED TO LOSE ONE HUNDRED AND FORTY POUNDS! THANK YOU, 'THIN NOW'!"

At this point, the following flashes across the screen: "Real user—not an actress. Atypical result." But the spacing on the word atypical is funny. There is a half a space between the "a" and the "t". It is actually kind of hard to say whether it reads, "Atypical," meaning not typical, or "A typical." In any event, the message quickly disappears.

"BUY 'THIN NOW' TODAY AT THESE FINE RETAILERS!" Grocery and drug store logos fill the screen. "BE LIKE ME! GET THIN——NOW!!!!!!!!!!!"

DISCUSSION QUESTIONS

1. Do any of the four examples amount to unethical ads, or are they all reasonable? If any strike you as wrongful, which one(s), and for what reason(s)?

_____

_____

_____

_____

2. Does the fine print in any of the ads make them any more or less acceptable? If so, which blocks of fine print influence your assessment of the ad?

_____

_____

_____

_____

3. Have you ever missed anything in fine print that cost you time, or money, or both? If so, were you upset at the company, or with yourself for not reading the fine print more carefully?

_____

_____

_____

_____

4. Some specific kinds of ads cannot be run without certain specific disclosures that run for a specific amount of time. For example, prescription drug ads are required by law to list common side effects. Ads for certain types of loans must carry prominent statements about whether the loans are "fixed" or "variable." Do you favor laws that would require more information from all kinds of ads? If so, should the information stay on the screen for a longer and defined length of time? Or would such regulations be too intrusive?

_____

_____

_____

_____

5. Aside from the four examples in this module, have you seen any other ads with quickly flashed fine print that are not acceptable? What kinds of products and services were being advertised?

_____

_____

_____

_____

Using Fear to Sell

Many advertisers seek to grab the attention of potential buyers by focusing on good things about their products and services. An image of a steaming-hot hamburger with melting cheese can go a long way toward someone getting in his car and going to the drive-through window. An ad that features an SUV handling off-road terrain at a recreational location can get customers in the showroom.

Other ads focus on discounts, financing, and other money matters. An offer of $3,000 cash back on a car, an offer of 0 percent financing with no payments for two years, or a wireless plan for "only $39 per month" can often convince a viewer that she really can afford the product advertised.

And many other techniques are quite effective.

As discussed in other modules, companies have a large amount of freedom in how they choose to communicate about their products. The free speech guarantee in the First Amendment does apply to corporations. In some ways, it applies more strongly to individual human beings, but corporations can run most kinds of ads, as long as they do not contain information that is false. Companies are not allowed to lie, but they are perfectly free to exaggerate.

So, if most ad types are legal, the question for our discussion becomes: Are there any ad types that are unethical? Are there any permissible yet unacceptably manipulative campaigns?

Some question whether it is appropriate to use *fear* to sell products. Is it OK to make people afraid, and to present an item as the thing that will make a consumer safe from something scary? Ads that use fear have become quite common and are often highly useful in boosting sales. In a typical fear-based ad, companies tend to present (often in a dramatic way) a *possible* but *unlikely* possibility.

Critics of such ads say that the ads do people a disservice, and that they make the world seem (to some viewers) a more dangerous place by making people wary of things that had never before crossed their minds. Companies defend themselves by saying people are afraid of lots of things to begin with, and that their ads merely introduce people to options that might guard against problems that people were thinking of in the first place. Critics say, "You guys manipulate people." Advertisers say, "Ridiculous."

The following scenarios examine different types of fear-based ads. All have become very common in recent years. And although fear-based ads show up in different places, all of the examples are standard 30-second television commercials. None of them presents a fraudulent statement of the type that strips a company of its free speech rights. These are perfectly legal ads, but are they acceptable?

SCENARIO

Ad 1—Big State Insurance

A 30-something woman sits at her dining room table and looks into the camera. She has a very serious expression. Children's voices can be heard in the background.

"As a single mom, I have a lot to think about," she says. "Getting them to school, work, then dinner and homework, the grocery store if I can fit it in." She smiles. "They depend on me for so much. What would they do if something happened to me?"

The camera pulls back to a wider view and the screen now includes three children playing in a living room. The woman watches them, and a soothing male voice-over says, "Big State Insurance offers a wide range of life insurance products. Agents are specially trained to match customers to the level of coverage they need."

The camera zooms back in on the woman. "I couldn't believe how affordable life insurance can be. I have a $500,000 policy from BSI for only $18 a month. Even with money as tight as it is, I hardly miss it. And the peace of mind is priceless." She smiles widely but humbly. "If there were a tragedy, at least they would have the money they need to go to college, and get a good start in life."

The smiling kids come into the kitchen and crowd around the woman. Now she turns up the wattage on her smile all the way and says, "They're worth it."

The odds of a healthy woman in the actress's age bracket dying in a given year are 8,000-to-1.

Ad 2—Senator Smith

Senator Smith is up for reelection, and he has spent millions on campaign ads. They have, for the most part, trumpeted his accomplishments. But, with only two months to go before the election, he is surprised to find himself trailing in the polls. He decides to switch his strategy and starts to run the following ad. Jan Jones is his opponent.

A man with a deep and menacing voice speaks, and a series of black-and-white photos shows on the screen. "It's a dangerous world," the voice-over says as a picture of soldiers in Iraq is shown. "Anything can happen at any time," he says as the image changes to show the Twin Towers. "It's an uncertain world…" the picture changes to a shot of the floor of the New York Stock Exchange. In the image, stressed-out-looking traders watch as the big board reads '-403.67' "…and families are hurting." Now the new image shows a man reading a letter with "Notice of Foreclosure" written across the top in large letters.

The images begin to repeat. "Jan Jones has never dealt with any of these problems. She has never been elected to a public office. She has never run a business. She is not qualified to handle the serious issues facing our nation today. We need proven leadership and a steady hand in these tough times."

Now the screen shows Senator Smith for the first time. He is well dressed and surrounded by his family. "I'll continue to fight terrorists and support our troops. I'll continue to fight for lower taxes for small businesses and for help for those who are struggling to find a job or make ends meet."

Senator Smith's campaign logo is superimposed on the screen, and the ad ends.

Ad 3—Super Light

A woman in a conservative nightgown and a sleeping mask rests on her bed. A silly-sounding voice says, "Amanda!" The voice is vaguely recognizable. The voice actor has done work for several cartoon shows.

The woman stirs slightly. The voice is heard again, louder this time: "A-MAAAN-da!!" The woman snorts, takes off her sleeping mask, and says (comically alarmed), "Who's that?"

"Down here," says the cartoonish voice.

The woman looks around her room. "Down where?"

"In your mattress!"

"Huh?!" the woman says. As she squints, the camera zooms in and shows a cartoon bug. He is multicolored and really gross, and he is surrounded by dozens of smaller bugs. They are dancing under a disco ball.

"It's just us, Amanda!"

"Bugs! In my mattress?" she exclaims.

"Just us dust mites. Millions of us!!" The camera zooms out and shows legions of bugs.

"Humph!" Amanda says. She walks to her closet and pulls out a wand with a large "Super Light" logo on the handle. With a determined look, she returns to her bed, strips the sheets, and turns on the Super Light. She then directs a dim beam of violet light onto her mattress and moves it slowly back and forth. The bottom third of the screen reads: "Super Light kills 99.9% of dust mites."

The perspective shifts back to the cartoon bug world. The disco-dancing bugs look skyward and shade their eyes from the violet light. Then they start to scream. One by one, they start to explode into little puffs of smoke. The disco ball crashes to the mattress floor and shatters, and the music comes to a halt. "And darkness and decay and the red death held illimitable dominion over all."[1]

Shifting back to the real world, the screen shows Amanda turning off the Super Light, nodding with satisfaction, and walking away.

All mattresses have some dust mites, and many do in fact have millions of the microscopic bugs. They are indeed creepy looking when viewed under a microscope. For most people, they are harmless, but they can trigger allergy symptoms in some. The light does in fact kill almost all dust mites.

Ad 4—Comfort Toothbrushes

A man brushes his teeth. When he spits his toothpaste out into his sink, he notices a light pink color in the fluid he spits out. "Honey," he says, "it happened again."

"Your gums?" she says from off-camera.

"Yeah. I thought I was done with this."

His wife enters the bathroom. She holds a new toothbrush in its original packaging. "Try this," she says, handing it to him. "I got this for you last time, remember?"

"Oh, I guess not," he says, sheepishly.

"Well, you should use it. Your old toothbrush is too harsh—it's no wonder your gums are bleeding. Comfort toothbrushes are made a new way, with a new kind of bristle. It cleans your teeth without irritating your gums."

"Huh. OK, I'll try it."

"You'll be glad you did."

Sometimes, bleeding gums are indeed caused by abrasive toothpastes or toothbrushes, or by people exerting too much pressure while brushing. But bleeding gums are also sometimes a sign of periodontal disease or of a nutritional deficiency.

Ad 5—Betapi Security Service

A woman sits on her couch at night watching a horror movie. From her TV, a woman screams as a knife-wielding madman menaces her. The movie cuts to a commercial break. The woman on the couch looks down and notices that she is out of popcorn. She heads to her kitchen for a refill. In her kitchen, she hears a sound, turns around quickly, and spots a knife-wielding burglar picking at her back door. The burglar is one

---

[1] Author's note: I apologize. I read "The Masque of the Red Death" among other Edgar Allan Poe tales while writing this section.

scruffy-looking dude, and he is wearing black gloves and a black ski cap. He gets the door open and says, menacingly, "Come 'ere."

The camera zooms in on the Betapi Security Service box next to the back door. The "enter code" light is flashing in yellow. The burglar takes a step toward the woman, and then another. She shrinks back in fear. The camera shifts back to the security box. The yellow "enter code" light blinks off, the red "alarm" light blinks on, and a loud siren blares.

The burglar stops his advance, indecisive for a moment. Then, he hears a dog barking outside and the sound of a neighbor's voice. He grimaces, and then turns and runs.

The woman's phone rings, and she says, "Hello?" in a shaky voice.

"Mrs. Smith, this is Betapi Security Service. Are you OK?"

"No, someone just broke in," she replies.

"I'm notifying the police now, Mrs. Smith."

"Thank you," she says. She slumps against her counter as the commercial ends.

In the ZIP codes where the ad was shown, the odds of a home burglary with forced entry happening in any given year are 500-to-1. The odds of such a burglary when a homeowner is in the house are 2,500-to-1. The odds of a burglary resulting in an assault against the occupant are 8,500-to-1.

DISCUSSION QUESTIONS

1. Rank the five ads, from #1 (most unethical) to #5 (least unethical).

   _____ Life insurance

   _____ Political attack ad

   _____ Dust mite light

   _____ Toothbrush

   _____ Home security service

2. Focus on your #1 and #2 rankings from the first question. What, specifically, do you find questionable about these ads?

   _____

   _____

   _____

   _____

3. Did any of the statistics in the scenario influence your assessment of the ads? If so, which ones? If not, would even longer odds (of, say, 1,000,000-to-1) have influenced your rankings?

   _____

   _____

   _____

   _____

4. Should any of these ads be disallowed/made illegal, or are none of them that bad?

   _____

   _____

   _____

   _____

5. Going back to an idea in the background section, do you think fear-based ads *create* fears in the first place, or do they merely inform people about solutions for things that they are *already afraid of*?

   _____

   _____

   _____

   _____

Celebrity Endorsements: What If the Celebrity Does Not Use the Product?

BACKGROUND

Advertising is an essential part of the mix for any company that relies on sales to individuals. Many ads do an excellent job of conveying a product's features or low price. The primary value of others is in letting customers know where products may be purchased.

But often, the game is different. A common and successful technique is to tell customers little about a product, but to leave them with the vague impression that something is interesting or that interesting people like it. Many companies do quite well by merely establishing product or brand recognition with large numbers of potential buyers. The best product in the world does not sell if no one has heard of it; mediocre products can generally sell quite well if everyone has heard of them. To execute these strategies—to make consumers remember a product and think that it is "cool"—companies often turn to celebrity endorsements.

Best-Compensated Celebrities

Lucrative opportunities are abundant for well-known actors, athletes, singers, and other "personalities" like Paris Hilton and Kim Kardashian, who are famous for reasons that are difficult to pinpoint.[1] Many famous people earn far more money endorsing products than they do for the activity that initially made them famous.

Before his well-publicized escapades, Tiger Woods had been the highest-paid celebrity endorser in the world for eight straight years. From July 2008 to June 2009, he earned $100,000,000 off the golf course. Many companies have dropped Tiger, so it appears that the next few races for highest-paid celebrity are wide open.

Among the highest-paid athletes in the world, only a few, such as Manny Pacquaio (boxing) and the hugely-unpopular-outside-of-New-York Alex Rodriguez, earn most of their money from sports. Much more common among athletic super-earners are Kobe Bryant, David Beckham, and LeBron James. All earn substantial portions of

---

[1] Is it possible to be famous for being famous? If so, how does one first attain this status?

their $45 million annual pay from endorsements. Off the field, Reese Witherspoon, Shakira, and Catherine Zeta-Jones all earn in excess of $20 million endorsing products and services to supplement their pay as performers.

Ethics Issues

Many celebrity endorsements are unquestionably effective. And, unless celebrities make flatly false claims in commercials, then, as with all spokespeople, no legal violation exists because the First Amendment provides fairly broad protection for corporate "speech."

Nevertheless, some ads that feature celebrities present interesting ethics questions. Is it wrongful for a celebrity to endorse a product that may be harmful to consumers? Is it wrongful if a celebrity endorses a product that he or she does not use? What about the companies that set up these deals? Do they have any responsibilities to the celebrities who sign on with them?

The following scenario examines these questions.

SCENARIO

Assume that Colby Johnson is an NFL phenomenon. In his rookie season, he led the lowly Buffalo Bills to the Super Bowl. His good looks and quick wit have made him one of the most visible athletes in America.

He has been rewarded with four substantial endorsement deals. He is now the spokesperson for Diet Pepsi, Miller Lite beer, Norelco electric shavers, and Jump Start Trainers, a line of workout shoes with unusual soles that the company claims increase strength and agility.

Ad 1—Diet Pepsi

Two professionally dressed women walk down a sidewalk in a downtown area.

"So I'll obviously never go out with him again," says the first.

"Ugh! Aren't there any decent guys in this town?" asks the second.

A man wearing a plaid polyester sport coat approaches from the opposite direction, carrying a bottle of another brand of cola. "Well, hellllll-o, ladies," he says, moving his eyebrows up and down. The two women grimace and brush past him, only to nearly collide with an extremely out-of-shape, sweaty man in a construction jumpsuit who is carrying a bottle of yet another brand of cola. "Oi, pardon me," he grunts. The women grimace again and move on.

Then, one of them stops in her tracks and inhales sharply. The other notices and follows her friend's gaze. The camera swings around to frame Colby Johnson approaching wearing a tight T-shirt. The camera speed goes to slow motion and the new Black Eyed Peas single starts to play. Johnson flashes a 1,000-watt smile, takes a long swig of Diet Pepsi, and says, "Aaah!"

The camera speeds up to normal, and as he passes the women, he smiles and nods nonchalantly to them. The women turn and watch him walk away, spellbound, as a Diet Pepsi logo fills the screen.

Ad 2—Miller Lite

An ad opens with a group of people at an apartment sitting on a large orange couch. They are watching a gigantic HDTV. The camera is positioned behind the TV and faces the group, and a voice-over can be heard. "Time for one last play. Four receivers in the game. Johnson out of the shotgun, takes the snap, and rolls right under pressure. Slips loose from a tackler, and HE'S GOT A MAN! Johnson heaves the ball to the end zone for Milner…TOUCHDOWN!!! BILLS WIN!!!" The fans on the couch go absolutely crazy.

In the second scene, the fans mingle in twos and threes around the orange couch. A doorbell rings, and the door is answered. Johnson enters dressed in street clothes. "Colby!" everyone in the apartment shouts. "Great game! Atta Boy! You're the man!"

say several people at more or less the same time. Someone hands Johnson a bottle of Miller Lite. "Thanks, bro," he says.

The remainder of the ad shows Johnson laughing and talking to friends while holding the bottle. He does not drink from it.

Ad 3—Norelco

Colby Johnson, wearing jeans and nothing else, stands at a bathroom sink. Most of the ad shows him shaving with a Norelco as a voice-over describes the electric razor's attributes. When he is finished shaving, a stunning young woman enters from stage right, rubs Johnson's freshly shaved face, and crinkles her nose in delight.

Before shooting the ad, he had two days' beard growth. He really did go from unshaven to clean-shaven by using the Norelco razor while the ad was being filmed.

Ad 4—Jump Start Trainers

The ad opens with Johnson lacing up a pair of Jump Start Trainers in a quiet locker room.

Then, with a strong beat playing in the background, the ad shows Johnson blasting through a series of drills with a trainer, running bleachers, and lifting weights.

In the last scene, his gray T-shirt wet with sweat, he throws his Jump Start Trainers back into his locker. The camera zooms in on them, and the Jump Start Logo is superimposed.

During all scenes filmed for the commercial, Johnson was really exercising wearing the Jump Start Trainers.

Early Monday Morning: 7-11 Store in "The Good Part of Town"

Colby Johnson pulled his Porsche into the parking lot and went into the store. He purchased a 20-ounce Diet Pepsi and a pack of Gillette razor blades. Because he is a star professional athlete with four major endorsement deals, he can afford to buy razor blades at a convenience store.

"Nice to see you, Mr. Johnson," said the regular early-shift clerk.

"Hey, Danny," Colby replied.

"Gonna beat the Bengals this weekend?"

"That's the plan."

The clerk scanned the items. "Your regular morning Diet Pepsi. (*beep*) Ay! I thought you were a Norelco guy *(beep)*," he said.

"Nah, not in real life. I just like to shave with a blade."

"Hah! Well, I won't tell anyone, Mr. Johnson."

"Thanks, Danny," Colby said as he swiped his credit card.

"See you tomorrow morning, Mr. Johnson."

"See you tomorrow morning, Danny."

Late Monday Morning: Bills' Practice Facility

Colby looked through his locker, but his workout shoes were nowhere to be found. An attendant walked through the locker room wheeling a large canvas laundry basket. "Hey, man," Colby said to him. "Can you grab me a pair of cross-trainers?"

"Sure thing," the attendant replied. "What size?"

"Fourteen."

"You want the Jump Start Trainers, right?"

"No way! Those things hurt my feet, man. Get me a pair of Nikes."

Monday Evening: 7-11 Store

Colby walked to the register with a six-pack of Miller Lite. A woman spotted him, walked over, and said, "Excuse me?"

"Hmm?" Colby rarely made it all the way home without signing a few autographs. He automatically reached for a Sharpie marker in his back pocket.

"Mr. Johnson, I'm Brenda."

"Hello."

"Mr. Johnson, I'm a member of Mothers Against Drunk Driving, and I wonder if I could have a moment of your time."

"Oh. Ah, look, I'm on my way home. If you call my manager…he's in charge of scheduling me for events and…" Colby made his way toward the cash register.

"But I'm interested in talking to you, not your manager."

"Oh. Well, hey, I can promise you I never drink a single beer if I'm going to be driving anywhere. I'm going to drink these at home on my couch." Colby paid for the beer and headed toward the exit.

"That's excellent, but I'd like to talk to you about the ads you run for Miller, there," she said, nodding at the six-pack. "Young people are very impressionable, and people like you who are in the public eye are very influential members of the community. Have you considered the message that your ads have on young people?"

Colby was through listening. He reached his car and opened the door. "Have you thought it over, Mr. Johnson?" the woman persisted. Colby closed the door. The woman continued talking through the closed window as he started the car. "Twelve thousand people died in drunk driving accidents last year, Mr. Johnson!"

At that, Colby rolled down his window. "That's not my fault," he said.

"Not entirely, of course not. But you play a part. I hope you'll call me," she said, offering a business card. Colby did not take the card. He put his Porsche in gear and drove away.

DISCUSSION QUESTIONS

1. When celebrities are paid hefty endorsement fees, products end up costing more money. Do you have any general opposition to celebrity endorsements? Is it acceptable, for example, if the wholesale price of Diet Pepsi is five cents more per bottle because of Johnson's role as spokesman?

   _____

   _____

   _____

   _____

2. Is it acceptable for celebrities to endorse products that they do not use themselves? Is there any difference in your mind between Johnson's endorsement of the razor or shoes he does not use and the beverages that he actually drinks?

   _____

   _____

   _____

   _____

3. Now consider the Miller Lite ads. Do celebrities have any obligation to avoid endorsing products that are entirely legal but may be harmful to some? Does the reason for a person's celebrity make a difference?

   _____

   _____

   _____

   _____

4. Is there currently an actual celebrity ad that seems wrongful to you? If so, what is it?

   _____

   _____

   _____

   _____

5. Many companies dropped Tiger Woods after his affairs came to light. Most would agree that if a celebrity's inappropriate behavior tarnishes his or her image, a company is not ethically obligated to continue making that person its public face. But what if something happens to tarnish an image that is not the celebrity's fault? What if Colby Johnson has a career-ending injury, and he no longer generates the same amount of interest? What if his girlfriend is caught having a fling, the paparazzi captures it on film, and in the end Colby looks less "manly"? What if, after playing for several years, his face has taken a beating, and he looks less youthful?

Do companies ever have an obligation to stand by their celebrities if endorsements become less profitable?

_____

_____

_____

_____

Marketing Unhealthy Food to Children

When she was First Lady of the United States, Nancy Reagan made the "Just Say No to Drugs" campaign the centerpiece of her public service. In more recent years, First Lady Laura Bush made a focused effort to improve literacy rates. Current First Lady Michelle Obama's attention has turned to childhood obesity.

Michelle Obama heads a task force that has an ambitious approach for controlling what has become an epidemic. The rate at which children in America meet medical definitions for being overweight or obese is up sharply in recent years to nearly one-third of all children. Mrs. Obama's goal is to reduce the rate to 5 percent by 2030.

It remains to be seen whether government agencies will pass new regulations that legally require changes. Michelle Obama has indicated that her first preference is not to seek new laws. The White House Task Force on Childhood Obesity will at least initially rely on using the "bully pulpit" to encourage voluntary changes. But it may not stop there.

Administrative Agencies and Regulations

For nearly one hundred years, Congress has, from time to time, created administrative agencies. The trend has been that when a problem becomes large and complicated, the government creates a new part of itself to specialize in addressing the problem. So, for example, when taxation became complicated, the Internal Revenue Service (IRS) was established. The Environmental Protection Agency (EPA) was formed to oversee new and elaborate environmental regulations. The Equal Employment Opportunity Commission (EEOC) handles discrimination issues, the Securities and Exchange Commission (SEC) is in charge of securities, the Federal Aviation Administration (FAA) regulates the airlines, and so forth.

When many people think of federal laws, they think of Congress. They assume that all national laws are passed by elected representatives and senators and are signed by the president. But an interesting aspect of many government agencies is that they have the power to pass laws themselves. When Congress passes a law, it is called a **statute.** When an administrative agency passes a law, it is called a **regulation.** Just like statutes, regulations are binding legal rules. If they are broken, negative consequences follow.

If, for example, the FAA requires a certain kind of safety inspection of large airplanes before every flight, and if an airline is caught by the FAA in failing to complete the inspections, bad things will happen to the airline. It might be fined or temporarily grounded. In an extreme case, it might lose its ability to operate altogether.

The point is that even though regulations are not passed by Congress, they are "real" laws that *must* be followed. Compliance is not optional.

Political Risks of Regulations

The decision facing Mrs. Obama and her task force is not an easy one. If administrative agencies are enlisted and regulations are passed, change will be required and will happen more quickly. The Federal Trade Commission may pass new rules if the food industry does not create new "responsible, industry-generated" changes. The Department of Health and Human Services (HHS) has taken a mostly similar approach. For now, no new regulations have been passed, but HHS has called for help in "bringing…the epidemic of childhood obesity under control."

Regulations might be the most effective road to travel, but the political risks of new laws aimed at childhood obesity may be substantial. Change might be expensive. Food companies have invested greatly in marketing strategies that are effective, and many of them won't want to follow new rules on how they may or may not advertise. Many of them will lobby Congress to prevent new legal requirements, and some of them will file lawsuits, claiming that any restrictions on advertising violate the Constitution's right to free speech. Such lawsuits may be effective; the Supreme Court has recently expanded the free speech rights of organizations.

Some politicians seek to capitalize on any expansion of government oversight by appealing to voters' sense of independence. Political ads with messages along the lines of "Why should government decide what your child may eat? Parents must be trusted to decide what their children may eat" might become common, and they might be effective.

Consumers may also be upset. Soft drinks sell well because people like them. The same is true for fast food and snack food. Some consumers may resent any efforts that have the effect of reducing choices, increasing prices, or changing the taste of their favorite treats.

Difficult choices await food companies. Until and unless new regulations are passed, their leaders will be free to make or not make the changes Michelle Obama advocates. The following scenario takes a look at some of the upcoming decisions that will need to be made.

Assume that Food Corp is a giant company with many holdings that have been acquired over the years. Among other things, Food Corp produces processed food and beverages, and it owns a chain of grocery stores.

SCENARIO

Food Corp

"So, anyway, the numbers look excellent for this quarter. We'll beat estimates by at least 5 percent," the CFO concluded.

"Excellent, really excellent. Nice work, everybody," said the CEO of Food Corp. "At this rate, we'll be up to #2 in, what, a couple of years?"

"We're on pace for that, yes."

"Maybe #1 someday."

"I don't see why not."

"Excellent, excellent."

"So while we're thinking long term, let me summarize something for you before I go."

"By all means."

The CFO pulled up a new file on her iPad. "I had John's group work up a report on how they think the Childhood Obesity Task Force might impact us."

"Here we go."

"It's not so bad. John thinks we can actually come out ahead."

"Humph. Just bugs me when we get the blame for parents who can't balance their kids' diet. But go ahead."

"OK. John's team makes four recommendations. First up: The team recommends that we phase out using cartoon characters to advertise our cereals and drinks over the next five years."

The CEO grimaced. "That'll kill us. We've spent a fortune building up those characters. Kids don't think of our cereals—they think of the Jolly Dwarf or Princess Cinnamon."

"In the short term, we might lose market share, yes. John's team estimates a 5 percent drop in our overall sales. But the team also believes that a ban on cartoon characters is a likely eventual outcome. There's precedent, of course. The Feds killed Joe Camel in the 1990s. If we adapt our marketing strategy now, we'll be ahead of everyone else if it becomes illegal to use cartoon characters in the way that we use them."

"I'm skeptical that will ever happen. I mean, it was one thing to use a cartoon camel to sell cigarettes, but we're selling cereal."

"But we're kind of the new scapegoat, at least to some people."

"Maybe. Unfortunately."

"Yeah."

"Dropping the characters would be a big step. But go ahead and at least have the advertising people run an analysis for me."

"Will do. So, John's second recommendation is to cut the added sugar in our cereals and drinks by 25 percent."

"People won't like the taste as much."

"A few won't, but John did a taste test between our existing products and 'low sugar' versions of them and found that most people couldn't tell any difference. He estimates a 4 percent drop in sales if we make the shift. He also estimates a 3 percent increase in sales if we cut sugar from consumers who would be more likely to buy a 'reduced sugar' item. We could experiment on a couple of products for a while. See if he's on the right track."

"OK. I'll think it over."

"Third recommendation," the CFO said, "is to offer our frozen dinners and soft drinks in smaller serving sizes. John thinks we should sell, for example, a 300-calorie frozen pizza next to a larger 600-calorie pizza, and 8-ounce mini-cans of our soft drinks next to the 20-ounce bottles."

"We make more money if people buy the big sizes."

"Yeeess, but…most people will probably still buy the large sizes. This is just a move to get in line with the Task Force's recommendations before it tries to change the law. If we give people a choice, the case that the government should require smaller serving sizes gets weaker."

"I guess so. What'll it cost us?"

"Probably nothing. John estimates a 3 percent drop in earnings from some consumers paying less for smaller sizes, but a 3 percent increase from new customers who are attracted to the smaller sizes."

"Hmm," the CEO checked his watch. "You have one more?"

"Yes. The last one involves the grocery stores. We might even make money on this one."

"I'm all ears," the CEO said, smiling.

"You've heard the term 'food desert'?"

"Ah...sounds vaguely familiar."

"It's a place with few grocery stores where fresh food is hard to come by. Some urban areas are like that, for example."

"OK."

"Part of the Task Force's recommendations focused on food deserts. It wants all kids to have access to healthier food."

"But we've run the numbers on inner-city locations before. They don't make money for us."

"That's true, but there's a new program that was buried deep in the budget that passed last week. It turns out that $40 million in funding is available to 'create incentives to encourage new market participants' in food deserts. If we open stores in underserved areas and make fresh produce and healthy food available, we qualify for a slice of the money. John thinks that if we are among the first to announce formal plans to expand our grocery operations into urban areas, we'll qualify for something like $3 million in government incentives. We might operate the stores at a small loss for a while, but we'd get a check up front. John thinks that, with the government incentives, the new stores would end up being less profitable than our existing locations, but still profitable. And it might improve our image."

"Hmm."

"Food for thought. And that's all of them."

"Yeah, OK. And think I will."

"OK. Until next time?"

"Yeah. And, again, great news on those second-quarter numbers."

DISCUSSION QUESTIONS

1. Set aside the specific company in the scenario and assess the four ideas in general. Rank them from most likely to help the problem of childhood obesity (#1) to least likely to help with the problem of childhood obesity (#4).

   _____ Eliminate cartoon characters used to advertise sugary cereal, snacks, and drinks.

   _____ Reduce added sugar itself in cereal, snacks, and drinks.

   _____ Expand offerings of lower calorie, smaller-sized portions.

   _____ Expand grocery store locations into "food deserts."

2. Now consider the same basic ideas from Food Corp's perspective. Rank the four ideas presented to the CEO from most worthy of consideration (#1) to least worthy (#4) of consideration for the company.

   _____ Eliminate cartoon characters used to advertise sugary cereal.

   _____ Reduce added sugar by 25 percent.

   _____ Offer lower calorie, smaller-sized portions.

   _____ Expand grocery store locations.

3. To what degree should parents and guardians bear responsibility for their children's diets? Are they more or less to blame for childhood obesity than food companies?

_____
_____
_____
_____

4. To what degree do food companies have an ethical obligation to try to reduce obesity in their customers, if in so acting their profits would decline? Is the obligation different if most of their consumers are adults and not children?

_____
_____
_____
_____

5. Do you expect real food companies to make the kinds of changes outlined in this module? If they fail to do so, should the government require the changes with new regulations?

_____
_____
_____
_____

MODULE 17

Children and Violent Video Games

BACKGROUND

I am not a "hardcore" gamer, but I have had a fairly new video game console or two in my home for roughly the last 30 years. Atari begat NES begat Sega Genesis, and so on. These days, a PS3 graces the small table under my TV.

Video games have been rated for some time. In most nonsports games, there are enemies that must perish before the game advances. These are my inexpert assessments for what the ratings mean where violence is concerned. (Of course, some games receive higher ratings for sexual content and foul language, but this module focuses on violence.)

In E-rated games, bad guys tend to be cartoonish. When they are killed, they are usually squashed in some fashion. They often say "Oof!" or the relative equivalent, before blinking out of existence or disappearing in a puff of smoke.

In T-rated games, human or humanoid enemies are killed realistically, and sometimes graphically. They are eviscerated with cutting, they are shot, or they explode with blood and gore. Shots to the head often kill more efficiently than shots to the body. But, in T-rated games, the enemies still tend to be unambiguous "bad guys." They are invaders from another planet intent on taking over the earth, or Nazis, or demons.

In M-rated games, one or both of the "limits" in T-rated games is exceeded. Sometimes, deaths are spectacular, with amazing levels of blood and gore. And, sometimes, the victims are not necessarily bad guys. Innocent bystanders may be taken out, for example. It may even be to a player's advantage just to kill everyone.

I myself don't play many M-rated games. I usually don't mind violent movies, but playing through extreme scenarios in first person is not all that appealing to me. But a lot of people enjoy a lot of things I don't enjoy, and vice versa. I don't want to go without the "MLB.com At Bat" app on my iPod; maybe you don't want to live in a world without *Grand Theft Auto*. Unless compelling reasons exist, it is difficult to justify laws that force restrictions on choices for everyone.

But the question becomes tricky where children, and especially young children, are involved.

Research

The idea that violent television leads to more violence in the real world is not a new one. In the 1970s, a Canadian researcher published a study on a village that, for a time, had no access to TV because over-the-air broadcasts were blocked by a nearby mountain range. When cable TV brought access to the village, violent behavior in the local school increased by over 150 percent. Current research shows that an average sixth grader has seen over 100,000 depictions of violence on TV.

In 1999, the massacre at Columbine High School brought attention to the possible link between violent video games and real-world harm. The two students who killed 12 of their classmates and a teacher were extremely avid players of *Doom*, an early first-person shooter game.

Several researchers have conducted studies in recent years that seek to determine whether there is a link between violent video games and violent behavior. To date, none has established a **causal** link that shows clear evidence that violent games transform a regular child into a violent child. But many have shown at least a **correlative** link between the two. It does appear from the studies that the more hours a child spends playing violent games, the *more likely* it is that he or she will act out in real life.

But there certainly may be other explanations than the games themselves. A child who is free to play graphic games for hours on end may often be unsupervised by parents, and the lack of supervision may be the primary culprit.

Supreme Court Case for 2010–2011 Term

As I write this edition, the Supreme Court has just agreed to review a California case that directly addresses the issue of selling violent video games to minors. By the time you read this, the case will have been decided. Google *Schwarzenegger* v. *Video Software Dealers Association* to find out what happened.

At issue in the case is a state law that the California Legislature passed. The law seeks to make it illegal to sell M-rated games to anyone under 18 and to require manufacturers of games to place additional information on game boxes. The fines are hefty: $1,000 per violation. The Ninth Circuit Court of Appeals struck the law down on free speech and equal protection grounds. The Supreme Court has been very protective of free speech rights in recent years, but because the California law is aimed at protecting minors, the justices may have a different point of view this time around.

To pass constitutional muster, a majority of the justices will have to be convinced that the law advances a "substantial government interest," and that it goes "no further than necessary" to directly advance that interest. The first argument should be easy. The second will be difficult but not impossible to make. The video game industry will point to its rating system and will argue that a total ban on selling violent games to minors goes "further than necessary."

The following scenario gets at the heart of the California lawmakers' justification for the law at issue in the case.

Galactic Games Headquarters

"And so," the president concluded, "it is my judgment that we need to refocus our attention on hardcore gamers. The sales of family games are centered on long-running, proprietary characters. We don't have Mario or Sonic in our stable, and we should leave kids' games to people who do."

Only one vice president spoke up. "But shouldn't we continue to make at least some games for younger players? If their only choices are extreme games, they'll play extreme games. Shouldn't kids have a chance to play something milder, at least for a while?"

"That's not our problem. Our shareholders expect solid returns, and our M-rated games make five times more money than our E-rated games. I'm pulling funding on the kids and family team after this development cycle."

Galactic Games Design Lab

"So," the game box designer said to his assistant, "this is the one I like so far for *Crime Wave 3*." He pulled an image up on his screen. "Whaddaya think?" It showed four cartoonish characters on a city sidewalk among skyscrapers. They had weapons and carried loot. One of them carried a gas can.

The assistant looked at the image for a long time. "I'm…surprised."

"But do you like it?"

"Well. I'm not sure. It's just so different from the last two. Those were, you know, rough looking. These look like manga."

"I was going for anime, but yeah."

"I mean, they look like kids. Do the characters in the game look like kids this time?"

"Not really. I just softened them up for the box cover."

"Yeah. Why?"

"I figure it like this. We get paid based on sales, right? And we're not making games for kids anymore, right? So I figure with a cover like this, the hardcore gamers who played *Crime Wave 1* and *Crime Wave 2* will buy it anyway. And it might look interesting to kids, too. And if a kid holds this box up to Mommy and Daddy, and if Mommy and Daddy just give it a quick glance, maybe they think it's just a cute kids' game and pat little Billy on the head and put it in the shopping cart. So, bingo! We sell more copies and make more money."

The Mall

"Mom, can I get this game?" Billy, age 11, asked.

His mom looked up from her iPhone briefly and gave it a casual glace. "Fine," she said.

Billy tossed the game into the shopping cart.

Later, while driving home, she said, "I'm going out tonight. Do you want to pick up something to eat?"

"Aw, Mom, again?"

"Mom needs some grown-up time."

"When will you be home?"

"Not too late. You can play your game as late as you want."

Billy's House

And so, Billy was left home alone at 7:00 PM while his mother met her girlfriends for drinks. A lot of drinks, it turned out. And on the big-screen TV, Billy played *Crime Wave 3*.

At 8:00 PM, Billy was beating security guards senseless with a baseball bat and robbing a bank.

At 9:00 PM, he was burning down the building of a character that refused to pay his character protection money after beating the character senseless with a baseball bat.

At 10:00 PM, he was beating up an old lady with his virtual bat and stealing her car.

At 11:00 PM, he was looking for characters that walked out of the game's nightclub and wandered off by themselves into isolated areas. When he found them, he beat them senseless with a baseball bat and stole their wallets.

At 12:00 PM, Billy took to wandering aimlessly around the game's landscape and attacking (with a baseball bat) any character that happened to be in the vicinity. Policemen, prostitutes, and panhandlers were perpetually pounded purposefully.[1]

At 1:00 PM, Billy's mom shuffled in. Her breath mint was utterly overpowered by the odor of coconut daiquiri and Benson & Hedges Lights.

Billy shut down his game and went to bed.

Billy's School—The Next Morning

"Hey, Coach!" the assistant shouted. "Phone call! It's the AD!"

The coach in turn said to the sixth grade P.E. class on the baseball diamond, "I've gotta take this. Keep playing—I'll be back in five minutes." The coach walked off the field and into the school building.

Billy's team was batting, and most of them were sitting on bleachers behind home plate. When the coach was gone, Billy took up one of the bats and casually wandered behind the bleachers, where a single sixth grader was sitting alone, bored.

"Hey," Billy said, mimicking the voice of his character in *Crime Wave 3*. "Gimme your !@#$%^& lunch money."

The other boy was startled, but said, "No way."

Quoting another line from the game, Billy said, "I'll give ya one… last… clear… chance." With each word, he patted the barrel of the bat in the palm of his left hand, just as the character in the game often did.

"Leave me alone," the other boy said as he started to stand up. Billy hit him in the leg with the bat before the boy was able to escape. The boy had a deep bruise, but it healed up nicely in a couple of weeks. Billy was sent to an alternate school for more than a couple of weeks.

DISCUSSION QUESTIONS

1. Do you think there is too much marketing of violent products to kids? Do you buy the notion that it creates or worsens any problems that would not have existed anyway?

   _____

   _____

   _____

   _____

2. Should a state like California be permitted to pass laws that restrict the sale of violent games to minors, or should the courts strike such laws down?

   _____

   _____

   _____

   _____

---

[1]Alliteration! Thank you!

3. From the scenario, rate the relative fault of the people involved in contributing to the injury.

	No Fault at All ←————————→ Significantly to Blame						
Game Executive	1	2	3	4	5	6	7
Game Box Designer	1	2	3	4	5	6	7
Parents	1	2	3	4	5	6	7
Clerk	1	2	3	4	5	6	7
Billy	1	2	3	4	5	6	7

4. Setting Billy aside, would it be fair for any of the adults in the scenario to face fines or other legal sanctions for their roles in getting the game into Billy's hands?

_____

_____

_____

_____

5. Is there too much violence shown on TV, in the movies, on the news, or anywhere else for your comfort level? As a consumer, do you avoid purchasing products or services from any companies that show too many graphic images?

_____

_____

_____

_____

Ethical Selling: Labeling Sleight-of-Hand

BACKGROUND

Selling processed food is a tough business. Competition for shelf space and loyal customers is intense, and profit margins are tight. Companies use a variety of entirely legal tactics to gain and retain market share.

But some groups have been highly critical of "big food" companies. They often argue that companies go too far in how they market to minors, disguise ingredients in some products, or cross the line in other ways.

The regulatory environment is constantly changing, but regulations are often lengthy and full of loopholes that can be found and cleverly used if a company is so inclined.

Natural Flavors

Entire aisles of the grocery store contain products that nearly all contain "natural flavors." Most soft drinks, packaged juices, and cookies list them on the list of ingredients. Many consumers, even those who read labels extensively, make the assumption that natural flavors are good for them, or at least not harmful. But consider the legal definition of "natural flavors" from the *Code of Federal Regulations*, Title 21, Section 101.22(a)(3):

> The term natural flavor or natural flavoring means the essential oil, oleoresin, essence or extractive, protein hydrolysate, distillate, or any product of roasting, heating or enzymolysis, which contains the flavor constituents derived from a spice, fruit or fruit juice, vegetable or vegetable juice, edible yeast, herb, bark, bud, root, leaf or similar plant material, meat, seafood, poultry, eggs, dairy products, or fermentation products thereof, whose significant function in food is flavoring rather than nutritional.

There is actually more, but you get the idea. (It is interesting to note that two of the words in the definition, "hydrolysate" and "enzymolysis," generate a red misspelled-word underline on my outrageously expensive word processor.)

Most natural flavors are perfectly harmless—concentrated fruit juice, spices, and the like. But under the legal definition, nearly anything can be creatively scored as a "natural flavor."

Calories and Serving Size

The Nutrition Labeling and Education Act of 1990 created modern food label requirements, but it, too, contains definitions that can be "massaged." Diet-conscious consumers often look first at the listing of calories atop the standard nutrition facts box. But calories are listed "per serving." Soft drinks of up to 360 milliliters must list the serving size as "1." Soft drinks of over 360 milliliters are not bound by that rule, and 361 milliliters equals 12.21 ounces.

Organic Products

Organic food is a big seller. The Organic Trade Association estimates that sales rose from $1 billion in 1990 to $23 billion in 2008. But the legal requirements for labeling food as organic allow for some wiggle room. Food sold in the United States must contain only 95 percent organic ingredients to use the USDA's certified organic logo, and food needs to contain only 70 percent organic ingredients to be allowed to use the phrase "Made with Organic Ingredients" on its packaging.

SCENARIO

Super Cola Conference Room

"So the boss didn't leave any doubt," said Max, the marketing director. "If we don't increase sales by 25 percent by this time next year, she's going to unload the soft drink operation. We need a new strategy, and we need it soon. I'll be working with the advertising people this week on a new ad campaign, but I need ideas from you about how we present our product on the grocery store shelves."

Max opened his briefcase and pulled out a red can of Super Cola. "We've been selling our drink in this exact can for 10 years, and in a can that looks more or less like this for 40 years." He pulled out a second, much older red can of Super Cola with an old-fashioned pull-ring on the top and placed it by the first. "We've had the same formula, too. We need bold ideas. I want to take chances, because we don't have much to lose here.

"And, we don't have time to develop a significantly different product—our timetable is too short. We have to get more people to buy *this* product, or something that is essentially the same as this product. A lot of soft drink consumers are very brand-loyal, of course, but building brand loyalty is a long-term game. We need something that grabs market share *now*." Max opened his hands and looked around the table at Alan, Beth, and Craig. "I want your best ideas presented at our regular meeting two weeks from today."

Two Weeks Later—Alan's Proposal

"A lot of dieters are extremely sensitive to calorie count. Some of these people opt for diet drinks with no calories, but a large number don't like the taste of artificial sweeteners, and so they're still in the game for regular soft drinks.

"We ran a table at the mall for two days last week. We put three small unmarked cups on the table and let anybody come up and do a taste test. One of the cups had our Super Cola, and the others had Coke and Pepsi.

"On the first day, 30 percent of the testers said our cola was the best.

"On the second day, we set things up in mostly the same way, but this time, we put an enlarged copy of a portion of the white 'nutrition facts' box on the table in front of each cup. We still didn't put any names down. We copied the boxes from the Coke and Pepsi cans, and each one said:

SERVING SIZE: 1 can CALORIES: 140."
"In front of the Super Cola, the box read:
SERVING SIZE: 6.1 ounces CALORIES: 70."
"Ah, Alan," Max interrupted.
"Yeah, boss."
"Our cans have 140 calories."
"In a 12-ounce can, yes, but 6.1 ounces has 70 calories."
"Can we do that?"
"Yes—I'll tell you how in a minute."
"OK, go ahead."
"So, anyway, on day two, with the nutrition facts boxes posted, 48 percent of the tasters liked Super Cola best. That's nearly two-thirds more!"
"So, back to the nutrition facts label. If a prepackaged drink has '360 milliliters or fewer,' it has to have a serving size of '1.' But for 361 and over, the rule doesn't apply and 361 milliliters is 12.2 ounces.
"A standard can has room for 12 ounces, even. But I found a manufacturer in Brazil that makes its cans flat and not curved on the bottom, and they hold 12.22 ounces. If we get our cans from them, we can split the serving size and make the calories per serving number small."
Max interrupted. "Come on, are people that dense?"
"People are used to looking at the calories number on the nutrition facts box. Some will notice, but a lot won't: 48 percent versus 30 percent, boss."

Beth's Proposal

"I was also working the table at the mall. After the two days Alan told you about, we spent one last day there. This time, the information card in front of the Coke and Pepsi had a copy of their ingredient list. 'High fructose corn syrup,' and so forth. The card in front of ours read: 'Made with Organic Ingredients.'"
"Ah," Max said, "we don't use organic ingredients, do we?"
"No. But, to put 'Made with Organic Ingredients' on the can, we only have to use 70 percent organic ingredients. The sweetener makes up more than 70 percent of the non-water ingredients in Super Cola, so all we have to do is swap out our current sweetener with organic sugar. All the other ingredients can stay the same.
"We had them mix up a 20-gallon batch of Super Cola with organic sugar at the bottler for the taste test. This time, 55 percent of the survey participants liked ours best."
"But organic sugar is expensive, right?" Max asked.
"It will raise our overall costs slightly, yes. But you said our task is to increase *sales* by 25 percent, not *profits*, correct? And everything other than the sugar stays the same."
"That is what I said, true enough."
"I think that if we reposition ourselves as an organic alternative, we can gobble up market share."

Craig's Proposal

"I think the last two ideas are good ones, and they should definitely be considered for our regular product. But I want to launch an additional product: an energy drink."
"I thought one of you would present this idea," Max said. "Double the caffeine, double the price?"
"Sort of. Actually, this is better. At least, I think it could be."
"Go ahead."
"One of my roommates in college was a biology major. He ended up working for a drug company, and he's doing research on Alzheimer's therapies. One of the things they've discovered over there is that nicotine helps, at least somewhat, in slowing memory loss in Alzheimer's patients. But, they've discovered another plant that contains a nicotine-*like* substance that helps a lot more. It's ... a lot stronger. It sharpened the patients' memory a lot in their study. They're working on a synthetic version of the substance that's more targeted to assisting with Alzheimer's.

"They got the plant from a grower in Australia. It's really not all that expensive. And the thing is, it's really, really addictive."

"Addictive," Max repeated.

"Super addictive. That's why my old roommate is working on a synthetic version. It wasn't useful as a therapy for the patients in the study. Their memory exercises went great, but they complained about headaches and feeling awful several hours later unless they got another pill. And there's something about Alzheimer's patients that makes them need a less regular ... 'delivery mechanism,' he called it.

"Anyway, the patients' memory was focused, and they reported feeling good during the tests themselves. This plant sounds *perfect* for an energy drink. Once somebody buys our new product with this new ingredient ... "

"Hold on," Max interrupted. "Isn't nicotine regulated? We can't put it in a soft drink, can we?"

"It's not nicotine, boss, it's *like* nicotine."

Max considered that. "OK, maybe so, but we'll have to list it as an ingredient. No one is going to want a drink with a mystery plant ... "

This time, Craig interrupted. "It's a plant *extract*, boss. We can list it as 'natural flavors.'"

"Hmm ... " Max said.

"It's not regulated?" Claire asked.

"Not at this time," Craig replied. He continued his presentation. "So, anyway, somebody buys a can of our new energy drink, and it works great. He *does* feel energized. His focus *is* sharpened, at least for a while. And, several hours later, he's going to crave another one! We'll sell two or three of these per customer per day, easy. Look, I like the other ideas fine, but I just don't see them increasing sales 25 percent in a year. We need to throw the ball downfield. This plan is the one most likely to boost our sales a lot in the next year."

DISCUSSION QUESTIONS

1. Is Alan's plan ethically acceptable, or unreasonably manipulative?

_____

_____

_____

_____

2. Is Beth's plan ethically acceptable, or unreasonably manipulative?

_____

_____

_____

_____

3. Is Craig's plan ethically acceptable, or unreasonably manipulative?

_____

_____

_____

_____

4. If you were Max, which of the three ideas would you be likely to approve or send up the line for final approval? All? Some? None?

_____

_____

_____

_____

5. Assume for this last question that the soft drink is not in trouble, and that there is no pressure to increase sales by 25 percent. Now which of the ideas would you be likely to approve or send up the line for final approval? All? Some? None?

_____

_____

_____

_____

Marketing in the Public Schools

BACKGROUND

In an early episode of *The Simpsons* from the 1990s, Pepsi thoroughly made its way into a fictional classroom as a joke. The teacher asked the second grade class a math question along the lines of: "If I had five Pepsis and take away three Pepsis, how many Pepsis do I have left?" A puzzled Ralph Wiggum tentatively answered, "Pepsi?" The teacher smiled and said, "Partial credit!"

At the time the episode aired, it was rare for companies to be successful in placing ads in public schools. But today, because of budget woes, such corporate presences are exceedingly common. And, as shortfalls deepen for districts, the trend is likely to accelerate. Schools are almost desperate for new revenue streams.

Corporations are eager to provide them. The ability to generate brand loyalty is an essential part of marketing. Many companies covet the chance to convince impressionable young people that their soft drink or candy bar or clothing line or pizza is the best. The dream is to gain lifelong customers who have decades of spending power ahead of them.

Thus, many private companies have now purchased a presence in public schools. Some products are merely advertised, as when companies sponsor school events. Other products are actually present and are for sale directly to children, as in the case of vending machines. One recent study found that over 80 percent of junior high schools sell soft drinks in vending machines on campus.

In one interesting development, traditional television ads are run in many classrooms with educational programming sandwiched around them. "Channel One," for example, is a service that broadcasts 12-minute programs that are watched in the classroom by over one-third of all schoolchildren in America. Traditional commercials are run during part of the 12 minutes.

Groups of parents have organized and offered various levels of resistance. "Is nothing sacred? Is there anywhere at all where my children can escape relentless advertising?" they often ask, exasperated.

In some places, lawmakers have taken notice. The states of New York and California have banned "Channel One." The cities of San Francisco and Los

Angeles, among others, have banned soft drinks and candy from school vending machines.

In most places, though, legal restrictions are few and companies are free to market their products and services in the schools. The question then becomes: Should they do so? Is it wrong to do so? Do they risk a backlash from consumers?

The following module examines these questions.

SCENARIO

Elementary School Conference Room

The elementary school vice principal spread his files on the conference table. The school's principal entered the room and shut the door behind her. "Hey, Ted," she said.

"Hey, Brenda," he replied.

"I'm so sorry to have sent you out there last-minute yesterday. I just couldn't be in two places at once."

"Not a problem."

"So how did it go?"

"Well, like we thought, the board wants to explore 'all untapped sources of additional revenue.' They're probably going to do whatever they want, but they're asking for input from all the principals before they make any final decisions."

"OK."

"They gave everyone a list of proposals. I copied it for you here," Ted said as he slid a document across the table. "They laid out everything under consideration, and the estimated additional revenue per campus. They want to know whether you find the items likely to be 'consistent with' or 'disruptive of' the 'educational mission of your campus.'"

"Well, we have to do something. I'm looking at laying off five teachers, and almost no room in the budget to replace the old computers or buy new books for the library. Not to mention maintaining the playground equipment or the field-trip budget."

"It's a mess."

"It is. You've looked these over?"

"I have. If we adopt all of them, we can close 80 percent of the budget shortfall. I'm not necessarily saying all of them are good ideas, but we do have a chance to make a big dent in the money problem."

"OK, well, let's go through them." The principals discussed the list item-by-item for the next 30 minutes. Portions of their conversation are outlined below.

Proposal 1—Vending Machines

Allow vending machines on all campuses. Districts will be compensated per machine, with significantly higher compensation for machines that dispense soda, and even higher compensation for machines that dispense energy drinks.

Solves 10 percent of the budget shortfall (20 percent if machines with soft drinks are allowed, and 30 percent if machines with energy drinks are allowed)

Brenda:	"These are fine, as long as they dispense milk or reasonable snacks. I'm not comfortable with selling sodas here. And certainly not energy drinks."
Ted:	"These kids have soft drinks at home for sure, and some of them probably have energy drinks. And, anyway, we have soft drinks at all of our events; it's not as if pop has never crossed the threshold of the building."
Brenda:	"But if the machines are here, some of the kids will drink one every day. Twenty ounces of cola is a huge amount of sugar for a young child."
Ted:	"As far as I know, the proposal doesn't require large serving sizes. Maybe we can recommend that they sell 8-ounce cans. Or maybe we can require a parent authorization before kids can buy soda."

Proposal 2—Flintstones Vitamins

Bayer proposes to sponsor a study room on each campus. The rooms would be in a central location and would be called "Flintstones Vitamins Study Centers." Each would have a prominent sign above the entrances and exits.
Solves 15 percent of the budget shortfall

Ted:	"I like this one."
Brenda:	"But you know what the PTA will say about corporate logos in the building."
Ted:	"But they'll complain more if we cut teachers and raise class sizes."

Proposal 3—Pizza World

Pizza World wants to sponsor a monthly "Pizza World Day." Once a month, every student would be given a colorful sticker at the end of the day to place on his or her shirt that would double as a Pizza World coupon, good for that night only.
Solves 15 percent of the budget shortfall

Ted:	"I like this one, too."
Brenda:	"You like them all so far."
Ted:	"I like being able to pay for everything we need."
Brenda:	"So do I. I guess I'm just lukewarm to actually putting ads on the children."
Ted:	"But they already have ads on themselves. Every kid who wears a soccer jersey to school has one. We have a lot of Samsung and UNICEF ads walking around already. And every kid with a designer shirt has a little Polo guy or whatever. And every sneaker has a logo on both sides. The ship has sailed on kids becoming walking billboards."

Proposal 4—Super Cola

Super Cola proposes to pay for a field trip to the bottler across town. Children would be given a tour of the factory floor and get to see how soft drinks are made, bottled, and shipped.
Solves 10 percent of the budget shortfall

Brenda:	"I like this one more than selling soft drinks themselves here. The kids might benefit from seeing how a production line works, how people work as a team."
Ted:	"This is the first one I don't like. The nature preserve field trip is so much better. The kids love it, and they get to learn about the environment. I'd rather change their minds about taking care of nature than change their minds about which soft drink to beg their parents for."
Brenda:	"I don't know if we can afford that one this year. The gas costs alone for 20 school buses going 70 miles round trip, I mean, it's just a lot of money."
Ted:	"I know, I know."

Proposal 5—Minor League Baseball

A local minor league baseball team proposes to send two players to every class for an hour. Players will sign autographs and distribute coupons for discount tickets.
Solves 10 percent of the budget shortfall

Brenda: "This one is just too much. I mean, we have to have some standards."

Ted: "I agree. These kids need to focus on learning when they're in the classroom."

Dean: (author of this module): "Come on, guys, lighten up. It's baseball."

Brenda: "Did … you hear something?"

Ted: "I, ah… I'm not really sure."

Brenda: "…"

After shaking off the feelings of eeriness, Ted and Brenda brought their meeting to a close.

DISCUSSION QUESTIONS

1. In your opinion, is there a fundamental difference between marketing to children in school and out of school? Is a "Flintstones Vitamins Study Center" any different from a billboard for the vitamins near a school, or a TV ad for the vitamins run during a cartoon that airs at breakfast time?

_____

_____

_____

2. Rate the proposals from most acceptable to most inappropriate. Place a #1 by the most reasonable proposal, a #2 by the second-most acceptable, and so forth. Then, circle the ideas you would recommend the school adopt, if you were the principal in the scenario.

_____ Vending machines on campus, without sodas

_____ Vending machines on campus, with sodas

_____ Vending machines on campus, with energy drinks

_____ Flintstones Vitamins Study Centers

_____ Pizza World Day

_____ Super Cola field trip

_____ Visit from baseball team

3. Would you be in favor of approving any additional ideas if the school in the scenario were a junior high school? Which ones, if any? What if it were a high school?

_____

_____

_____

4. Assume once again that the proposals are being evaluated by an elementary school principal. What if the school were facing no budget shortfall and no funding cuts? Would you now be in favor of fewer proposals? Which ones, if any?

_____

_____

_____

5. Assume that the school district adopts all proposals. As a parent, would you be angry? Would you go so far as to avoid purchasing products from any of the companies?

_____

_____

_____

UNIT 4

Workplace Ethics: Treatment of Employees

Unit Background

Good employees are an essential part of any successful operation. How should they be treated? Should a company go beyond legal minimums and seek to treat workers "well"?

Module 20

Weight Discrimination. [In the last unit, we examined the obesity epidemic and the marketing of unhealthy food and beverages. In this module, we examine the treatment of obese employees and customers. Weight discrimination is generally legal, but is it ethical?]

Module 21

Extreme Hours. [Many professionals work very long hours. Some people argue that extreme hours have negative effects on workers and their families, and the law ought to change to perhaps not prevent, but at least discourage, extreme workweeks. Is there merit to this point of view?]

Module 22

Layoffs in Good Economic Times. [Sometimes, struggling companies must cut jobs in order to survive. But what if a company is doing well? When are layoffs reasonable if a company is operating successfully?]

Module 23

Workplace Diversity. [Countless major companies have adopted diversity policies in recent decades. Such policies are usually legally allowed but not legally required. In what circumstances are they most and least justified?]

Module 24

No-Compete Agreements and Arbitration Clauses. [Employees are often surprised to learn that, when they started with an employer, they agreed not to work for competitors for a fixed amount of time if they ever left the company. Others are surprised that an old contract prevents them from suing a company. Are these common clauses reasonable parts of employment contracts?]

Module 25

Layoffs and Health Care. [If a company will cut workers, are health care needs a valid consideration? What if a particular worker has unusual health care requirements that cannot be met if he loses his company-sponsored health insurance?]

Workplace Ethics: Treatment of Employees

A merican workers are substantially better off than they were 100 years ago. They have many rights that have been created by modern laws and court decisions. Many kinds of discrimination are not legal. Workplace safety laws are numerous. Companies must allow for medical leaves of absence in many circumstances.

But there are also many "gaps" in worker protection law. In the end, most workers are *employees at will,* which means that they can be treated in any way that is not specifically legally prohibited.

And so, for example, companies cannot discriminate based on race because a specific law (the Civil Rights Act) prohibits the practice. But companies can often discriminate against an obese worker because the Civil Rights Act and similar laws fail to require them to act differently. Two of the modules in this unit examine discrimination issues where the law does not require or prohibit action.

Other modules examine many other common practices that are legal but that may nonetheless be unethical. Requiring employees to work long hours, sign covenants not to compete, and sign arbitration clauses are among the topics presented.

We will also look at layoffs. Sometimes, corporations must let workers go in order to survive, but how should the terminations be handled? What kinds of factors ought to be considered? Productivity? Longevity? Special needs? Often decisions about retaining employees are quite complicated.

Employment decisions frequently allow for many legal possibilities, and the trick is often selecting the best and most ethical choice.

Weight Discrimination

BACKGROUND

Before 1964, racial discrimination by private companies was entirely legal. Why? Because no laws existed yet that made such a practice illegal. If a corporation said to a man, "You are qualified, but we won't hire you because you aren't white," there was essentially no possibility of a successful lawsuit, even if the statement were made in writing or before 100 witnesses. It is true that a small handful of plaintiffs won race discrimination cases in this era by "stretching" the Constitution and the guarantee of equal protection to cover a few private businesses, but such cases were rare.

In 1964, Congress passed the Civil Rights Act. It prohibits discrimination based on race, religion, gender, and national origin in all workplaces with 15 or more employees. Since 1964, Congress has passed similar laws that ban discrimination based on age, specific disabilities, and certain kinds of genetic tests. But it is important to note that there is no broad law that generally prohibits discrimination at work. The several specific types mentioned in this paragraph are prohibited; other types are not, at least at the national level.

And so, for example, if a worker is fired because he is gay, he cannot file a federal lawsuit, because there is no federal law that makes such a firing illegal. About 20 states make sexual orientation discrimination illegal at the state level, and many cities do the same, but the U.S. government does not.

One common type of discrimination that is rarely protected even at the state level[1] is that which is based on obesity.

The Overweight and Obesity "Epidemic"

The definitions of overweight and obese are tied to a person's body mass index (BMI), a common measure of weight to height. A person is classified as overweight with a BMI of at least 25, and obese if the BMI exceeds 30. Calculators are widely

---

[1] The only exception is in Michigan, at the time of this writing.

available online if you wish to check your BMI. To give a quick reference, I entered my own statistics. I am 6 feet tall, and I would be considered overweight at about 190 pounds and obese at about 230 pounds.

Currently, roughly 67 percent of adults in the United States are either overweight or obese. By 2030, the number will rise to an estimated 86 percent. This trend, which shows utterly no signs of slowing, will create any number of genuine policy dilemmas for companies and the government.

Many people are trying to address the "epidemic" of obesity, particularly as it relates to children. First Lady Michelle Obama's "Get Moving Campaign" is one high-profile attempt to change habits and help people lose weight.

Legislation

Under current law, winning a lawsuit based on weight discrimination is not impossible, but it is very difficult. No federal law directly prohibits the practice. Lawsuits that stretch the Civil Rights Act are remotely possible. Lawsuits based on the Americans with Disabilities Act are somewhat more plausible winners, but extra weight alone is insufficient to meet the definition of "disability" under that law, and, in any event, employers are required only to make "reasonable accommodations."

If weight discrimination is to be curbed by law, a new antidiscrimination statute would be required. Congress passes such laws from time to time—on average, about every 15 years. But a new law at this time appears to be a politically improbable event. Congress is focused on economic issues and probably will be for the life span of this textbook's edition. Even if Congress does turn its attention to a new antidiscrimination law, one that addresses sexual orientation seems more likely to be next up for debate.

So, for the time being, weight discrimination is generally legal. Companies, then, are left to address issues as they see fit, which makes this topic, for now, a question of ethics.

SCENARIOS

Policies That Would Impact Customers

Business #1 is a chain of women's clothing boutiques. The stores sell high-priced business wear and stylish casual clothing. The business has been increasingly profitable in recent years. Prices have been raised significantly, but sales volume has remained strong. It is considering "capping" its sizes offered at size 14. It has, until this point, carried several sizes larger than 14.

The boutique's CEO has been pushing a marketing strategy of "exclusivity." Stores are located only in a few markets: New York, San Francisco, Dallas, and Miami, among others. She believes that selling fewer sizes fits in with the exclusivity strategy and will allow her to raise prices still higher, and that her chain will be more profitable, even though it sells fewer articles of clothing.

The boutique would lose customers who currently shop there and wear a size above 14. But, overall, the supply of clothing of all sizes would be almost completely unaffected. Even in the towns in which the boutiques operate, they sell far less than 1/100 of 1 percent of the women's clothing sold in the area.

Business #2 is a commercial airline. The airline's standard "coach" seat is 27 inches wide from armrest to armrest. In recent years, it has received an increasing number of a particular type of complaint from passengers. The airline's CEO recently made a call to one complaining customer to talk about the issue personally.

"Hello," Rick Adams said as he answered the telephone.

"Mr. Adams?"

"Yes. Who's this?"

"Mr. Adams, my name is Will Rodriguez. I'm the CEO of National Airlines."

"Oh. Well, ah, how can I help you?"

"Mr. Adams, I asked my assistant to look for complaints like the one you made online last week. I'm considering a new policy, and I wanted to talk to people directly before I make any decisions. Can you tell me about your Houston to Boston flight last month?"

"Oh. You know, I'm actually kind of embarrassed now that I made a complaint. I was just bugged at the time and I had an hour to kill in my hotel room, you know. It wasn't really as bad as I said it was."

"That's quite all right. I just want to hear everyone's experience firsthand."

"OK. Well, so I had a window seat. The gentleman next to me—this would be in the center seat—he couldn't, ah, you know..."

"Go on," the CEO encouraged.

"Well, he was really heavy. He couldn't put the armrest down between my seat and his, you know. He, ah, he took up his seat and some of my seat. I, ah, I couldn't really set up my laptop, and it was about a four-hour flight. I was just kind of uncomfortable, but like I said, it wasn't as bad as I made it out to be on my complaint. And he was a nice guy; we ended up talking for a while. I just..." Adams trailed off again.

"It's quite alright, Mr. Adams. And I'd like to personally offer you two round-trip tickets anywhere we fly for your trouble."

"Oh. Well, ah, that'd be super. Thanks. Thanks a lot."

After the call, Rodriguez made several additional calls and heard similar stories. He then looked down at the draft of a policy on his desk. "*It is the policy of National Airlines that passengers who are unable to fully lower both armrests of their seats must purchase a second fare,*" it read. Rodriguez sighed and thought about whether or not he should approve the proposal.

Policies That Would Impact Employees

Business #3 operates a factory with long and physically taxing shifts. It is adding a third shift and will be hiring 100 new workers for its assembly line. The production manager chose to address his senior human resources team.

"OK, and when you hire, give a thought about whether it seems like someone will be able to work in a hot factory for an eight-hour shift, five days a week.

"I'm not saying to knock out anyone with some specific disability that can be worked with, but if an applicant is just, you know, excessively out of shape, then give a harder look at someone else, especially for the assembly line positions.

"We need to operate at peak capacity if this new shift is going to make money, and we need everyone to work at top speed.

"And I'm not talking about someone who is a bit out of shape. Frank here is fine," he said, gesturing to one of the HR people who was overweight but not obese. Some quiet laughs were heard around the table.

"Frank plus 100 pounds is not OK. Are we clear?"

Business #4 is a gym. Its head personal trainer (Ally) is talking to its owner (Steve).

"I'm just saying that he can bench press more than anybody on our staff," Ally said.

"That may be so," Steve replied.

"And he's really into it. He won't have a problem motivating anyone."

"That may be so, but those aren't the only things to consider."

"If you're worried about him not being able to get through a workout, I think you're wrong. I worked him out pretty hard, and he kept up fine. And we're not hiring cardio people, we're hiring trainers for the weight room."

"I appreciate the fact that he impressed you, Ally, I just think we should pass on him."

"Because of his weight."

"Because of his weight, yes. He's not just a little bit overweight, Ally. He's at least 200 pounds overweight."

"I think that's a little high..."

"It's not, and you know it. Look, we have an image to maintain. People pay us a lot of money to work them out, and they expect to be trained by someone who is fit. If our own employees are extremely out of shape, why will our customers expect our services to help them? I'm willing to let it slide a bit on the weight room trainers, but there's a limit. The answer is no. Find somebody else."

"All right, Steve."

Business #5 is a coffee shop. Assume that its owner and a subordinate just had the same basic conversation as the gym owner and his head trainer in the last example. The coffee shop owner says that he wants to project a "fit and hip" image to his customers, and he tells his manager not to hire an extremely obese applicant who has just interviewed.

DISCUSSION QUESTIONS

1. Assume that Business #1 and Business #2 adopt the policies under consideration. Rate the decisions.

	Completely Unacceptable ←——————→ Entirely Reasonable						
Business #1	1	2	3	4	5	6	7
Business #2	1	2	3	4	5	6	7

2. Now, assess the actions of the three companies that adopted policies in hiring.

	Completely Unacceptable ←——————→ Entirely Reasonable						
Business #3	1	2	3	4	5	6	7
Business #4	1	2	3	4	5	6	7
Business #5	1	2	3	4	5	6	7

3. Which two of the five policies did you rank highest? What specific facts made them more acceptable to you than the others?

_____

_____

_____

_____

4. Which two of the five policies did you rank lowest? What specific facts made them more acceptable to you than the others?

_____

_____

_____

_____

5. The original Civil Rights Act was passed to protect the rights of minority groups. Interestingly, a law banning weight discrimination would protect a significant *majority* of people. Would you favor such a law? If so, would it be more important for the law to protect consumers or workers?

_____

_____

_____

_____

Extreme Hours

BACKGROUND Americans work long hours. Looking at workers in nations that are major trading partners with the United States, only employees in Japan and Mexico have reasonably equivalent average workweeks, and only South Korean workers put in significantly more hours.

Workers in many European nations—Germany, France, Norway, and Sweden, among others—average nearly 10 fewer hours per week than U.S. workers. Many of those nations have laws that require six weeks of paid vacation per year.

How do the long hours pay off? Americans, when compared with others in the world, make a lot of money. We earn an average of $46,000 per year. In France, per capita income is $34,000.

But shorter workweeks don't necessarily translate into lower earning power. Norwegians, while putting in about 500 fewer hours per year than their U.S. counterparts, have a higher per capita income at $52,000.

And longer workweeks don't necessarily lead to higher earnings. South Koreans work 500 more hours per year than Americans and 1,000 hours per year more than Germans, but they earn an average of $28,000 per year.[1]

Societal Problems?

There are many negative trends in the United States. Divorce rates are higher than they were a generation ago. Health problems related to obesity are markedly higher. Some place part of the blame on long workweeks. They argue that people spend too much time away from their families and don't have enough time to eat well and exercise. But, for now, these ideas are definitely in the "correlation without proven causation" category.

---

[1] All figures are International Monetary Fund (IMF) estimates of per capita income, 2009.

What is definite is that workers report being "stressed out" in larger numbers, and job dissatisfaction is on the rise. People take fewer vacations and report greater anxiety about being away from the office. "Work-life balance" programs that seek to help people juggle careers, families, and personal time are increasingly popular. Featured stories on Yahoo! and other high-traffic websites often involve strategies for working smarter and spending more time enjoying life.

America generally does reasonably well in "quality of life" surveys. We usually rank about 15th out of the world's 200-plus nations. But the top ten are almost always dominated by nations with shorter workweeks—Holland, Norway, Belgium, and others.

Has the time come to reduce the number of Americans working long hours, or would that be a giant mistake and counter to the American work ethic that has built the nation?

The Fair Labor Standards Act

Since the 1930s, the Fair Labor Standards Act (FLSA) has placed a legal deterrent on making people work long hours. Under the FLSA, if an employee works more than 40 hours per week, she must be compensated at 1.5 times her normal rate of pay for the hours over 40.

Assume that Ed earns $20 per hour, and that he works 50 hours per week. He must be paid $20 an hour for the first 40 hours, and $30 for the last 10 hours of his workweek.

The FLSA has long required employers to pay a premium for long workweeks.

The limitation of the FLSA is that it fails to cover most salaried employees. If an employee is paid, for example, $50,000 per year as opposed to $20 per hour, she probably cannot seek additional compensation for working more than 40 hours per week.

For those who favor shortening workweeks in the United States, the simplest legal change would seem to be closing this loophole in the FLSA. Congress could at any time amend the law to require additional compensation for *all* workers who work beyond 40 hours per week (or perhaps a modern version would say "beyond 50 hours per week"). If this came to pass, many companies wouldn't make employees work long hours, because the cost would be too high. Now, there certainly might be any number of economic drawbacks from this kind of a shift in policy, but people certainly would average fewer hours at work.

The following scenarios look at four people who all put in an average of 70 to 80 hours per week at work, and the reasons for which they are required to work the extended hours.

SCENARIOS

Diana

Diana is a doctor in a residency program. She works three 24-hour shifts per week for a total of 72 hours.

During a recent dinner party, a friend of the director of Diana's program asked about the legendary hours worked by residents. The director answered the question this way:

"It's always been that way, or at least, it's been that way for the last 100 years or so. Residents are worked hard, and anything they need to know about is thrown in front of them so that they can learn how to do everything.

"It's a boot camp of sorts. A physician's work tends to come in waves. A surgeon might have several emergency procedures within a week or two, and then might have a stretch of time that is comparatively quiet. We need to be trained to work long hours.

I would be delighted if patients only became critically ill between 9 AM and 5 PM, but alas, illnesses surface at inconvenient times.

"And, let's face it—residents are cheap. They are still students, to a degree. Highly skilled students, but they are still learning. I can get all the residents I need for salaries under $40,000 per year. They, in turn, can care for many patients at a reasonable cost. And that matters. Insurance reimbursement is not a sure thing, and many patients lack insurance in the first place. It doesn't hurt to get a lot of work for a small price. And I don't feel the least guilty about it. When the program is done, most of the residents will cash in."

Lewis

Lewis graduated from law school two years ago, and he is an associate lawyer in a very large law firm. He works 12 hours per day Monday through Saturday, and 4 hours on Sunday afternoons, for a total of 76 hours.

During a recent dinner party, a friend of a partner in Lewis's firm asked about the legendary hours worked by associates. The partner answered the question this way:

"It's about money, mostly. Associates bill clients $300 per hour. We pay them a nice salary, but it works out to something like 20 bucks an hour. The more work they do, the more they bill, and the more the partners make."

"But," the friend asked, "couldn't you hire more people and cut the hours for all of the associates?"

"I guess we could do a lot of things. But there are only so many law students who might be worth our time. And, besides, we like the long hours. We want to weed out anyone who's not willing to do whatever it takes for the firm, you know? We all had to do it to get where we are. Why shouldn't they go through the same thing? No easy shortcuts."

Carl

Carl is an assistant coach for an NFL team. During football season, he works 12 hours per day Tuesday through Friday, 18 hours per day on Saturday and Sunday, and 6 hours on Monday, for a total of 90 hours. During the off-season, his workweek is closer to 50 hours long. Over the course of a full year, then, he averages about 70 hours per week.

During a recent off-season dinner party, a friend of the head coach asked about the legendary hours worked by NFL coaches. The head coach answered the question this way:

"Yeah, we work practically around the clock during the season. And do you know why? Because that's what they're doing in Dallas, and Miami, and Green Bay, and Oakland, and everywhere else. We usually win or lose games on three key plays. Sometimes less than that. And when a big play comes up, how are things gonna go if their offensive coordinator has spent 10 more hours watching game film than my offensive coordinator?

"We get to coach football for a living, and we're paid like kings. And there's plenty of time to go fishing with the grandkids in the off-season."

Penny

Penny is a police officer. She averages about 25 hours per week of overtime. Unlike most salaried workers, Penny is covered by the Fair Labor Standards Act. And so, unlike the first three people discussed, she receives 1.5 times her normal rate of compensation for her overtime hours.

During a recent dinner party, she was asked about her long hours. She answered the question this way:

"I have four kids, and I'm going to pay for college for all of them. If I take all the overtime, I can usually almost double my pay. The hours are long, but we make it work just fine."

DISCUSSION QUESTIONS

1. Should any of the employers in the scenario take steps to reduce the extreme workweeks of their employees? If so, which ones, and why?

_____

_____

_____

_____

2. Looking at the NFL assistant coach specifically, is there anything different about his position? Is his team more justified in expecting a long workweek from him based on the fact that its direct competitors are working extremely long hours? Or is that irrelevant? Is a law firm that expects long hours of associates because it can simply make more money as justified?

_____

_____

_____

_____

3. Should the government amend the FLSA to require additional compensation for all kinds of workers who put in an average of more than 50 hours a week and require employers to pay more for longer hours?

_____

_____

_____

_____

4. Are countries in Western Europe right to create laws that require several weeks of paid vacation per year, or do such policies place them at a competitive disadvantage? Should the United States have a legally required minimum number of vacation days? We currently have no law in this area—should we have some minimum? Maybe two weeks paid time off?

_____

_____

_____

_____

5. Do you believe that extreme hours are harmful to people and families, or does it seem like people make it work and do just fine? Are you concerned or unconcerned about your own ability to balance work and the rest of your life?

_____

_____

_____

_____

Layoffs in Good Economic Times

BACKGROUND

When money is tight, the need to trim the payroll can be urgent. But even if times are not tough, a company's leaders can usually try to streamline the operation and improve its profits if they choose to do so.

Most workers in the United States are **employees at will**. This is the legal idea that there is no legally required security in the employer-employee relationship. A company can fire a worker at any time for any reason. It is not necessary to show that the company is struggling, or that the worker has done something terrible. In fact, no justification at all is required. Workers serve "at the pleasure of their employers." Workers enjoy the same freedom; an at-will employee can quit his job at any time for any reason.

The employment at-will doctrine is not without exceptions. Some workers do have legal job protections and cannot be fired unless there is a strong reason. Common exceptions exist in:

- **Contracts.** If an employee's contract includes a specific duration (stating the job will run from January 1, 2011, through December 31, 2014, for example), then she cannot be fired without valid cause until the end of the contract.

- **Discrimination Statutes.** A worker cannot be fired due to his race or religious beliefs, for instance, because such a firing would violate the Civil Rights Act. Many similar laws exist.

- **The Common Law.** If a worker is fired in retaliation for doing "something good," such as reporting illegal activity at her company to the government, some protections exist.

- **The State of Montana.** If one happens to work in Montana, no one there is an at-will employee.

But, again, most workers are employees at will. Decisions to lay off most workers, even if no strong reason for the layoffs exists, are generally completely legal.

Many corporate leaders will go to great lengths to protect jobs unless a compelling need exists to eliminate them. Others regularly purge their employees.

118 UNIT 4 • Workplace Ethics: Treatment of Employees

General Electric's (GE) strategy for years was to identify the top 20 percent of employees and reward them, and to also identify the bottom 10 percent of workers. The workers in the bottom tenth were usually terminated.

Over a stretch of several years in the 1980s, GE laid off over 100,000 employees. But over the same period, GE's investors saw a return of over 250 percent on their investment.

In the end, if layoffs are to be considered, decisions are easier if there are workers who are clearly poor performers. But even in the absence of "bad" workers, there are always workers who perform poorly relative to their peers. Even on an all-star team of 50 players, someone is the 50th-best athlete.

It is also easier to decide to terminate positions if doing so is a necessity, because the company is struggling. But even during good times, such things must at least be considered.

SCENARIO

Super Grocery

Stephen, the new store director of Super Grocery #14, opened a file. "So, all of our department managers have reported back to me. I asked them to identify their "stars," "solid workers," "acceptable workers," and "underperformers.""

"Yeah, I heard you had put out some kind of survey," said Gene, the longtime assistant store director. "There's some chatter about it."

"I imagine there's chatter about just about everything around here."

"That's true enough."

"Yeah. Well, not surprisingly, not one worker was rated as an 'underperformer.'"

Gene smiled. "I do a pretty good job of getting rid of people who don't want to work."

"I'm glad to hear it. But what I really wanted from this was the list of 'acceptable workers.' I've spent a lot of time the last couple of days looking over those workers' files."

"Ah. OK."

"I've taken an interest in several of them. Write them down, will you?"

"OK." Gene took a pen from his pocket.

"Ann Adams, the checker. She scans about 30 percent fewer items per hour than average."

Gene wrote down her name. "Yeah. She's a little slow, but the customers seem to like her."

Stephen did not comment. "Brad Beard, the stocker. He's missed six shifts in the last few months."

"Yeah, I've talked to him about that. His mother has some kind of problem. I think he has to go across town to take care of his little brother sometimes. But he's a hard worker when he's here, which is most of the time."

"Carol Carlson in floral. She spends a lot of time on the phone, I'm told."

"That's true, but sometimes there's not much to do back there. She always promptly attends to customers, when she has any."

"Um, hum. Dan Davis in home and garden. Takes long breaks. He's supposed to have 30 minutes for lunch. Looking over our time clock records, he takes an average of 46 minutes, highest average in the store."

"I'll talk to him about that."

"Ellen Edmonds in health and beauty. Refuses to cover anything on weekends."

"She does like to keep her weekends free."

"Our busiest days are weekends. Her manager says she has to scramble to cover the weekend shifts."

Gene had no response to that.

"Fred Ford, the sacker. Drops a lot of bags, breaks a lot of items."

"Fred's clumsy, no doubt about it. But he's a really nice guy."

"And, last, Gerald Green in produce. Does a lousy job of separating rotten fruit from good fruit. His manager says customers avoid produce altogether if there are a few 'bad apples' on top, and that Gerald can't seem to get rid of them."

"Yeah. He's kind of an enviro-type guy. He says, and he's absolutely right, that apples with a few spots are perfectly good to eat, and that he doesn't want to waste food."

"We waste a lot more food if we don't sell any of it."

"Maybe so."

Stephen snapped his file shut. "OK, that's all of them for now."

"So what do you want me to do, give them a warning? Whip them into shape?" Gene grinned.

"No, I want you to let them go."

Gene's eyebrows shot up. "Let them go? Seriously?"

"Yes."

"But…this is all pretty minor stuff. And we haven't laid anyone off in a long time. I mean fired, sure, we've fired lots of people for doing a lousy job, but these people are all doing OK. We let some people go years ago when we were really struggling. But we haven't just…sacked anyone during good times in ages."

"Well, we're going to start now."

"But why? The store's doing great! The numbers look great! We don't need to cut our costs."

"A business always needs to cut costs."

"I disagree with that."

"I know you do, and that's one of the reasons you've been an assistant store director and not a store director for the last, what is it, fifteen years?"

Gene got quiet. "I never wanted to be a store director."

"That's OK by me. But I *am* a store director, and I want to be a regional manager within three years, and after that, who knows? And the way for me to do that is to do what the home office wants and what the shareholders want, which is to make as much money for the company as possible. And part of doing that is trimming the fat on the payroll."

Gene considered that. Eventually he said, "We have good people working here. If you'd been around a little longer, gotten to know them better…"

"I value good people, Gene, and I value having good working relationships with them. I'm not talking about letting our best workers go, or even letting our average workers go. I'm talking about eliminating marginal workers in positions that we can do without."

"And I'm for that, too, if there is a need. Ten years ago we laid off a lot of people because we were struggling, and we needed the money to renovate our stores and increase our advertising. I broke the news to everyone myself, and I didn't like it one bit, but I could see that we needed to do it to have a decent chance to grow. But we've grown, and we're making buckets of money. It's not the same situation."

"But who says it has to be the same situation? I say, and I do get the final say here, that anytime a company can save payroll costs, it should do so."

"I think you're wrong."

"Don't forget that *you* work for *me*, Gene."

"All right, you're right. I'll take that back and say that I disagree with you."

"And that's what I want you to do. But you've made your position clear, and I still think that this is something we should do. And we are going to do it." Stephen smiled slyly. "I'm the 'decider.'"

Gene squinted his eyes for a moment. "Where have I heard that before? Movie?"

"President Bush."

"Ah, that's right."

"Yeah. Friends?" Stephen extended his hand.

Gene paused, and then shook it. "Agreed," he said. Stephen nodded. Without another word, Gene stood, left the office, and closed the door behind him.

DISCUSSION QUESTIONS

1. Discuss the general idea presented in this module. If a company is doing well, should workers who are doing a reasonably good job be retained? Or should a company's leaders always seek to eliminate positions of marginal performers?

    _____
    _____
    _____
    _____

2. Of the seven employees described, which would you decide to terminate? Why?

    _____
    _____
    _____
    _____

3. If all seven are laid off, would you anticipate a drop in morale among the remaining workers? Or would you expect the remaining employees to think, "Ah, they weren't any good anyway," and not worry about it?

    _____
    _____
    _____
    _____

4. Now discuss the seven employees described, assuming that the grocery store is struggling. If times are tough, which of the seven would you lay off?

    _____
    _____
    _____
    _____

5. In previous generations, it was somewhat common for workers to spend entire careers at a single company, and very common for them to spend careers at three companies or fewer. Is the old model better? Would we be better off with more long-serving workers around? Or is the newer model better, in which companies and workers feel less loyalty toward each other and job changes are much more common?

    _____
    _____
    _____
    _____

MODULE 23

Workplace Diversity

For the last 30 years, many businesses and universities have sought to increase diversity in their workforces and student populations. Many argue that different points of view are an essential part of a classroom experience and that companies miss out on maximizing their talent pool if groups of workers are overlooked.

The law surrounding affirmative action programs is somewhat complicated. Many "reverse discrimination" lawsuits have been filed by plaintiffs who were not offered a seat in a freshman class or a job at a company. They often claim that they were at a disadvantage because they were male, Caucasian, or both. Of the numerous lawsuits, two court cases are essential.

The Supreme Court first examined the issue of diversity programs in the 1978 case *Regents* v. *Bakke*. Bakke was white and was not offered a seat in the medical school class at the University of California, Davis. In the 1970s, UC Davis had a nearly 100 percent white student body, and the Board of Regents put this policy into practice: for every 100 seats, 84 were "open" and 16 were "set aside" for members of underrepresented minority groups. Bakke argued that if he had been of another race and had been able to compete for 100 percent of the seats and not 84 percent of them, he would have gained admission.

In the end, the case set two precedents. The system at UC Davis was found to be an unconstitutional "quota system." The majority of the justices did not like the fact that 16 percent of the seats were set aside and would go to minority applicants "no matter what." But the Court also decided that if a diversity program considered the race of applicants as one factor among many, then no constitutional problem was created. So, if UC Davis modified its system to evaluate an applicant's race alongside his MCAT score, college GPA, personal statements, and personal interview, then affirmative action would be just fine.

As is often true, the case turned on the Supreme Court's *interpretation* of a key legal idea.

Appellate courts are made up of human beings, and each has his or her own idea of how laws should be interpreted or applied. The media often calls certain judges "liberal" or "conservative," but such labels can be misleading. "Conservative" judges often agree with Republicans on issues, but they sometimes do not. By the same token, "liberal" judges often agree with Democrats, but not always.

A much more accurate and useful way of thinking of judges is *literalist or nonliteralist*. Some judges believe that the Constitution, statutes, and any other laws they review, should be applied exactly as written, no more and no less. Others believe that it is important to consider the purpose of a law, and they are sometimes willing to go beyond the specific language in a law when they apply it to a case. Both groups strongly believe that they are acting in the most appropriate way.

On the issue of affirmative action, literalist and nonliteralist judges disagree. If one reads the exact language in the key laws, one can make a plausible case that race, gender, and other factors are not supposed to be considered in making admissions and hiring decisions. "Conservative" or literalist judges conclude, then, that many diversity programs are illegal.

"Liberal" or nonliteralist judges often ask: "Why do we have the Fourteenth Amendment?" "Why do we have the Civil Rights Act?" They will often answer, "to end discrimination," or "to act as a remedy to past discrimination," or both. They will then often conclude that diversity programs are legally acceptable. As one Supreme Court justice notably put it, "it would be ironic" if these laws, meant to be a remedy to past discrimination, were read so literally as to prohibit voluntary programs that seek to remedy past discrimination.

The importance of the "balance of power" between these two groups of judges to the issue of affirmative action cannot be overstated. When nonliteralists have a majority on a reviewing court, affirmative action tends to be allowed. When literalists have a majority, it tends to be restricted or prohibited. In the 1990s, some lower courts controlled by literalists did just that. Colleges in Texas, Louisiana, and Mississippi were ordered to end diversity programs as a result. Some lower courts justified breaking with Supreme Court precedent on the grounds that there was much more diversity in the 1990s than there had been in the 1970s, and so the time for legal diversity programs had passed.

The Supreme Court revisited the issue in the 2003 case *Grutter* v. *Bollinger*. *Grutter* featured essentially the same facts as *Bakke* had 25 years earlier. This time, a white applicant who was denied a seat at the University of Michigan brought the case. The Supreme Court decided that, in spite of the presence of more diversity, affirmative action programs were still acceptable as long as they considered the race of applicants alongside other factors. The lower court opinions that restricted affirmative action were overturned.

For now, the legal issues surrounding diversity programs are settled, and they are the same nationwide. To summarize two key points:

1. Affirmative action programs are generally acceptable under the law because of the Supreme Court decisions just outlined; but,

2. Affirmative action programs are rarely required. It is true that to be eligible to bid on a few kinds of government contracts, a company must have such a program. It is also true that, in rare cases involving longstanding and flagrant racism, a few courts have ordered companies to adopt affirmative action. But the overwhelming majority of companies and businesses that have adopted diversity programs have done so voluntarily.

On this issue, companies can go either way. The options are neither required nor prohibited, and so the question falls into the realm of ethics. Many organizations have intense discussions about which path to take.

SCENARIO

Omega Corporation

On the top floor of the Omega building in Dallas, Texas, an executive of Omega Corporation was finishing his presentation.

"And so, to summarize, we have a great deal of diversity. We don't discriminate in hiring, *period*. Five percent of our applicants are African American, and 5 percent of our hires are African American. Fifteen percent of our applicants are Hispanic, and 15 percent of our hires are Hispanic.

"We also compensate workers equally and give everyone an equal chance to earn a promotion. It is true, granted, that in the past this company acted indefensibly. But those days are long gone. I urge you not to fix a problem that doesn't exist. The best thing for us to do is to be fair to every applicant and to always hire the best applicant for every position. Thank you."

At the head of the conference table, the CEO said, "Thank you, Richard. Ann will now present the other side of the issue. Ann?"

Omega's CFO rose and walked to the opposite end of the conference table. She plugged a cord into her laptop, straightened her jacket, and began her argument.

"In many ways, Omega Corporation is a diverse organization. Our officers are 45 percent female, and our overall workforce is 48 percent female. But we lag far behind our competitors in other areas.

"We do have 5 percent African-American workers, but Texas's population is 12 percent African American. We do have, as Richard pointed out, 15 percent Hispanic employees, but Texas's population is 33 percent Hispanic.

"Minorities are significantly underrepresented at Omega. And, whether we talk about it or not, we all know why." She paused. "It's because Mr. Smith wanted it that way." She pointed squarely at the oversized portrait of the company's founder that hung on the conference room's wall.

"That's not fair at all!" Richard said. "You can't..."

The CEO interrupted him. "You've had your say, Richard."

Richard fell silent. Several people at the table shifted in their seats.

"Please continue, Ann," the CEO said.

Ann clicked her mouse and brought up a new screen that was dense with small text.

"I scanned a page from an old newspaper into my laptop this morning," she said. "You are looking at an index page from the help wanted ads. This particular page is from 1963, so it is old, but not *that* old.

"Omega used to rely heavily on ads like these to generate applications. I know the words are hard to make out, but I really only want to call your attention to two items in the second column." Ann clicked again. Her computer zoomed in on a small area of the page and enlarged it to fill the screen.

A boldface heading read: **Employment.** Beneath it were many subheadings such as "Manufacturing, p. 15, column D" and "Clerical, p. 16, column B." The next boldfaced heading read: **Colored Employment.** Beneath it were many subheadings with different page numbers.[1]

"Take a look at those two headings. Can you imagine? This is from long ago, perhaps, but not from *that far* in the past. *This* is how it used to be.

"*This* company, for decades, ran ads in the 'employment' section. Not once did we run an ad in the 'colored employment' section. Don't think for a second that we, and a lot of other companies, didn't make it absolutely clear who was welcome to apply for a job.

---

[1] Although this scenario is hypothetical, the classified ads described were very real in a number of newspapers before the passage of the Civil Rights Act of 1964.

"I am not out to make anyone feel badly, and everyone of you knows how committed I am to this company, and how proud I am of what we do. But if we are to do what is right today, we must look squarely at our history."

Ann paused for a moment. "That kind of discrimination was legal until 1964. When the Civil Rights Act passed in 1964, newspapers stopped dividing help wanted ads in this way." Ann touched a button and blanked the screen.

"From 1964 until he stepped down in 1981, Mr. Smith continued to push an unwritten policy of discrimination against minorities. I've interviewed many retirees and a couple of our most senior people who are still around and confirmed that this is so. We had essentially no minority employees at all until 1982. We were sued more than a few times, but Mr. Smith spent millions in today's dollars fighting the claims in court and at the Equal Employment Opportunity Commission. When it looked like someone might win a case, he settled it and kept it out of the papers.

"I agree with Richard on one point: We don't discriminate in hiring today. Two equally qualified graduates of different races do have an equal chance of being hired. There are no racists working here that turn people away unfairly.

"But, nevertheless, because of our past, we attract fewer minority applicants in the first place. We still have a negative image in the minds of enough people to matter. Some terrific students don't drop a resumé with us. Some who do interview with us take a job with another company. If you have an office visit here, you will certainly see less diversity than you do in other places.

"We need an affirmative action policy that embraces everyone and makes it clear that we welcome everyone. Our competitors all have such a policy. We don't. I firmly believe that we are missing an opportunity to attract exceptional employees. I also firmly believe that our customers will respond favorably to such a policy. I have no study specific to our company, but all the research shows that enough consumers pay attention to corporate diversity initiatives to matter.

"Adopting one or more of the policies we are debating today is the right thing to do, and this company will benefit from any or all of them. Thank you."

"Thank you, Ann," the CEO said. "OK, that's both sides. I want to remind everyone of the three policies that are up for an up-or-down vote at the end of this meeting.

"One," the CEO held up one finger for emphasis, "we will consider whether to spend more time and money doing on-campus recruiting at colleges with large minority student populations.

"Two, we will consider ending our policy of interviewing only applicants who are in the top 25 percent of their college class.

"These first two policies are designed to help us get a look at a broader range of applicants.

"Three, we will consider increasing signing bonuses to match or exceed those offered by our competitors. This policy, if adopted, would also include making more promises to pay off student loans if new workers stay with us for at least three years.

"This last policy is designed to help us close the deal when we interview an outstanding applicant. If you are a 22-year-old kid with a lot of debt, I imagine Omega doesn't look so good if you also have an offer from a company that will give you $20,000 up front.

"I am going to refrain from further comment. I will do nothing other than call on people to speak for the remainder of the meeting, and the vote we take will be by secret ballot. Please speak your mind and vote your conscience.

"OK. Discussion?"

DISCUSSION QUESTIONS

1. Consider the three main justifications given for affirmative action at Omega.

   a. Omega's history
   b. Omega's workforce is 5 percent African American and 15 percent Hispanic, and the population of Texas is 12 percent African American and 33 percent Hispanic.
   c. Omega's competitors have affirmative action programs.

   Which of the three do you find most and least persuasive? Why?

   _____
   _____
   _____
   _____

2. If you had a seat at the meeting described, would you argue for or against adopting an affirmative action policy? Why or why not?

   _____
   _____
   _____
   _____

3. If a different company could *only* raise the argument you found *most persuasive* in the first question, and the other two factors did not apply to them, would you be in favor of the other company adopting an affirmative action policy?

   _____
   _____
   _____
   _____

4. If Omega does adopt some diversity program, which of the three items the CEO specifically described at the end of the scenario do you find most and least justifiable? Why?

   _____
   _____
   _____
   _____

5. Is a public university more justified in adopting diversity programs than a corporation? Why or why not?

   _____
   _____
   _____
   _____

No-Compete Agreements and Arbitration Clauses

The fact is that most people don't read contracts thoroughly before signing on the dotted line. When presented with a delivery agreement, medical consent, lease, or even employment contract, people typically scan the page, and perhaps flip through the pages if there are several of them, but they absorb little before scribbling a signature at the bottom or clicking "I agree."

Sometimes, this is not a big deal. Laws exist that protect consumers and renters from some kinds of agreements and make some terms in contracts unenforceable. Sometimes, this is a very big deal. People often sign contracts in haste and live to regret it. Companies, on the other hand, usually know precisely what contracts contain.

Even when people bother to read agreements from beginning to end, negotiations between people and companies tend to be uneven. Usually, when a person signs a written contract, it has been entirely written by a business. The person is then left to take it or leave it—to sign the deal as presented or walk away.

Consumers sometimes have some power to "drive a hard bargain," but even in these cases, almost all terms in a contract are not addressed. For example, you may have negotiated a price on your new car that was $3,500 less than the sticker price, and the contract you signed with the dealer may have reflected the lower price. But everything else in the multipage document—the warranty, arbitration clause, service agreement, and so on—was probably unchanged.

Employment Contracts

At the time of this writing, the job market is lousy. Applicants are often delighted to receive job offers and willing to work for any reasonable terms. Now, more than ever, prospective employees are unlikely to turn down jobs over clauses "in the back of the contract."

This module addresses two specific kinds of clauses that have become increasingly common in employment contracts: arbitration agreements and covenants not to compete. Both are completely legal, and companies are free to include either or both of them in job contracts. But both are controversial and raise the ethics question: Is it *right* to make prospective employees agree to them?

Arbitration Clauses

You are familiar with arbitration, even if you don't think that you are. The wide range of "real courtroom" shows on daytime TV—*The People's Court, Judge Judy,* and all the rest—are really forums for arbitration, which is a process for settling cases outside of court.

When people or companies have a dispute, they have many options. You are always free to work out a problem without any outside help, and this is what usually happens. When property is damaged, people are hurt, or money is lost, usually people who have disagreements work them out. When an agreement can't be reached, the injured side often decides just to forget the whole thing. At the other end of the spectrum, people are sometimes moved to file a full-blown lawsuit over a disagreement. Arbitration lies somewhere between these two extremes.

In an arbitration, both sides in a dispute sign a contract in which they agree not to go to court over their dispute. Instead, they name an arbitrator (Judge Judy or whomever) to hear evidence and render a decision. They also usually lay out rules for presenting evidence according to their preferences. On TV, the sides might agree to have six minutes each. In a corporate arbitration, the process might be made nearly as formal as a full-blown trial.

When an arbitrator renders a decision, it is important to note that it is "real" and binding. If an arbitrator orders you to pay $1,000, you have to pay the money as much as if you had just charged $1,000 on your credit card.

Traditionally, arbitration contracts were signed after some incident happened. Two people would first have a car accident and then agree to arbitration. But arbitration contracts can also be signed *before* any problem comes up in the first place. Two sides can sign a contract that essentially says, "If we have any disputes in the future, we agree to solve them through arbitration." Many companies have started to require that employees sign arbitration agreements in their employment contracts.

The companies benefit in several ways. If cases stay out of court, they generate less bad publicity for the firm. Arbitrations are concluded much more quickly than trials, and the media is less interested in them. "Walmart Sued by Workers" makes for a bold headline; "Walmart, Workers Agree to Arbitrate Dispute" is much duller. Also, arbitrations tend to cost less in legal fees and, perhaps, in ultimate payouts, because some arbitrators are less likely than juries to give large awards in cases with difficult-to-estimate damages.

Critics argue that employment clauses in employment contracts are unfair. They say that workers should not be forced to sign a "blank check" to get a job, and the wronged workers should always "have their day in court" and not be forced into arbitration. A few courts, especially in California, seem to find this point of view legally valid. Most courts do not. In most places, if a worker signs an arbitration clause and then wishes to sue his company, his only option is arbitration.

And so, arbitration clauses are legally binding, but are they *fair*?

No-Compete Agreements

Another controversial clause that is sometimes found in the back of a long employment contract is a covenant not to compete, or a "no compete." These clauses prohibit a worker from taking a similar job with a competitor for a fixed amount of time after leaving a company. So, for example, a news anchor might sign a contract with a local NBC affiliate that includes a six-month no-compete clause. The anchor might get strong ratings, and the local ABC station might offer twice as much money. The anchor is free to leave the NBC station, but she cannot start broadcasting the news for ABC for six months.

No competes are usually legal as long as they are not overly long, and many companies make use of them. Some of the companies have stronger justifications than others. Drug companies, for example, defend no competes with arguments like this one: "We are constantly racing our competitors to develop new drugs. We simply can't have a researcher on one of our teams go across the street to our competitor for more money and have him put his inside knowledge about our research to immediate use. We need a mandatory cooling-off period to protect our intellectual property." High-tech companies often make the same kinds of arguments.

Other companies seem to use no competes simply to discourage workers from leaving. A worker who knows she cannot take a similar position without taking a "time-out" might stay with a company for longer than she otherwise would.

An important final note is that no competes are usually enforceable regardless of the circumstances under which a worker leaves a company. If a worker quits, is downsized, or is fired, a company can usually enforce a covenant not to compete against him.

SCENARIO

Alpha Company—Part 1

Alpha Company, a corporation based in Austin, makes most of its money designing cell phone chips and selling cell phones. Its primary competitor is Beta Company, which also has a design lab in Austin. Alpha requires all of its employees to sign a one-year no-compete agreement.

Recently, the executives at Alpha Company have become aware that three of the company's former workers have violated their no-compete agreements and have taken jobs with Beta Company without waiting for a year after leaving Alpha. The workers are:

- Rachael Smith, a senior-level electrical engineer. She has detailed insight into how the next-generation chips under development at Alpha work. She is now working as a senior-level electrical engineer at Beta and is actively helping them design their own next-generation chips. Beta doubled her salary to get her on board, and she left Alpha under bad circumstances. She claims the no compete doesn't apply to her, even though under the law it clearly does.
- Tony Jones, a human resources manager. Jones is a single father who lives 30 miles from Alpha Company's headquarters. Because of traffic, he was unable to pick up his children from after-school care until 6:30. He has taken a new HR job with Beta, which is located two miles from his house. He is now able to pick up his kids at 4:30. Beta also gave him a 10 percent raise. Tony has significant knowledge of specific characteristics that Alpha seeks in new hires, but no specific insight into the design of cell phone chips. He knows a lot about who Alpha hires, but not a lot about what those people do.
- Mark Rodgers, a sales representative who was laid off from his job when Alpha reduced the size of its direct sales team. After being unemployed for three months, he was delighted to find a sales position with Beta and is very successful there. He has been named Beta's Employee of the Month twice in the last three months. He has single-handedly helped Beta gain one-quarter of a percent market share on Alpha by selling several large orders to corporate clients.

The executives have been asked whether Alpha's lawyers should go to court to seek an injunction that would order the former employees to stop working for Beta until the expiration of their one-year no-compete agreements.

Alpha Company—Part 2

Alpha is also dealing with employee anger over arbitration agreements. A popular worker was passed over for a promotion, and she has vocally complained that it was a case of discrimination. The company strongly disagrees. The employee has been particularly vocal in expressing her anger that the dispute will be settled in arbitration. "I want to tell my story in open court! I want this company to answer to a jury, and to change its ways," she says.

When they signed their contracts, hardly any employees took notice of the arbitration agreement on page six of Alpha's standard contract. Now, everyone is talking about it, and more than a few have accused the company of being "sneaky" and of forcing workers to "sign away their rights."

Since the controversy began three months ago, nine people have left Alpha. This is uncommonly high turnover; usually, three or fewer people leave in a quarter.

Even recruiting has been impacted. A highly sought-after design engineer was made an offer last week. He verbally accepted but has balked at the arbitration clause in the contract presented to him. He has refused to sign unless the arbitration clause is removed.

DISCUSSION QUESTIONS

1. Should the company go to court and enforce the no-compete clause against Rachael Smith (the senior electrical engineer)? Why or why not?

_____

_____

_____

_____

2. Should the company go to court and enforce the no-compete agreement against Tony Jones (the HR manager) or against Mark Rodgers (the laid-off sales rep)? Why or why not? Is the fact that Mark Rodgers was laid off and did not leave voluntarily relevant?

_____

_____

_____

_____

3. Would you personally be less likely to take a job if the company's employment contracts included a no-compete clause?

_____

_____

_____

_____

4. Should Alpha release the worker who is currently claiming discrimination from her arbitration agreement and allow her to sue the company in court? Should it release other workers from their possible future claims? Should it take the arbitration clause out of the sought-after recruit's contract?

_____

_____

_____

_____

5. Are arbitration clauses fair? Would you be upset if you signed one and then were unable to sue your employer in court? Should arbitration clauses in employment clauses be legal, or should they be legally unenforceable?

_____

_____

_____

_____

MODULE **25**

Layoffs and Health Care

In the spring of 2010, the U.S. Congress passed a health care bill that it had debated for most of the previous year. President Obama promptly signed the bill into law. At the center of the political debate were the roughly 50 million uninsured Americans. The costs associated with this problem are astronomical. The costs of fixing the problem may be at least as and perhaps even more astronomical.

This module will focus on Americans who *currently* have health insurance, but who *may* lose it. Many people have coverage for themselves and their families through work. A typical policy costs about $3,000 per year per person. So a single person's policy is about $3,000, and a policy that covers a family of four costs about $12,000.

When companies offer health coverage to employees, companies usually pay a significant portion of the total premiums. A company often pays about two-thirds of the cost of the health plan, and the employee picks up the other one-third.

About 60 percent of U.S. firms offer coverage. Job losses are traumatic in many ways, but one of the most significant fears that many soon-to-be laid off workers experience is, "What will I do if I lose my health insurance?" The next two sections examine a law that is designed to mitigate these fears.

COBRA Coverage

In 1985, Congress passed the **Consolidated Omnibus Budget Reconciliation Act (COBRA)** in an attempt to cover "gaps" in insurance coverage when employees find themselves between jobs. If an employee has health insurance through work at a company with 20 or more employees, he can usually[1] stay on the company's plan for as long as 18 months.[2] The catch is, when he no longer works for a company, he

---

[1] Unless he is fired "for cause."

[2] The maximum time doubles to 36 months if you are a dependent on a health care plan that one of your parents has at work, and you lose your status as a dependent. A student who finishes an undergraduate degree and takes a first job that does not offer benefits may find this provision particularly useful.

has to take over paying his entire premium himself. For example, assume that John is single and has health insurance through his employer. He pays $100 per month toward the cost of the policy, and his employer pays $200 per month. John is then laid off and applies for COBRA coverage.

Under normal circumstances, John would now pay the full $300 per month himself, rather than the $100 he was paying before. He would likely continue with the arrangement until he had a new job with new health coverage, and then he would cancel the COBRA coverage through his former employer.

The 2009 "Stimulus Bill"

Very early in President Obama's administration, Congress passed the **American Recovery and Reinvestment Act**. It carried a price tag of several hundred billion dollars, and the press dubbed it the "stimulus package," because it was designed to stimulate the sagging economy. Among many other things, this law made temporary adjustments to COBRA.

Importantly, it capped a laid-off worker's COBRA bill at 35 percent of his total premium for the first nine months of COBRA coverage. Revisiting John from our example, he would face paying $105 of his $300 monthly bill for nine months, and the government would cover the remaining $195 with stimulus dollars. The act was modified later in 2009 to extend the same 35 percent deal to the first 15 months of COBRA coverage.

Although all stimulus-bill-related provisions were scheduled to end on February 28, 2010, at the time of this writing the Congress has passed an extension that runs to the end of 2010, and further extensions may be created.

The Specific Problem

Despite the existence of COBRA and its generous temporary modifications, it doesn't last forever. A laid-off worker who is unable to find other employment with a firm that offers health coverage often finds herself out of options after 18 months and joins the ranks of the uninsured.

This situation can present an ethical dilemma for companies, particularly when a worker has unusual health care requirements. The following scenario presents just such a case.

SCENARIO

Sales Director's Office

"I don't like layoffs any more than you do, but…" Carl said.

"We have to do it," the sales director finished.

"Yeah."

"Yeah. How many?"

"I'd recommend five. No, six. If we lay off six, we probably won't have to do this again, at least not this year."

"OK."

"So, do you want to go by seniority?" Carl asked.

The sales director thought about it for a minute. "No," she said, "let's stick with the numbers. Rank everybody from top to bottom, first place to…how many do we have?"

"Forty-one."

"First to forty-first. Let's average the last three years if they've been around that long, just this year if not. The bottom six will go."

Carl made some notes on his laptop. "I'll get right on it."

Two Days Later

"Here's the report," Carl said. "Benjamin is tops, of course. Over $350,000 a year."

"He's a machine," the sales director said.

"He is. The, ah, bottom six are highlighted. Below the line."

The sales director looked over the spreadsheet. The bottom portion read:

34. Roger	$143,000
35. Susan	$140,000
36. Javier	$126,000
37. Ellen	$120,000
38. Terry	$110,000
39. Fred	$92,000
40. Irene	$90,000
41. Stan	$52,000

"I didn't know Stan was this bad," she said. "I mean, this is just dreadful."

"He hasn't been pulling his weight for some time."

"We should have cut him loose a long time ago."

"I can't argue with you on that."

"OK. Ellen's been with us a long time."

"That she has."

The sales director looked over the numbers for a while longer. "All right. The decision's been made, so let's get this done."

"Agreed."

"Stop by human resources, and tell Jane what's going on."

"Will do."

Later that Day

"Hi, Jane," the sales director said as she looked up from her screen. "What's up?"

"Can I close the door for a minute?" Jane asked.

"Sure."

"Carl told me about the layoffs."

"Yeah. I hate to do it, but we're sunk if we don't get our costs under control."

"Yes, I know. And I don't want to argue against all of them. Just one of them."

The sales director took off her glasses. "Which one?"

"Terry."

"Terry's a great guy, and I'd keep him on if the company was in better shape, but his numbers just aren't there."

"True, but I know something about him that I don't think you do."

"Which is..."

"Terry's a hemophiliac."

"OK. That's...a bleeding disorder, right?"

"Right. He's had the condition since birth."

"OK, but...that's never been an issue here. He's got low numbers, that's it."

"The issue is that Terry's condition is one of the most expensive health problems there is. He has to receive regular injections to help his blood clot, and each round of treatment costs thousands of dollars. His medical bills are over $150,000 per year. Without health insurance, he can't possibly cover that amount."

"And he has our insurance."

"Of course."

"Well...he'll get another job. And he can get COBRA coverage in the meantime, right?"

"For a while, yes, but COBRA doesn't last forever."

"But it lasts for, what, 18 months?" Jane nodded. "He can find another job with health coverage in 18 months," the sales director said.

"A mediocre salesman in this economy? Perhaps, but it's hardly a sure thing."

"But aren't there…special programs for problems like his? Won't the government pick up the bill?"

"Maybe so, maybe not. It's hard to say whether someone can enroll in something like that, or what level of coverage they'll receive if they are enrolled."

"But nobody gets turned away from the ER, even if they don't have any insurance at all."

"Yes, but Terry might not make it to the ER. If he doesn't get his regular injections, even a small cut can be life-threatening. He can literally bleed to death in minutes because, without the injections, he can't stop bleeding."

The sales director's phone buzzed. "Your three o'clock is here," her assistant's voice said over the speaker.

"That's all I had to say, anyway," Jane said. "It's your call, of course. I just thought that this was something you should know."

"Yeah, you're right," the sales director said. "I'll think it over, Jane."

DISCUSSION QUESTIONS

1. If you were the sales director, would you lay off Terry?

_____

_____

_____

_____

2. If Terry is not laid off, how should the other "below-the-line" workers featured on the partial spreadsheet be treated? Is it fair to terminate Javier and Ellen, when they had higher numbers than Terry? Should Susan now be terminated, since she is in the bottom six among the "not-Terry" employees?

_____

_____

_____

_____

3. If Terry's job is spared, should the company create a policy for layoffs and workers with unusual medical needs, or should it just make exceptions on a case-by-case basis?

_____

_____

_____

_____

4. If Terry's job is spared, what should be done if Terry's performance slips even further at some point? Say, for example, that next year he bills only the $52,000 that last-place Stan billed in this scenario. Should he be terminated at that point?

_____

_____

_____

_____

5. Assume now that Terry is not a hemophiliac. Rather than a genetic condition that he has had since birth, suppose that he instead has huge medical bills because of a problem created by his behavior. Assume that Terry was driving drunk, ran his SUV into a concrete pillar, and that he has ongoing substantial bills related to physical therapy and a series of reconstructive surgeries that are not yet complete. Would you give less consideration to his potential problems if he loses his health insurance? Why or why not?

_____

_____

_____

_____

UNIT 5

Responding to Employee Behavior

Unit Background

Employees misbehave in a variety of ways, both at and away from the office. When rules are broken or bad things happen, how should a company respond?

Module 26

"Don't Be a Hero" Policies. [Most banks, and many other organizations, strictly prohibit employees from resisting criminals. What should a company do if an employee breaks such a policy, apprehends a criminal, and "saves the day"?]

Module 27

Company Perspective: Sexual Harassment Policies and Workplace Dating. [Some business leaders are highly concerned with the possibility of sexual harassment lawsuits. Some of them choose to implement policies that ban workplace dating. Are such rules appropriate?]

Module 28

Employee Perspective: Sexual Harassment Policies and Workplace Dating. [If a company does adopt a no-dating policy, and if coworkers become romantically involved, how should a company respond?]

Module 29

The Family and Medical Leave Act and "Fake Illnesses". [The FMLA is a much-appreciated law among workers dealing with serious illnesses. But what if a worker takes FMLA leave and it comes to light that he was never ill in the first place?]

Module 30

Firing Workers Responsible for a "Big Problem". [Bad decisions can lead to catastrophic results. If a specific person plays a major role in creating a disaster, should she be fired?]

Module 31

Resumé Fraud. [The economy has made some job applicants more desperate than usual. Some of them will seek any possible advantage to get a job. Is "stretching the truth" on a resumé harmless, or does it always indicate that a person is unfit to work for a company?]

Module 32

Employee Behavior Away from the Office. [Employees have personal lives. What should happen if, far away from the office, a worker does something that is highly embarrassing to a company?]

Responding to Employee Behavior

he last unit examined workplace issues that are independent of how employees act. This unit focuses on situations that are created, at least in part, by employee behavior.

If an "at-will" employee violates company policy or behaves badly in some other way, what should a company do? Should it fire workers, or would that make remaining workers disgruntled or paranoid? Should a company discipline workers without terminating them? Or perhaps do nothing at all?

Does it matter if an employee who violates company policy thinks that he is helping the company? The first module in this unit looks at such a situation. What if the violated policy seeks to control behavior away from the office?

What if the bad behavior results in substantial losses for the company by generating lawsuits? What if an employee lies? What if there is no violation of any specific company policy, but an employee does something in her personal life that embarrasses the company?

These issues are examined in detail in the next several modules.

MODULE **26**

"Don't Be A Hero" Policies

Bank robberies are a reasonably common occurrence. And although bank robbers are often eventually caught by police, very few of them are confronted at banks themselves. Almost all large banks have strict policies for employees to follow in such cases. Tellers are instructed to comply with requests to "hand over the money," regardless of whether a weapon is displayed or a robber seems physically intimidating. Convenience stores, liquor stores, and other businesses at an increased risk of being robbed have implemented similar rules for quite some time.

The reasoning behind such policies is clear. A robber may pull out and use a weapon if confronted, and the life of a clerk or bystander is not worth the several thousand dollars in a typical bank drawer. Also, video surveillance tapes usually give authorities a good chance to eventually find and apprehend the suspect. Increasingly, even ordinary retailers are creating "don't be a hero" policies that are primarily aimed at shoplifting situations.

Shoplifting

Shoplifting is terribly expensive. It is so common that retailers lose as much as several billion dollars a year to it. Estimates are that every item for sale in grocery and department stores costs 1–3 percent more than it would if there were no shoplifting, as stores must raise their prices somewhat to offset losses from merchandise that leaves without being paid for.

But store owners fear violent confrontations, just as owners of banks and liquor stores do. They might wish to stop shoplifting but not at the price of the safety of their workers and customers.

Another concern for store owners is tort law. If a person is held against his will, he can often sue for **false imprisonment.** It is true that shopkeepers have some legal freedom under tort law to detain suspected shoplifters, but in most states the "shopkeepers' exemptions" contain one or more "reasonableness" standards that generate more questions than answers. When is a shoplifter who tries to flee detained "reasonably"? Can he be grabbed? Tackled? Punched? Dragged to a back room and searched? If so, can clothing be searched? If so, must it be done by a security guard of the same gender as the suspected shoplifter?

If a mistake is made, the consequences can be costly. False imprisonment is an intentional tort, which means that plaintiff's lawyers can ask for *punitive (punishment) damages* on top of ordinary *compensatory damages*.

Many storeowners have simply given up. They implement strict policies that their employees are not to detain or pursue shoplifters. Some stores go so far as to instruct employees not to touch customers in any circumstances.

Employment-at-Will

The policies discussed so far can be backed up with essentially any threats that employers wish to make. Most employees in America are *employees-at-will*, which means that they can be fired at any time, for almost any reason. A company does not have to have a "good reason" to terminate an at-will employee as long as no specific law is violated. Consider the following two examples:

a. *A worker is fired because of her race.* In this case, the company has acted unlawfully, because there is a specific law (the Civil Rights Act, and perhaps others that would apply as well) that prohibits firing because of race. The terminated worker could sue her former employer and win.
b. *A worker is fired because his boss does not like his tie.* In this case, the company has acted lawfully, because no law creates job rights for those who wear ugly neckwear. The firing is frivolous, unjustified, and silly, but not illegal.

As in the second example, no law exists that gives rights to workers who are disciplined for violating "don't be a hero" policies. If a company has a strict policy of this kind, and if a worker violates it, he can be disciplined in any way the company finds appropriate. If the policy is important enough to the company, the worker can legally be fired.

Although the law is clear, many question whether the policies described in this module *should* lead to harsh consequences. There is a tendency for people to admire anyone who tries to "stop the bad guys."

The following scenario is inspired by an Austin case in 2009. An employee of a Randalls supercenter chased a thief who had taken a customer's purse from her shopping cart. The pursuit continued through the store, the parking lot, and ended in a field adjacent to the Randalls. The worker was fired, and the case generated a great amount of debate on the Internet discussion boards of Austin news stations.

SCENARIO

Supercenter Management Office—First Case

The store director pushed "play" on the console in front of him. The screen showed sharp black-and-white images of the home and garden department.

"Here you are, correct?" he asked as he gestured to an image of a man in a dark apron.

"Yes, sir," Hank replied. He looked nervous.

"The security guys spliced this together for me—they used footage from two different cameras. I just want for you to talk me through how things seemed to you at the time."

"Yes, sir."

On the screen, a man in a hooded sweatshirt approached a woman from behind, looked over her shoulder, and grabbed at the woman's purse. The strap caught on her arm, and the man pushed her to the ground and ripped the bag from her shoulder.

"So I was restocking the potting soil, and I heard a woman start screaming. I looked around, and I saw this guy standing over her and yanking at her purse; it looked like he was hurting her. So I dropped everything and started heading over there and shouting at the guy. He finally got her purse and took off."

On the screen, the man ran out of the frame.

"And you took off after him?"

"Ah, yes, sir."

"Why didn't you stay with the customer? See if she was OK?"

"She was yelling, 'He stole my purse! Stop him! Stop him!', and she looked OK to me. It just happened so fast. I guess I just followed her orders."

"He could have been armed."

"Well, I guess so. It was kind of just instinct to try to help."

"OK, so then what happened?"

The screen went blank for a moment, and then shifted perspectives to show an image of the store's parking lot, shot from a new camera.

"Well, he took off out the side door, and I followed him out into the parking lot, shouted for him to stop. I ran halfway through the parking lot, but, ah, he was pretty fast, and I knew after awhile that I couldn't catch him." The security tape confirmed his story.

"And then?"

"Well, I went back to make sure the customer was OK, and then I helped her call the police. The cops asked me a lot of questions—helped me remember what I saw, you know? When I was chasing the guy, I got close enough to notice that he was wearing Levi's, and that he had white Reebok shoes with a scuff mark on the left heel. They seemed glad to have that information."

The store director made notes as Hank talked.

"Hank," he said, "you know we have a strict policy against doing this kind of thing, right? It's in the employee handbook, and it was part of your training, correct?"

"Ah," Hank looked even more nervous, "yes, sir. I just…I just didn't have time to think of that. I mean, I was just minding my own business, and then…it just happened so fast."

"What was your plan? If you caught up to him?"

"Well," Hank considered the question for a moment, "I mean, for sure I was going to get the lady's purse back. And I guess, ah…I hadn't really thought about it after that."

"OK, Hank."

Supercenter Management Office—Second Case

A week later, the store director rolled a new spliced-together video for another employee.

"And this is you?" he asked as he pointed to an image of an employee in the electronics department.

"Yes, it is," Blake answered.

"OK. This tape will show the incident from different angles. Just talk me through how things looked through your eyes."

"Will do. So this dude here," Blake said, pointing to the screen, "I'd seen him around before. Never bought anything, just spent a lot of time looking at the iPads."

"OK."

"So the day all this happened, he comes in wearing a coat, and, man, it was like 75 degrees that day. So I kept an eye on him."

"Did you notify security?"

Blake rolled his eyes. "No offense, sir, but those guys are the laziest guys in the store. I mean, I didn't even bother, because I *have* called them before, and they never even show up for, like, an hour, and then they fill out a form, and that's it."

"OK." The screen showed the man in the jacket walk rapidly to the Apple display and pull something from his pocket.

"So I notice that he's got something—they look like wire cutters to me—and sure enough, that's what he has! He cuts through the cable holding the iPad demo and slides the whole thing under his jacket." The surveillance tape clearly showed the theft. "So I walked over to him and said, 'Hey!' and he tries to take off." The tape now showed the shoplifter take three rapid steps away. "So then I tackled him."

The screen showed Blake making a nice, clean takedown. When he saw the image, Blake smiled in spite of himself. The store director noticed.

"You seem amused," he said.

Blake's grin vanished, but then returned. "Well, come on, it was a pretty good tackle."

"Hmph. So go on with the story."

"Well, like the tape shows, I just kind of sat on him. He struggled at first, but then he mostly gave up. Somebody must have called for security, and eventually the guys actually did show up, and they took him away. And I got the iPad back, and it still worked! I ran a new cable through it, and it's still our demo."

"Yes. Blake, do you know how much an iPad costs us?"

"Ah, I don't know. We sell them for $499, so maybe $399?"

"That's about right. Do you know what a single lawsuit costs us? If a customer had been hurt in this scuffle, or if this guy sues us for false imprisonment?"

"It wasn't false anything! You saw him steal from us right on the tape!"

"That's not the point. A single lawsuit costs us tens of thousands of dollars in legal fees. More if we lose a case and have to pay a judgment."

Blake thought about that for a moment. "OK, but how much do we lose to shoplifting in a year?"

"That doesn't matter."

Blake pressed him. "Would you say it's more than $50,000?"

"Well, perhaps so…"

"I heard it's more like $500 a day. Maybe a couple hundred grand a year."

"That might be accurate."

"Sir, if more people acted like I did, you'd have a whole lot less shoplifting."

DISCUSSION QUESTIONS

1. Rate the degree to which you find "don't be a hero" policies sensible in the following types of businesses.

	Completely Reasonable ←————————→ Completely Unreasonable
Bank	1 --- 2 --- 3 --- 4 --- 5 --- 6 --- 7
Liquor Store	1 --- 2 --- 3 --- 4 --- 5 --- 6 --- 7
Supercenter	1 --- 2 --- 3 --- 4 --- 5 --- 6 --- 7

2. Do you agree with this statement made by some critics of "don't be a hero" policies: "If robbers and shoplifters expected to be confronted by clerks, and perhaps by armed clerks, then there would be far fewer robbers and shoplifters"?

_____

_____

_____

_____

3. Should Hank be fired, disciplined without being fired, or commended? Should Blake be fired, disciplined without being fired, or commended?

_____

_____

_____

_____

4. If you had been shopping at the store when the incidents presented in the scenario unfolded, would you have wanted the clerks to act as they did, or would you have preferred for them to do nothing?

_____

_____

_____

_____

5. Assume that Hank and Blake are fired. If you saw a news report of the incidents and the firings, would you be angry at the store in either case? If you were a regular customer, would you be less likely to shop there in the future?

_____

_____

_____

_____

Company Perspective: Sexual Harassment Policies and Workplace Dating

BACKGROUND

The oldest and most important of the major discrimination laws is the Civil Rights Act. Congress passed the act in 1964, and it prohibits workplace discrimination based on race, religion, gender, or national origin. In the 1980s, the Supreme Court recognized sexual harassment as a form of gender discrimination.

Sexual harassment lawsuits can generate significant problems for companies. Although the average verdict is much lower, million-dollar payouts are not unheard of. The lawsuits generate bad publicity and often lower office morale. More than ten thousand such complaints are filed with the Equal Employment Opportunity Commission (EEOC) in a typical year.

There are two types of sexual harassment lawsuits: "quid pro quo" and "hostile work environment." In **quid pro quo** cases, a manager, owner, or other authority figure in a company demands sexual contact in exchange for something job-related. The authority figure can offer good things (raises, promotions) or can threaten bad things (firing, cancellation of benefits, difficulty in getting promoted). The sexual contact does not have to be forced as it does with sexual assault; pressure is enough.

In **hostile work environment** cases, a worker is distressed by a "sexually charged atmosphere" in a workplace. Dirty jokes about sex or conversations about sex can lead to complaints. Sometimes, plaintiffs file after being asked out on dates by coworkers. Some lawsuits start after a groping incident or some other kind of sexual touching.

Except for the last item (sexual touching), there usually has to be a longstanding pattern of offensive conduct before plaintiffs have a reasonable chance to win in court. Today, it is rare for a plaintiff to win a case because of a handful of dirty jokes. There are some cases from the 1990s with judgments against companies over small incidents, but these have largely disappeared as courts have better defined the law.

Companies have become keenly interested in avoiding sexual harassment lawsuits, and many have come to rely on a standard legal defense that the Supreme Court created. If a company has a legitimate sexual harassment policy that encourages complaints to be filed internally, the company legitimately investigates the

149

complaints that are made, and if a plaintiff files a complaint with the EEOC without first following the company's internal policy, then the defense is generally met. In effect, companies can create a "last clear chance" to fix things in-house. It is worth noting that this defense does not apply to quid pro quo cases.

A strongly worded policy that is vigorously enforced is often enough to change a corporation's culture. But some companies choose to go even further. "Love contracts," for example, have become standard HR documents in some businesses. They require two employees who wish to become romantically involved to submit paperwork first. These contracts often require the workers to waive any legal rights to sue the company if their relationship goes wrong or at least agree to only take action against the company in arbitration and not in court.

Love contracts sometimes help a company avoid sexual harassment lawsuits. But they can come with costs. Professionals, especially new professionals, often spend more waking hours at work than they do anywhere else. The office is a natural place to meet romantic interests. Placing strict prohibitions on dating can lead some workers to seek employment elsewhere or just ignore the rules.

Love contracts themselves can be laughable. Some are perfectly fine, but the lengthy legal definitions that some contain for basic concepts like "a date" or "a kiss" are genuinely incredible. And as with any action that seeks to regulate the behavior of employees away from the office, some workers resent having invasions of their "personal lives."

Policies that define and discourage sexual harassment directly are always a good idea. Policies that require love contracts require careful deliberation. The following scenario raises some of the relevant considerations.

SCENARIO

Mr. Green's Office

"And so it's really over?" asked the CEO.

"She took the settlement, Mr. Green. It's really over."

"And it won't be in the papers, that kind of thing?"

"She signed a confidentiality agreement as part of the settlement. She can't talk to the press."

"And we didn't admit any wrongdoing on our part?"

"No. You can put this behind you."

The CEO let out a long breath. "What was the final total?"

"Two hundred thousand."

"Ouch!"

"You authorized me to negotiate up to three hundred."

"That's true."

"All things considered, it's not a bad result. I did my best to keep it lower, but…"

"It's OK. I know you did your best. It's just, you know, this whole thing blindsided me."

"It usually works that way. I have a lot of clients in the same boat. They can't believe it."

"I mean, a *sexual harassment* lawsuit. We've been sued before, but it was always because we played hardball and somebody didn't like being outplayed. But being sued from the inside…and for this…we're just so *professional* around here…"

"I know it stings, Mr. Green. But take it from me, you handled it the right way. It might feel lousy right now, and you have to write a big check, but trust me, this one could have been much more damaging to you."

"I suppose so. Well, thanks for your efforts." The CEO rose and offered his hand, and the lawyer shook it. "Did you use up your retainer working on this?"

"Not sure. Call my secretary."

"Will do."

"Anything else, Mr. Green?"

"No, that should do it…well…actually, I'd ask you one more thing, yes."

"OK, shoot."

"Do I have the power to just put an end to romantic office relationships? Can I just decree that dating coworkers is against the rules, legally speaking?"

"You can, yes. You can put limits on what's OK, or ban workplace romances altogether. You can put clauses into contracts if you want to or just put the rules in the employee handbook."

"Nobody can sue me for keeping them from their 'true love'?"

"Anybody can sue you for anything, but they can't sue you and win."

"Interesting. I'm going to think about that. Well, thanks again."

"My pleasure, Mr. Green."

Lunchroom

"He was completely wasted—you should have seen this guy. By the time we left…"

"Shut up," Dan interrupted Eric, quietly but urgently. Eric looked at him, puzzled. Dan widened his eyes and nodded his head slightly toward a spot over Eric's shoulder. He turned around and saw the company's founder right behind him.

"Mr. Green," he managed, getting awkwardly to his feet.

"Oh, sit down, sit down. Eric, isn't it?" Mr. Green asked.

"Yessir."

"And, ah," Mr. Green said, looking at Dan.

"Dan, sir."

"Dan!" Mr. Green said, snapping his fingers. "Of course. Do you gentlemen mind if I join you?"

"Ah, no, sir," Eric said.

"Not at all," Dan agreed.

"Excellent! I always make it a point to spend a little time with our interns if my schedule allows for it. So, tell me, how are things going?"

The three made small talk about the internship program for a while.

Lunchroom—10 Minutes Later

"Well, I'm glad to hear things are going so well," Mr. Green said. "So I have to admit, gentlemen, that I had an ulterior motive to join you for lunch today. You're both aware that we're being sued in a sexual harassment lawsuit?"

"Yes, sir," the interns said, uncertainly.

"Well, the good news is: that case just settled. But even so, I'm left to decide how to keep something like that from happening again, if I can. What I don't have that I *need* to have is a picture of what kind of…romances, yes, let's say romances, are going on around here."

The interns sat in silence.

"No one wants to gossip around the boss, which, by the way, makes my life much less interesting. I would have liked to hear the rest of the story you were telling when I walked up."

Mr. Green looked at Eric, who swallowed uncomfortably. "Ah…"

"It's OK. It's perfectly natural," Mr. Green smiled. "The saying is right. It IS lonely at the top. But no matter…or, at least, it *usually* doesn't matter. But this time, maybe it does. So look, I'm asking you for a favor, and if you're uncomfortable with it and say no, then I promise you it won't hurt your chances to be hired full-time next year. You don't have to use anybody's name—nobody's getting in trouble. I just want you to tell me what kinds of relationships there are between people who work here. I need to know so that I can come up with a sensible policy, and I'm asking you because it's my experience that interns know everything when it comes to stuff like this, correct?"

Eric smiled sheepishly. "Ah, I guess so, Mr. Green."

"Uh, huh," Green said smiling. "Do you concur, Dan?"

Dan exhaled. "Yes, I agree. I know who's with who. Or, with whom? Ah..."

"It doesn't matter!" Green said, laughing now. "So, will you help me out, gentlemen?"

They both agreed. Over the next 10 minutes, Eric and Dan described the following to Mr. Green:

1. A pair of employees who have had a committed relationship for the last eight months.

2. A supervisor and an employee who works directly with the supervisor who have had a secret, committed relationship for the last three months.

3. A pair of employees who have "hooked up" several times but have no relationship.

4. A manager and an administrative assistant in another department who have "hooked up" several times but have no relationship.

5. Sean and Ann, who met at the office and have now been married for five years.

Mr. Green was only aware of the last item. He thanked the interns and left the lunchroom.

Mr. Green's Office

Green returned to his office and scribbled on a yellow notepad, outlining different policies that he might put in place. After half an hour, he had the following rough ideas for rules sketched out:

1. No dating coworkers.

2. No dating between high- and low-level employees.

3. No dating between high- and low-level employees if the high-level employee directly supervises the low-level employee.

4. No dating coworkers unless both employees sign a document ahead of time agreeing not to sue the company over anything related to the relationship.

5. No policy—just forget about it.

Ann's Office

"So that's my dilemma," Mr. Green said. "And I want your input for obvious reasons." Mr. Green pointed to a wedding picture on Ann's desk. "How long have you and Sean been married, now?"

"Five years."

"Wow!"

"I know. Time flies."

Green pointed to another picture, "And how old is Carol Ann, now?"

"She just turned two."

"What a great age. I remember my boys at two. So full of energy!"

"You can say that again."

"Well...," Green spread his hands. "So what do you think, Ann? I don't want to keep people like you and Sean apart. Of the plans I'm thinking about, which of them would have done that?"

Ann thought about the question. "All of them," she eventually answered.

"All of them?"

"I think so, yes. I can't speak for anybody else, but in my case...Sean's so shy before he gets to know someone. If there had been any company policy at all about dating, even if it didn't really apply to the kind of coworkers we were, I just don't think he would have ever asked me out."

"Huh," Mr. Green said. "Even if I had a clear policy that only prohibited supervisors from dating supervisees? And if I explained it thoroughly to everyone?"

"In our case, I just don't think he would have asked me out. But maybe others would be different."

"OK. Well, thanks very much, Ann."

DISCUSSION QUESTIONS

1. Rate the first four relationships the interns described as either "inappropriate" or "no big deal." Elaborate on why you scored each as you did.

   _____ A pair of employees who have had a committed relationship for the last eight months.

   _____ A supervisor and an employee who works directly with the supervisor who have had a secret, committed relationship for the last three months.

   _____ A pair of employees who have "hooked up" several times but have no relationship.

   _____ A manager and an administrative assistant in another department who have "hooked up" several times but have no relationship.

   _____

   _____

   _____

   _____

2. Rate the policies that Mr. Green is considering as either "reasonable" or "unreasonable." Elaborate on why you scored each as you did.

   _____ No dating coworkers.

   _____ No dating between high- and low-level employees.

   _____ No dating between high- and low-level employees if the high-level employee directly supervises the low-level employee.

   _____ No dating coworkers unless both employees sign a document ahead of time agreeing not to sue the company over anything related to the relationship.

   _____ No policy—just forget about it.

   _____

   _____

   _____

   _____

3. If you were an employee, would any policy be likely to influence your actual behavior? In other words, would you date other employees anyway and hope that you didn't get caught?

   _____

   _____

   _____

4. What would an appropriate penalty be for violating each of the first four policies that Mr. Green is considering? Should a worker be fired? Disciplined in some other way? Should the punishment be more severe for violations of some policies rather than others?

   _____

   _____

   _____

   _____

5. Many companies try to control some things that employees do when they are away from the office. Compare policies that try to discourage office romances with policies that require employees to submit to drug tests and nicotine tests and seek to discourage the use of drugs and tobacco.

	Completely Reasonable ⟵⟶ Intrusive and Unacceptable						
Dating Policies	1 --- 2 --- 3 --- 4 --- 5 --- 6 --- 7						
Drug Testing	1 --- 2 --- 3 --- 4 --- 5 --- 6 --- 7						
Nicotine Testing	1 --- 2 --- 3 --- 4 --- 5 --- 6 --- 7						

Employee Perspective: Sexual Harassment Policies and Workplace Dating

In the early 1990s, Clarence Thomas was nominated by President George H. W. Bush to be a Supreme Court Justice. During his Senate confirmation hearings, things got ugly. Anita Hill, a former coworker, accused him of sexual harassment. Thomas denied the claims, and Hill provided no evidence other than her own testimony. In the end, the Senate confirmed Thomas, and he was seated on the Supreme Court. But after the hearings, sexual harassment was definitely "on the map."

The number of people aware of sexual harassment law and who filed sexual harassment lawsuits skyrocketed throughout the rest of the 1990s. Today, the increases have leveled off, but even so, more than ten thousand complaints are filed with the Equal Employment Opportunity Commission in a typical year.

Types of Cases

Sexual harassment lawsuits can generate significant problems for companies. There are two types of sexual harassment lawsuits: "quid pro quo" and "hostile work environment." To repeat a key distinction from a previous module (Module 27): In quid pro quo cases, a manager, owner, or other authority figure in a company demands sexual contact in exchange for something job-related. The authority figure can offer good things (raises, promotions) or can threaten bad things (firing, cancellation of benefits, difficulty in getting promoted). The sexual contact does not have to be forced as it does with sexual assault; pressure is enough.

In hostile work environment cases, a worker is distressed by a "sexually charged atmosphere" in a workplace. Dirty jokes about sex or conversations about sex can lead to complaints. Sometimes, plaintiffs file after being asked out on dates by coworkers. There usually has to be a longstanding pattern of offensive conduct before plaintiffs have a reasonable chance to win in court. It is rare for a plaintiff to win a case because of a handful of dirty jokes.

Companies' Responses

Companies have become keenly interested in avoiding sexual harassment lawsuits. Although the average verdict is much lower, million-dollar payouts are not unheard of. In any event, the lawsuits tend to generate bad publicity, and they often lower office morale.

In an attempt to reduce the number of possible sexual harassment incidents, some companies have banned workplace relationships. The thinking goes that supervisor–subordinate relationships can lead to quid pro quo cases, and flirting can lead to hostile work environment allegations. These particular companies threaten workers with termination if they are found to be romantically involved with a coworker.

Another module in this series (Module 27, if you are using the textbook) examines whether a business leader should adopt a no-dating policy in the first place. In the scenario that follows, a company has already implemented such a policy, and an employee must decide what to do.

SCENARIO

Lunchroom

The 40-ounce soft drink made Jim's lunch tray difficult to balance, but he did his best as he navigated the cafeteria. He spotted his friend, Mike, across the room. Actually, he noticed Claire, who was just getting up from a seat next to Mike. Then he noticed Mike. Jim hesitated for a moment, and when he was sure that Claire was really leaving, he walked over to Mike's table. When he arrived, Mike didn't notice. He was watching Claire walk away.

"Mike?" No answer. "Mike? Hey, Mikey!" Jim said, raising his voice.

Mike slowly turned his head. After a second, he said lazily, "Oh. Heyyy, Jimbo. How are ya, buddy?"

"Not as good as you. May I join you, good sir?"

Mike replied with the same mock formality. "By all means, good sir." He gestured to an empty chair with a flourish.

Jim sat down. "Saw you talking to Claire."

"Ah, Claire," Mike said, grinning wide. "I," he said, "just asked her out. We're going to dinner. On Friday. How about that?" he asked, grinning even wider.

"Ah, that's great, buddy. Except, ah, you know…"

"Know what?" Mike looked suspicious. "She's not married or something, is she?"

"No, nothing wrong with Claire. You know, the other thing."

Mike's grin disappeared. "You're killing my buzz, Jimbo. What are you talking about?"

"Have you ever read the employee handbook?"

Mike grimaced. "Why the hell would I read the employee handbook?"

Jim groaned. "Never mind. Short version: Your contract says you agree to live by the rules in the employee handbook, and the employee handbook says that you can't date your fellow employees."

"You're a liar."

"No. Haven't you noticed that nobody really dates around here?"

"I don't hang out with anyone around here after work. Except you. I have no idea who's hooking up around here."

"Well, nobody is—at least not with each other."

"Jim," Mike said, steering the conversation in another direction. "You've seen Claire."

"I have."

"And how would you describe her?"

"As a happily married man who is not after her, I believe I can give an unbiased opinion."

"Which is?"

"She's smoking hot."

"That is correct."

"Which doesn't change the fact that your contract..."

"Wait," Mike said, holding up a finger. "Let me finish."

"All right, Mike."

"And how many hours a week do we work here?"

"I dunno...55?"

"Ah, it must be nice to have some seniority. But a new employee like me puts in more like 65 or 70. And, Jim, if I'm always here, then where else am I going to meet anyone?"

"Not sure. Bookstore?"

"Yes, yes, everyone knows you met your wife in a bookstore. I can't pull that off, OK? Everyone at the bookstore can tell that *I don't read anything.*"

"So...somewhere else."

"No. I'm always here. I need to meet girls *here.* Surely anyone can see that."

"I sympathize with you, but here's another summary for you. Four years ago: The company loses a big sexual harassment lawsuit and partners freak out. Three-and-a-half years ago: The no-dating policy goes into the employee handbook. Three years ago: A fairly high-level guy and gal *both* get fired for taking a trip to the Bahamas together. Ever since: No one dates around here."

"That's outrageous!"

"I'm not saying it's a *good* policy. But it is the policy."

"But I'm not *harassing* Claire. She *wants* to go out with me! And if she didn't, I'd leave her alone."

"I know that. But they don't know that. Look, all the executives care about is that they 'do something' to make sure that we don't lose 1.3 million dollars in another sexual harassment lawsuit. The no-dating policy lets them show the board that they've 'done something.' That's it. End of story."

Mike thought for a while. Then, determined, he said, "I don't care. I'm going out with her anyway. I'm not doing anything wrong."

"All right. I won't rat you out. But what if you guys get together? How long do you really think you can keep it a secret?"

"I don't know," Mike said, sullen.

"What will you do if you get caught?" Jim prodded.

"I don't know!" Mike was highly irritated now. "Find another job, if it comes to that."

"In this economy?" Mike was silent. Jim continued. "And what about Claire? Will she 'find another job' too?"

Mike's expression turned icy. "You know, this is all really easy for a married guy to say."

Jim turned his palms up. "Hey, I'm on your side here. I just want for you to think it through, that's all."

"Yeah, all right, I know. It's just that, you know, five minutes ago...man, Claire's just terrific. I couldn't believe she wanted to go out with me. And now..."

"I know. It's not fair. It's not fair at all."

The two ate in silence for a while. "Maybe I can," Mike said eventually, "ah, you know, talk to somebody in human resources. Explain everything. Maybe they'd give us an exception."

Jim, frowned. "Yeah. Or, you could just wear a sign that says, 'I'm planning to violate company policy. Please fire me!'"

"So...bad idea."

"Doesn't seem good to me. Not if you want to try to get away with it."

Mike groaned. "So, what, I just tell the hottest girl who's liked me in...forever... that I'm sorry, but we can't go out after all?"

"Not necessarily. Look, man, I told you that I'm on your side. And finding somebody is important. I was a sad, hopeless idiot before I got married. Ah, not that you're a sad, hopeless idiot."

"Thanks."

"And, look, the lawsuit happened four years ago. Everybody was hypersensitive about it right after it happened, but maybe everyone's kind of forgotten about it by now. And maybe you can keep it a secret. Or maybe Claire will hate you if you take her to dinner, and it will be a moot point."

"Again, thanks." Becoming less sarcastic, Mike then said, "Actually, thanks. For real. I had no idea about the policy. It's good to at least know about it.

"Yeah," Jim said, nodding. "You're welcome."

Mike looked at his watch. "Oh, man! I've got a meeting in five minutes. I'll see you around, Jim, OK?"

"See you around, Mike."

DISCUSSION QUESTIONS

1. If you were in Mike's position (or Claire's position), would you find a way to go on the date, or would you decide to cancel because of the company's policy?

   _____

   _____

   _____

   _____

2. If you would keep the date, would you try to talk to someone at the company and be made an exception to the rule? Or would you try to hide the relationship? If you would break the date, would that impact your ability to do a good job for the company?

   _____

   _____

   _____

   _____

3. A small but nontrivial number of companies have no-dating policies, and they are usually justified as a tool that will reduce the chance of a sexual harassment lawsuit. The policies are completely legal, and courts have backed up real companies that have fired workers for violating them. In your opinion, are no-dating policies for coworkers reasonable? Do you think that they would actually make sexual harassment less likely?

   _____

   _____

   _____

   _____

4. Some firms have "light" no-dating coworkers policies that ban supervisors from dating subordinates altogether but allow other coworkers to date provided that both employees sign an agreement before they become romantically involved. The agreements are usually awkwardly worded documents that boil down to this idea: "I will hold the company legally blameless if anything goes wrong with this relationship." If you were in Mike and Claire's position at a company with a "light" no-dating policy, would you feel comfortable signing such a document before you went out with someone? If not, would you break the date, or just try to hide the date from the company?

   _____

   _____

   _____

   _____

5. Assume that your next job is with a company that has no particular policy on dating coworkers. The majority of companies don't have such a thing. Would you be reluctant to become involved with a coworker for some other reason, or does it make no difference if you meet someone interesting at the office or anywhere else?

_____

_____

_____

_____

MODULE **29**

The Family and Medical Leave Act and "Fake Illnesses"

In 1993, Congress passed the Family and Medical Leave Act (FMLA). The law seeks to help American workers who find themselves in specific "between a rock and a hard place" situations. Under certain medical circumstances, workers can *demand* to be allowed to take a leave of absence from work. If workers qualify, covered companies must allow for the leave and place the employee back in his "old job," or an equivalent job, when he returns to work.

Before the FMLA, many workers faced difficult dilemmas. A parent with a sick child might have thought, "Well, I can stay home with my child, but if I miss too much work, I might lose my job. Or I might go into the office every day, but my child could suffer." With the FMLA in place, many people are no longer required to make this difficult choice.

FMLA Coverage

The FMLA applies to companies with at least 50 employees. It does not apply to workers who have worked at a company for less than one year on a full-time basis. The law covers women who are pregnant and also workers with a "serious illness" in their "immediate family."

Serious illnesses are problems that require hospitalization or a series of visits to a doctor. Immediate family members as defined by the FMLA are yourself, your spouse, your parents, and your children.

If a worker qualifies under the conditions above, she is entitled to take up to 12 weeks of unpaid leave per year. A woman taking time off because of a pregnancy can definitely take the entire 12 weeks. An employee taking time off because of a serious illness can take as much of the 12 weeks as is medically necessary.

In the end, a covered worker can address his medical situation without fear of being fired. But because companies do not have to pay workers during the leave of absence, he must have some other means of paying his bills while he is away from work.

The Problem

Because workers miss paychecks during FMLA leave, most people take time off only if they have a compelling need. But in some cases, unfortunately, workers try to exaggerate health problems. Sometimes, they make up serious illnesses altogether. Statistics on "fake illnesses" do not exist, but there is strong anecdotal evidence that some companies deal with them on a repeated basis.

The FMLA lays out a way for a company to "call a worker's bluff" if it seems like the employee is trying to take FMLA leave when she is not actually ill. The process, though, is not an easy one if the worker is persistent in claiming an illness.

First, a company can demand a doctor's note verifying the illness. Usually, such a note ends any controversy, but not always. Most doctors are completely honest, but in any town, there are a few health care providers who seem willing to write any note a patient wants regardless of whether the patient is actually ill.

If a dubious note is produced, the FMLA allows for a company to require a worker claiming a serious illness to visit a second doctor of the company's choosing. But two problems can arise with this option. First, the company must pay for the visit. Second, if the company doctor says that the worker is fine, then the company must pay for a third medical appointment. Only if the third doctor agrees with the second doctor that a worker does not have a serious illness can the company deny the leave of absence. Eventually, a company can deny FMLA leave to even a stubborn worker who claims a fake illness. But the process is costly and time consuming.

The following scenario looks at further issues that come up in a typical "suspected fake illness" situation.

SCENARIO

Vince's Office

Pam, a human resources chief, knocked on Vince's door. Vince, a recently hired senior manager, looked up from his desk. "Oh, hi. Ah...Pam, right?"

"That's me. Do you have a minute?"

"Sure. Come on in." Pam closed the office door behind her and sat down. "What's up?" Vince asked her.

"I want to talk to you about Al Smith. He's in your department, correct?"

"Right. I, ah...I think he's been out for a few days, actually. Bad cold, or something."

"Yeah. That's actually what I'm here to talk about. He called in to one of my guys this morning and said he'd be out with a 'highly contagious upper respiratory virus' for at least three weeks and that he wants to claim FMLA leave."

"Wow. I guess he's pretty sick."

"Yeah," Pam said under her breath.

"So, ah, what's the problem?"

"The problem is that I don't think he's sick."

Vince squinted his eyes and seemed more attentive. "Why is that?"

"He did the exact same thing in early June last year. Right when the warehouse folks were starting their big inventory and maintenance period, Al called in sick with a 'highly contagious upper respiratory virus' and took three weeks of FMLA leave. He came back—all smiles and with a tan—the day after inventory and maintenance was over. The warehouse guys hate the inventory and maintenance weeks. They were ticked off because they thought Al played hooky and skipped them, and they had to do even more work than usual because they were shorthanded."

Vince thought for a moment. "But, well, maybe he's just...susceptible to getting really sick. I have an aunt like that—she has a heart problem, and when she gets sick, she stays sick for a while."

"Maybe."

"But you still don't think so."

"The timing is just unusual. Al hasn't missed a day of work in three years, except for the stretch right around the last super-busy time in the warehouse."

"But didn't he bring in a doctor's note, or something?"

"No, he didn't. And his last manager told me not to press him for one. He said, 'we have to trust our workers,' and so forth."

"Hmm."

"So can I ask him for a note?"

"Yeah. Yeah, go ahead. I'm sure he'll send one in."

"And if he doesn't?"

"Well…let's cross that bridge when we come to it.

One Week Later

"Hi, Vince."

"Oh, hey, Pam. What's the word?"

"Al Smith faxed in a note today."

"Oh, good. You know, I talked to him on the phone at the end of last week. He sounded really miserable."

"Yeah," Pam said under her breath.

"But you're…still skeptical?"

"Take a look at the note." She handed a fax to Vince. "You'll notice that the physician's assistant has diagnosed Al with 'Acute Medical Illness.'"

Vince read the note. "Huh?"

"I called the doctor's office after this note came in. The person on the phone said she couldn't elaborate."

"Well, that's probably true. Aren't patient records confidential?"

"This is the absolute fakest-looking diagnosis I've ever seen. 'Acute Medical Illness'? Are you kidding me? That sounds like something a seventh-grader would write on a forged note from his parents after he cuts school."

"But it is from an actual medical office? I mean, it does exist?"

"Yes," Pam admitted. "It does exist."

"So isn't that the end of it?"

"It doesn't have to be. The FMLA allows for us to make Al go to a doctor that we choose for a second opinion. I want to send him to Dr. Franklin. He has offices across the street from us. I've seen him before, and he won't write an excuse for work unless Al is really sick."

"I don't know, Pam. He sounded pretty sick to me on the phone."

"The guys in the warehouse are furious. They all had to come in on Saturday because they're shorthanded again. We can't let Al get away with this again. If we do, everyone is going to get 'sick' next June."

"Maybe."

"So can I set an appointment for Al with Dr. Franklin?"

Vince thought for a long while. "Yeah. Yeah, go ahead," he said eventually.

Call Between Vince and Al

Later that day, Vince answered his phone. "Hello?"

"Hello, sir," said a gravelly voice.

"Al?" Vince asked.

"Yes, sir, it's me. (*Cough*.)"

"Al, you sound terrible."

"I feel terrible. I just want to stay in bed all day."

"Well, then that's what you should do."

"I'd love to. The problem is that Pam just called me."

"Ah."

"She told me that I have to visit some company doctor. Doctor Franklin, I guess? What gives?"

Vince rubbed his forehead. "Look, Al, I don't have to tell you that it's a busy time down at the warehouse, and Pam just wants to verify your illness."

"I already did (*ah-choo!*)... I already did that, boss. I faxed her a note this morning."

"Yes." Vince paused. "Yes...she, ah...wasn't sure what an 'acute medical illness' might be. She just wants to make sure..."

"Look, I'm sorry the guy was in a hurry when he wrote the note!" Al cut him off. "Pam said she needed a note, so I (*hack!*) dragged myself out of bed and (*hack! hack!*) and I went back to the doctor's office and waited for nearly an hour. Eventually, the guy wrote the note in between looking at other patients. (*Ah-choo!*)"

"Yes, well, again...Pam just wants to make sure. You know, verify your illness."

"I was trusted last time I got sick. I didn't have to bring a note then. In fact, I can't think of when anybody has been asked to bring in a doctor's note. Much less (*cough!*) visit another doctor. Come on, boss, have a heart. I'm dying here. Why should I have to keep this appointment with Dr. Franklin?"

DISCUSSION QUESTIONS

1. If you had been in Vince's position in the middle of the scenario and had seen the "acute medical illness" note, would you have required Al to visit a company-selected doctor, or would you have left it alone?

2. If you were in Vince's position as the scenario ended, would you insist on Al keeping the appointment with Dr. Franklin?

3. Assume that Al goes to see Dr. Franklin, and that the doctor finds nothing wrong with him. Assume further that the company sends Al to a second doctor, who also finds nothing wrong. Should Al then be fired? Disciplined in some other way? Or would you allow him to escape punishment if he showed up for work?

4. If a worker has *never* applied for FMLA leave before, is it sensible to require additional doctor visits after a doctor's note is produced? What if it is a dubious-looking note like the one in this scenario?

5. In the late 1990s, when the economy was roaring along, there was some talk in Congress about changing the FMLA to allow for workers to take *paid* medical leave. "Workers who live paycheck-to-paycheck can't afford to take advantage of this law," some members of Congress argued. But then the tech-bubble bursting in the early years of the twenty-first century and the mortgage meltdown a few years later put any discussion about paid FMLA leave on the back burner.

Assume that, five years from now, the economy is again doing great. Would it be a good idea for Congress to revise the FMLA to require that workers be paid during medical leaves of absence, or would such a change make the kind of situation described in the scenario above become more common?

_____

_____

_____

_____

Firing Workers Responsible for a "Big Problem"

BACKGROUND

Sometimes, bad things are the result of a single person. A man snaps and punches someone. An employee decides to take money from her company's petty cash drawer. A person parks on a steep hill, forgets to set his parking brake, and his car rolls down the hill and crashes into a tree. But often, injuries, accidents, and financial losses result from a series of events in which many people play a key role. Bad results often would not happen at all if any one of several people behaved differently.

As an example, it is estimated that there are as many as two hundred thousand cases of medical malpractice in the United States every year that result in *death*. Two hundred thousand! By comparison, about forty thousand people die in car crashes in the United States annually. About three thousand people died in the September 11th terrorist attacks.

In a number of these cases, the ultimate cause of death is the fact that errors have been made prescribing drugs. The side effects of one drug combine with those of another, causing disaster. Or a drug is prescribed in an improper dosage, and a medicine that would help a patient at 1 unit per day kills a patient when given at 10 units per day.

In an average case of accidental overdose, at least five people and groups might come into play. Many incidents unfold more or less like this: A prescription is written by a *physician's assistant (PA)*, and the PA might write down an inappropriate dose on his prescription pad. The mistake is not caught immediately because the medical *office where the PA works* is not equipped with software that automatically double-checks dosing. The *doctor* who is charged with supervising the PA does not thoroughly check all prescriptions that he writes. The *pharmacist* who fills the prescription does not notice that the dose prescribed is unusually high, and the *pharmacy where she works* is not equipped with software that automatically double-checks dosing.

If the patient then overdoses on the prescribed medication and dies, who is to blame? Everyone? Only the person at the beginning or end of the "chain of events"? It is sometimes hard to say.

167

Legal Ideas: Foreseeable Harm and *Respondeat Superior*

The scenario in this module focuses, as always, on questions of ethics. There is no requirement that you apply legal doctrines to it. However, there are two relevant legal ideas that might be helpful in assigning blame to the characters. The first relevant legal standard is *foreseeable harm*.

If you are injured by another person and choose to go to court, you file a **tort** lawsuit. Tort cases cover most any personal injury situation. To win, you need to show, among other things, that the person you sue caused foreseeable harm. In the end, if a jury thinks a defendant should have known better, expected someone else to be harmed, and been more careful to prevent the harm, then he will probably be found to be legally responsible for the plaintiff's problems. If, on the other hand, a jury determines that a defendant had no reasonable way of knowing that someone would be harmed by his actions, he is probably not liable for the harm.

The second relevant legal standard is the doctrine of **respondeat superior**, which literally translates to "let the master respond." It is the legal notion that, if someone is working for you and makes a mistake, you can be sued for the mistake just as much as your employee can. Legally, companies are usually liable for the "at work" errors of workers.

Employment Issues

Legal issues aside, when employees make mistakes that lead to financial losses, injuries, and other problems, companies often face ethical dilemmas. The key question often becomes: What *should* we do to the workers involved? The law rarely requires companies to hire or fire workers. And so, if workers make costly errors, should they be disciplined? Removed from positions of authority? Fired? Or should they pay no specific price at all? Often, the answer is not entirely clear.

In the following scenario, five people act carelessly. Any one of them could have prevented the ultimate harm that comes to a customer, but none did. You may, but are not required to, apply legal doctrines to the questions that follow the module.

SCENARIO

The Red SUV

Ron works on the assembly line at an auto plant. He installs the assembly that connects the windshield wipers to the driver's controls on the turn signal. Ron installs 30 units per hour for eight hours, every day. Part of the assembly requires him to insert a clip with four wires into the casing that surrounds the small windshield wiper motor, and it is ordinarily an easy task. However, when he is working on a red SUV at the end of a long shift, he accidentally inserts the clip upside down. He tries to remove it, but it has become stuck. Frustrated, and falling behind, he jerks on the wires trailing from the clip, finally gets it loose, and inserts it in the proper direction, but one of the four wires is no longer attached to the clip. It dangles below the windshield motor, with copper clearly exposed.

Bill is an inspector on Ron's shift. His job is to do a visual inspection on 60 specific things that are done in Ron's part of the assembly operation. He has four minutes to do each inspection. The assembly line is halted every two hours for a ten-minute break. It is 2:00, and the next break is at 2:50. Unfortunately for Bill, he had a 44-ounce "Thirst Bust-R" Mountain Dew Code Red during his lunch break, and he is in desperate need of a restroom break. This is not a surprise to Bill; he often has a "Thirst Bust-R" with his lunch, and he rarely makes it to the 2:50 break without needing to use the restroom. When he is confident that no one is looking, Bill hustles to the men's room. He returns quickly but has only 90 seconds to do the inspection on the red SUV that would normally take four minutes. Checking the windshield wiper assembly is near the bottom of his checklist.

Ordinarily, he would spot the dangling wire that Ron left behind, but in his rush, he doesn't notice this time. He stamps the red SUV "passed" and moves on to the next vehicle.

Anna sells cars at Smith's Car Country. She accompanies a customer on a test drive of a red SUV in the rain. Thirty minutes after the test drive, Anna goes outside to move the car back to its original parking space. Before she starts the car, she notices a faint buzzing coming from behind the instrument panel. She listens more closely and eventually opens the hood. The buzz seems to be coming from the base of the windshield wipers. She goes back to the drivers' seat and discovers that, after the test drive, the customer left the switch controlling the wipers in the "high" position. Anna pushes the switch to "off," and the buzzing sound immediately stops. After she parks the car, she reports the buzzing sound to her manager.

Max Smith is Anna's manager and the son of the owner of Smith's Car Country. Either Max or Max's father sign off on all new car sales. When Anna tells him about the red SUV, he makes a note to have it checked out, but he never gets around to doing anything about it.

A week later, the customer who took the red SUV for a test drive returns to Smith's Car Country and wants to buy it. Anna is eager to make the sale and starts the paperwork. She does not ask Max whether anyone inspected the windshield wiper assembly, and she does not take another look at the red SUV herself. Max vaguely remembers that someone had a problem with the SUV, but he signs off on the deal.

Doug is a mechanic at Smith's Car Country. Among other things, he is in charge of inspecting all new vehicles just before they are delivered to customers. He has a 140-point inspection that he is supposed to do, and a visual inspection of the windshield wiper assembly is one of the items on his checklist. But it is Saturday, and Doug's new best friend is ESPN 3. During almost the entire hour he is supposed to be inspecting the red SUV, he is watching a college football game online. During one commercial break, he pops the hood, starts the car, and listens to the engine run for a minute while he looks it over. He does not notice the exposed wire, but he would have noticed it if he had made a reasonable inspection. Satisfied, he kills the engine and returns to the game without missing a single play.

The customer takes the red SUV home and is very happy with it for a week. Then she drives it on a rainy day and parks it at work. She leaves the windshield wiper switch in the "high" position. Four hours later, a coworker runs in and shouts, "A car is on fire in the parking lot!" The fire department is called, and they arrive before the fire spreads, but the customer's red SUV is a total loss.

DISCUSSION QUESTIONS

1. Rank the five people discussed in the example above from #1 to #5, with #1 being the person *most* responsible for the SUV fire, and #5 being the person *least* responsible.

   _____ Ron (installed the assembly improperly in the first place)

   _____ Bill (did a lousy job inspecting Ron's work)

   _____ Anna (did not double-check the buzzing sound before selling the car to a customer)

   _____ Max (did not tell a mechanic to look into the problem)

   _____ Doug (does a lousy inspection at Smith's Car Country)

2. Focus on your top-two people most responsible for the SUV fire. Why are they in the top positions? If the story can be reconstructed, and specific blame can be placed on them, should they be fired? Disciplined? Neither?

   _____

   _____

   _____

   _____

3. What if the red SUV had not caught fire in a parking lot? Assume that the car had ignited with the customer inside and that the customer had been killed. Should more people in the chain be fired if their mistakes resulted in a fatality?

_____

_____

_____

_____

4. Speaking generally now, when a chain of errors in the workplace leads to bad results, do you tend to place more blame on the people who make the initial mistake or on the people who supervise them and fail to correct the mistake?

_____

_____

_____

_____

5. Now, assume that only one person is to blame. Assume that the car was manufactured correctly and had no problems until it was prepped for delivery by Doug, the mechanic at Smith's Car Country. While going through his inspection in a hurry, he accidentally pulled the wire loose from its socket and left bare copper exposed. If the car ignites, should the mechanic be fired?

_____

_____

_____

_____

MODULE **31**

Resumé Fraud

BACKGROUND

Everyone is looking for an edge. It is the nature of people, or at least of most people, to seek out advantages. This is particularly true in the business world. Competition forces companies to drive hard bargains.

Workers these days are particularly motivated to find the inside track. The job market is substantially worse than average, and most openings have more applicants than usual. Both new college graduates and established workers have to work harder to find the right job.

Some people do extra work to find employment. They scour hiring websites, send out resumés, pay close attention to personal networking, or earn new degrees or certifications. Others cheat.

Resumé fraud, broadly defined, is making intentional misrepresentations on a resumé in the hopes of increasing the chance of being hired. The degree to which the phenomenon exists is difficult to determine. Employers double-check resumés unevenly—some thoroughly and some not at all. One recent major study estimated a 1-in-4 chance of a "major" discrepancy on a resumé. Other smaller studies have set the estimate even higher.

Although it is remotely possible that lying on a resumé could lead to legal liability, the greatest harm usually comes in gaining a reputation as an untrustworthy person. Whatever an applicant's field, word about resumé fraud tends to get around more than people think it will. Competitors know each other. They attend the same meetings of the same professional organizations, eat lunch at the same restaurants, and attend the same charity functions. In most professions, it really *is* a small world, and news of resumé fraud does spread.

Where Is the Line?

Another common characteristic of people is that most try to paint themselves in a positive light. I do know one guy who will tell you that he's no good at anything, but he's very odd. Most people will talk about their accomplishments and achievements, especially if asked about them, and many exaggerate from time to time.

171

So where is the line between harmless exaggeration and resumé fraud? Sometimes, it is hard to say. In the following scenario, a company looks into several specific kinds of claims applicants make.

SCENARIO

Mary's Office

"We look like idiots," Mary said as she looked at page one of the newspaper's business section. "Look at this—front page today." The headline read: "Smith and Jones Partner Lacks Degree, Transcript Shows." "How could we not know this for 10 years?"

Mary's assistant sat quietly and let her rage without interruption.

"I mean, we've already lost two clients over this. One of them was Baker. Do you know what he said to me on the phone this morning? He said, 'How the hell can I trust anything you guys tell me? What kind of an operation are you running over there?' That's half a million a year, out the door. And who knows how many other clients will bail out on us? This is just…" She seemed to lose steam as she searched for the right word. Eventually, she went with "intolerable."

"All right, so I need approval from the other partners before we decide how to check up on the people who already work here, but the hiring decisions are mine. So, Richard," she said to her assistant, "I want you to go down to HR, and I want you to get a copy of every resumé from every applicant we have who has made the first cut. And I want you to spend the next couple of days going over them line by line. Drop everything else you're working on."

"Nobody gets an offer until you're finished and we've talked about what you find. Check all the references. Confirm all the degrees and all the previous employers. I want to know what people are trying to pass off. OK?"

"Right away."

Three Days Later

A somewhat more relaxed Mary talked to her assistant again. "Well, at least for now, the rest of our clients seem more understanding than Baker was. But we still have to make sure that nothing like this ever happens again. So, anyway, tell me what you found."

Richard began his report. "OK. I checked 40 resumés, and 32 of them checked out perfect. Eight of them had a questionable item, or at least something I thought I should bring up. The first four are from our college applicants, and the other resumés were from people with industry experience. Most of the college ones have to do with grades."

"Anderson rounded her GPA up. Her resumé lists a 3.7, her actual GPA is a 3.65. Benson's resumé says that his 'Major GPA' is 3.9, which is true, but his overall GPA is 3.2, and his resumé doesn't say anything about that. Caldwell just flat-out lied about his GPA. He listed it as a 3.5, and it's really a 2.8."

"Davis was, ah, his deal was different. One of his references was his boss during an internship. He listed the manager as 'James Cox' and gave a phone number. I called it and talked to 'James Cox,' and he gave Davis a really terrific reference. But he didn't seem to know a lot about our industry."

"So after I hung up, I looked up the phone number, and it belonged to someone named 'Avery Sanderson,' who is also listed as a senior at Davis's college. So I called the number again from my cell phone so that, you know, the company's name wouldn't come up on the guy's caller ID. He answered and said, 'S'up?' Same voice as 'James Cox.' And I said, 'Avery? Hey, man, it's John.' And he said, 'John who? Miller? S'up, dog?'"

Mary was smiling. "Very creative. This is why I like you."

"Thanks."

"What did you say then?"

"I, ah, I just hung up on him. I couldn't really think of anything else. But, anyway, then I found the number for the real James Cox and talked to him. He said that Davis did intern for him over the summer and that he was not a standout but not terrible. He didn't really recommend or not recommend him."

"You did well. That's all the college applicants?"

"Yes. Then there were the four others with previous industry experience."

"Edwards listed his current position as '2006–present,' but he was laid off three months ago."

"Franklin is currently employed, but she stretched her dates of employment twice in the work history section of her resumé. Reading through it, it looks like she's always had a job, but she wasn't working for one stretch of six months in 2006 and another stretch of ten months in 2008. So she would claim she worked for a company January 2006–January 2008 when she really only worked 18 of those 24 months—that kind of thing."

"Green exaggerated his job duties. His resumé claims that he supervised 20 people at his last job and managed a budget of three million dollars. His former employer disputes that. She told me that he might have supervised a total of 20 different people over the three years he worked there, but never more than 7 at a time. And she also said he never had a personal say in more than about $750,000 of the budget."

"And last was Henderson. She listed 'to start my own business' as her reason for leaving her last employer. She did start a business, but her former employer told me that she didn't leave voluntarily. She was fired for cursing out a supervisor after he confronted her about being late repeatedly."

"And, ah, that's all of them. These people were all finalists for positions. What do you want me to tell HR?"

DISCUSSION QUESTIONS

1. Rate the resumé discrepancies of the four applicants who are soon-to-be college graduates.

	Unacceptable ←					→ Not a Problem	
Anderson	1	2	3	4	5	6	7
Benson	1	2	3	4	5	6	7
Caldwell	1	2	3	4	5	6	7
Davis	1	2	3	4	5	6	7

2. Now, rate the resumé discrepancies of the four applicants who are workers with experience.

	Unacceptable ←					→ Not a Problem	
Edwards	1	2	3	4	5	6	7
Franklin	1	2	3	4	5	6	7
Green	1	2	3	4	5	6	7
Henderson	1	2	3	4	5	6	7

3. If you were Mary, which of the eight would you tell HR to no longer consider for employment? Why?

_____

_____

_____

_____

4. Assume that Mary and the other partners decide to examine the resumés of people who *currently* work for the firm. Now assume that the same eight resumé tricks are uncovered. Should any current workers who are otherwise doing reasonably good work be fired or disciplined over these kinds of "old" resumé discrepancies?

_____

_____

_____

_____

5. Do you think that when resumé discrepancies exist, it is more often an oversight or deliberate? Or is it perhaps most commonly a deliberate thing that could be explained as an oversight?

_____

_____

_____

_____

Employee Behavior Away from the Office

BACKGROUND Employees who are caught doing bad things at work are usually disciplined or fired, and this is perfectly sensible. Companies face a range of legal problems derived from misbehaving employees.

Respondeat superior is an ancient common law tort doctrine that means "let the master respond." It allows for plaintiffs to sue employers when employees make on-the-job mistakes.

Assume that you own a restaurant. If your custodian mops the restroom floors and forgets to put up a "wet floor" sign, and a customer slips on the wet restroom floor and breaks her wrist, she can sue you just as much as if you had been careless yourself. If tax accountants do a lousy job preparing clients' tax returns, their firms can be sued. If a cable guy knocks over a vase at a customer's home when he is installing cable service, the cable company can be made to pay for it.

In addition to the broad risks presented by *respondeat superior*, companies face many specific legal problems if workers are up to no good. When employees engage in sexual harassment or create an unsafe workplace, for example, other workers can often sue the company.

Thus, bad judgment at the office often carries justifiable consequences. But what if an employee misbehaves in his or her personal life? Companies are rarely legally liable for behavior that is not work related. If an employee is involved in a drinking and driving accident, the drunk driver's employer can't be sued unless special circumstances exist.[1]

What should a company do if there is no legal threat but the reputation of the company is tarnished by bad employee behavior away from the office? For some businesses, image is everything. A negative story in the press can cost companies

---

[1] Such as if the worker had too much to drink at a company event and his attendance at the company event was understood to be required.

millions in lost sales. Consumers don't like to support organizations that they believe to be run by "bad guys."

As always, when assessing job security issues, it is worth stating the **employment-at-will doctrine,** which is the legal idea that workers can be fired at any time for any reason. The doctrine is not without exceptions. Workers cannot be fired because of their race, for example. But in the absence of a specific legal protection, employers can fire workers whether or not the workers' work performance is poor.

The scenario that follows presents a series of off-the-job incidents that are exceedingly unlikely to fall under any legal exception to the employment-at-will doctrine. Therefore, the executive in the scenario is legally free to terminate any or all of the workers without fear of losing a lawsuit over the decision. Instead, she faces an ethical dilemma. She is permitted to go either way in deciding the fate of each worker, but what *should* she do?

SCENARIO

Jim's Gym

Assume that Jim's Gym is a successful operation that has 30 locations. It focuses on boxing and markets itself as a "no frills" place to work out. Many of its locations are in inner cities, and many of the people it serves are children and teens. The current heavyweight champ credits Jim's Gym for keeping him away from bad influences while he was growing up and teaching him the skills and work ethic that have made him the champ.

Jim Jackson founded the company 25 years ago. It has since gone public, but Jackson continues to serve as the chief operations officer (COO). He makes personnel decisions, and he is rarely overridden by the CEO.

But recently, employees at several locations have been involved in incidents that have generated media attention. In response, Jackson assigned his deputy to collect all negative press about Jim's Gym employees from the previous 12 months.

Jim Jackson's Office

"So I found seven specific incidents that made a local newspaper," said the deputy COO. "I haven't yet searched for additional reports that might have made TV news."

"That's fine," Jim replied. "We don't have to find everyone right away. I think I really just want to send a message of what's OK and what's not."

"OK," the deputy continued. She laid a stack of printouts of newspaper articles on the desk. For some time, she described each article as Jackson took them in hand and looked them over, one by one. "And these are all people who still work for us. I have a few others in my office that have moved on."

"OK."

"OK. So case one, one of our office admins got a DWI. Her car was weaving, and she was pulled over, and she blew a .11 on the breathalyzer. No one was hurt."

"The second one is another DWI, but this one was a wreck. A personal trainer in L.A. hit a family in a station wagon. No fatalities, but some of the injuries were pretty bad. He was arrested at the accident site, and they drew his blood. I think he was .23 or something; he was way over the legal limit."

"Case three was a fight."

"Putting those boxing skills to a field test," Jim grinned.

"Yep. And our guy won the fight."

"Excellent! But *why* was he fighting?"

"It looks like our guy probably started the fight. The blurb in the *St. Louis Post-Dispatch* describes him as an 'attacker.' The other guy went to the hospital. The DA looked into it but never filed charges."

"Mmm hmm."

"Case four was from Atlanta. Our employee's girlfriend called the cops and said her boyfriend hit her. When they showed up, she changed the story, but she had a black eye. Georgia law required that the cops make an arrest, so they did. The paper picked it up and put his mug shot in the paper."

Jim looked at the newspaper. "And the Atlanta director hasn't fired him?"

"I called him. He says the guy's been on staff 10 years and that he's the best youth trainer that they have. He also said he didn't believe the girlfriend's story."

"Uh. Ah, all right, who's next?"

"Number five: A personal trainer got caught with a marijuana cigarette and an unlicensed .22 under his seat. He pleaded no contest to a misdemeanor for the gun, and the drug charge was dropped. No jail time."

"Number, ah, six." The deputy turned her legal pad to a new page. "Oh, yeah. She was protesting something at the governor's mansion in Tallahassee. The death penalty, I think. Anyway, she got past the security line and actually got inside the mansion. She was nabbed by the security detail before she actually found the governor, but he was upstairs at the time. She's been charged with criminal trespass. She's saying her right to free speech is being violated."

"I'm not surprised that one made the paper." Jim scanned the lengthy article. "But this doesn't mention us as her employer."

"No. None of these cases so far has a mention of the person's employer."

"That's something, at least."

"Yeah. So I have one more. This one isn't an incident like the others, really, but I turned it up when I was researching everything. A trainer in our Philadelphia location was profiled in a piece for *The Philadelphia Inquirer*, and he had some bad things to say about the company."

"Such as?"

"Such as 'We do help some kids get off the street and stay off the street, but the majority of kids who come through our doors don't want our help and aren't helped by us. They box a couple of times, mess around with the punching bags, and then they move on.'"

"That's not so bad. I mean, it makes for a lousy ad campaign, but it's true enough."

"He also said, 'I'm tired of all of this trying to get girls into the ring. You're a girl, you go to a girl's gym, that's what I think. Our place is for serious boxing.'"

"That," Jim said, "is, ah...different."

"Yep." The deputy clicked her tongue on the roof of her mouth a few times. "Well, that's all of them. What's next?"

"I need to think about what to do to these seven. Then, we need to draw up a policy for this kind of thing. But I want to start with you—what do you think we ought to do?"

DISCUSSION QUESTIONS

1. How harmful do you think each of the incidents will be to Jim's Gym?

2. Now assume that each of the newspaper articles described did mention Jim's Gym as the employer of the person who got into trouble. How harmful do you think each of the incidents would be to Jim's Gym?

3. Assume that the described incidents happened and that the newspapers named the employers of everyone who got into trouble, but now assume that instead of an operation that works with children, the employees all work for a standard professional services firm (a law firm, accounting firm, consulting firm, etc.).

Read the first and second questions again. Now, taking into account the assumptions of this third question, use the blanks below to assess the characters in this scenario (Q1: Jim's Gym, newspapers don't name employer; Q2: Jim's Gym, newspapers do name employer; Q3: Professional services firm, newspapers do name employer). For all three questions, on a scale of 1 to 10 (with 10 being the most harmful), how damaging do you think each event described in the scenario is likely to be to the company?

Q1 Rating	Q2 Rating	Q3 Rating	Incident
_____	_____	_____	DWI (no injury)
_____	_____	_____	DWI (with injuries)
_____	_____	_____	Fight
_____	_____	_____	Domestic Violence
_____	_____	_____	Marijuana and Handgun
_____	_____	_____	Trespass at Governor's Mansion
_____	_____	_____	Criticizing Company's Efforts to Attract Female Fighters

4. Now draw the line, taking into account the guidelines issued in the first three questions again. Which workers should be fired? Which should be merely disciplined or just left alone? Indicate whether you would fire, discipline, or leave the employee alone in the blanks below.

Q1 Result	Q2 Result	Q3 Result	Incident
_____	_____	_____	DWI (no injury)
_____	_____	_____	DWI (with injuries)
_____	_____	_____	Fight
_____	_____	_____	Domestic Violence
_____	_____	_____	Marijuana and Handgun
_____	_____	_____	Trespass at Governor's Mansion
_____	_____	_____	Criticizing Company's Efforts to Attract Female Fighters

5. At the end of the scenario, Jim mentions future plans to create a sort of employee code of conduct that defines off-the-job behaviors that are not acceptable to the company. Legally, the company can fire any of the workers in the scenario, even if it has no code of conduct in place. But does the presence or absence of such a policy make a firing more or less fair? Or are there some things that people should just know not to do?

_____

_____

_____

_____

UNIT 6

Workplace Privacy

Unit Background

The law offers little privacy protection in most workplaces. Companies are permitted to engage in all kinds of "snooping," but should they do so?

Module 33

Monitoring Software. [Is it reasonable for companies to use software to track what employees are doing on their computers throughout the workday?]

Module 34

Email Surveillance. [Is it reasonable for companies to read employees' email, and if so, what disciplinary steps should be taken if inappropriate messages are found?]

Module 35

Drug Testing and Polygraph Testing. [Should employees be required to take drug tests if their work performance is acceptable? Should workers ever be required to take lie detector tests?]

Module 36

Background Checks and Social Networking Websites. [Nearly everyone has a Facebook page. Is it acceptable for employers to check applicants' Facebook pages when making hiring decisions?]

Module 37

Job Applicants and Credit Reports. [The economic downturn has resulted in millions of new Americans having significant debt problems. Is it appropriate for companies to run credit checks as part of the hiring process?]

Workplace Privacy

The constitutional right to privacy is probably the most controversial of all constitutional liberties. Loosely stated, it is the legal idea that there are certain areas of one's life that should be free of government regulation and that the government should not have the ability to influence certain decisions.

The Supreme Court first weighed in on the right to privacy in the 1965 case *Griswold* v. *Connecticut*. Before this case, a Connecticut state law made it illegal to use birth control or even to give others advice about the use of contraceptives. The state of Connecticut prosecuted an employee of Planned Parenthood (Griswold) who had counseled couples on methods of contraception. The Supreme Court reversed the conviction of Griswold, reasoning that the state law violated the privacy rights of Griswold and those seeking information from her.

The interesting thing about the Court's decision is that the Constitution does not directly mention a "right to privacy." Other constitutional liberties are mentioned by name—one can find specific mention of free speech in the First Amendment, due process in the Fifth Amendment, and the right to be free from cruel and unusual punishment in the Eighth Amendment. But the Supreme Court accepted the idea that when the Constitution is viewed as a whole, it creates certain "zones of privacy."

Not all justices agreed. Justice Stewart notably called the Connecticut law "silly," but he also thought that is was acceptable to have such a law under the Constitution. The controversy about the existence, and the reach, of the implied right to privacy continues to this day.

For our purposes in this unit, the ability of employers to keep tabs on their employees is the central theme. Should businesses be able to look through employee email? Or monitor the websites that employees visit? Or require workers to submit a urine or hair sample for a drug test? Or take a lie detector test?

Often, privacy rights at work must come from statutes or other kinds of laws that mirror or supplement the constitutional right to privacy. In many key areas, there are no statutes, so many privacy issues fall within the realm of ethics.

Monitoring Software

In December 2009, four employees at Fidelity were terminated. Layoffs in 2009 were all too common, but the reason for these four terminations was uncommon: The four were fired for playing in a $20 fantasy football league. A Fidelity representative told the press, "Participation in any form of gambling through the use of Fidelity time or equipment or any other company resources is prohibited."

The majority of comments posted on Internet discussion boards were negative. Many called the action "ridiculous" and "outrageous." A few even called for a boycott of Fidelity. Other posts praised the action. A production line worker commented that he and other workers like him can't "mess around" during the workday without being fired and that workers with a "desk job" shouldn't be able to either.

While posters on message boards were free to debate the appropriateness of the firings, the law in this area is reasonably clear.

On one hand, corporations have a measure of constitutional rights. Corporate speech such as advertising is protected by the First Amendment, for example.

But in another sense, constitutional law does not usually apply to corporations. Employees of corporations cannot generally sue their employers for violations of their liberties. The Supreme Court has decided that free speech, due process, privacy, and other constitutional rights generally exist to protect people from government tyranny but not to protect people from each other.

If the police prevent a citizen from peacefully spreading a political message, then the citizen probably has a strong case; if a private employer bans spreading political messages at an office, then the worker probably cannot sue.

The "big" right to privacy has constitutional origins, and it does not cover most private-sector workers while they are at work. Workplace privacy rights, if they are to exist, must come from statutes and other kinds of laws. Sometimes, such laws exist and grant rights: There is reasonable privacy protection when companies wish to give lie-detector exams at work because of the Employee Polygraph Protection Act, for example. Often, though, employees have few rights because no law exists that grants them.

Email and computer privacy rights are virtually nonexistent where corporate employees are concerned. In the landmark case *Smyth* v. *Pillsbury*, Smyth was fired after his employer found offensive emails Smyth sent to a coworker. Before the incident, Pillsbury leaders went so far as to promise their employees that their emails would not be searched or used against them in any way. A federal judge ruled in favor of Pillsbury and opined that Smyth had no "reasonable expectation of privacy," despite his employer's promises. Other similar cases have gone the same way. Congress could pass legislation tomorrow prohibiting companies from monitoring employee email, Internet usage, and computer activities. So far, though, they have not. Therefore, corporations have a wide range of options if they wish to use technology to keep tabs on their workers. Most methods are legal, so the question becomes whether companies *should* make use of them.

About 78 percent of U.S. firms monitor their employees' computer usage. Almost all of those (90 percent) inform their employees of specific monitoring activities.

Nearly two-thirds of American companies have disciplined workers for inappropriate email or Web browsing. About one-third have fired a worker.

SCENARIO

Break Room—September 8

Gary sat in the empty break room and ate a sandwich at his favorite table. The room had been maintenance space before it had been remodeled, and it was oddly shaped. Gary's table sat alone around a corner from the door and the coffee pots. He scanned a file and ate in silence.

The door to the room opened. "...on Drudge Report every time I'm there. Every day! I can't believe he's still here," said one voice. "I know. There's a guy on my floor named Phil," said another. Gary listened.

"Oh, Phil! He's the worst!"

"He's just in there watching ball games on ESPN. He'll mute them if you knock, but..."

"Not with me—he just keeps on watching. Decaf?"

"Ah, no. Leaded, please." From his table, Gary could hear mugs clinking.

"He's the worst during March Madness. When does he work?"

"Dunno. I heard his numbers are really good, though. Me? I'd get fired in a second if I got caught messing around like that."

"Yeah. Here you go."

"Thanks. Where are you off to?"

"Meeting. You?"

"New client coming in."

"Ah."

"His last advisor must have been the absolute stupidest..."

The break room door closed, and Gary was alone again. He opened a notebook on his table and scribbled a few notes to himself on a blue notepad.

CEO's Conference Room—September 9

Gary listened to his colleague's argument as he scanned the notes on his blue notepad.

"Productivity is down significantly—we're just not getting as much done," she said. She clicked a mouse, and a chart appeared on a large screen behind the conference table. "Adjusted for inflation, we're billing 12 percent less per person per hour than we were five years ago. People are here, but they hole up in their offices and fool around. We need to get rid of the individual offices. I think we should remodel—move everyone together. People will stay more focused if they are out in the open and not behind a closed door."

"Remodeling sounds expensive," someone offered.

"So is sliding productivity."

Gary spoke up. "I agree—productivity *is* down, and I agree we need to do something about it. There's no reason to accept this trend," he said, pointing at the graph on the screen. "In this economy, we get ten well-qualified applicants for every opening we post. If somebody is slacking, we should replace him with someone who won't."

"Money's tight," the CEO said. "And a remodel usually messes up productivity even more while it's going on."

"That's true, but I think we can solve most of the time-wasting issue for a few hundred dollars."

"How?"

"Most of the nonsense, or at least a lot of it, is online. I overheard two guys in the break room today complaining about coworkers messing around on their computers all day, and I've heard that kind of chatter before. Most of our competitors monitor their employee's website activity. The software is practically free. I think we should install it on our network and let it run for a month—see what everybody's up to."

"Spy on them, then?"

"Monitor them. Make sure they are doing ten hours of work for ten hours of pay."

The CEO turned to the lawyer at the table. "Can we do this kind of thing?"

"Yes," the lawyer said.

"Hmm..." the CEO thought about it. "Do we have to notify them before we start?"

The lawyer shook his head. "It might be polite, but, no, you don't have to."

"Hmm..." The CEO turned back to Gary. "And you can set this up fairly quickly?"

"No problem."

"OK, let's do this: Set it up as soon as possible and collect data for 30 days. Put together a report, but don't use anyone's name—just call people 'Employee#1, #2,' that kind of thing."

"And should I notify everyone that they'll be monitored?"

"No. Let's see what they're up to. I'm not looking to discipline anybody...yet. After we look at the first round of results, we'll draw up a disciplinary policy and then let everybody know about the monitoring."

"I'll get right on it," Gary said.

CEO's Conference Room—October 14

Gary connected his laptop to the umbilical, clicked on a file marked emps.net.sept, and began his presentation. "I installed tracking software on our network after our last meeting. I let it gather data for the 30 days, which ended on Friday. I've selected eight employees for discussion today who are either representative of several employees or interesting cases. Their names are not included."

(*Click.*) The conference room's screen showed a slide titled, "Employee #1," which framed a picture of a spreadsheet. A caption read ":00 per day."

"Employee #1 visited a total of zero off-task websites during the past 30 days," Gary said. "He was the only person out of 75 in the company with no personal Internet usage."

"Tony!" said the controller, and everyone in the conference room laughed.

"Perhaps," Gary said smiling. "But these are anonymous. I cannot confirm that employee #1 is Tony."

"Oh, go ahead and confirm it," said the CEO.

"All right, Employee #1 is Tony." More laughter.

(*Click.*) The screen now read "Employee #2," showed a screenshot of Amazon.com's homepage, and had a caption reading, "<:10 per day."

"Employee #2 spent between five and ten minutes off-task on most days. She most commonly checked her credit card balance, visited her child's school's website, and browsed biographies on Amazon. About 40 percent of our workers had similar patterns."

(*Click.*) The screen now showed Derek Jeter. "Employee #3 spent an average of 15 minutes per day on Major League Baseball's website."

"You monitored MY computer!" the CEO said loudly, pretending to be outraged. The laughter around the conference table was louder than before.

"*Everyone* was monitored, sir, as per your orders."

"Well," the CEO said," I don't think it's any secret that I read the box scores during my coffee break." He smiled and made a circular motion with his finger. "Now, let's go ahead to Employee #4, shall we?"

"Right away." *(Click.)* "Employee #4 spent an average of 30 minutes per day off-task. He usually went to news websites and tracked the stock market."

"Does #4's job have anything to do with the stock market?" The CEO asked.

"No, sir. I was fairly generous in assembling this presentation; if I thought there was any chance that website was related to the employee's job, I did not include it in these statistics."

"OK," the CEO said.

"About 45 percent of our workers showed a pattern and an amount of time off-task that was reasonably similar to Employee #4. A total, then, of 85 percent used their computers for personal business for an average of 30 minutes per day or less."

(Click.) The screen now showed a Facebook page. "Employee #5 spent an average of 1 hour per day off-task. The most common visits were to social networking sites, Yahoo! Mail, and vacation-planning sites. About 10 percent of our workers were off-task for in the neighborhood of an hour a day."

(Click.) A screenshot showing five cards—three 4s, a Queen, and a Jack—filled the screen. "Three of our 75 employees spent substantially more than an hour per day on personal business. This one, Employee #6, spent an average of two hours per day, most often on a fantasy football website and on Poker.net."

"Who is it?" asked the controller, sounding irritated.

"No names now," said the CEO. He wrote something on his notepad. "Gary, is Poker.net a, ah…is he placing actual bets there, or is it just for fun?"

"No actual bets on that website, sir."

"OK." The CEO nodded and added to his notes.

"The last two slides are unique cases. Neither one of them spent nearly as much time as some others did off-task, but I thought they still ought to be discussed." *(Click.)* "Employee #7 spent an average of 30 minutes per day on actual gambling websites. He seems to be spending most of that time looking at betting lines, and then placing one or more bets most days, usually on basketball."

The CEO grunted and made more notes.

(Click.) The last slide had a blank box where the last several slides had showed a screenshot. "Employee #8's slide obviously has no illustration," Gary began, looking somewhat uncomfortable. "He was one of the final employees I reviewed last night. He's been spending roughly 30 minutes per day on, ah, pornography websites."

Several people around the conference table shifted uncomfortably. "What kind of pornography?" the CEO asked.

"Pornography pornography, sir. Um, triple-X-rated stuff."

"Huh," the CEO said. He tapped his pen rapidly on his notepad. "Every day?"

"Most every day, yes, sir." Gary stood silently for awhile.

The CEO turned to the lawyer. "This last one—what if somebody sees that on #8's screen? Is that a sexual harassment situation?"

"Could be," the lawyer said. "Depends on what's on the screen, and what a jury thinks a 'reasonable person' would think of it. A lot of people might lean toward calling it a 'hostile working environment.'"

"Gary," the CEO said, "is #8's monitor visible to anyone in his office?"

"Ah…no, sir, anyone who is not behind his desk can't see the screen."

"Hmph."

Gary clicked one last time. A slide with the word "Discussion" filled the screen.

DISCUSSION QUESTIONS

1. Was it reasonable for the company to install the tracking software in the first place? Should the company have given notice to workers that their activities would be monitored?

_____

_____

_____

_____

2. Although the CEO said in the first meeting that he was "not looking to discipline anyone yet," he is not legally bound by that remark. If he has a change of heart, should Employees #4–7 be given a reprimand, suspended, or terminated?

	No Punishment	Reprimand	Suspension	Termination
Employee #4	_____	_____	_____	_____
Employee #5	_____	_____	_____	_____
Employee #6	_____	_____	_____	_____
Employee #7	_____	_____	_____	_____

3. Assume for this question that the CEO decides not to discipline anyone this time but that he issues a clear policy banning personal use of the Internet at the office. Now evaluate the same workers, with the addition of Employee #2. What punishments, if any, should they face if they are "on notice"?

	No Punishment	Reprimand	Suspension	Termination
Employee #2	_____	_____	_____	_____
Employee #4	_____	_____	_____	_____
Employee #5	_____	_____	_____	_____
Employee #6	_____	_____	_____	_____
Employee #7	_____	_____	_____	_____

4. Consider the case of Employee #8, who viewed pornography at work. What should happen to him at this point?

_____

_____

_____

_____

5. If you owned a business and were drawing up a policy to cover this kind of scenario, what would it look like? How much personal use of the Internet would you allow?

_____

_____

_____

_____

Email Surveillance

BACKGROUND

Email and computer privacy rights are virtually nonexistent where corporate employees are concerned. In the landmark case *Smyth* v. *Pillsbury*, Smyth was fired after his employer found offensive emails Smyth sent to a coworker. Before the incident, Pillsbury leaders went so far as to promise their employees that their emails would not be searched or used against them in any way. A federal judge ruled in favor of Pillsbury, and opined that Smyth had no "reasonable expectation of privacy" despite his employer's promises. Other similar cases have gone the same way.

Congress could pass legislation tomorrow prohibiting companies from monitoring employee email, Internet usage, and computer activities. So far, though, they have not. Therefore, corporations have a wide range of options if they wish to use technology to keep tabs on their workers. Most methods are legal, so the question becomes whether companies *should* make use of them.

SCENARIO

CEO's Office

"Sir?" the human resources manager asked as the corporate lawyer knocked softly.

The CEO looked up from his spreadsheet. "Joyce, Bill. Come in."

"OK if we close the door?"

"By all means. What's up?"

The two visitors took a seat. The lawyer began. "We may have a situation."

"I'm listening."

"We think we have a leak in research and development."

The CEO took off his glasses and exhaled. "You have my full attention."

"As you are well aware, we've lost out on the race for a patent three times this year to AlphaMed, at a cost of..."

"Billions," the CEO completed his sentence. "A couple of billion each for the allergy drug and the acne treatment, maybe several billion for the blood pressure medicine."

"It might be an unusual run of bad luck. I mean, even the Yankees lose three-in-a-row once in a while, right? But it might also be something else. Joyce, ah..."

The HR manager said, "I heard an interesting story this morning. We have an intern named Jason. Tall kid, dark hair, makes copies and runs errands for the research staff. He slipped into my office early this morning…"

Earlier That Day

"Ms. Stevens, I need to talk to you."

"Jason. Come in, sit down. What's on your mind?"

The intern wiped sweat from his forehead with his sleeve and looked over his shoulder. "I, ah…" He couldn't get the words out.

"Just relax," Joyce said as she shut her office door and drew the blind shut. "Better?"

"Uh, yeah. Thanks, Ms. Stevens."

"Why don't you start at the beginning?"

"OK." Jason took a deep breath. "So I went out last night. I know, it's only Wednesday, but I got talked into it, and I didn't get drunk or anything."

"Your time is your business."

"So, anyway, I went with my roommates to see this band. They were playing at this place that I'd never been to before. We got there at about 11:00. It was pretty crowded. I watched the band for about an hour, and then I started talking to this girl at the bar."

"Jason," Joyce smiled, "you know I like talking to you, but I'm backed up today. Can you bottom line this story for me?"

"I'm just about to, Ms. Stevens. So, anyway, I look up, and I can't believe it, but Mr. Randolph and Mr. Sullivan are sitting at a table at the back of the place."

"The science guys who work here?"

"Yes, ma'am. I couldn't believe it either. I mean, you'd expect them at a *Star Wars* convention or something, but not at a bar."

"OK. And, what, they were drunk? High? I can't really do anything if…"

"No, ma'am, nothing like that at all. I watched them for a while, and I would have gone over to say hi, but this girl I was talking to was really hot, er, good looking. And so, anyway, after a while, this guy slides into the booth with them. Mr. Randolph and Mr. Sullivan looked really nervous when he showed up. They started looking all over the bar. The guy only stayed a minute, but he handed Mr. Randolph an envelope. It had money inside. I saw it when Mr. Randolph checked it."

Jason fell silent, and Joyce considered her next question for a moment. "How sure of that are you? That there was cash in the envelope?"

"Absolutely sure. I saw it."

"From across a bar?"

"Yes, ma'am."

"Do you see the little framed certificate on the wall over there?" Joyce pointed across her office.

"Yes."

"Under the big 'Joyce Stevens,' read what it says."

"'In recognition of ten years of leadership in the Association of Human Resource Managers.'"

"Hmm…"

"And Ms. Jenkins?

"Yes?"

"Below the signatures, on the bottom edge it says, 'AHRA—PO Box 1217—Jacksonville, FL 32231.'"

Joyce crossed the room halfway, squinted, and saw that the organization's address was indeed listed in small print. She paused again to collect her thoughts. "And you weren't drinking?"

"No, ma'am. I had to work today. And I was driving, anyway."

"I believe you. What happened after Randolph and Sullivan took the envelope?"

"The other guy nodded and left. They waited about a minute, and then they got up and left, too."

MODULE 34 • Email Surveillance **189**

"Did they see you?"

"No, ma'am. I, ah, I kind of turned away from them. I didn't really want them to see me, after that. It was just so weird."

"You did the right thing coming to tell me, Jason."

CEO's Office

"So that's what he told me," Joyce concluded.

The CEO made a steeple with his fingers. "Hmm…" he said. "And I suppose Randolph and Sullivan would have been able to get their hands on the working papers for all three drugs we failed to patent?"

"Between the two of them, yes, sir."

"Hmm…so we have a string of bad luck and a kid who thinks he saw two of our guys take a wad of cash. Course, he might be mistaken."

"He convinced me, but, yes, he might be mistaken," Joyce said.

"OK, Mr. Lawyer, what's your advice for me?"

"If the intern is right, and if they're selling inside information on our drugs in development, it's almost a sure thing that we can find evidence of it on their computers."

"And it's legal to snoop around like that?"

"Yes."

"Go on."

"We don't do any of this stuff right now, but a lot of our competitors do. Before you came aboard, our founder was against 'snooping' in all forms. But I'd recommend some changes, starting immediately. First, we need to go through Randolph's and Sullivan's computers tonight, after hours. We should pay particular attention to their email. Our tech guys can reconstruct anything that has been deleted."

"Have we given anyone notice that we might do that kind of thing?" the CEO asked.

"No, but we don't need to do that. Not legally, I mean."

"OK."

"Second, we need to start filtering everyone's email. The software is practically free. We can set it to scan for any keywords we can think of that have anything to do with drugs in development—code names, ingredients, chemical chains, whatever. We can see if anyone is sending communications about any of our works in progress."

"Not that we have any hard proof they're up to no good yet, but what if Randolph and Sullivan send messages through a personal email account from work… Gmail or something?"

"As long as it comes from a company computer, we can filter that, too. And that brings me to my third point. We issued Sullivan a laptop last year. We should ask him to bring it in for a 'routine software upgrade' or 'inventory' or something and give it the once-over. If he is in fact selling information, he'd be more likely to communicate about it from home on his laptop.

"Last…well, last for now…I think we should install a keystroke logger on everyone's machine."

"What's that?"

"Software that stores every keystroke that everyone makes all day. It would let us see everything Randolph, Sullivan, or anyone else is up to, regardless of what program they were running. You can delete text from a screen, but you can't delete the characters you've entered from the keystroke logger unless you're an expert, and these guys are definitely not experts."

"Hmm. Joyce, what do you think?"

"I'm convinced that Jason at least thinks he really saw something. So, if it's done legally, I think we can make a better case for snooping around Randolph's and Sullivan's computers. I'm not sure about filtering everyone's email. Some people might get upset at that, especially if we don't tell them what we're doing."

The CEO turned to the lawyer. "She makes a good point, Bill."

"If these guys are doing it, others might be as well. We should have started doing this a long time ago."

The CEO's Blackberry vibrated, and he glanced at it. "Ahh, 2:00 already. Joyce, Bill, I've got to make an appearance at an event across town, but I'll be thinking about this. I'd like for you both to be back here tomorrow morning at," he checked his BlackBerry, "10:15. I'll tell you how I want to proceed then."

"Thank you, sir."

"Thank you."

DISCUSSION QUESTIONS

1. If you were the CEO, would you order the desktop computers of the two suspicious employees searched?

2. Should the company search Sullivan's laptop?

3. Should the company passively monitor everyone's email for keywords and phrases that might indicate an information leak?

4. Should the company log every employee's keystrokes? If your answers to this question and the previous question are different, why are they different?

5. Should the company notify workers of any plans to monitor their computer activities? Would you be upset if your employer monitored yours without notifying you?

MODULE **35**

Drug Testing and Polygraph Testing

BACKGROUND

Most people feel strongly about their "privacy." Some are most concerned about sensitive documents such as medical records and bank statements. Others feel strongly that they should be able to live as they wish, free from government interference. When some people speak of privacy, they refer to the importance of time alone.

Legally speaking, privacy has a specific meaning, and few legal ideas are more misunderstood.

The most well-known, and most passionately debated, Supreme Court decision of the past 50 years is certainly *Roe* v. *Wade.* In that case, the plaintiffs argued that some laws prohibiting abortions violated the Constitution. The Supreme Court agreed, citing privacy rights. There is no part of the Constitution that refers to "privacy" in so many words, but a majority of the justices agreed that several parts of the Constitution, when taken as a whole, *implied* privacy rights. Applying these rights, the Supreme Court legalized early-term abortions. The right to privacy has since been applied to many other issues, especially those related to how far police can go in monitoring the activities of suspected criminals. Thus, constitutional privacy rights have been protected by the Supreme Court for decades.

Constitutional rights usually don't apply to corporations in the sense that employees usually cannot base lawsuits against their employers on constitutional rights. The Supreme Court decided long ago that the primary purpose of the Constitution is to protect people from government tyranny, and not to protect people from each other. If the government wishes to change the behavior of private people or private companies, it must pass some other type of law.

Usually, when the federal government wants to regulate companies in a "big picture" way, it enacts a statute. Almost any idea can become a statute if it passes the House of Representatives and the Senate, and is signed by the president. Statutes are flexible. They can be applied to whatever and whomever the government wishes. Countless times, statutes have been passed and have prohibited new kinds of corporate action. In the last 50 years, companies have been ordered not to

191

discriminate based on race and several other factors. They have been required to make workplaces safer, take better care of retirement benefits, and allow workers time off to take care of family medical emergencies. But Washington has not had a great deal to say about privacy rights at work.

Most employees are "employees at will," which in the end means that most employees can be treated in absolutely any way at all, as long as the treatment is not specifically prohibited in law. Corporate decisions surrounding privacy are often a question of ethics and not law, because no statute exists to require or prohibit a given action.

A question often facing leaders is, "How much should we monitor our employees?" Many corporations have heated internal debates surrounding the issues of drug testing and polygraph testing.

Beginning with the Reagan administration in the 1980s, the "war on drugs" was ratcheted up. Since then, Washington has very deliberately refrained from creating drug testing rights for employees. With only a few restrictions, it is legal to make employees take drug tests and to fire employees who refuse or fail drug tests. Thousands of companies have adopted tough zero-tolerance policies.

Privacy rights groups and some employees complain about drug testing. They often argue that even if someone does use drugs, it is not a company's business unless job performance is suffering. Recreational drug use on the weekend should not have job consequences, they often say.

In defense of testing, corporate leaders argue, "We need drug testing. If our workers make mistakes on the job, the company can be sued. Maybe some people who abuse drugs can do their jobs just fine, but if you have a drug problem, you are statistically more likely to do poor work and miss a lot of work days, and embezzle from the company, for that matter. We need to know if someone is developing a habit that puts the shareholders' money at risk."

It is worth noting that despite the sizeable number of companies that have drug testing, a majority do not. Executives of nontesting companies often say that the expense is too great, or that they just don't care to look into personal lives, as long as employees do good work.

A second frequently debated issue is whether or not to make use of polygraph exams. Almost everyone has seen a "lie detector" test. They have been featured on any number of reality TV shows and in the hilarious Ben Stiller movie *Meet the Parents*. Polygraph testing at work may seem exotic, but over four *million* employees took a lie detector test at work last year. Many companies have turned to this device for help in finding an employee who has stolen money, equipment, or intellectual property. Some have even used them to prevent crimes before they occur.

The central idea behind polygraph science is that most people cannot control certain body responses when they lie. Polygraph machines measure heart rate, blood pressure, and the amount of sweat on the fingertips of test subjects. Even people who are "smooth liars," people who can look a person in the eye and tell a lie that seems believable, can't usually control things like their own blood pressure.

When operated by a licensed professional, polygraphs can be about 95 percent accurate in the sense that, 95 times out of 100, the machine correctly identifies whether a person is being truthful or deceptive. However, polygraph science is called "junk science" by some critics. The Supreme Court has called polygraph evidence "unreliable," and the result of polygraph exams usually cannot be introduced as evidence in court.

A statute does exist that gives employees some rights when they are asked to take a polygraph exam. But the law usually allows companies to use polygraph machines if they are investigating a crime, and some kinds of companies are exempt from the law altogether.

SCENARIO

ER Waiting Room

Marty, a manager at Greentown Bank, rushed through the double doors and absently brushed the snow from his hair as he looked around the ER. He soon spotted a familiar face and walked over to her.

"Is Carl…" he began.

"OK, I think. The doctor came out a few minutes ago and said he's awake."

"Thank God. What happened?" When his coworker didn't reply, he added, "It wasn't…"

She nodded. "I think it was."

Marty slapped his gloves into an empty hand and exhaled heavily. Not knowing what else to do, he sat down to wait.

Marty's Office

Three days later, Marty sat in his office. The Chief Operating Officer knocked on his slightly open door.

"Got a minute?" the COO asked.

"Sure."

The COO closed the door and sat down. "Hey, Marty, I just wanted you to hear this from me."

"OK."

"I just let Carl go."

"But he just got out of the hospital…"

"After another overdose."

"We don't know if that's why…"

"He admitted it, Marty. He admitted it. I'm sorry."

"Ah. Cocaine?"

"Yep."

"He promised me—promised me, after last time…"

"I know. I'm sorry. But it gets worse."

"How so?"

"When we knew he was back in the hospital, and we guessed why he was there, we took a look at the records. A close look."

"And?"

"Carl's been supplementing his pay."

"What do you mean?"

"Marty, he stole almost $50,000 from us."

"What?!"

"When we confronted him with the evidence, and we have a lot of it, he broke down crying. He blamed it on the drugs and begged us not to go to the cops."

"No." Marty sat silently for a moment. Then he asked, "Are we? Going to press charges?"

"That's not my call."

"Ah."

"Listen, Marty, I know you really tried to get him back on track. Sometimes things just don't work out."

"Yeah, I guess they don't."

The COO checked his watch. "Sorry, but I've got a meeting."

"Sure, sure. Hey, thanks for coming by."

"You bet, Marty." The COO shook Marty's hand and left.

Greentown Bank's Executive Conference Room

The next day, a furious CEO sat at the head of the long conference table.

"And we will never, I repeat *never,* allow something like this to happen again. We will never place our customers' and shareholders' money at risk. We will never again risk our reputation. We got lucky this time, and nothing showed up in the papers, but next time we might not be so lucky.

"I am implementing two policies, effective immediately.

"First, effective in 60 days, we will implement a random drug testing policy. Every employee, including me, will be asked to submit a urine sample several times per year. The tests will not be announced ahead of time. This will be a zero-tolerance policy, and the penalty for failing a test or refusing to take one will be immediate termination.

"I have decided on a 60-day delay because I want any of our workers who have a problem similar to Carl's to have a last clear chance. I am told that urinalysis tests can usually detect drugs for only about 30 days after they are used. The message: 'If you want to keep working here, knock it off right now!'

"Second, when we begin drug testing, we will start asking all of our employees to take a quarterly lie detector exam. We have retained the services of a licensed polygraph examiner. Anyone who fails an exam or refuses to take one will be dealt with harshly, but our lawyers and I are still working on specific punishments. No one is ever going to steal $50,000 from us again because we'll catch him before he is able to carry out his plan.

"These policies will go out to all employees later today. That's all, everybody."

Marty's Office

"Got a minute, boss?"

Marty looked up from his monitor. "Sure thing, Ernie. Come on in."

"Thanks. I just read the new policies, and I'm not happy."

"I knew you wouldn't be."

"I've been here for 30 years. I've never used drugs, and I've never stolen a penny."

"I know that, Ernie."

"Look, we're all sorry about Carl, but I'm not going to be held under suspicion."

"I feel your pain, Ernie, I really do, but it's the new policy."

"I won't do it."

"You have to."

"No, boss, I mean I really won't do it. I've got enough to retire, if it comes to that. I won't be treated like a criminal."

"Ernie…"

"Look, boss, I'm just letting you know. I'm going to refuse to take both tests. If I get fired, I get fired."

"I hope you'll reconsider. I'd hate to lose you."

"I'd hate to go. But I won't take those tests."

Vacant Office

The polygraph examiner had set his equipment up in an empty office. Marty sat on a stool with straps and wires dangling from his chest, upper arm, and fingertips.

"Is your name Marty?" the polygraph examiner asked.

"Yes." The polygraph's needles softly scratched across a scrolling page.

"Are you originally from Antarctica?"

"Yes," Marty replied. The needles scratched swift, angry arcs. Marty chuckled.

"Have you ever stolen money from Greenville Bank?"

"No."

"Are you wearing a white shirt?"

"Yes." Marty was.

"Do you have any plans to steal from Greenville Bank in the future?"

"No."

"Is today Monday?"

"Yes." It was.

"Are you aware of any plan by anyone else to take money from Greenville Bank?"

"No."

The questions continued. Although he was always truthful, a bead of sweat formed on Marty's brow. It grew larger, moved slowly down his nose, paused, and fell from the tip of his nose onto his tie.

CEO's Office

A week later, the CEO's assistant called Marty and asked if he could come down to the CEO's office right away. When Marty arrived a few minutes later and was seated, two files lay on the CEO's massive desk. He consulted one of them, and then looked over his glasses at Marty. "I asked you to stop by because I want input from my managers before I make any final decisions."

"Yes, sir."

"I am considering—just considering, for now—softening my position on failed tests. It seems we have, ah, more than a few."

"Yes, sir."

"Five of your subordinates are on my lists."

"Five." Marty could think of nothing else to say.

"Don't worry, Marty, other managers have about the same numbers." Marty was somewhat relieved. The CEO continued. "Anderson tested positive for marijuana. Bates tested positive for cocaine. Cooper failed the lie detector on the 'have you ever stolen from Greenville' question. Daniels failed the lie detector on all three key questions. And then there's the guy, what's his name…"

"Ernie?"

"Right, him. He wouldn't even take the tests. Either one."

"Good grief."

"Look, Marty, these are your people. You know them. Carl was one of yours, too, which makes me particularly interested in what you have to say because he started all of this. What would you do if you were in my shoes?"

DISCUSSION QUESTIONS

1. Did the CEO overreact when he implemented the drug testing policy, or was his decision appropriate?

   _____

   _____

   _____

   _____

2. Did the CEO overreact when he implemented a policy of giving polygraph exams to all employees, or was his decision appropriate?

   _____

   _____

   _____

   _____

3. How should Anderson and Bates be disciplined, and should they face the same punishment?

   _____

   _____

   _____

   _____

4. How should Cooper and Daniels be punished?

_____

_____

_____

_____

5. How should Ernie be punished?

_____

_____

_____

_____

Background Checks and Social Networking Websites

BACKGROUND

Things change in a hurry. This module is being written on a 2007 word processor, and "Facebook" comes up as a misspelled word. It reminds me of first-generation Amazon Kindles made in the same year that have no idea how to pronounce President Obama's name (and now "Obama" has just come up as a misspelled word).

Facebook has taken America by storm. At the time of this writing in 2010, it has over 400 million members. Its founder Mark Zuckerberg (yet another "misspelled word," according to the 2007 word processor) has an estimated net worth of $1.5 billion. Facebook has changed the way that people communicate, especially among people under age 25.

Countless corporations, universities, and charitable institutions have tried to ride Facebook's momentum. "Follow us on Facebook!" has become a mainstay of advertising.

Other social networking sites are also immensely popular. Although it has been overtaken by Facebook, MySpace remains in second place in overall Web traffic. Twitter rose as high as third place in 2009.

These sites and others have a significant upside: By making it easier to stay in touch, they can bring people closer together. Facebook does today what the post office did in the 1800s and the telephone did in the 1900s. Many would argue that human relationships are the most important thing there is and that anything that enhances them is to be commended.

But the upside does not come without potential downsides. Some people spend long hours on these websites daily, to the exclusion of other activities. Some argue that without face-to-face interaction, online interaction is not healthy. Cyberbullying and cyberstalking cases make the news with some regularity. Hate groups sometimes use the Internet to further harmful messages before their posts are removed.

The focus of the scenario that follows is a pitfall that many users of social networking sites fail to consider. It is easier than ever for universities, employers, and potential employers to peer into a worker's or applicant's private life. By taking privacy settings seriously, someone can often make such glimpses more difficult, but many people simply don't bother with such things.

Some companies and universities look up workers and applicants online and take note of what they find. Others promise not to do so. Legally, there is nothing wrong with looking at publicly available information on the Internet. Ethically, people have different opinions about where the line should be drawn.

SCENARIO

Conference Room

"Hey, Jim."

"Abby…hi. Sorry I'm running late."

"No problem—I'm just getting organized."

Seven packets bound with paper clips were spread out along one side of the conference table. Each had a photograph placed on top with a name written beneath in blue marker: Anderson, Baker, Cooper, Daniels, Evans, Franklin, and Gordon.

Jim took off his overcoat, laid it across the back of a chair, and sat down. "So these are the finalists?" he asked.

"Yep. Seven folks, three openings."

"It's always nice to see names matched with faces," Jim said, looking over the photographs. "Dale interviewed them and gave me his rundown of them, but this is the first time I've seen pictures. They get younger every year."

"I think it's us who are getting older."

"Perhaps," Abby said, smiling.

"OK, well, before I tell you what Dale had to say about what he thought of these folks in person, I want to know what you've found."

"OK. So I did what you asked me to do. No aggressive data mining. I just looked at their Facebook pages, Twitter accounts, and things like that. I didn't try to use any sneaky back doors to get around privacy settings; I only looked at the stuff they posted and that anyone in the world can have a look at."

"Excellent."

"Starting off with Anderson. Nothing much. Some party pictures with friends. Some show her with alcohol. She's 22 now, and on some of the shots, she might be under 21, I guess. Nothing wild. Some poetry, quotes from movies, that kind of thing. She seems nice."

"Dale thought so too. He ranked her fifth out of the seven. 'Pleasant in person, decent grades, resumé a little thin,' he told me."

"OK, moving on. Baker had, ah, substantially more party pictures."

"Substantially?"

"Really, really substantially. Lots of booze. Bonging beers. Chugging whisky with no shirt on. Ah, what's it called when your friends lift your legs over your head and you chug beer out of a keg upside down?"

"Can't remember. An inversion, maybe?"

"Anyway, Mr. Baker seems to have been very active on the party scene."

"Interesting. He has a 4.0 grade point average."

"Huh."

"Any drugs in those photos?"

"Not that I saw. Cigarettes, yes. Alcohol, tons. No drugs."

"OK. Dale ranked him fourth overall. Decent interview and weak internship to go with the GPA."

"On to Cooper. He's the last of the party boys. More party shots than Anderson, less than Baker. The only new thing with him was that he posted a photo of a topless girl."

"Really?"

"He had a series of photos labeled 'New Orleans Road Trip.' Looks like a Mardi Gras trip—he had lots of beads."

"Is the girl in the background?"

"No, she's the only thing in the picture."

"Might the girl be underage?"

"She doesn't appear to be."

"Hmm. Anything else?"

"No. Just run-of-the-mill party pics."

"OK. He had a great internship. Dale had him ranked third."

"Next we have Daniels. No party pictures, nothing controversial. One tweet worth mentioning."

"Ah, a tweet."

"She sent this an hour after her interview with Dale."

Abby handed Jim a piece of paper with the following highlighted: "Just interviewed with giant bald dork at Smith and Morian. Think the loser liked me. We'll see. Hope I get an offer from Tess Brothers. Can't imagine working for that guy."

Jim fought it, and then cracked a smile. "This really isn't funny," he said.

"No," Abby agreed.

Jim stopped smiling, paused, and then burst out laughing. Abby joined him. "I mean, we're Plan B for her, and she's talking about her potential boss behind his back."

"Yep," Abby agreed.

"But she's, you know, right."

Abby laughed harder. "SO?!" Their laughter eventually trailed off.

"Well, Dale didn't much like her either. He ranked her sixth. So what about Evans?

"Mr. Evans. I think Mr. Evans might have…an anger problem."

"Oh," Jim seemed taken aback. "How so?"

"Well, lots of things. He posts angry song lyrics. He talks a lot about his guns on his Facebook page. One of his photos shows him holding a pistol of some kind. He says derogatory things about his girlfriend, and she just looks…really sad in every picture of her on his page. I don't like him."

"OK, but anything specific? Anything to indicate he uses the guns inappropriately, or hits his girlfriend, or anything like that?"

"Nothing specific, no."

"OK. He did pass our standard background check. No criminal record."

"That's something, I guess."

"But your gut says 'bad guy.'"

"My gut says 'bad guy.' I could be wrong."

"Maybe so, maybe not. Dale ranked him second. Really liked him."

"Like I said, I could be wrong."

"OK. I appreciate your candor. What about Franklin?"

"Ah. Now, Franklin, he does have a specific issue."

"Dang! Dale ranked him first—he thought Franklin was absolutely terrific."

"I'm sorry to hear that, Jim."

"Ah. So, go ahead."

"OK. So on his page, one of the pictures shows Franklin without a shirt on and kind of from behind. He has a tattoo about the size of a playing card around his right shoulder blade…"

"That's it?" Jim asked. "Abby, lots of these kids that interview with us probably have tattoos. If it's not visible when he's in a suit, I really don't see…"

"Look, it's not a regular tattoo, or I wouldn't make a big deal about it."

"Ah. Hey, I'm sorry for interrupting you. It's just—Dale was so keen on this guy. I think I'm rooting for him to not have any problems."

"That's OK. So the tattoo, it's very distinctive. It seemed like I had seen one like it before somewhere, maybe on TV. So I started looking around on the Internet and eventually I found it."

"So what is it? Devil worship or something?"

"It's a hate group."

"A hate group," Jim repeated. He took off his glasses and rubbed his eyes. "And who do they hate?"

"Jewish people. The group started in Europe and has spread over here."

"Are you sure it was a match? I mean, might he have a similar tattoo?"

"One hundred percent sure. The coloring, design, script, and motto were absolutely identical. This isn't something generic that Franklin got out of a catalog some night at a tattoo parlor."

"And they're really bad?"

"They're very into Hitler."

"I see." Jim stared into space for a while.

"Look, maybe he got it without knowing much about the group. Maybe he did just see the design and thought it was cool. Maybe he doesn't know anything about what it represents."

"Possibly, I suppose. Are there any anti-Semitic statements on his page?"

"No. No links to anything, either. Just the tattoo."

"And you're 100 percent positive that it's him in the picture?"

"It's him."

"OK. Is the picture still up, do you think, on Facebook?"

"I looked at his page yesterday, so probably so."

"I want to look at it myself later when I get a minute." Jim scribbled a note on his pad. "Let's do the last one, ah…"

"Gordon."

"Gordon, right. What's the scoop on Ms. Gordon?"

"There is no scoop on her. No Facebook page. No MySpace. Nothing. She hardly comes up if you Google her. Very low profile online."

"I don't have any social networking stuff."

"You're 45. She's half that. I'm not saying it's a bad thing, but she is the only one in this group without a substantial online presence. Might be a loner."

"Or she might just interact with humans in person. Or she might really value her privacy."

"Maybe so."

"OK. Well, Dale was noncommittal on her. Ranked her seventh overall. 'Bland personality, bland resumé he told me. She does have good grades."

"Seems about right. Well, that's all of them. It's up to you now."

"That it is." Jim checked his watch. "And I've just got time to run over to Starbucks before my 2 o'clock. Thanks very much, Abby. I really appreciate it."

"You're welcome. Let me know which three you decide to hire."

"I will."

DISCUSSION QUESTIONS

1. Is it reasonable for employers to screen applicants by searching social networking sights in the first place?

   Completely Reasonable ⟵——————————⟶ Absolutely Unfair
   1 --- 2 --- 3 --- 4 --- 5 --- 6 --- 7

2. Which (if any) of the applicants should have Abby's report held against him or her? In other words, which applicants (if any) should have at least a somewhat lower chance of being hired?

   _____

   _____

   _____

   _____

3. In the scenario, Dale ranked the applicants according to the left column. In the blank column to the right, give your assessment of how Jim should rank the candidates taking the information from Abby's report into account. (The top three will be made offers.)

Dale's Rankings (Potential Problem)	Jim's Rankings Should Be…
1. Franklin (hate group tattoo)	*1. _____
2. Evans (angry-looking)	*2. _____
3. Cooper (topless photo)	*3. _____
4. Baker (lots of party photos)	4. _____
5. Anderson (mild)	5. _____
6. Daniels (sarcastic tweet)	6. _____
7. Gordon (no information)	7. _____

4. Assume now that the seven people listed above *already work for the company* in the scenario and that Jim is given the same information. Should he discipline or fire any of them if they are current employees who are doing a good job?

_____

_____

_____

_____

5. Would it reasonable for a *university* to screen applicants in this way, by searching social networking sights?

Completely Reasonable ◄——————————————► Absolutely Unfair

1 --- 2 --- 3 --- 4 --- 5 --- 6 --- 7

Job Applicants and Credit Reports

When applying for a new job, applicants are often asked to list previous employers. Some companies merely scan over a person's employment history and use it to help determine whether or not the person has the kind of experience required for the current position. Other companies contact former employers seeking insight into whether an applicant is a good worker.

A generation ago, former employers tended to be more forthcoming when asked to comment on a former employee's job performance. Whether the report was favorable or negative, many "reference checks" generated a significant amount of information. Today, many companies are much more cautious, particularly when asked to give a reference for a poor ex-employee.

Tort lawsuits can be brought against private people and companies for most any kind of problem that is not related to a broken agreement. If you have had an injury to your body or damage to your property, and if you want to sue someone and seek compensation in court, you can file a tort lawsuit of one kind or another.

The tort of **defamation** allows for a plaintiff to sue over a false statement that causes an injury to his reputation. Ex-employers have long feared that if they say negative things about former employees, they will be accused of making false claims and sued for defamation. This can be a particular problem for two reasons.

First, there is a subcategory of defamation called *slander per se* that covers, among other things, verbal false statements that harm someone's *professional* reputation. *Slander per se* lawsuits eliminate a key requirement for a plaintiff's case—the plaintiff does not have to specifically identify a particular injury in order to win damages.

Second, all defamation lawsuits are considered **intentional torts**. This matters because juries have the option of awarding **punitive damages**, which are available in some types of lawsuits to "punish" a defendant, on top of damages designed to compensate plaintiffs for actual losses. Punitive damages are vaguely defined in most states and can be quite large.

As a result, for years, most employers have avoided saying negative things about former employees. But even saying positive things about former employees can now lead to legal trouble. What if a company gives a favorable review to a former employee who was violent? The courts are currently divided on this issue.

In one Michigan case, *Moore* v. *Joseph Nursing Home*, a woman's husband was killed at work by a violent coworker. The violent coworker had previously been fired by Joseph Nursing Home after being disciplined two dozen times for violent behavior and use of drugs and alcohol. The victim's wife sued, arguing that her husband's employer had done a reference check on the violent coworker and that Joseph Nursing Home should have said something about the violent behavior but did not. The court held that there was no duty to do so without a "special relationship," and it upheld the dismissal of the wife's lawsuit.

A similar case in New Mexico came out differently. In *Davis* v. *Commissioners*, the plaintiff was sexually assaulted during therapy sessions by a mental health technician who had been reprimanded at his previous job for having sex with female inmates as a detention sergeant at a jail. His supervisor recommended him as an "excellent employee" who "displayed considerable initiative and imagination." The New Mexico court held that the plaintiff could sue the former employer over the positive reference because it misrepresented material facts and ignored a substantial risk of foreseeable physical harm.

In the end, many employers are sensibly reluctant to say much of anything about former employees. Many companies have strict policies that allow for only basic facts, such as dates of employment and job title, to be given out when references are requested.

The "New" Tool: Credit Checks

Employers remain eager for information about job applicants, and a growing number have turned to a new source. The Society of Human Resource Management recently conducted a survey and found that 60 percent of companies made at least some use of credit checks in the hiring process.

Nearly everyone has seen his or her credit report. Companies such as TransUnion compile the reports, which include credit scores and credit histories. Banks and other lenders are the heaviest users of the reports. A borrower with a high credit score can usually qualify for a larger loan and pay a lower rate of interest than a credit applicant with a low credit score. Increasingly, new credit cards with limits of over $1,000 are issued only to consumers who have at least decent credit scores.

But the widespread use of credit reports to screen candidates for a job is a fairly new phenomenon. The general assessment that many employers seem to make is, "An ugly credit report shows that you don't have your life in order. If you can't handle your own money, we won't trust you with ours." Some will admit that they fear embezzlement by employees who are in financial trouble, and that they avoid hiring workers with bad credit reports to fill positions that would allow them to have direct access to cash.

Critics argue that there is no proven link between poor credit scores and embezzlement, or between poor credit scores and being a subpar worker. At least one lawsuit was filed in 2009 that alleged that a company's use of credit reports in hiring amounted to illegal discrimination. That case is unresolved at the time of this writing.

For now, the question of whether to use credit reports to screen job applicants is generally legal and is therefore a question of ethics.

SCENARIO

Pharmaceutical Company—CEO's Office

"Have a seat, Ron," the CEO said to her head of human resources.

"Thanks, Ms. Jenner. How are you?"

"Not good," the CEO replied grimly. Ron raised his eyebrows. "I just got absolutely hammered by the Board of Directors."

"Over the, ah…"

"Yeah. 'How did two employees manage to walk out the door with a total of SEV-EN HUN-DRED THOUS-AND DOL-LARS worth of narcotic painkillers before you caught them?!' they said. I mean, the chairman was shouting at me."

"Ouch."

"Yeah, ouch. The chairman had one of our little embezzler's credit reports at the meeting. 'Why did no one notice that this guy was financially desperate? Why was he ever permitted to have access to the books in the first place? Why did his accomplice have access to the warehouse?' he asked me. I had nothing for him."

Ron sat silently, waiting.

"So, obviously, we have to make some major changes," the CEO finally said.

"What do you want me to do?"

"For starters, I want your team to get a credit report on everyone."

"Everyone?"

"Everyone, Ron. And I want you to pull a credit report on every applicant who gets to the point of being a finalist for any position."

"OK, Ms. Jenner. Won't be cheap."

"I don't care, I want it done."

"I will. Ah, what do you want to do with the, ah, bad credit scores?"

The CEO thought for a moment. "Put together a report with details on the worst cases. Bring it to me in two weeks, and we'll put a policy together."

"OK, Ms. Jenner."

Two Weeks Later

"Hi, Ron, give me a second," the CEO said without looking up from her computer.

"OK, Ms. Jenner." Ron sat patiently for several minutes. Eventually, the CEO said, "OK, that fire's put out. I think. Let's sit at the table, OK?"

"Sure." Ron placed two files on the CEO's conference table.

"I'm sorry, Ron, I only have about ten minutes."

"No problem.. This report looks at what we determined to be the 'worst 10 percent' of the credit reports in the bunch. The reporting companies can't send us credit scores for this kind of thing, so we had to make our own calls."

"OK. So this is the worst 10 percent of whom? Our employees? Applicants?"

"Both."

"OK."

"So we grouped them into five categories. Category 0 people have no plausible access to the drugs we make. They work at the call center, home office, somewhere other than the manufacturing plant."

"I don't care about them."

"I didn't think you would. Category I people work on the floor of the plant. They work on the assembly line, or mix the ingredients, or do quality control. They could get some pills, but probably not a lot of pills without being noticed."

"OK."

"Category II people have access to large quantities of our drugs. They work in the warehouse, drive our trucks, that kind of thing. They can get hold a lot of the drugs, but they'd have a tough time covering their tracks for long because their paperwork wouldn't match up. At least, they'd have trouble without help."

"Mmm-hmm," the CEO said knowingly.

"Category III people control the documents that verify that no drugs have gone missing. They enter the raw data from written records into our systems, and they're supposed to prevent theft. Some of them also generate government reports, especially for the narcotic prescriptions."

"So by your definitions, a Category II guy working with a Category III guy got us last time."

"That's correct, yes."

"OK. And the 'fours' are the managers and above?"

"Right. Category IV people have access to both large quantities of the drugs and to our information systems. These folks could plausibly act alone and get away with stealing from us, at least for a while."

"OK. How many of your bottom 10 percent people were in each category?"

"In Category I, we have 15 workers. Category II had 5, Category III had 2, Category IV had 1."

"I was hoping you'd say zero for Category IV at least."

"Sorry."

"Is it Jim?"

"Yes."

"How bad?"

"Just from his credit report? Terrible. I can't believe he hasn't lost his house yet."

"Or his Porsche."

"Or his Porsche," Ron agreed.

The CEO sighed. "What do you think about all of this, Ron? I mean, the board is all over me. I have to do something, but is this it?"

Ron thought for a moment. "I'm not sure, Ms. Jenner. I get the idea that if someone is on his last leg financially, he might make a desperate move. But we're putting a lot of systems in place that should make that more difficult without getting rid of people with bad credit scores."

"It's hard when it's a specific person you know, isn't it?"

"Well, yes. But Jim aside, I mean, it might be that someone with money trouble is a better worker."

"How so?"

"What I mean is, you might be more loyal to the company if you really need the income. I won't say his name, but we both know who the laziest guy in this building is."

The CEO smiled and nodded her head.

"He's financially independent—his credit report really proves it, by the way—and he doesn't care if he gets fired."

"He may get fired soon, after I sort this mess out," the CEO said.

"Yeah, well, maybe somebody who can't miss a paycheck would work extra hard."

"Maybe. Or maybe that person isn't reliable in his personal life or when he's here."

"Maybe." A silence stretched out. "So, ah, Ms. Jenner, what do you want me to do?"

She thought for a moment. "Let me think this over for a few days."

"Will do, Ms. Jenner."

"Thank you, Ron."

DISCUSSION QUESTIONS

1. Should the CEO have ordered credit checks on the various categories of workers in the first place?

Category I	Yes // No
Category II	Yes // No
Category III	Yes // No
Category IV	Yes // No

2. Now that she has the information, should the CEO fire the workers with the lowest scores in the various categories?

Category I	Yes // No
Category II	Yes // No
Category III	Yes // No
Category IV	Yes // No

3. Is it more reasonable to start using credit checks on new applicants? For new applicants, should a low credit score be not considered at all, be considered as one part of the overall application, or be a deal breaker that automatically prevents someone from being considered any further?

Category I	Not Considered // Considered in Part // Deal Breaker
Category II	Not Considered // Considered in Part // Deal Breaker
Category III	Not Considered // Considered in Part // Deal Breaker
Category IV	Not Considered // Considered in Part // Deal Breaker

4. Compare two job applicants with equally poor credit scores. The first is 24 years old and is a recent college graduate. The second is 39. As a manager, would you make different assumptions about whether the applicants were likely to be reliable workers based on their credit reports? Why or why not?

_____

_____

_____

_____

5. Two bills have been introduced in Congress at different points in the last decade. Neither has passed at the time of this writing.

Proposal 1: Make ex-employers at least partially immune (exempt) from defamation lawsuits while giving references to former employees unless they maliciously attempt to prevent the former worker from gaining employment elsewhere.

Proposal 2: Ban companies from using credit reports for the purposes described in this module.

Would a combination of these two ideas be a reasonable proposal? Would you favor a law that granted immunity during reference checks and banned the use of credit checks for hiring and firing? Or would you worry that former employers would have too much leeway to block you from gaining employment elsewhere?

_____

_____

_____

_____

UNIT 7

Employee Compensation

Unit Background

Everyone would like to make more money, and organizations operate in a world of limited resources. How can a company fairly allocate salaries and wages?

Module 38

CEO Compensation. [Are American CEOs paid too much? How much is too much? Under what circumstances should large compensation packages be considered?]

Module 39

Taxes and Salaries: Egalitarian and Libertarian Policies. [When allocating scarce resources, should people be treated equally, or should they be rewarded according to the wealth that they generate?]

Module 40

Rawls's Veil of Ignorance and Fair Compensation Systems. [Noted thinker John Rawls proposed the idea of a "veil of ignorance" as a justification for egalitarian policies. Is his point of view reasonable?]

Employee Compensation

Americans are keenly interested in how much money they are paid relative to others. Newspaper articles about salaries are a constant because people find them interesting.

Companies have limited resources, and they are never in a position to give every worker every dollar he or she would like to have. Salary trade-offs are a constant struggle for many businesses.

American CEOs earn tidy sums. In many nations, a typical CEO earns 20 times what an entry-level employee makes. In the United States, the multiplier is several hundred. Boards of directors justify large pay packages by pointing to the tremendous difference in revenue between well-led and poorly led organizations. But many politicians, reporters, and workers remain unconvinced. The first module examines extreme CEO compensation and whether it is justified for all leaders, only for successful leaders, or for no leaders at all.

The remaining modules look at pay for "regular" workers. Libertarian and egalitarian thinkers have different points of view on compensation policies, and the two philosophies are contracted. John Rawls's "veil of ignorance" is one of the more useful tools for thinking through these issues, and it is presented in the unit's final module.

CEO Compensation

It pays to be at the very top. Bestselling author Stephen King brings home $50,000,000 per year. David Beckham earns about the same. And large numbers of CEOs earn sums north of seven figures.

Chief executive officer (CEO) compensation has long been a hotly debated issue, and critics have become more vocal during the current economic downturn. As "regular" workers are laid off, and wages of most workers who stay employed remain stagnant, many in the press have sharp words for executives with large compensation packages.

Corporate compensation committees seem to be paying attention. In 2009, total pay for the leaders of America's 500 largest companies fell 11 percent. But the average CEO of a top-500 company, even with the reduction, still pocketed an average of $11.4 million. Critics continue to call for consumer boycotts and new government regulation.

CEOs seldom defend themselves in on-the-record interviews, but when they do, they argue that their strategic decisions can make the difference between a company that thrives and one that files for bankruptcy. CEOs are paid handsomely, but their compensation totals less than 3 percent of a typical company's profits. If a CEO's vision helps a company earn extra billions, the argument goes, then why shouldn't he or she be able to earn millions?

Later in this unit, we will look at trade-offs between concentrating raises among top earners and spreading them out more evenly among all workers. This module, however, focuses only on the level of CEO pay itself.

CEO Pay and Average Salaries

Until 1994, ice cream maker Ben & Jerry's had a well-known rule that the CEO could earn no more than 5 times the wages of the company's lowest-paid worker. Today, Whole Foods Market has an internal policy that caps CEO pay at 19 times the pay of the average employee. Although a handful of other companies set similar voluntary limits, most do not.

Around the world, there is wide variation in the relationship between executive compensation and the pay of average workers. In Japan, a typical CEO is well paid, but he or she earns only 11 times what the company's average worker earns. So if an average worker at a company earns $40,000, the typical Japanese CEO pockets a very nice but nonshocking sum of $440,000. In the United Kingdom, the multiplier is 22, and a typical executive might earn almost, but not quite, $1 million.

In the United States, the multiplier is substantially higher. A generation ago, it was already 40 times the average worker's salary. Currently, it is 150–200 times higher. Critics argue that this is a harmful disconnect and that CEO pay is unconscionably out of step with an average worker's pay. Critics say that workers are less motivated and that they feel less part of a team when such salary disparities exist.

Others argue that there is no substitute in an organization for excellence among top leaders and that CEOs are extremely well paid because they are irreplaceable.

The Beginnings of Broad Regulation? The Troubled Asset Relief Program

To date, the government has declined to pass laws that place broad limits on CEO pay. However, there has been recent regulation of the pay of the leaders of some companies that have received a new kind of government assistance.

When the housing market collapsed and sparked the current recession, Congress threw several hundred billion dollars at the problem in the form of the **Troubled Asset Relief Program (TARP)**. The essential problem addressed was this: Large numbers of borrowers ("subprime" and otherwise) became unable to pay their mortgages. Banks and others faced tremendous losses as the value of their mortgages and the mortgage-backed securities they held plummeted.

TARP money was used to buy these "toxic assets" and to help keep financial institutions afloat. In return, the government took an ownership stake in bailed-out businesses. In addition, TARP recipients had to accept new regulations.

In June of 2009, President Obama appointed Kenneth Feinberg the TARP program's Special Master for Executive Compensation. The press sometimes refers to Feinberg as the "pay czar." He has broad authority to regulate the pay of the top 5 executives and the next 20 most highly compensated employees of companies that have received TARP funds. CEO pay is not strictly limited to any defined level, but Feinberg can and often has rejected proposed compensation packages.

Some members of Congress have argued that TARP program restrictions on CEO pay should be significantly expanded to cover all publicly traded companies.

In the following scenarios, several people have taken in the same amount in the past year. The questions that follow will ask you to approve of or condemn their large paydays.

SCENARIOS

Consider the following companies. Assume that all CEOs described took home total compensation of $50,000,000 last year.

Company 1

CEO Jane Smith leads the most profitable pharmaceutical company in the world. When she took over five years ago, its performance was average. She made a series of bold moves and assembled a team of researchers who lead the industry in patents. Her marketing department and network of sales representatives are also considered second-to-none. Her pay is a total of less than 1 percent of the company's annual profit.

Company 2

Javier Vazquez is CEO of a bank that was in deep trouble when he took the helm four years ago. At that time, the bank was near bankruptcy. Foreseeing the mortgage collapse, he instituted a strict policy of making no loans to applicants with low credit scores and set about reshaping the bank's image. Today, the bank has become very profitable again. Vasquez recently received an offer to take over a larger competitor at a salary of $65 million. When the board of his current employer offered him a new package worth $50 million, he decided to stay. His new compensation amounts to 5 percent of the bank's total profit from last year.

Company 3

Jerome Smith is CEO of an oil company. It has held steady for several years as the nation's fifth largest oil company. He has brought the company through a difficult strike among refinery workers and a significant drop-off in crude oil prices. His pay is about 1 percent of the company's annual profit.

Company 4

Randy Roberts is CEO of a struggling software company. When he took over seven years ago, the company was thriving and was a leader in creating and selling business applications. Today, the company is substantially less profitable than in its heyday; 15 percent of its workforce has been laid off. Roberts has argued repeatedly to the board of directors that "it could be worse" and that his leadership has prevented the company from collapsing altogether in a changing market. His pay is about 6 percent of the company's total profit.

Consider also these non-CEOs.

Al

Al Harris was badly hurt in an auto accident when his car's steering malfunctioned. He is partially disabled from the accident and probably always will be. He is able to care for himself, but he will never again be able to resume his job as a construction worker. He sued the maker of his car and won $50 million.

Jan

Jan Linus is a genius day trader. Over the last 15 years, she has built an initial stake of $200,000 into $100 million. She had a particularly good year last year, snapping up undervalued assets and increased her net worth by $50 million.

Franklin

Franklin J. Moneypenny inherited $50 million from his grandfather.

Betty

Betty Goodfortune won $50 million in the Powerball lottery.

DISCUSSION QUESTIONS

1. How justifiable are the large compensation packages for the CEOs discussed above?

	Completely Unreasonable ⟵ ⟶ Completely Reasonable
Pharmaceuticals	1 --- 2 --- 3 --- 4 --- 5 --- 6 --- 7
Bank	1 --- 2 --- 3 --- 4 --- 5 --- 6 --- 7
Oil	1 --- 2 --- 3 --- 4 --- 5 --- 6 --- 7
Software	1 --- 2 --- 3 --- 4 --- 5 --- 6 --- 7

2. Is it reasonable for the government to regulate companies that have received TARP money? If so, should the government go further and regulate the CEOs of all corporations? If not, should the government never set legal maximums for salaries?

_____

_____

_____

_____

3. Do you give any weight to the criticism that CEO salaries are too many multiples of the salaries of average workers? Is Japan more reasonable with a multiplier of 11, for example, than the United States is with a typical multiplier of 150–200? What should the multiplier be? Or is this a nonsensical comparison?

_____

_____

_____

_____

4. This module opened with Stephen King and David Beckham. Compare their $50 million to the $50 million the CEOs in the scenario earned. On a gut level, do you find it any better or worse when a celebrity or entertainer makes a large amount of money than when a CEO does the same?

_____

_____

_____

_____

5. Now consider the $50 million that the non-CEOs received. If you were the king or queen and had total authority, who would you allow to keep all of the $50 million, less regular income taxes that everyone pays? Circle everyone who you think should be able to keep the entire $50 million, and leave blank anyone on whom you would impose a "special extra tax."

Al Harris (lawsuit)	Jan Linus (stock market)
Franklin J. Moneypenny (inheritance)	Betty Goodfortune (lottery)

Taxes and Salaries: Egalitarian and Libertarian Policies

In case you are working on this module by itself and not as part of the complete series, a brief recap of egalitarian and libertarian thought follows.

Egalitarians do not generally favor *complete* equality, but they do favor providing everyone with reasonable access to the wealth that a nation or a company has to divide. Egalitarians in politics favor, for example, universal health care, welfare systems, and a progressive tax system. In business, they tend to favor across-the-board raises for all workers and a smaller concentration of wealth among top executives and owners.

Libertarians often argue that people should keep the wealth that they generate. In politics, libertarians tend to favor low taxes and fewer social programs, and they often campaign against governments "redistributing wealth." In business, they tend to advocate large salaries for employees who add large amounts of value to a firm in some measureable way. To libertarians, an employee who brings in a large number of clients, makes strategic decisions that increase profits, or creates valuable intellectual property ought to be compensated handsomely, and perhaps very handsomely. The same holds true, they argue, for owners who create enterprises in the first place.

Taxes in the United States

For decades, income taxes in the United States have been "progressive." The more money you earn, the higher your "tax bracket." A low-income worker might pay 10 percent in taxes. The highest tax bracket in 2010 for top earners is 35 percent.

The degree to which taxes are progressive sometimes swings rapidly as the balance of political power shifts between egalitarian thinkers and libertarian thinkers. Under President Carter, a worker making over $100,000 per year paid 70 percent in taxes. Under President Reagan, who followed Carter, the tax bracket for a $100,000 salary became 33 percent. Thus, the top tax bracket may no longer be 35 percent by the time this book goes to press.[1]

---

[1] The highest U.S. income tax bracket of all time was 94 percent during World War II. Ouch!

Some politicians advocate a "flat tax," in which all Americans pay the same percentage of income tax. Such a system would effectively create one tax bracket, and everyone would pay, say, 20 percent. Egalitarians oppose this idea, arguing that it would be overly hard on lower-income workers and that it would prevent a reasonable share of America's wealth from going to all workers. Libertarians tend to favor the idea of a flat tax.

Corporate Compensation Policies

Corporate salaries are a hot topic in business ethics journals. Authors debate whether salaries for top executives are excessive and whether wages paid to entry-level workers are too low. Generally speaking, egalitarians favor lower pay "at the top" and a more equal distribution of salaries. Libertarian thinkers have no problem with enormous paychecks for a firm's most valuable employees.

Sometimes, the best way to work through a complicated system is to simplify everything. For the next scenario, we're off to a very small nation, located somewhere in the tropics.

SCENARIO

Tiny Island is an independent nation with 501 adult residents. A software company is the only private employer, and 401 of the island's residents work there. The salary structure is simple.

200 employees earn $25,000 each as phone operators, data-entry clerks, and support staff.

100 employees earn $50,000 each as junior programmers and sales staff.

100 employees earn $100,000 each as senior programmers.

1 man—Mr. Smith—owns the business and earns $10,000,000 per year.

The total annual income of all workers at the software company is $30,000,000.

In addition to the software firm's workers, there are 100 government workers on Tiny Island. The salary structure for them is also simple.

40 workers earn $25,000 as custodians, junior clerks, and landscapers.

40 workers earn $50,000 as firefighters, police officers, and teachers.

20 workers earn $100,000 as supervisors, principals, and high-level administrators.

The total annual income of all government workers is $5,000,000.

In addition to the $5,000,000 needed for salaries of all government employees, the government needs an additional $2,000,000 per year to pay for maintenance on the school and other government buildings, electricity, road repairs, a ferry service that runs off the island, and the like.

Tiny Island's Constitution requires that all tax revenue come from an income tax. The total government budget is $7,000,000. The total income of all residents of Tiny Island is $35,000,000. In order to fund all current needs, the tax must average 20 percent (a "flat tax" of 20 percent on all salaries would fund all needs).

DISCUSSION QUESTIONS

1. Where should the $7,000,000 in taxes come from? Create an ideal system for spreading Tiny Island's tax burden on its residents, and support your system with egalitarian or libertarian thinking.

Percent Paid in Taxes	×	Total Amount Earned by All Workers Earning this Salary	=	Tax Revenue Raised
Workers earning $25,000 will pay	_____ %	× $6,000,000	=	_____
Workers earning $50,000 will pay	_____ %	× $7,000,000	=	_____
Workers earning $100,000 will pay	_____ %	× $12,000,000	=	_____
Mr. Smith will pay	_____ %	× $10,000,000	=	_____
		(Total Tax Must Equal $7,000,000)		

2. Is your system more egalitarian or more libertarian? Why? Is your system reasonably similar to the current U.S. system of taxation? If not, what makes your system better?

_____

_____

_____

_____

3. Now, let's apply the libertarian and egalitarian ideas to the company's compensation policy. Focus on the software company's compensation policy. Mr. Smith takes home one-third of all pay in the 401-person company, but he owns the business that employs 80 percent of Tiny Island's residents. Is his large payday justified? Or should more of his annual take "trickle down" to lower-level employees?

_____

_____

_____

_____

4. Suppose that Mr. Smith was not the owner of the company but had been hired by the owner to be the CEO. Mr. Smith made excellent strategic moves and helped the company experience substantial growth. Would your answer to the third question change?

_____

_____

_____

_____

5. Assume now that Tiny Island's political leaders are debating raising taxes for various reasons. The proposed new programs are egalitarian in nature and must be funded directly from the incomes of the 501 workers. Indicate your approval (or lack of approval) for the ideas proposed.

Idea	Annual Cost	Approve/Reject
Create a Government Pension for All Citizens Over Age 65	$2,000,000	_____
Government-Run Health and Dental Care for All Citizens	$2,000,000	_____
Pay Raises for All Government Employees	$1,000,000	_____

If you approved any of the ideas, where would you raise the tax revenue to pay for them? Work through a simpler system than in the first question:

Additional revenue needed to pay for approved programs: _____

Source: $ _____ total from $25,000 per year workers

$ _____ total from $50,000 per year workers

$ _____ total from $100,000 per year workers

$ _____ total from Mr. Smith

MODULE 40

Rawls's Veil of Ignorance and Fair Compensation Systems

BACKGROUND

Corporations have limited resources, as do governments, families, and any other identifiable assembly of people. The reality is that leaders can allocate only so many dollars among a firm's employees. **Distributive justice** ideas provide models for thinking about how to divide wealth fairly. This module will examine two of them.

Libertarians often argue that people should keep the wealth that they generate. In politics, libertarians tend to favor low taxes and fewer social programs, and they often campaign against governments "redistributing wealth." In business, they tend to advocate large salaries for employees who add large amounts of value to a firm in some measureable way. An employee who brings in a large number of clients, makes strategic decisions that increase profits, or creates valuable intellectual property ought to be compensated handsomely, perhaps very handsomely.

Egalitarians do not generally favor *complete* equality, but they do favor providing everyone with reasonable access to the wealth that a nation or a company has to divide. Egalitarians in politics favor, for example, universal health care, welfare systems, and a progressive tax system. In business, they tend to favor across-the-board raises for all workers and greater job security.

The Veil of Ignorance

John Rawls was a philosophy professor at Harvard and a noted egalitarian thinker. He created a unique tool for thinking about egalitarian ideas. He called it the **veil of ignorance,** and he intended it as *a justification* for egalitarianism.

The veil of ignorance requires a kind of thought experiment. It asks that you imagine yourself in a state of limited information. Specifically: What kind of distributive justice rules would you want *if you had absolutely no idea of how you stand relative to everyone else*? What if, for example, you simply didn't know how intelligent you were compared to other people? Early in life, people in the real world start to sense whether they are gifted, average, or below average. But what if you had no basis for comparison? What if you didn't know whether you were a hard worker relative to others? Or whether you had a likeable personality? Or were attractive? Or lucky? Or …anything at all?

Rawls argued that people's notions of distributive justice were clouded by their sense of their own competitiveness in the world. He believed that the only fair way to set rules for dividing up limited resources was to do so from behind a veil of ignorance. Rawls believed that if a person genuinely carried out his thought experiment, he would naturally conclude that egalitarian principles were better and more desirable than the alternatives.

Raise Policies

Corporate executives must set policies on how raises are to be determined. Often, they arrive at a common and fundamental "fork in the road"; the libertarian path favors top producers, and the egalitarian path offers more equal benefits to everyone. Rawls, of course, believed in the second option. The majority of large companies lean more toward the first option.

Rawls believed that a rational person behind a veil of ignorance would *want* an egalitarian system. He thought that, in the absence of a sense of your own competitiveness, you would desire an environment that rained rewards on everyone.

The following scenario is more unlikely than any other in this series. But if you really want to go all the way and test the veil of ignorance idea, you have to be *unable* to assess your relative standing in society. In the next scenario, although a character like Jack ordinarily appears only on soap operas, he is useful for testing Rawls's idea.

SCENARIO

(All scenes take place at University Hospital in Geneva, Switzerland.)

ICU Room 104—March

The patient opened his eyes. He saw only a blur at first, but in time, the images around him resolved. In front of him, he saw a blue wall with a flat-screen TV mounted on it. Bright sunlight shone through a window to his right. An open door stood to his left.

He hurt. Everywhere. Moving took great effort. He seemed unable to open his mouth.

Something lay by his hand. He reached out, fumbled the object in his fingers, and grasped it. It was an IV tube. *So,* he thought, *a hospital, then.*

A doctor with a dark gray goatee entered the room. He picked up a chart from the end of the patient's bed and started to flip through the pages. He made a notation, glanced at the patient, then glanced back at the chart. He squinted his eyes and looked back up at the patient, surprised. "*Monsieur?*" he ventured, stepping around the bed.

"Yes," the patient croaked through parched lips.

"*Monsieur* is awake! *Très bien!* Wonderful! How do you feel?"

The patient mustered his strength. "Awf…awful."

"Of course you feel awful! You have been unconscious for three weeks. But now you are back!"

"Ugh," the patient said.

"You must rest, regain your strength. But first, *monsieur*, tell me your name *s'il vous plaît.* You are, how do you say, a riddle to us. You had no wallet when you were brought here, and no one has come looking for you."

"Jack," the patient said.

"Jack! Excellent! I am so delighted to know your name!" the doctor said. "And I am Dr. Van Bergen, Jack." He wrote JACK in large block letters at the top of his chart. "And, Jack…what is your last name, *monsieur?*"

A startled look crossed Jack's face. "I'm, ah…I'm not sure," he said.

Dr. Van Bergen's Private Office—April

"Your examination results are excellent, Jack," said Dr. Van Bergen as he read from an open file. "You are the picture of health. I am thrilled to see you walking, if only for short distances. In a month, maybe two, I am confident that you will fully regain your physical strength."

"And then we'll be down to one problem," Jack said.

"Perhaps, perhaps not. Amnesia is a strange condition. It can persist indefinitely, yes, or it can switch off in an instant." Van Bergen snapped his fingers for emphasis. "If only we could figure out where you belong. Sometimes being around familiar faces and settings is useful therapy. But with you...you are an enigma, Jack."

"Well...at least I am an enigma who is getting better."

"Yes—just so!"

Recreation Room in the Long-Term-Care Wing—May

Jack sat alone at a table. He wrote carefully and deliberately in the margin of a large hardback textbook. Dr. Van Bergen approached him, unseen. "Hello, Jack," he said.

Startled out of his concentration, Jack looked up. "Doctor," he said. "I didn't hear you come in."

"I'm just ending my rounds, and I saw you through the window. What are you working on?"

Jack closed the textbook. Its cover read *Advanced Calculus*. Jack slid the textbook across the table. "I found it here on the shelves. I, ah...maybe I shouldn't write in it..."

"Shh, shh, not a problem," Van Bergen was turning through the pages. "Jack!" he said, "you've worked through most of the equations in this book. And they appear to all be correct."

"Yeah. I've, ah, I've been working on a chapter every day for a few weeks now. It ...all seems to make sense to me."

"You have an aptitude! You use this in your profession, perhaps!"

"Perhaps. Whatever it is," Jack said.

"Jack," the doctor said, "this is wonderful. I hope you'll complete the book, and I would be delighted to buy you another at any time. This may be a key to helping you remember who you are."

Dr. Van Bergen's Office—June

"Please excuse my voice today, Jack," Van Bergen said quietly. "I cannot believe that we beat Spain at the World Cup yesterday. I watched the game with my brothers, and I have not screamed so loudly and for so long since...well, since I can remember."

"Yeah. That was a good game."

"Bah! You are entirely uninterested in the World Cup. You must be an American!" the doctor said, smiling. "I must redouble my efforts to search for missing persons in America!" The doctor sighed. "Anyway, hoarse or not, 'the show must go on,' eh?"

"I suppose so."

"So, Jack, the reason I wanted to see you today is this: I can't keep you here indefinitely. Your memory is missing, but you are strong and in good health. You have the ability to care for yourself. And you have no health insurance! At least, none that we know about. I cannot bill the treasury for your care indefinitely."

"I understand. I sort of guessed that this day was coming."

"Yes. But the news is not all bad. My wife is on our school board. She knows about your case and about your calculus aptitude. She presented it to the board, and I am pleased to tell you that they have taken an interest in your unique circumstances. Jack, they have extended you an offer to teach high school mathematics!"

"Wow. Well...hey, that's great, doc."

"It is, isn't it? And it is a win-win situation. The board needs three high school math teachers for the upcoming term. All we need to do is select the school for you." Van Bergen spread his hands.

"Well, OK, then. Ah, what can you tell me about the schools?"

"Each offers the same starting salary to a new teacher—50,000 euros. Each offers a three-year contract. Also standard for new teachers. At the end of three years, you will either be offered permanent employment or asked to find…other employment. The difference is in the type of school, and the, ah, opportunities for advancement at each.

"The first school is a standard public school. Unless you are dreadfully unreliable, you will be offered permanent employment after three years. Frankly, even marginal teachers have perfect job security. The downside is that your salary will not increase by much. After three years, you can expect to be making, at most, 60,000 euros per year.

"The second school is a competitive school. Parents choose a more rigorous program for their children, and they expect expert instruction because they pay for it. About half of the teachers are not renewed after three years. But those who are renewed get a salary bump up to 90,000 euros.

"The last school is an elite academy. Only students with test scores in the top 2 percent of all schoolchildren are allowed to attend. New teachers are paired with senior teachers, and they are given a chance to prove their merit. Almost everyone is released at the end of the initial contract. But for the 10 percent who are skilled enough to earn permanent employment, the rewards are high. Promoted instructors are paid 250,000 euros per year, which, I don't mind telling you, is more than I make.

"So that is your choice, Jack. You need not decide today, but I will need to forward your preference by this time next week."

Jack let it all sink in. "I'm speechless, doctor," he said. "I…well, I'm good at math. I wonder, though, if I'll make a good teacher."

"I don't see why not, Jack. I have every confidence in you."

"Thanks, Doc," Jack said. "Thanks so much for everything."

DISCUSSION QUESTIONS

1. Place yourself in Jack's shoes behind the veil of ignorance. Which of the three schools would you choose as your employer? Why?

_____

_____

_____

_____

2. Which of the schools do you think most people would select? Why?

_____

_____

_____

_____

3. Place yourself in Jack's shoes again, but suppose that you are able to recall one additional fact about yourself: Before the accident, you were a math teacher for ten years. Now which of the three job offers would you choose? If your selection changed, why did it change?

_____

_____

_____

_____

4. Now suppose that you are able to recall another new fact about yourself: You were a highly decorated math teacher before the accident. In fact, you clearly remember being named "teacher of the year." Now which of the three job offers would you choose? If your selection changed, why did it change?

_____

_____

_____

_____

5. After working through this module, do you find the veil of ignorance idea to be a useful tool? Why or why not?

_____

_____

_____

_____

UNIT 8

Special Obligations to Customers

Unit Background

Customers are the lifeblood of any business. Does this reality create any special obligations? If a company does not violate the law, and it does not act so badly that its customers will leave, does it nonetheless owe ethical duties to its patrons?

Module 41

Customer Deception: Who's to Blame? [When customers are misled, does the primary blame lie with top-level policy makers, or are lower-level workers who directly interact with customers more at fault?]

Module 42

Lending Practices. [The recession caused millions of Americans to go to unusual lengths to "make it work" financially. Some forms of credit, although very expensive, can be appealing to those with few options. What obligations, if any, are owed to customers who seek high-interest loans?]

Module 43

"Microinsurance". [Just about everything priced at over $50 comes with an offer of an "extended service plan." Customers on tight monthly budgets are often willing to insure even small purchases. Does the practice of selling "microinsurance" raise any ethical issues?]

Module 44

Using "Bad" Things to Boost Profits. [There are many products and services that are perceived negatively by large numbers of people. Cigarettes are legal, but nonsmokers generally dislike them. Many forms of gambling are legal but unloved by nongamblers. If a company can profit from a legal but "bad" activity, should it do so?]

Module 45

Store Cards, Search Engines, and Customer Data. [Many businesses track and store data on customer purchases. Is a company obligated to tell its customers about such practices? Is a company obligated to keep the data to itself?]

Module 46

"Least-Profitable Customers". [Companies love big spenders. But what about small spenders and other customers who generate little or no profit? Does a company have any obligations to its "worst" customers?]

Special Obligations to Customers

Companies are often accused of taking advantage of their customers. Sometimes, the accusations are reasonable. In other cases, customers seem to simply make poor decisions.

This unit opens with a scenario in which a company regularly lies to its customers. It then asks whether top executives, store managers, or low-level workers are most responsible for the deception.

Many of the remaining modules look at products and services that arguably take advantage of people. Payday loans, which are usually made at tremendous rates of interest, are the subject of one scenario. Another explores "microinsurance," and a third focuses on boosting profits by using items that may be bad for consumers or society.

The last two units look at acceptable and unacceptable uses of customer data and whether organizations have any obligations to their "least-profitable" customers.

MODULE **41**

Customer Deception: Who's to Blame?

At my local grocery store …

First standard question: "Did you find everything you needed?"

Second standard question: "Are plastic bags OK?"

Third standard question: "Do you need any_____ today?"

The "_____" is sometimes shampoo or toothpaste, often some unappealing kind of candy, occasionally disposable cameras, and, at least once, an item I could not readily identify. Whatever the item is, it is always contained in a large wire basket under the monitor on which my purchases are listed as they are scanned.

Checkers compete to sell the largest number of items from their baskets. Daily winners receive a small bonus, and those who are caught failing to ask customers if they need any of the "daily item" are disciplined.

Many retailers have similar programs in place designed to help clear out overstocked items. Does your grocery store have 5,000 candy bars that are about to expire? Simply spend a week during which every cashier asks every customer if he or she would like to buy one, and watch excess inventory disappear.

Other businesses push some products over others because they have higher profit margins. Does your car dealership make $3,000 on the sale of a large SUV and $500 on the sale of a compact car? Train salespeople to push the SUVs, and watch your profits soar.

Such practices are entirely legal and above board, as long as no misrepresentations are made.

Fraud and Sears Auto Center

There is no evil inherent in commission-based systems. Many salespeople are much more motivated when they receive a cut of every item they sell, and, as such, will work much harder when paid on commission. And most of them don't deceive their customers because they want to establish good relationships and good reputations, or because they fear legal consequences.

Sometimes, lower-level employees are trained (or at least encouraged) to be deceptive while pushing products. **Fraud** occurs when a person misstates a material (important) fact with the intention of deceiving another person. In most cases, even aggressive salespeople do not commit fraud. But there are, of course, exceptions.

In the 1990s, Sears Auto Center got into hot water with the state of California. Thousands of service advisors were taken off salary and were switched to commission-based compensation. The advisors received more pay for meeting quotas, which were often expressed in terms of "repair dollars billed per hour."

Over the next year, hundreds of consumers complained to the California Department of Consumer Affairs that Sears Auto Center aggressively sold them repair work. Eventually, California officials conducted an undercover operation.

The state replaced all worn brake components on many old cars and then made the new parts look aged by rubbing grime onto them. The state then visited various Sears Auto Center locations a total of 38 times with the cars that had perfect braking systems. In 34 of the 38 cases, the service advisor recommended repairs to the undercover state employee at an average cost of over $200.

California accused Sears Auto Center of fraud and threatened to revoke the company's right to operate in the state. In the end, the case settled out of court for $8 million.

Who's to Blame?

When an employee who is paid a commission does cross the line and commit fraud, it raises an interesting question: Who is at fault for the deception? Does the bulk of the blame sit with the low-level employee who most directly lied to a customer or with the executives who established the compensation policy in the first place?

This is more than an abstract question. Society's perception of the responsible party can influence whether customers will ever again do business with a company, what kind of action government regulators will take, and whether and how much the media reports a story and heaps bad publicity on a company. The degree to which a jury deems actions foreseeable can even affect legal liability. In these ways and others, people's gut feelings about who is "wrong" can broadly impact an organization.

In the following scenario, assume that Samuelson Watch Repair Company owns and operates 100 stores in the United States. They are located mostly in shopping malls. A typical store has a manager, two repair technicians, and between three and six salespeople.

The stores earn $20 on a typical watch battery replacement, and an average of $120 on a typical watch repair.

SCENARIO

Samuelson Headquarters

"And so," the CFO concluded, "without additional revenue, we'll likely have to close at least 10 locations, and possibly as many as 15 locations, by the end of the fiscal year."

"So," the CEO asked, "are you suggesting we raise our prices?"

"I don't think we can raise our prices, at least not by much. The market won't bear it. Customers will pay $24 to have us replace a watch battery because it's just easier. But if we go higher than that, some of them will figure out that they can get the same battery at Walmart for $5, and that it isn't that hard to swap it out with the old one."

"What about the prices on our repair jobs?"

"We might be able to go a little higher there, but the main problem is that 80 percent of our customers just stop in for a simple battery replacement. We make a lot of money on watch repairs, but we need to get more of that kind of job in the first place."

"I agree," said the deputy CFO. "Here's how we'll do it." All heads turned toward him. "We put everybody on commission. No salary, limited guaranteed wages. Everybody goes on commission."

"People will quit," the CEO said.

"I don't think so, not in this economy," the deputy CFO replied. "And if they do, we can find replacements who want a job whatever the terms are—that's an advantage of high unemployment."

"OK, so say everybody's put on commission. So what?"

"So we tie their pay to the number of watch repairs they bring in per week. If a salesperson sells, or a tech repairs, let's set it at, maybe, 10 percent more watches than before, then he or she makes the same pay as before we switched them to commission. Same deal for the managers, except we measure the whole store. If the store's numbers don't go up, managers will make less. If the store's repair numbers go up by more than 10 percent, they'll make more money than ever."

"But merely making people's livelihood dependent on selling watch repairs won't make customers magically appear at the door," the CEO said. "We need better marketing, better customer service, and new kinds of services…maybe push our discount club. You know, increase repeat business."

"We've tried those things, and we need more business than they can generate," the deputy CFO replied. "And I disagree that we need more customers walking through the door. We just need for them to spend more money when they show up in our stores."

"I still don't see how your plan will do that."

"The employees will figure it out."

Samuelson Store #37—Workroom

Vincent looked at the Omega watch. It sat atop a pink order slip that read, "Repl. Batt.—Cust. Back 2 PM." He flipped the Speedmaster Professional over and started to hum the James Bond theme song.

When he had the back unscrewed, he focused a pencil beam of light from the flashlight on his headband onto the watch's innards. His fingers deftly removed tiny screws, and he replaced the battery without effort. He made subtle movements and shone his light over the mainspring, balance wheel, and the rest of the movement. All were in perfect working order. He replaced the watch's back, rubbed his fingerprints off with a cloth, and set the watch gently aside.

Vincent took the pink slip and began to write in the comments box. "Batt. replaced. Mainspring shows damage—recommend replacement—Vincent." He sighed. The mainspring probably wouldn't fail for another 20 years at least, he knew. But he also had to complete seven more repairs to meet his weekly quota.

Samuelson Store #37—Main Lobby

Jenny handed the Omega back to the customer. "All done," she said.

"Excellent," the customer said as he took his watch.

Jenny took the order slip over to the cash register. "Oh," she said, reading the comments section. "It looks like our repair tech found a problem."

"What kind of a problem?"

"He says your mainspring is damaged, and he recommends replacement. Have you noticed having to reset your watch more often than usual lately?" This was a line she had used on hundreds of customers in recent months.

"Not really…" the customer started. "Well, maybe." He seemed puzzled. "I mean, is it about to stop running? It seems OK."

"Hold on. I'll go ask the tech." She exited the lobby through a door behind the counter and made her way to the workroom. "Hey, Vince," she said.

"Oh. Hey, Jenny."

"Customer wants to know whether the Omega's about to stop running on him." Vince shrugged his shoulders and said nothing. "Gotcha," Jenny said. She returned to the lobby.

"He says it could go at any time," Jenny said to the customer. "He says that if it snaps, it could damage the other little parts in there—kind of like shrapnel, you know?"

"Oh," the customer said, sounding indecisive.

"We had a guy in here last month with an Omega with a broken mainspring. His bill was $500."

"Ouch," the customer said. "How much would it be to replace the mainspring today?"

Jenny flipped through a price book on the counter. "Let's see…Movado…Ulysse Nardin…here we go—Omega. Mainspring repair is…$99. But since you already brought your watch in for the battery replacement I can discount that 10 percent, so $89."

"OK…well…I guess I better get that done, then." The customer handed his watch back over.

"Better safe than sorry," Jenny said. *Only two more repairs and I've met my weekly quota*, she thought to herself.

Samuelson Store #37—Manager's Office

"That's not what I'm saying," said Lewis, the store's manager. "See here," he said, pointing to a spreadsheet. "Everyone else has met the quota for at least six of the past eight weeks. You only met it twice."

"But that's not my fault," Alan replied. "I'm unlucky. I don't get a lot of people who need a watch repair during my shifts."

"The others can usually make quota whether I schedule them morning or afternoon, weekday or weekend. You need to make your own 'luck' and sell people on maintaining their timepieces."

"I try, but I won't lie to them."

"Whoa! Nobody's telling you to lie, here. What I'm telling you is that it's part of your job to sell our more expensive services when you have a chance to do so."

"And if somebody's watch is in perfect working order?"

"Then, of course, out they go with a battery change only and a 'thank you' from us."

Alan sat silently for a moment. "I'll do my best," he said eventually.

"Step it up," Lewis said. His own pay depended on the total revenue his store brought in, and Alan was not helping in the slightest.

DISCUSSION QUESTIONS

1. If Samuelson Watch Repair Company's customers are misled and sold watch repairs that they do not need, assess the amount of blame that falls on each of the following:

	Little Blame ←					→ Substantial Blame
Deputy CFO	1 --- 2 --- 3 --- 4 --- 5 --- 6 --- 7
Vince (repair tech)	1 --- 2 --- 3 --- 4 --- 5 --- 6 --- 7
Jenny (clerk)	1 --- 2 --- 3 --- 4 --- 5 --- 6 --- 7
Lewis (manager)	1 --- 2 --- 3 --- 4 --- 5 --- 6 --- 7

2. In the background material, the example of a grocery store "hard selling" small items like candy bars was raised. Is the Samuelson practice any worse? Is there any difference between aggressively selling simple items like candy bars and complex services like watch or auto repairs?

_____

_____

_____

_____

For questions 3–5, assume that Samuelson gets in trouble with the government of Florida in the same way Sears Auto Center did in California.

3. If you paid $89 for a watch repair at Samuelson and afterward you saw a news report of the suspected fraudulent overselling of watch repairs by the chain of stores, how would you react? Being realistic, would you try to get your money back? Do nothing? Seek to sue? Would you ever go back to the store? Would you complain to others about Samuelson and encourage them never to go there?

_____

_____

_____

_____

4. Suppose that a lawsuit was brought against Samuelson and that you were selected as a juror. Suppose further that the plaintiffs laid out a strong fraud case. In fraud cases, juries usually have two options. First, they can choose to award plaintiffs only compensatory damages, which are meant to cover their losses (pay them back for the money spent on unnecessary repairs, in this case). Second, juries can award compensatory and punitive damages. Punitive awards are piled on top of compensatory damages, and they are meant to punish a defendant beyond payment for the losses actually caused.

As a juror, would you award compensatory damages alone to the fraud victims, or would you add punitive damages as well? If you would award punitive damages, would they be small, large, or extremely large?

_____

_____

_____

_____

5. What remedy should the Florida government seek against Samuelson? A cash penalty? Should it seek to prohibit Samuelson from operating in the state?

_____

_____

_____

_____

MODULE **42**

Lending Practices

After many years of record profits, the bottom fell out of the credit card industry in the fall of 2008. Too many cards were issued to consumers with poor financial track records. Too many of these consumers spent more than they could ever realistically repay. When the financial meltdown hit, the results were disastrous: Issuers of credit cards had to write off over $20,000,000 as "uncollectible" bad debt in the closing months of 2008 alone.

A credit card lender is in a weak position when a customer can't pay his or her balance because credit card balances are rarely "secured" by anything. If a bank makes a loan that is used to buy a car or a house, the contract usually secures the loan with the purchased item. This means that if payments are missed, the bank can eventually repossess the car or foreclose on the house. The car or house can then be sold, and the bank can get at least a reasonable amount of its money back.

If a borrower can't pay his or her unsecured credit card balance, the credit card company can't seize any property. It can sue, but lawsuits are generally more expensive than the unpaid bill. It can hire a collection agency to harass its customer, but if the customer just doesn't have the money, that is also ineffective.

Furthermore, when a consumer declares bankruptcy, credit card lenders typically receive 5 percent of their balances at the most. Unsecured lenders are near the bottom of the list that bankruptcy courts use to decide which creditors are paid first and last. So the industry has problems collecting when push comes to shove.

A positive for the industry is that credit cards loans are less regulated than mortgage and car loans. There is more "wiggle room" in the law, which gives options to companies looking to increase revenue or cut costs.

States have usury laws that set maximum rates of interest. But the law that applies to a credit card company is the law of the state where the company's headquarters is located, not the state of each individual credit card holder. It is easy enough for a headquarters to be placed in a "friendly" state. Credit card companies are generally able to charge high fees, raise their customer's rates for the smallest of reasons, and lower credit limits without violating the law.

The industry is often grilled by the press, consumers' rights groups, and, from time to time, Congress. "How can you charge 29.99 percent interest?" and "How can you charge $35 late fees?" are among the more commonly asked questions.

Card issuers defend themselves with vigor. They argue that they are in business to make a profit and that lower rates and fees would make the industry unprofitable. They argue that no one is forced to make a late payment and that everyone can avoid interest altogether by choosing to charge no more than can be paid off in full at the end of the month. They argue that their customers are adults and that adults are fully capable of making reasonable financial decisions.

In the end, the law seems unlikely to change in dramatic ways, so the practices of credit card companies fall largely within the realm of ethics.

Payday Loans

At the far edge of the lending frontier are payday loans. When advertised, these are usually characterized as "emergency loans." TV spots open with an unhappy character with a broken-down car, a sick child, or some other problem. In the next scene, a clerk counts new $100 bills into the same character's hand. "Instant cash" and "no credit check" are promised.

A typical payday loan is for $300 to $500. It is usually due to be repaid on the borrower's next payday, or two weeks after the money is loaned.

The catch is the fee charged for the short-term loan. It is usually about $15 per $100 borrowed, which amounts to a staggering 400 percent annual rate of interest. Most states exempt payday loans from even the loose regulations placed on credit card loans, making 400 percent interest perfectly legal.

Studies show that an average person who takes out a payday loan "rolls it over" almost 10 times per year. A person borrowing $500, and paying a $75 fee 10 times, pays $750 to borrow $500 for 20 weeks. Some borrowers roll their payday loans over around the calendar and pay the fee 26 times per year.

Payday lenders argue that the fees are necessary because their clients have a high default rate and the lenders must be profitable to stay in business. "We'll lend someone money when no one else will," they argue. This is perfectly true, but many remain skeptical of the industry.

The following scenario presents a series of tough ethical dilemmas many in the consumer credit industry face.

SCENARIO

Thanksgiving Night

Eric reclined in a lawn chair and watched the stars spin slowly overhead. He felt at peace in the backyard of his childhood. A radio play-by-play commentator told him that Texas had a big third down at the Texas A&M 35-yard line.

A voice came from behind him. "Looks like you found a good spot."

Eric turned around and smiled at his father. "Sure did. Kids asleep?"

"Finally. I don't know how you keep up with them every night."

"Less sugar, pop."

Eric's father laughed. "Nice to have you home, Eric."

"Nice to be home."

"I'm proud of you, boy. You and Ann and those kids all look so happy."

"Thanks, Dad."

Father and son listened to the game and made small talk about football until halftime. When the radio station cut to a long commercial break, Eric's father turned the radio off. "Son?"

"Yeah, Dad?"

"You're pretty quiet. Everything really OK?"

"Oh, sure." Eric's father held his gaze and let an uncomfortable silence stretch out. "Well, mostly OK."

"Mm hmm?"

"No, really. I mean, Ann and I are great, and the kids are doing great."

"But at work?"

"Ha! At work! Yeah, that's…" Eric trailed off. His father waited patiently for him to continue. "I like a lot of things about my job. But lately…I'm just not sure what to do."

"Want to talk about it?"

Eric thought for a moment, and then he began to talk. His father nodded and listened but did not interrupt his son.

"OK, so here's the thing. We've had to write off two hundred *million* dollars in bad credit card debt this year. People just aren't paying their bills. Most of them just can't. And that's bad news for the Vice President of Consumer Credit Operations, who happens to be my boss.

"So the board members are breathing down his neck. They want him to cut our losses to no more than one hundred million dollars next year and make our division profitable again within three years. And they've been breathing down my neck, wanting options fast. Honestly, this is the first day I haven't worked in the last six weeks. I've been dying to get to the Thanksgiving holiday.

"Anyway, there *are* a lot of ways to cut our losses and even start making money again. I've got the numbers to prove it. But I'm not sure which of the options to push. I mean, people more important than me will decide in the end, but my recommendations will carry a lot of weight, and I've got to decide what to say at our meeting next week.

"The thing is that everything with a fast impact will hurt somebody. The options aren't illegal or anything, but I don't know if they're fair, and…" Eric trailed off and collected his thoughts for a moment.

"So the obvious thing we can do is to raise our interest rates and fees. Everybody else is higher than we are, so we won't lose many customers if we do. Right now, our customers usually pay 17 percent interest. We can raise that to as high as 24 percent without a significant loss of customers. We can also raise our standard penalty for late payments from $25, where it is now, to $35. Again, no big drop in customers would be likely because there aren't any better deals out there. Those two actions would improve our bottom line. Not dramatically, but some.

"But those are obvious things to do, and I'm not getting paid to give obvious answers. To really stop our losses, we have to do more. We have to figure out which of our customers are likely to never pay us back, and we have to *stop lending them money*.

"The thing is, we don't know who they are until they miss payments, go over their limits, or declare bankruptcy. By then, it's too late. We don't have enough people to go line by line over everybody's habits, anyway. We have to look at our customers in groups and in ways that can be analyzed by software. And we have to predict who is likely to be a problem for us before he starts showing that he is a problem.

"So I've been analyzing mountains of data, and there are definitely patterns to be found. For example, if you live in a Zip Code with a lot of home foreclosures, you are 20 percent more likely to default on a credit card in the next five years. The same is true if you spend a lot of money on clothes and electronics at high-end stores. And it's especially true if you have a job in an industry that has had a lot of layoffs lately.

"So if we take all of our customers in those groups—"high-foreclosure neighborhoods," "big luxury spender," and "at-risk industry"—and if we cut their credit limit on our cards, from say an average of $5,000 each down to an average of $3,000 each, we save a ton of money. When some of them default on their debts, we lose less.

"The problem is that a whole lot of people in each group haven't done anything wrong. Most of them won't be laid off. Most of them will never default on their cards. They just happen to be in a demographic that has a larger-than-average number of people who will spend our money and never pay it back. But everybody gets the same notice in the mail if we go with this plan: 'Sorry, but your credit limit has been decreased.'

"And here's the worst part, Dad. When we decrease somebody's credit limit, her credit score goes down. It doesn't matter why we did it, the score drops just the same. And that means that, in addition to having less of a credit line from us, she'll have a harder time getting a new one from anybody else.

"So, anyway, I've got to decide whether or not to recommend that stuff. It would improve our bottom line a lot. But there's one other idea I've got that would make us even more money. A lot more.

"We're obviously set up to loan people money. Our infrastructure makes it fairly cheap for us to expand into other types of lending. I think we could make a fortune making payday loans.

"They're much riskier than our credit card operations. Tons more defaults. But because they are short-term loans, they are usually exempt from state laws that cap the interest rates we can charge on them. We can go as high as a $20 or $25 fee on a $100, two-week loan. That's on the order of a 500 percent return, so even if we have a staggering number of customers who never pay us back, so what?

"I think payday loans alone could move us back to being profitable at least a year ahead of schedule, maybe more. But I don't know how I feel about them..." Eric trailed off again. This time, he seemed to be finished.

His father ended the silence. "Well, it's true that people do like to gripe about high interest and late fees. But nothing's stopping them from paying their balances off, and paying on time.

"Cutting limits on groups of people is tricky—you're right. But if it helps the company, it helps the company. I did a great many things in my career that I might not have done if I'd been playing with my own money. Of course, sometimes I said 'the heck with the shareholders.'

"I've read about payday lenders. Some columnists call it usury. Quick: Which circle did Dante put the usurers in?"

"What?"

"*Inferno*, son, *Inferno*. Which circle?"

"Oh, man. You made me read that, what, 20 years ago?"

"True enough. Which circle?"

"I dunno. Third?"

"Third! What, with the Gluttons?"

"OK, OK! Fifth?"

"What?! With the Wrathful and Sullen?"

"I give up! I yield!" Eric said, holding his hands before his face and laughing.

"Seventh. The Usurers are in the seventh circle."

"Ah. With the...Harpies?"

"You DO remember! My boy!" They were both laughing, now. "Of course, it...might not be wise to let a fourteenth-century poet guide your decisions on twenty-first-century finance."

"You think, Dad?"

"I do, I do. Look, Eric, payday loans have high fees, that's true. But if you have no money, and you need it, and if you can't get it anywhere else, then who's to say that you shouldn't get a payday loan? If your customers are adults, and if the fees are worth it to them, then I don't know..."

Both men fell silent for awhile.

"Look, Eric...you've been a good boy all your life. You'll know what to do."

"Thanks, Dad. You know, I think you're right."

"Of course I'm right. And I'll bet the third quarter is just about ready." Eric's father turned the radio back on. The Aggies had the ball on their own 20. Father and son leaned back and listened to the second half.

DISCUSSION QUESTIONS

1. Do you favor Eric's company raising the standard interest rate on their credit cards from 17 percent to 25 percent? Why or why not?

   _____

   _____

   _____

   _____

2. Do you favor lowering credit limits for customers in "at-risk" demographics?

   _____

   _____

   _____

   _____

3. Is there any difference in lowering the credit limit for someone whose personal behavior has placed him or her in an "at-risk" demographic? For example, is it more fair to cut the limit of someone who buys a lot of luxury items than it is to cut the rate for someone who is in a profession that recently laid off a large number of workers?

   _____

   _____

   _____

   _____

4. Should Eric's company get into the payday loan business?

   _____

   _____

   _____

   _____

5. Although a few states make high-interest payday loans illegal, the majority do not. Should Congress or state lawmakers in the other states place limits on acceptable interest rates? If so, what is the maximum annual rate of interest that you find acceptable?

   _____

   _____

   _____

   _____

MODULE **43**

"Microinsurance"

When I was an undergraduate, and then a law student, I expected to have a wide variety of new expenses come my way after graduation. I expected a car payment when I upgraded my aging car. I expected to spend a fair amount on professional clothes. I expected to have a larger entertainment budget to cover nicer restaurants and football season tickets. But one big expense I didn't see coming, which now eats up a sizeable portion of my overall budget, was insurance.

I am 37 years old and in good health. My family is also in good health. I have never had a claim on my car policy, and my home is within $5,000 of the national median value. Yet…my family's health insurance policy is $12,500 per year. Fortunately, my employer picks up all but about $5,000 of that. Our car insurance is about $1,000—$500 per car. (This is the only one that is actually cheaper than when I was a student. In a single year, I got married, turned 25, and traded in my Z28 Camaro on a Volvo. I was rewarded with a stunning reduction on my next bill.) Our home insurance is about $2,000. For dental insurance, we pay about $1,000. For long-term disability and a couple of other things, we pay about $1,000 total. We lay out about $10,000 per year out-of-pocket for "basic" insurance coverage.

Although I'd prefer to pay less, on a fundamental level I'm not bothered by these policies because they cover potential situations that I can't afford to handle on my own. If my car is stolen, for example, I can't conveniently buy another one.

To members of past generations, this was generally the reason for buying insurance. In recent years, though, there has been a significant shift in the way Americans think about money, and it has resulted in a thriving new business that I think of as "microinsurance."

What Is Microinsurance?

Whenever I buy electronics, furniture, or most anything that costs over $100, I am asked by a clerk or an online ordering system if I'd like to buy an "extended warranty" or an "extended service plan." These kinds of offers on smaller items have proliferated dramatically in recent years.

Most products come with manufacturers' warranties at no charge. If a product doesn't work properly when purchased because of a manufacturing defect, most items are covered. Extended warranties enhance and extend typical manufacturers' warranties for an additional charge. They cover situations that basic warranties don't. Many of these plans cover power surges and "ordinary wear and tear." Some offer to replace items for almost any reason other than reckless or intentional destruction.

I've just finished my Christmas shopping for this year. The two "big" items I bought were an $800 TV and a $200 Nintendo Wii. The extended warranties for these things were $90 and $35, respectively.

"The House Always Wins"

As long as odds are correctly assessed by actuaries, experience, luck, or some combination of the three, businesses that offer insurance make money. Many are very profitable. As they say in Las Vegas: "the house always wins." A casino may lose money one weekend if a player hits a big jackpot. But over time, the odds of blackjack, roulette, and everything else favor the casino and generate profits.

In the same way, an insurance company that covers drivers may have a bad month in which many policyholders have accidents and it pays out more than it takes in. But over the long term, it will take in more in premiums than it pays out in claims. Microinsurance involves smaller amounts of money per transaction, but the idea is the same.

A generation ago, there was a much smaller market for microinsurance, primarily because people saved more money. An average household saved over 10 percent of its income in the 1980s. For some years in the 2000s, households had an average negative savings rate—they spent everything they made and a bit more. Also, an average household today carries more than $10,000 in credit card debt.

A generation ago, a typical customer would have declined microinsurance on a $500 item because he would likely have thought, "Well, even if this breaks, I can afford to buy another one." Today, customers are much more likely to pay a bit extra for microinsurance because they typically have little in savings and are thus much more likely to think, "I can't conveniently cover the $500 cost of a new one if this one breaks."

Insurance, regardless of what it covers, offers predictability and peace of mind. It smoothes out peaks and valleys in one's financial life. Two interesting ethical questions arise: (1) how much of a profit should an insurance company typically make? and (2) how should risks be presented to customers? The interesting trick, as is often the case, is to draw the line between offering a valuable service and gouging customers.

Note: Most of the large companies that offer extended service plans make a smaller profit than the one described in the scenario in this module.

SCENARIO

Big Al's Electronic Emporium

Alan punched in his code above the door handle, heard a faint click, and opened the door with the "Employees Only" sign. He left the showroom floor behind him and headed up a staircase to the second floor of Big Al's Electronic Emporium. On the top floor, he passed a security room where a bored guard watched customers through one-way glass on the floor below.

"Any action today?" Alan asked him. The guard turned slowly, shook his head, and turned away.

Alan passed two managers' offices and came to the break room, which also offered a view of the first floor through one-way glass.

"Kid!" Alan was enthusiastically greeted by a man in a plaid blazer. A gold nametag on the coat pocket read "Morty" in large capital letters and "25 years of service" in smaller letters below. "Siddown!" Morty patted the chair beside his, and Alan wandered over to it. "How are ya, kid?"

"Fine, Mr. Johnson."

"Morty! How many times do I have to tell you it's Morty?!"

"Fine…Morty."

"There you go!" Morty took a heroic bite of a ham sandwich. A small dab of mustard was left clinging to his lower lip. "So, kid. How's business today?"

"It's good…Mr.…Morty," Alan said. "I sold a refrigerator and two HDTVs this morning."

"Say, that's great! How big?"

"The TVs? Ah…46 inches."

"Not bad! What kind?"

"Sony."

"Sony!"

"Yeah. Yeah, I think I'm starting to get the hang of this. One of the ladies told me that her friend bought a TV from me last week, and that she ought to…"

"Yeah, referrals are great, kid," Morty interrupted. He trailed off and took another bite of his sandwich. Alan decided not to continue with his story and ate in silence.

"Hey, kid. Lemme ask you a question."

"OK, sure."

"How long do you want to work here?"

Alan paused and gave a quick glance at the "25 years" part of Morty's nametag. "Um…well, I guess at least until I graduate. I'm a sophomore now. The money's pretty good, and it would be nice to take out smaller loans. I…"

"I was talking to Big Al about you a couple days ago."

"You were?"

"Oh, sure. Big Al and I have been tight from the beginning. I was the third person he ever hired, you know. We talk about everybody."

"Wow. So what did he say?"

"He likes you, kid. He thinks you're a natural with the customers. He told me that you move a lot of merchandise for a new guy."

"Hey, that's good. Good to hear."

"Yeah. But you've got a problem, kid."

"I do?"

"Yes…you do. And you won't last six months if you don't fix it. You want to know what your problem is, kid?"

"Yes. Definitely."

"OK. When you sold that fridge today, did you sell 'em an extended service plan?"

"No. No, I offered it, but they just didn't want it."

"Uh, huh. And what about the two HDTVs? Service plan for either one?"

"Ah…no. They didn't want one, either."

"Do you realize that Big Al makes most of his money off of service plans?"

Alan thought about that for a while. "Really?"

"Really."

"But those things are cheap compared to…practically everything we sell."

"True, but practically everything we sell is sold at cost. Big Al has to compete with Walmart and Best Buy. His prices have to stay at least in the neighborhood of their prices, so he marks up a TV that costs him $900 to maybe $939, but probably not even that much."

"Wow."

"Yeah, but the service plan, that's almost pure profit. We sell a big TV for $939, and sell them a service plan for $99 on top of that if we can, right?"

"Right."

"OK, so do that 100 times. That makes for about $10,000 in service plans. Now, out of the 100 customers, maybe one guy has a problem that we have to cover where his set has to be replaced. The manufacturer's warranty covers a lot of replacements because, if a new set doesn't work at all, it's usually because it was defectively made. But sometimes one gets broken in a way that we have to pay for. So, OK, we're out $900 on that one."

"OK." Alan had forgotten his lunch altogether.

"OK, so maybe 5 out of the 100 have a repair of some kind that we have to cover."

"Only 5?"

"Maybe a few more, but people—most people—take good care of their big TV. It's their baby! So, anyway, a few repairs—say another grand down the drain, total. That leaves Big Al with $8,000 out of the $10,000 extended service plan money in his pocket. So Big Al...can you do the numbers, kid?"

"He makes $39 from the TV, and $80 from the service plan," Alan said.

"Bingo! He gets it!"

"Wow. I had no idea."

"Now you know. So, you see, the amount of merchandise you sell is OK. It's about average. But you're only making one-third of each sale because you almost never sell somebody on the service plan."

"That's true. I mean, I always offer it like they said to in training, but..."

"What do you say when you offer it?"

"Well," Alan thought. "I guess I just ask if they want the plan, and give them a price."

"Oh, kid," Morty said, shaking his head. He checked his gold watch. "Look, I've got 15 minutes left on my break. How about a crash course in selling those plans?"

"Oh, I don't know, Morty. I mean..."

"Kid, this is a limited-time offer. I'm trying to save you here—you've got to sell those plans."

"I appreciate it. It's just...is it fair to charge them?"

"Oh! Moralizing on me! Is this what they're teaching in college these days?"

"Well, actually, I am taking an ethics class this semester. I've got this guy, Bredeson—he's really goofy-looking, but the class..."

"Yeah, they've got lots of bright ideas at colleges. Look, do you want the advice or not?"

Alan looked through the one-way glass at the customers below. His focus shifted, and he studied his own reflection in the glass for a moment.

"OK, Morty," he watched himself say.

On the Sales Floor–Later that Day

Alan sold three more HDTVs that afternoon. All three customers initially declined when he offered them an extended service plan. Alan talked them into buying the service plans with the following statements.

Customer 1

The first customer was a woman with two small children. As she and Alan were talking about the extended service plan, one of her children bumped into a display table and nearly knocked it over. Alan said, "You know, if he knocks the TV over and it breaks, the extended service plan will buy you a new one."

This was a true statement. Earlier, Morty told Alan, "Most of the time when we have to cover a broken set, somebody's kid has knocked it over or thrown a ball at it or something like that."

Customer 2

When the second customer declined the service plan, Alan said, "You know, these new 1080p sets have a lot of pixels. Sometimes one freezes up or goes dark—makes it kind of irritating to watch, especially with sports. You said you'd be watching a lot of sports on this set? The extended service plan would fix or replace your TV if anything like that happened."

His statement was again true. The customer thought for a moment and then agreed to buy the service plan.

Earlier, Morty told Alan, "I've only had one guy who ever had a frozen pixel, and that was five years ago. The TVs we sell are rock solid by the time the manufacturers get done testing them. But customers will buy the idea that one little spot *might* fail, and you're not lying when you tell them the warranty would cover that kind of problem, even though it's a 1,000-to-1 odds that it happens to them."

Customer 3

When the third customer declined the service plan, Alan again said, "You know, these new 1080p sets have a lot of pixels. Sometimes one freezes up or goes dark—makes it kind of irritating to watch, especially with sports. You said you'd be watching a lot of sports on this set? The extended service plan would fix or replace your TV if anything like that happened."

This customer then asked him, "Does that happen very often?"

Alan replied, "I don't know. I just started working here."

DISCUSSION QUESTIONS

1. In this scenario, the store sells a service plan for about $100 on a $900 HDTV. On average, it pays out $20 for actual service and replacements and keeps an average of $80. Is the $100 price appropriate?

_____

_____

_____

_____

2. Building on the example in the first question, what is the highest charge that would be appropriate? Circle your answer below.

$20 --- $40 --- $60 --- $80 --- $100 --- $125 --- $150 --- $200 --- $250 --- As Much as People Will Pay

3. Is Alan's statement to Customer 1 ethical?

_____

_____

_____

_____

4. Is Alan's statement to Customer 2 ethical?

_____

_____

_____

_____

5. Is Alan's statement to Customer 3 ethical?

_____

_____

_____

_____

Using "Bad" Things to Boost Profits

Sports are big business in America. The NFL, NBA, MLB, and NHL had a total revenue of over $10 billion in 2008. TV is also big business. The major networks—ABC, CBS, NBC, and Fox—brought in a similar amount of revenue in 2008. But by many estimates, pornography brought in more money than either the four major sports leagues combined or the four TV networks combined—nearly $14 billion in the United States, and nearly $100 billion worldwide.

This fact is surprising to many people. After all, there is no pornography section in the newspaper. People don't wear pornography jerseys around town. Major cities don't have pornography stadiums that seat 80,000 people. It seems impossible that a largely hidden industry can be so large, yet it is.

The largest barrier to the widespread dissemination of pornography—an unfriendly legal environment—has largely disappeared in recent decades. For much of our nation's history, pornography was regulated quite heavily. Puritans did not have *Penthouse*. At one time, possession of "lewd images" could bring public flogging and lengthy stretches of hard labor. Even into the mid-1900s, many states had laws covering pornography with harsh punishments attached to them. This began to change with a series of Supreme Court decisions involving the U.S. Constitution and free speech rights.

The Constitution contains absolute rules; no other kinds of laws can violate constitutional standards. The First Amendment to the Constitution says that "Congress shall make no law…abridging the freedom of speech." For most of the nation's history, the Supreme Court applied free speech rights to political discussion but not much else.

As the twentieth century unfolded, though, the Court began to apply First Amendment protection to pornography, extremely insensitive works of art, and demonstrations involving burning the American flag in protest, among other things. The justices began to take the view that almost any form of communication that does not do direct harm to others ought to be protected as "free speech."

With pornography, there remain a few lines that cannot be crossed. The Court will allow for the regulation of some violent images, for example. Child pornography can be banned as "obscene," but in recent years, a number of laws that have sought to ban pornography more broadly have been deemed unconstitutional by the courts and voided.

Many groups argue that pornography is exploitative and harmful to society and that it ought to be less widely available. But until and unless the Supreme Court revisits its views on the First Amendment, substantial new regulation of the industry is unlikely.

SCENARIO

Mr. Allen's Office

"Glen, good to see you."

"Good morning, Mr. Allen."

"My father always spoke highly of you. 'When in doubt, listen to Glen,' he would say."

"He was a remarkable man, Mr. Allen."

"That he was. So you have some ideas for me?"

"Yes, sir, I do. I should start by telling you that I presented these same ideas to your father several years ago, and he rejected them. But in my opinion, there is an even stronger financial case to be made for them now."

"I loved my father, but I am not him. Go right ahead."

"Yes, sir. Looking at the two largest assets you've inherited—the hotel chain and the trust fund—the largest single revenue booster would be from…" Glen trailed off.

"Would be from…?" Allen encouraged him.

"Pornography. Sir."

"Pornography?"

"Yes, sir."

"As in, videos…and such…of people…"

"Yes, sir."

"You're serious?"

"Yes, sir."

Allen made a grimace, but said, "Go on."

"Yes, sir. Your hotels already have pay-per-view devices in nearly every room. Guests pay on the order of $10 to watch movies that have recently been in theaters and $5 for kids' movies. You more or less break even on them—the cost of maintaining the infrastructure is nearly identical to the revenue produced. But if you add pornography…"

Allen interrupted him, "And when you say pornography, just to be clear, you are not talking about R-rated films."

"Correct."

"These would be…films…of…"

"People having sex."

Allen grimaced again. "Proceed."

"Yes, sir. If you add pornography to the mix, your revenue will increase dramatically."

"Why?"

"Because people will pay more, a lot more, for adult films. We can charge $20–$40 per film, and an average viewer of pornography will be more likely to order more than one film per stay. An average guest now on a three-night stay watches one movie for one of the nights he stays, so he spends $10. An average pornography viewer will spend, we estimate, $95 during a three-night stay."

"But the others, I mean the big hotel chains, don't offer this kind of thing…"

"A lot of them do, sir. Some do and some don't, and it's not as if those that do make it part of their ads, but many of your competitors do indeed offer pay-per-view porn in-room."

"And how much do they make?"

"About an extra 10 percent in overall revenue. More than the extra take from their minibars, for example. And the 10 percent would be almost pure profit for you because there is nothing for you to buy. You already have the hardware in your rooms."

"And what would an extra 10 percent be in, you know, dollars?"

"$20 million per year, straight to your pocket."

Allen's mouth came open. "You're kidding."

"Give or take."

"$20 million?"

"Yes, sir."

"But won't we lose some of our customers who don't like that we offer porn? Maybe start a boycott against us?"

"We will lose a few, Mr. Allen. Based on the experiences of our competitors, I'd estimate that we'll lose perhaps 1 guest in 200 who stays somewhere else specifically because of the porn issue. The risk of a more organized boycott is small. Remember that a lot of our competitors—larger competitors—already offer this service. Even if there is an organized boycott, surely a bigger fish would be the target."

Allen sat still for a moment. "No legal problems?"

"No, sir."

"Hmm…" Allen thought for awhile, and Glen let him think. Eventually, Allen said, "You have other ideas for me, you said?"

"Yes, sir. Your other major new asset is the trust fund. It is substantial, and it is invested conservatively. Lots of bonds, some blue-chip stock. I would advise you to consider putting a portion of its assets into investments with a higher yield. There is no reason to settle for a 4 percent return."

"I suppose not. And your ideas for the money involve pornography?"

"It's the issue of the day, sir. I have two items for your consideration. First, there is a company for sale at a very good price that distributes pornography. You could acquire it by liquidating about 25 percent of your trust fund. This company is the major supplier of magazines and DVDs on the East Coast, and it has a major presence in Internet distribution. As with the pay-per-view idea for your hotels, I estimate that this investment would increase your annual return by roughly $20 million."

"But Glen, with both of these ideas…don't get me wrong, $20 million each sounds terrific, I mean, I'd like to buy a nice European soccer club someday…but doesn't pornography…hurt people?"

"Some make that assertion. Look, Mr. Allen, I can come back next week with a presentation on anything you want if this makes you uncomfortable. But consider two things. First, if you don't do this, someone else will just do it anyway. And, second, there is nothing illegal about anything we'd show in the hotels or distribute. Nothing with underage actors, nothing with violence, just mainstream, 100 percent legal stuff."

"I don't know, Glen."

"Some people condemn tobacco companies, alcohol manufacturers, and casinos. All three are highly profitable industries providing legal goods and services that people want and that employ tens of thousands of people each."

"I just don't know. What's your other proposal?"

"Another company up for sale. The founder wants to cash in his chips and retire. This one produces pornography…"

"Oh, come ON!"

"Sir?"

"I'm not going to, you know…MAKE this stuff."

"That is your decision to make, sir. I am merely presenting options."

"I mean, what would my father have said?"

"He rejected all of my proposals along these lines."

"Yeah. Dad just wouldn't have gone near anything like this."

"That is very true, sir."

"And I suppose the production company is the most valuable of your ideas?"

"It is, sir."

"OK, go ahead and give me the numbers."

"For a price that can be met by liquidating a further 25 percent of your trust's assets, I would estimate an additional $45 million in your pocket per year."

"Forty-five?"

"Yes, sir. Actually, perhaps more. Think of the benefits of controlling all three parts of the supply chain, Mr. Allen. Think of the possibilities if you adopt all three of my proposals. You can assess what kinds of films your customers want by analyzing the data from your hotel's pay-per-view sales. You can then create more films that will appeal to your customers' tastes. And by owning the distribution company, you would eliminate the middleman. Individually, these ideas are worth something on the order of $85 million. Together? Comfortably into nine figures additional annual income. That's Manchester United money, sir."

"Don't like the Red Devils."

"OK, so buy Liverpool. Or any team at all."

"I appreciate what you're trying to do, Glen, but my reputation..."

"Mr. Allen, can you name a single person involved in the pornography industry?"

"Name one?"

"Yes, sir. Do any 'famous' pornographers come to mind?"

"Ah...at the moment, no."

"And yet, there must be thousands of millionaires out there. It is a $100 billion global business."

"I...suppose so."

"I assure you that it would all be very anonymous. The production company isn't called 'Porn, Inc.' It has a generic name, and it produces some independent films that are strictly PG. The distribution company also has a generic name and distributes plenty of 'regular' entertainment. Your hotels would still provide all of the lodging services that have always been provided. No one will pay attention to the fact that you hold a stake in the adult film industry."

"But what if the press turns it up? Does a feature story?"

"No one will care."

Allen sat without speaking for a long while. Eventually, Glen brought him out of his silent musings. "I'll leave you with some supporting documents, Mr. Allen," he said. "I have no stake in this. If you reject these ideas, I'll propose other ways to grow your money whenever you request."

"Yes. Yes, thanks for coming by, Glen. I do need to do some thinking. Thanks very much."

"My pleasure, sir. I'll show myself out."

Glen picked up his briefcase, stood, and left the office. Allen stared blankly straight ahead.

DISCUSSION QUESTIONS

1. Should Allen approve the showing of X-rated pay-per-view movies in his hotel's rooms?

   _____

   _____

   _____

   _____

2. Would your answer to the first question be any different if the hotels were failing and the addition of X-rated movies was a way to keep the hotels out of bankruptcy?

   _____

   _____

   _____

   _____

3. Should Allen acquire the pornography distribution company? Why or why not?

_____

_____

_____

_____

4. Should Allen acquire the pornography production company? Why or why not?

_____

_____

_____

_____

5. Rate tobacco companies and producers of pornography on the following scale:

	Should be Illegal ←————————→ Completely Acceptable
Tobacco Companies	1 --- 2 --- 3 --- 4 --- 5 --- 6 --- 7
Pornographers	1 --- 2 --- 3 --- 4 --- 5 --- 6 --- 7

If your ratings are different, why is one higher than the other?

_____

_____

_____

_____

Store Cards, Search Engines, and Customer Data

Several years ago, I switched grocery stores. I had been a loyal customer at, let's call it "Store A," for many years. But then the store began pushing hard to have all customers sign up for a store discount card. At the register, the first question wasn't "Did you find everything you needed?", "How are you?", or even "Paper or plastic?", but rather, "Can I have your discount card?" When I replied, "I don't have a discount card," the reply was generally, "Here, you can apply for one while I scan your groceries." When I said I didn't want a store card, it usually took a few rounds of discussion before the checker started scanning my food. Eventually, I gave up and started going to "Store B."

My reason for declining the store card was this: I don't like junk mail. I really, really don't like it. I do not want store circulars. I do not want coupons. I do not want catalogues. I do not want anything other than my magazines, checks from my publisher, and holiday greetings from my family and friends. It depresses me when I receive pound upon pound of trash.

Store cards often generate junk mail. Stores use them to create a record of everything customers buy on every visit. Sometimes, the stores themselves use this data. But often, stores sell the data to others who are willing to pay handsomely for lists of customers who use their products or who use their competitors' products. And the lists usually include home addresses.

This use of store card data is an old one. But, recently, some data has been used in a new way that bothers me less but seems to bother some people more.

Salmonella Outbreak

In 2010, the Centers for Disease Control (CDC) investigated an outbreak of salmonella. When such an outbreak occurs, the CDC frequently questions ill patients and seeks to determine whether they have purchased similar foods or eaten at similar restaurants. By working backward, the CDC can often pinpoint a source that is causing widespread illness.

But interviews that rely on the recollection of patients who are feeling poorly are notoriously inexact. Patients often give incomplete or even incorrect answers, which can delay pattern recognition. During the 2010 outbreak, the government tried a new tactic. It asked for grocery store card data on patients with salmonella poisoning. After analyzing the data, the CDC was able to efficiently pinpoint the likely cause as a particular brand of salami and then place the blame on the pepper that was an ingredient in some varieties of the salami.

In all cases, the CDC asked for the patients' permission to access the store card data. But some privacy advocates feared a slippery slope; they feared that, because of the success of the salmonella inquiry, the government might not ask next time. The CDC dismissed such concerns.

Beyond Store Cards

Lots of companies have mountains of data on their customers. Credit card issuers know what you buy, and your cable company knows what you watch on television. Your Internet service provider knows where you go online, and the search engines you use know what you are interested in. Many people hire services that back up *all* data on their computers online.

In some cases, laws exist that require companies to give out information on customers. But in others, companies are free to comply with or refuse requests. The following scenario portrays a company responding to the CDC story summarized in the previous section. Assume that LightSpeed is a search engine, and that like most search engines, it creates and retains a record of every search done by every user. LightSpeed is run by its founders Dan and Laura Smith, who are brother and sister.

SCENARIO

LightSpeed

"Did you see this?" Dan asked his sister.

"What's that?" Laura replied as she spread cream cheese on a bagel. Dan tossed a newspaper across the table. Laura gestured at her eyes. "No glasses. Summarize."

Dan sighed. "All right. So remember that salmonella outbreak last month?"

"Yep," Laura said, chewing.

"The CDC solved it by tracking customers' purchases from store card data. They figured out that it was pepper, or something."

"Mm hmm. OK, so…what's your point?"

"My point is, what should we do if the government asks for our customers' data? What if the CDC wants to know the names of everyone who has been searching for information on particular symptoms? That's happened to Google already. What if they want to sift through all the searches that everyone has made?"

"Well," Laura said, "I guess we hand it over."

"Yeah, yeah, if it's required. If a judge orders us to release data, we'll release data. But the thing about the salmonella outbreak is that the stores *didn't have to hand it over*. The CDC just asked them for it, and they chose to give it up."

"Oh."

"Yeah. So the question is: What if it's optional? What if we are asked for our customers' data, and we are allowed to either release it or not?"

"Well, I guess…we should ask the customers' permission."

"We already have it for all the people who had LightSpeed preinstalled on their computers. They clicked a long 'I agree' box, and it included complete rights for us to track and make use of their search data."

"We should ask them more directly than that."

"Maybe. But we don't need to, not legally. But, anyway, what if the government asks us for data, and our customers say, 'No, thanks'? Or what if the government needs data right away to make any use of it, and we don't have time to ask everyone for permission?"

"Well…" Laura said as she started on the second half of her bagel. "I guess it depends on what they need it for. I mean, if they say, 'terrorists are planning an attack, and we need to see who has been searching for a particular chemical that we think might be used to make a bomb,' then I'm OK with it."

"But that's just the thing. Hardly anyone searching for information on the chemical would be an actual terrorist, and a lot of our customers would fall under suspicion."

"Maybe."

"Here's a more specific example. Last month, you looked up 'methamphetamine ingredients.'"

"I wanted to know what's in that stuff after we saw that thing on the news."

"Right. Did you find the, ah, recipe?"

"Yeah. All right, point taken. Like almost everyone who does a search on meth, I was not doing so for the purpose of cooking up a batch myself. Blah, blah, blah. But if I haven't actually done anything wrong, why would I worry if someone knew that I looked up methamphetamine ingredients?"

"Because you, my friend, are a nerd."

"I have a husband who disagrees. Nerd."

"I am also a nerd. No question. But, Laura, you don't care if the cops see that you have been searching for meth ingredients because absolutely no one on earth would suspect you of being a meth dealer. You feel 'safe' because…because, it's just laughable…"

"It's not that laughable."

"It is. But you might *not* want the government to know if you had been searching for 'offshore tax havens' or 'avoiding income taxes.'"

"I haven't done searches on those things."

"But if you had innocently looked something like that up after seeing a news report, you might be more uneasy."

"Maybe. Maybe so—I'm not sure, really."

"See?"

"I said 'maybe.'"

"Look. I just think that our policy should be that, if it is optional, we should always keep our customers' data private."

"You know I don't like 'always' and 'never' rules, Dan. I mean, sometimes, yes, I can see that it would be sensible to turn the government down. But other times…I mean take the salmonella outbreak, since you just brought it up. That was a good thing. They used data to figure out what was causing the salmonella, they got it off the shelves, and a lot of people avoided a serious illness, right? A few people probably literally had their lives saved. If something like that comes up, why wouldn't we try to help?"

"I just think the potential for abuse is too high. The store cards at least track…real things that real people acquired in the real world. But we deal in information. Our customers leave a record of what interests them, but not what they've done. If we turn over our data, we're revealing what our customers are *thinking*."

"That's true. Sort of. But I can still envision a scenario where knowing what people are thinking might help people in the real world. I think we should just decide what to do if and when this ever comes up. I don't think we need a policy ahead of time."

"But what if our customers want one? More and more companies release their customers' data to the government all the time. What if some customers are concerned by that? What if some of them would be more loyal to us if we told them up front, 'we will never voluntarily release any information about you to anyone outside of LightSpeed.'"

"Well, if *that's* true, then we should talk about it more. I'm assuming that you are just speculating that it *might* be something our customers want?"

"Yeah."

"Well, assign someone to cook up a survey. If the market *really* wants a strict privacy policy, then I would be delighted to consider creating one. Fair enough?"

"Fair enough, Laura," Dan said.

DISCUSSION QUESTIONS

1. Did the CDC make appropriate use of store card data in the real salmonella case outlined at the beginning of this module?

_____

_____

_____

_____

2. Would you be comfortable with the CDC accessing store card data in a future case if it did not ask permission of sick patients ahead of time?

_____

_____

_____

_____

3. Should LightSpeed create a policy against ever voluntarily turning over customer data?

_____

_____

_____

_____

4. Assume that the search engine you use most often released a list of all searches done by all users to the government. Assume further that users' names were attached to each list. Would you be at all uneasy? Would you be less likely to use that search engine in the future?

_____

_____

_____

_____

5. The government aside, are you bothered by companies that sell your information to other companies? Are you less likely to buy items and services from companies that spread around your phone number, address, and other personal information?

_____

_____

_____

_____

"Least-Profitable Customers"

In 2010, tremendous media attention was focused on Congress and proposed changes to the health care system. In the end, by a small number of votes, a substantial new law was passed and signed into law by President Obama. This module is not about the new law, but it opens with an example that is related to it.

Cancelled Policies

Behind the scenes in 2010, other parts of the government were aggressively pursuing health insurance companies accused of cancelling the policies of sick patients. Regulators accused WellPoint of using software to flag all policyholders who had been diagnosed with breast cancer and then seeking to invent justifications for dropping them from coverage. Similar accusations were made against Assurant Health for its alleged actions toward HIV-positive patients.

Rescission of policies is perfectly legal if a policyholder has lied to an insurance company and committed fraud, but government investigators found that some companies were overzealous in their claims of sick patients' misrepresentations. The game, they said, was to seek out very small errors on complicated application forms whenever patients were diagnosed with certain expensive-to-treat conditions.

In cases involving life-and-death, moral judgments are easier to make. If a patient becomes ill, has her insurance coverage cancelled on a pretext, and dies because she cannot afford proper treatment, it is easy and natural to call the insurance company's actions "bad."

But all companies must remain profitable in order to continue to exist.[1] Health insurance companies may have an unusual relationship with their customers, and it may be wrongful that a few of them seem to attain profitability on the backs of their sickest patients, but a path to profits must be found.

---

[1] Even those like Chrysler that receive government bailouts must eventually recover or perish, one would presume.

The Broader Issue

This module examines more mundane situations in which the consequences are not life-and-death. This central issue for debate is, *What obligations, if any, does a company have to its least-profitable customers?* Most businesses make a large share of their profits from a fairly small percentage of customers. "Regulars" are often rewarded with discounts, special attention, and other perks. But what about customers in the bottom 10 percent? What about customers from whom a firm makes no money, or even loses money from dealing with them? Is a "regular" firm obligated to treat all of its customers the same, or is it ethically acceptable to identify and drop those customers who are not profitable?

This issue cuts across virtually every industry. Some kinds of businesses have an easier time finding their least-profitable customers, and some businesses have an easier time disentangling themselves from their least-profitable customers than others. But, in the end, most all companies deal with a "drag" from customers who must be either run off or compensated for.

Specific Company Types Profiled in the Scenarios

Several types of companies are more inclined to try to get rid of "deadbeats." Among them are:

Credit Card Companies: Large issuers of credit cards earn billions in late fees and interest payments on balances that are "carried forward." Customers who pay balances in full every month generate a small amount of revenue (retailers pay credit card companies a small fee with every transaction), but not enough to keep the credit card company going. Some companies in this industry may be the first anywhere that internally referred to responsible customers as "deadbeats."

Oil Change Businesses: To the chagrin of grandfathers everywhere, most Americans do not change their own oil. But oil change businesses make relatively little profit from oil changes themselves. Most make $10 or less per customer per oil change, and some aggressively price the service to make almost no profit at all. The real profits come from changing air filters, performing scheduled maintenance, conducting emissions testing, and the like. Employees have been known to give customers who order only an oil change the stink eye.

Sports Franchises: Countless professional sports stadiums have been demolished and replaced in recent decades. (I still get somewhat nauseated when recalling images of the original Busch Stadium being imploded. I mean, come on, I went to games with my Dad there. I'm still really quite bloody angry about the whole thing.) The driving force behind many stadium upgrades has been skyboxes and other premium seating that generate substantially more revenue per fan.

Apartment Complexes: Landlords deal with two kinds of "least-profitable customer." The first type can be created when rents fluctuate. If a city grows rapidly, and if the construction of new apartments does not keep up with demand, rents can spike upward sharply. In such a scenario, a landlord may have, for example, established tenants paying $700 a month for a one-bedroom apartment, but the landlord may be able to set the rent for new tenants at $1,000 per month. Additionally, owners of apartments face losses from tenants who do not care for their apartments. Security deposits can sometimes help owners avoid losses, but if a tenant causes $1,500 in damage and originally had only a $750 security deposit, a landlord may have to pay the difference out of his own pocket.

Fast Food Restaurants: Businesses that offer cheap food have a tendency to attract large numbers of young people, particularly at night and on weekends. And when large numbers of young people mingle at night and on weekends, interesting developments sometimes ensue...

Department Stores: "Compulsive shopping" is a genuine medical diagnosis that is more common than most people realize. A surprising number of people regularly take massive shopping sprees and then return most or all of their purchases later. And large numbers of returns can be an expensive problem. Clerks are tied up, and items may be difficult to resell because they are no longer in mint condition or because their applicable season has passed.

SCENARIOS

Credit Card Company—Boardroom

"We don't see much more room to increase revenue from the balance-carriers," said the vice president. "We need to explore increasing revenue from our customers who pay their balances off every month. Effective immediately, we will flag all accounts that have paid the last 12 consecutive statements on time and in full. Those customers will get notices that will require them to pay an annual fee of $125 in order to continue as cardholders."

"Most of them won't stand for that," a junior executive said. "They'll cancel their accounts."

"That doesn't bother me in the slightest," the vice president replied. "We are a business. We offer a service, and we have the reasonable expectation of making a reasonable profit from it. If a customer's habits and inclinations do not provide that reasonable profit, we don't want them."

Super Fast Oil Change—Manager's Office

"You wanted to see me, Mr. Magee?" asked the associate.

"Bob, come in, sit down. And close the door."

"Yes, sir."

"Got something for you," Mr. Magee said, pointing to a sort of wheeled podium that had a laptop secured to the top. "Your new mobile workstation."

"Ah. Thanks, Mr. McGee. It looks great."

"Yes. Now here's how I want you to use it. Wheel it back about halfway between the entrances to the service bays and the start of the parking lot. We'll set up a little area for you with a stop sign. Now, when a customer pulls up to you, you type in her license plate number, and a record of all her past visits will pop up on your screen."

"OK," Bob said, scribbling on a notepad.

"Right. So if it's a new customer, or if she's purchased a lot of services from us on her previous visits, I want you to direct her to service bay 1 or 2, whichever has the shorter line."

"OK."

"These will be our...kind of...express lanes. We're going to have a full crew and will try to work fast in those bays."

"Yes, sir."

"Now, if somebody pulls up, and your screen tells you he only orders oil changes when he visits us, you direct him to bay 3."

"Bay 3," Bob mumbled as he added to his notes.

"Right. That's going to be our slow lane. No three-man crews—we're just going to have Roger down in the pit."

"Ha!"

"Hey! Roger'll get it done...eventually."

"But boss, don't'cha think the bay 3 people will be mad?"

"Eh," Mr. Magee replied, shrugging his shoulders.

Baseball Team—Executive Offices

"What about bleacher seats?"

"We're deemphasizing them in the new ballpark. I think the latest plans call for 1,000 of them."

"We have 5,000 of them right now."

"The luxury suite holders want a giant HD scoreboard and landscaping beyond the outfield wall, and that's what they're going to get."

"Won't that price a lot of fans out of coming to games?"

"Well, yeah, but don't worry. Our models show that we'll still sell out regularly."

Apartment Complex—Property Manager's Office

"If I'm going to get a good price for this property when I sell it in a year or two, I need more cash coming in," the owner said to her property manager. "So for now, I want you to do two things. Number one, I want you to send a notice to every month-to-month tenant who is paying less than $900 per month. We're not having any trouble renting every available unit at $1,000 per month. Give them a choice: agree to pay $1,000 per month or move out within 30 days. OK?"

"Can do," said the property manager.

"Number two, I want you to send the maintenance guys around to every unit. Anybody with anything more than minor damage inside who has a month-to-month lease gets a notice that he has 30 days to move out. Anybody with a long-term lease who has damage inside doesn't get renewed when the lease is up. No exceptions. I'm tired of taking a bath on repairs when some of these people move out."

"I'll start this afternoon," the property manager said.

Super Taco—Parking Lot

"You're banned from the restaurant," the manager said to the teenager with the ripped T-shirt.

"What do you mean I'm banned?" the teen replied.

"I mean you fight in my parking lot, you drive away my customers, and I won't stand for it!"

"You can't ban me from the restaurant!"

"You're banned! If you come back here, I'll have you arrested for trespassing. Now beat it!"

Department Store—Returns Register

"I've warned you before, Mrs. Smith," said the store director. "Repeatedly."

"Yes, but I've changed my mind."

"You've changed your mind many dozens of times this year."

"Your policy," Mrs. Smith said, pointing to a sign, "allows for returns for 60 days with receipt. I bought these clothes yesterday, and here's my receipt."

"We allow returns as a courtesy to our valued customers. The law does not require us to do so."

"I have my receipt," Mrs. Smith repeated, ignoring him. "Are you going to take these clothes back or not?"

"Yes, Mrs. Smith, we are going to accept your return."

"Well," she said. "That's very good."

"But after today, you are not welcome to return to the store."

"What?"

"I will be circulating a picture of you from our surveillance cameras to all clerks this afternoon. They will be instructed to refuse to ring up any purchases for you."

"You can't be serious!"

"I am quite serious. We are a private business, and we have the right to refuse service to any customer. I am refusing further service to you. Finish getting your refund and do not return."

DISCUSSION QUESTIONS

1. Many forms of discrimination are illegal. If a company treats customers differently based on race, for example, the company is in big trouble. But many forms of discrimination, such as those featured in this scenario, remain completely legal. Overall, does a company have an ethical obligation to treat all customers the same regardless of how much they spend, or does no such obligation exist?

_____

_____

_____

_____

2. Rate the moves the companies made that will be detrimental to classes of "low revenue" customers who did nothing "bad."

	Outrageous ←					→ Completely Reasonable
Credit Card Company	1 --- 2 --- 3 --- 4 --- 5 --- 6 --- 7					
Oil Change Business	1 --- 2 --- 3 --- 4 --- 5 --- 6 --- 7					
Baseball Team	1 --- 2 --- 3 --- 4 --- 5 --- 6 --- 7					
Apartments (low rent)	1 --- 2 --- 3 --- 4 --- 5 --- 6 --- 7					

3. Have you felt like you've been treated disrespectfully by a business because you failed to spend enough money? If so, what happened?

_____

_____

_____

_____

4. Rate the moves the companies made that will be detrimental to classes of "low revenue" customers who behaved badly. Are you more comfortable with companies targeting individuals with destructive behavior, or does that not make a difference in your mind?

	Outrageous ←					→ Completely Reasonable
Apartments (damage)	1 --- 2 --- 3 --- 4 --- 5 --- 6 --- 7					
Super Taco	1 --- 2 --- 3 --- 4 --- 5 --- 6 --- 7					
Department Store	1 --- 2 --- 3 --- 4 --- 5 --- 6 --- 7					

5. If a company chooses to try to purge its least-profitable customers, special care must be taken when _health and safety_ are involved. Affected customers are more likely to sue in such cases, they are substantially more likely to find a valid legal basis for their lawsuits, and large jury verdicts are also more likely to occur.

Consider the health insurance example in the background information. Assume that you are on a jury in a case in which you believe that a health insurance policy was wrongfully terminated and that a policyholder ultimately died as a result of being unable to afford proper treatment. Assume further that you are instructed that you may assign any amount you wish in the form of punitive damages.

How much money would you award the deceased person's family?

_____

_____

_____

_____

UNIT 9

Environmental Ethics

Unit Background

Few issues generate more passion than those surrounding the natural environment. People generally like conservation efforts, diminished levels of pollution, and "green" practices. But these things can be quite costly. Once a company has complied with the law, is it morally obligated to actively care for the environment?

Module 47

Dumping. [Some offshore practices are lightly regulated. What should a company do if it can save millions by "throwing things overboard"?]

Module 48

Environmental Disasters from the *Exxon Valdez* to BP. [What should a company do before an environmental disaster strikes to prevent a possible disaster? And if bad things have already happened, what should a company do to try to make things right?]

Module 49

Sustainability: Renewable Energy and "Green" Buildings. [Many companies purchase energy generated by renewable sources, and many more adopt environmentally friendly building and maintenance policies. But at what point, if any, do cost concerns override a desire to be green?]

Module 50

Animal Rights. [Do animals have rights? If so, are companies obligated to observe these rights? Are they the same for mammals as for insects?]

Module 51

"Perfectly Good" Items: Wasteful Business Practices. [In many situations, companies throw items away because it is cheaper than finding a way to make use of them. Should businesses go further to avoid wasteful practices?]

Environmental Ethics

Global warming, carbon footprints, greenhouse gases, cap and trade, pollution credits, renewable resources, sustainability: Many environmental causes have become everyday items for discussion. These issues are extremely important to vast numbers of people, and the modules in this unit deal with them.

Law tends to set minimum standards of conduct; it is fairly unusual for laws to require the "best" behavior. So, while there are many environmental regulations, companies can often go much further than the law demands. But, often, it is far cheaper to merely comply with the law, and do nothing further.

The opening module presents a simple decision about dumping waste. The second module takes a look at an environmental disaster along the lines of the *Exxon Valdez* leak and the BP problems in the Gulf of Mexico in the spring and summer of 2010. It examines ethical decision making in addressing environmental harm and decisions that can *prevent* the harm in the first place.

Sustainability and green building practices are the focus of the third module. Companies are often faced with choosing building practices that are either cheaper (at least in the short term) or that are more expensive but better for the environment.

The fourth module in this unit covers a topic that seems to have fallen off the radar in recent years: the protection of endangered species. General animal rights are also addressed.

The last module looks at wasteful business practices. Companies often dispose of "perfectly good" items that could be put to use simply because it is the cheapest or the most convenient thing to do. But do companies have obligations to be less wasteful and make an effort to see that someone is able to use "no-longer-wanted" items?

Dumping

Few issues generate more passion and debate than those surrounding the environment. People like green spaces; we are hardwired to like nature. But many things that generate pollution are essential to our society. We need computers. We need roads and vehicles to get us from place to place. We need affordable energy. Often, there is no easy answer to environmental questions.

A majority of companies face difficult environmental decisions. Often, leaders must balance laws, profits, the expectations of their customers, and their own desire to do what is right. Let's look at each of these issues in turn.

There are a large number of environmental laws, but many of them are fairly new. Until 1970, there was essentially no environmental regulation from Washington. Before then, companies generally operated in the cheapest way possible, even if it meant creating massive and obvious pollution. Factories were specifically located near rivers so that any waste materials the factory created could be dumped into the river and washed away. Cars had no emission control systems. Absolutely everything, toxic or not, was thrown away in the same garbage piles. Many companies have had to change their ways substantially during the careers of the people who now lead them.

Profits and meeting customers' expectations often go hand-in-hand. In recent years, many consumers have started to pay close attention to the environment. They often demand that the companies with which they do business respect ecology. Often, sales increase dramatically if a company gains a reputation as being "green." As a result, many firms strive to operate more cleanly and efficiently and to support environmental causes with corporate donations.

But the decision is an easy one in win-win cases. If a company can both care for the planet and make more money in doing so, there is no ethical dilemma to process. The real choices come when profits and the environment seem to be at odds.

For example: What should a CEO do if an environmental project does not seem likely to generate increased sales? Should she pass on the project and keep hold of the shareholders' money? A great many business leaders argue, often off-the-record, "Look, we'll take care of the planet, but only if the law requires it. If we do things that

265

our competitors aren't required to do, and if we don't generate revenue by doing them, we place ourselves at a competitive disadvantage. If the environment needs protecting in a new way, the law needs to change so that everyone plays by the same rules."

Some decisions are even harder. What if the likely costs and benefits of an environmental action are not uncertain? What if the green option will definitely *lose* large amounts of money? If a company does not break the law, and if its customers don't seem to mind, can losing money on green projects be justified? Can "the Earth" be a stakeholder that takes priority over shareholders and others?

Returning to the law, two of the first major environmental statutes passed in the United States were the Clean Air Act and the Clean Water Act. The two laws take fundamentally different approaches to the regulation of pollution.

The Clean Air Act actually allows for a large amount of air pollution. The Environmental Protection Agency (EPA) has set "attainment levels" for a number of pollutants: ozone, carbon monoxide, and dozens of others. As long as cities don't have too much of a substance in the air, the government requires no action. In theory, states can then lose federal highway funding if their cities have persistent attainment problems, but the grace periods allowed for even the most polluted cities are remarkable.

The Clean Water Act, on the other hand, requires action up front. If a business wishes to dump anything into a waterway, it must first obtain a permit from the EPA. Fines for dumping without a permit are substantial. But some companies have found and explored an interesting loophole in the Clean Water Act, as the next scenario describes.

SCENARIO

Sigma Cruise Lines

The new CEO of Sigma Cruise Lines sat at a small but expensive conference table. The Vice President of Operations knocked at her office door.

"Mike," she said. "You're right on time."

"Hi, boss. Can I close the door?" The CEO nodded, and he eased the tall door shut. The VP took a seat at the table. "Thanks for seeing me."

"My pleasure," the CEO replied. "So, let's hear your plan to 'substantially increase revenue by next quarter.'"

"OK. I should start by saying that I pitched this to your predecessor last year, and he said 'no.' I still think we should do it, but if you disagree, I won't bring it up again."

"Fair enough."

"What do you know about the Clean Water Act?"

"Refresh my memory."

"In the 1970s, Congress cracked down on water pollution. Basically, if you get caught dumping anything into water without a permit, you pay a big fine. Lakes, rivers, the ocean, anything. But…it doesn't apply more than 12 miles offshore. Other laws extend a little farther, but where we operate…"

"I don't like where this is headed, Mike."

"Just hear me out."

The CEO sighed. "Go ahead."

"Most of our bigger competitors have been dumping for years once they get out to sea. Every day, one of our big boats generates," he paused to find a document, "350,000 gallons of water from showers and sinks, toilets, and the engine room. And 10 tons of garbage. That's a heavy extra load, and the heavier our boats are, the more fuel we burn. And it's expensive to pay a contractor to haul that much away if we keep it until we reach port. The ocean can take it all away for free, and it's not illegal to dump when they get away from the coast."

"Wait…those guys have all paid big fines…"

"Yes, yes, but the fines were for faking records and lying to investigators—almost all of them. And a few of the fines were for dumping too close to the coastline. If you avoid those traps, no fines."

"And so, we'll have, what, an open policy of dumping?"

"Open, no. But we won't lie if we get caught."

"But if we admit it to the Feds, the press will get the records, and we'll be on the front pages like Exxon was for the *Exxon Valdez* 20 years ago."

"That's exactly what your predecessor said."

"Sharp guy. Well, except for the, you know, embezzling." The CEO smiled. "But look, Mike, I won't risk our good name to save a few bucks."

"First off, it won't be another *Exxon Valdez* situation, even if we get caught. There will be no oily otters for the front pages because we won't dump any oil. The engine room waste is 1 percent of the total waste we generate, and even I don't advocate dumping that overboard. And there won't be any trash washing up anywhere because we won't dump that either. It's also only 1 percent of the total. We can still get rid of 98 percent of the weight without those two things going overboard. If we get caught, and if the media grills us, we'll say, and we'll be completely honest, 'we only discharge water into the ocean.'"

"People will still be angry."

"They won't. Our competitors have been caught doing much worse, and their profits are soaring. And when there are no oily otters or Sigma Cruise Lines napkins washing up on the beach to photograph, I doubt the media will even be interested."

"Maybe so. But, again, I won't risk our reputation to save a few bucks."

"It's more than a few bucks, boss. I wouldn't have bugged you otherwise."

The CEO sighed for a second time. "How much do we save?"

"Per year?"

"Per year."

"Twelve million dollars."

The CEO took off her glasses and rubbed her eyes. "Twelve *million* dollars?"

"Twelve million. Minimum. Maybe more."

The CEO seemed more interested. "That would have doubled our profit last year."

"Yes."

A lengthy silence followed. Then, the CEO asked, "What about the passengers, Mike? They won't be excited to see wastewater dumped overboard."

"We'd do it strictly between 3:00 AM and 5:00 AM. Even the drunks are in bed by then."

The CEO fell silent again. "What about wildlife? Soapy water can't be good for fish."

"Minimal impact. Most fish flee from our ships—we're big and noisy."

"But some don't."

"True."

"What about foreign laws?"

"There are some that affect a few places, but we know where the places are, and we wouldn't dump there. There are lots of other parts of the ocean."

"Hmm…"

"And, boss—OK, this is where the last CEO laughed at me and ended our meeting—on balance, it might not be bad for the environment at all. Yes, the water immediately around our ships is temporarily more polluted until the ocean disperses what we dump. But less weight means we burn less fuel, which means fewer greenhouse gases. And we don't have to hire contractors to dispose of the waste, so they burn less fuel, which again reduces greenhouse gases. Water quality goes down, air quality goes up. They offset."

"That…seems farfetched."

"But it's true just the same, I believe." The VP checked his watch. "I'll leave you in peace, but one more thing?"

"Go ahead," the CEO said.

"I was talking to Fran, and I know that we're on target to miss Wall Street's expectations this quarter. We're off by about $2 million—true?"

"True," the CEO acknowledged.

"We can implement this plan in a week. We can save the $2 million this quarter, and $3 million every quarter after that. Keep the share prices where they are, you know?" When his boss didn't reply, he checked his watch again and said, "I won't keep you. Thanks for your time."

"Thank you, Mike," the CEO replied. After he left, she began looking through some of the documents he left behind.

DISCUSSION QUESTIONS

1. If you were the CEO, would you give a green light to dumping? Why?

   _____
   _____
   _____
   _____

2. At what specific point in the dialogue did you become sure of your decision?

   _____
   _____
   _____
   _____

3. Do you view the vice president unfavorably for raising this idea in the first place?

   _____
   _____
   _____
   _____

4. Do you consider "the Earth" or "the environment" to be a stakeholder worthy of consideration?

   _____
   _____
   _____
   _____

5. Should Congress change the law to make dumping by U.S. companies illegal worldwide?

   _____
   _____
   _____
   _____

MODULE **48**

Environmental Disasters from the *Exxon Valdez* to BP

BACKGROUND

In the summer of 2010, the BP oil spill dominated news coverage. In April of that year, an explosion on BP's *Deepwater Horizon* rig in the Gulf of Mexico caused 11 deaths and started a seemingly endless flow of oil from the floor of the Gulf. There turned out to be no quick fix to the leak, and it was four months later when the oil flow was finally slowed to a trickle. An estimated 200 million gallons of oil spewed into the gulf. BP share prices took a beating: They fell more than 50 percent before rebounding somewhat later in the year.

Before the BP disaster, the 1989 *Exxon Valdez* crash was widely cited as the worst human-created environmental disaster in U.S. history. The oil tanker struck a reef off the coast of Alaska and some 20 million gallons of oil eventually spilled into the remote waters. Pictures of oily otters were widely circulated in newspapers, and Exxon's public image took a significant hit.

In retrospect, both disasters were very preventable. Lots of specific actions could have averted catastrophe. But without the benefit of hindsight, it is sometimes difficult to spot the "key thing" in time. Companies could always take more time and spend more money on safety issues. The difficulty often lies in deciding what level of caution to exercise. The first half of the scenario in this module examines this kind of "before-the-disaster" decision.

Reactions

Once bad things happen, companies are left to clean up the mess, literally and figuratively. Exxon has faced cleanup costs, settlements, and lawsuits for more than 20 years after the *Exxon Valdez* crash. The total bill stands at several billion dollars, and it would be significantly higher were it not for a favorable Supreme Court ruling on punitive damages.

BP agreed to set aside $20 billion toward the cleanup efforts, but that sum may be the tip of the iceberg as BP faces a future filled with legal actions.

A large-scale environmental disaster is in some ways like an out-of-control forest fire: Executives must choose where to allocate resources to best control damage. The

269

second half of the scenario in this module examines these kinds of "after-the-disaster" decisions.

One problem with the BP spill is that the area affected was so large that it can be difficult to visualize. This module's scenario involves a much smaller area and a smaller number of impacted people.

SCENARIO

PART 1

The Greentown Widget Factory sits atop a wide hill. It has been operating for nearly 100 years. In fact, it is fair to say that the widget factory is the reason that Greentown exists. The factory came first. Homes to house, and businesses to support, the workers sprung up around the factory.

The factory burns a lot of coal as it turns out widgets. The byproduct of the coal is a thick sludge that contains high levels of mercury, cadmium, and other harmful elements. The sludge is channeled into a "storage pond" that can hold several million gallons of the nasty stuff. A dam contains it. Once a year, the factory pays an environmental disposal company to drain the pond into large tankers and haul the sludge away.

Greentown Lake sits one-half mile away at the bottom of the hill on which the factory is located. No other large lakes exist in the immediate area. Many waterfront homes have been built on the side of the lake farthest from the factory. Most of them are quite expensive. Several waterfront restaurants have also opened, and they do a booming business. The lake has become a very popular spot for fishing and recreational boating.

CEO's Office—Greentown Widget Factory

"OK, but bottom line it for me, Ken," said the CEO. "Is the dam on the storage pond sound or not?"

"Here's how the guy put it to me," Ken, the plant's manager, replied. "'It probably won't go today. It probably won't go tomorrow. But it probably won't last another 50 years.' He recommended that we reinforce it."

"And that we hire his company to reinforce it."

"Naturally."

"And how much is that going to cost us?"

"Lots, in terms of dollars."

"In terms of dollars, he says," the CEO muttered to himself. "And how else would we think of the costs?"

"Well, in this case, I think it would be better to think of it as a percentage. I know you don't like to spend money."

"All right, tell it your way."

"OK. We make about a 7 percent total return for our shareholders, year in and year out, right? The engineer wants us to reinforce the dam and have it redone every ten years. If we spread out the cost of the job over ten years, it would reduce our shareholders' return by 1 percent, to 6 percent."

"That's a lot of money."

"But it's not a big percentage, especially when you think of how much we might lose if the dam gives way. Which will 'probably' happen in the next 50 years if we don't do anything."

"But not for sure."

"No, not for sure. The engineer said, 'more likely than not, on a 50-year time horizon.'"

"Ugh. That thing has held up for decades. I'm not sure why I should have to be the one to fix it."

"Somebody has to, eventually."

"Yeah." The CEO sat and thought for awhile. "As long as we're talking about spending money on it—just for the sake of argument—how much would it cost to just get rid of the storage pond?"

"As in, pack the sludge into drums as soon as it's produced?"

"Yeah—have a weekly pick-up or something."

"It would cost more. I had a guy give me a proposal on that a few years ago before you took over. The appeal of the storage pond for all these years is that it's cheap. If we got rid of it, it would cost about twice as much as the dam reinforcement idea. Knock the shareholders' return down to 5 percent."

"But it would permanently fix the problem. I mean, even a reinforced dam can fail."

"That's true enough."

DISCUSSION QUESTIONS

PART 1

1. If you were the CEO, would you decide to reinforce the dam, change how you dispose of waste so the company could eliminate the storage pond, or neither?

_____

_____

_____

_____

2. Now assume that each option is *twice* as expensive as originally presented. Reinforcement will now reduce the shareholders' return from 7 percent to 5 percent, and eliminating the storage pond will reduce their return from 7 percent to 3 percent. Now would you pursue reinforcing the dam, eliminating the storage pond, or neither?

_____

_____

_____

_____

3. Now assume that each option is *half* as expensive as originally presented. Reinforcement will now reduce the shareholders' return from 7 percent to 6.5 percent, and eliminating the storage pond will reduce their return from 7 percent to 6 percent. Now would you pursue reinforcing the dam, eliminating the storage pond, or neither?

_____

_____

_____

_____

SCENARIO

PART 2

Assume that the CEO gives the green light to reinforcing the dam, but the dam collapses before work begins. Millions of gallons of sludge flow downhill, straight into Greentown Lake. The lake becomes unsuitable for swimming and fishing. Boating is not dangerous, but the stench keeps most people away.

CEO's Office—Greentown Widget Factory

"So here's what we've got," Ken said to the CEO. Both men seemed to have aged 20 years in the last month. "We can make $20 million available right away. Any more than that and we'll probably have to declare bankruptcy. We should be able to make more money available in future years. The question is how to use the first pile of money."

"Yeah," the CEO said. He opened his desk and took out a bottle of Pepto-Bismol. He poured himself a generous shot of the pink stuff and drank it down. "You have estimates?"

"Yeah. The thing is, we can only do about half of what we need to do, at least this year."

"Yeah, OK. Go ahead."

"Cleaning up the lake to make it swimmable again will cost about $10 million. If we want to completely restore the, you know, ecosystem, that's another $5 million. The homeowners with lakefront homes have lost a lot of property value. To fully compensate them would cost $10 million."

"But won't their homes be worth as much as ever if we clean the lake up?" the CEO asked.

"Maybe over the long term, but something like this...it gives the lake a bad reputation, you know? Buying prices might take years to come back to where they were. And they might never come back."

"OK."

"We can also think about compensating businesses on the lake. The restaurants are hurting. Not many people want to drive out here to eat next to a lake that smells bad. The boat rental and tour companies are down to practically nothing. The tackle and bait guy said his regulars stop by to talk to him and sympathize, but they don't buy much."

"But those businesses will come back quickly once the lake is open for business again, right?"

"That's more likely. To compensate them for the next year's lost profits would cost $10 million."

"OK," the CEO said as he made notes.

"Last up are the businesses near the lake. They've taken a hit, too. Gas stations, convenience stores, boat storage places...basically everything on the two roads leading up here. They're off between 10 percent and 40 percent with fewer visitors to the lake. 'It makes summer seem like the offseason,' one guy told me."

"Even 'Naughties'?" the CEO asked.

"I, ah, I didn't research the strip club."

"Liar," the CEO said, smiling for the first time during the conversation.

Ken eventually smiled back. "They're off 33 percent."

"Hah!" the CEO clapped. "I knew it."

Ken shrugged. "What can I say? They have a good lunch buffet."

"Yeah," the CEO said.

"At any rate, compensating the businesses around the lake would cost $5 million."

The CEO tallied up his figures. "So that's $40 million worth of ideas for a $20 million pot?"

"Right. So...where do you want me to set our priorities?"

DISCUSSION QUESTIONS

PART 2

4. Spend the $20 million. The proposals, and the amounts needed to fully fund them, are listed below. You may choose to partially fund any or all of the choices. In the blanks, write in how much of the available money you would spend on each project.

$ Millions Spent	Amount Needed	Project
_____	($10 million)	Cleanup—make the lake swimmable
_____	($5 million)	Cleanup—fully restore ecosystems
_____	($10 million)	Compensate lakefront homeowners for lost property value
_____	($10 million)	Compensate lakefront businesses for lost profits
_____	($5 million)	Compensate businesses near the lake for lost profits

Total: $20 million

5. Of the choices listed in the previous question, which was your top priority? Why? Which was your lowest priority? Why?

_____

_____

_____

_____

Sustainability: Renewable Energy and "Green" Buildings

"Sustainability" has become a tremendously powerful idea in recent years. Governments, citizens, interest groups, and corporations have taken an interest in making wise use of limited natural resources. Oil will not "run out" in our lifetime, but it will run out eventually, and our ability to increase annual supply may well end in the near term, so sensible energy conservation efforts are entirely reasonable. Water for household use and irrigation is already in woefully short supply in many parts of the world, and problems are starting to pop up in the United States. "Rare earth" minerals that are essential in the manufacturing of hybrid cars are in short supply, as are many other commodities.

A number of sustainability efforts are simple and cheap and have been widely adopted. Recycling, for example, is becoming universal. Recycling bins for plastic bottles, aluminum cans, and newspapers are everywhere, and most garbage companies offer curbside pickup for home recyclables.

Other ideas are useful for conserving resources, but they often come with a higher price tag.

Green Buildings

Many options exist for building facilities that have less environmental impact. Leaders who evaluate new construction choices must make decisions about energy, wastewater, materials, and a range of other things. This introduction will not detail them; instead, they are discussed by the characters in the scenario that follows.

The basic trade-off tends to involve costs. A state-of-the-art "green" building tends to cost about 10 percent more than a "regular" building to construct.[1] A building that is designed to send less waste to sewers and landfills costs more money. A building designed to make use of renewable energy also costs more up front.

---

[1] I am using 10 percent because that seems to be an average estimate. Groups that favor environmental causes and have an interest in promoting them tend to estimate a 5 percent premium. Others that are organized around the opposite point of view tend to estimate building premiums of about 15 percent.

But many leaders have been persuaded to look at long-term costs. Green build-ings cost more to build but, depending on features, can cost less to operate. Some environmental upgrades can "pay for themselves" over time. And cost issues aside, many leaders have decided to go green, because they decide that it is the right thing to do.

In the following scenario, two executives at an expanding company look at sev-eral options available for a new office building. They will definitely approve the con-struction of the space. The only question is whether they will adopt some or all of the suggested modifications.

SCENARIO

CEO's Office

"I'm not saying 'no,' I'm saying 'convince me,'" Ron, the CEO, said to his vice presi-dent. "But convince me today—I want to sign off on everything by tomorrow afternoon so we can start taking bids while I'm in Singapore."

"All right," Jack replied. "I thought we might go through what I think are the best ideas that the consultants presented last week."

"Fair enough."

"So water usage is the biggest problem around here. The restrictions we had this summer are only going to become more common. I think that our clients will particu-larly appreciate water conservation efforts."

"Any data on that? Any evidence of our competitors winning clients because of those kinds of efforts?"

"Ah, no direct evidence, no. But people are aware of the issue. It can't hurt."

"I'll grant you that—it can't hurt. I'm just wondering if it can help. But go ahead."

"OK, well, the 'good' ideas, to me, were these. First, we ought to install the rain-water collection system on the roof. It only adds $50,000 cost to a $15,000,000 build-ing, and it can save a great deal of water, which we would have to pay for otherwise."

"I agree—I had notes on that being a sensible idea as well. Let's add it."

"Done. The next water saver is the landscaping idea. I agree with the consultants that we ought to have limited grass on the grounds of the building and that we should use native plants and native rock wherever possible. That artist's rendition looked really good, and we can water 50 percent less."

"But people like lawns," Ron said. "Everybody has lush green lawns around their space. I don't want our building to be landscaped like a desert."

"I'm not saying we shouldn't have any grass—just that we should strategically limit the amount of grass. Maybe a nice lawn surrounding the clients' parking lot, and native landscaping in other places."

"Maybe. What's it cost, again?"

"About $100,000 for the initial landscaping. But then it costs less to maintain—no mowing, less watering costs."

"OK. What else do you like?"

"The last water idea I liked was to use packed gravel and not concrete for the employees' parking lot. That lets rainwater return to the aquifer much more efficiently—it doesn't puddle and evaporate back into the air as much as with concrete. And the cost is about the same."

"Yeah, but do people want to walk on gravel every day? Scuff up their shoes?"

"They'll get used to it."

"You ever try to walk on gravel in high heels, Jack?"

"Ah, no. But it's packed gravel. It's not the loose gravel stuff they used to use."

"Maybe. Moving on…"

"Right. The next few ideas are related to energy usage. I know you don't like solar panels on the roof."

"Ugly," Ron said.

"But I would argue that no one will see them on top of a five-story building with a flat roof, so what does it matter what they look like?"

"Expensive," the CEO countered.

"Up front, yes: $200,000. But if we can generate our own power, we'll make money off of them eventually."

"How much of our power can we generate with a roof full of solar panels?"

"Fifteen, maybe 20 percent."

"Uh, huh."

"If you want all of the power from solar cells, we also have that option."

"Yeah, but if we buy our energy from the, what, the solar energy farm, then we pay 30 percent more than if we buy it from the city."

"If energy prices don't go up. The solar farm is offering us a 15-year deal. Their prices might start to look pretty good if 'regular' energy prices double."

"That's true. I'll think about that one."

"The next energy idea is to use local building materials. If we bring in less stone, steel, carpets, and fixtures from far away, then the builders use less energy to get everything to the building site. We should buy local whenever we can."

"What was the price premium on that one?"

"Three hundred thousand dollars."

"OK," the CEO made some notes.

"The last two energy ideas that I like are the efficient windows and the upgraded insulation. They're expensive—$400,000 and $200,000—but our heating and cooling costs will go way down. We'll definitely recapture our full costs in six years or less."

"Yeah, I noted those as well during the presentation."

"I thought you might. That's almost everything I wanted to bring up. Just two more things with the restrooms."

"Oh, no," the CEO said.

"Now I know you're probably..."

"You're not going to bring those up. Nobody wants those."

"You have the final say, but I am going to bring them up."

Ron groaned. "So go ahead."

"In a company our size, bidets would save a tremendous amount of toilet paper per year."

"No one wants to use a bidet."

"That's only because they're not common. They're very standard in many countries."

"We're not in those countries, Jack," Ron interrupted.

"You'd save $50,000 a year on toilet paper, and the sewers would have..."

"Fifty thousand dollars isn't worth the amount of grief I'll get."

"So just make them an option—people can use another stall if they want toilet paper. One bidet per restroom, that's all I ask, with $100,000 added to the building costs."

The CEO grunted but didn't say anything. Eventually, Jack continued.

"So, ah, the other restroom idea I liked was the hand driers. We can save $100,000 per year on paper towels and send a lot less to the landfill. The new models are very energy efficient, and it's more sanitary."

"Yeah, people are used to hand dryers. But they were expensive, weren't they?"

"Not really—$150,000 for the building. They pay for themselves in a year and a half."

"Yeah, OK. So all of your proposals total," the CEO checked his notes, "a million and a half?"

"That's right. But don't think of it in terms of construction costs. A lot of these ideas make money eventually."

"That's true, but I still pitched $15,000,000 to the board last quarter. I have to have good reasons to OK a higher figure."

"I think all of these ideas are in our shareholders' best interests."

"I know you do. I have to think over whether or not I agree."

DISCUSSION QUESTIONS

1. Rank the ideas presented, from #1 (best) to #10 (worst).

   _____ Rainwater collection system ($50,000)

   _____ Native landscaping ($100,000)

   _____ Packed gravel parking lot ($0)

   _____ Solar panels on roof ($200,000)

   _____ Contract to buy solar-generated energy ($0 up front, future cost depends on energy prices)

   _____ Energy efficient windows ($400,000)

   _____ Upgraded insulation ($200,000)

   _____ Local building materials ($300,000)

   _____ Bidets ($100,000)

   _____ Hand dryers ($150,000)

2. Focus on the ideas you ranked as the two best. What specific fact makes them particularly good choices?

   _____

   _____

   _____

   _____

3. Focus on the ideas you ranked as the two worst. What specific fact makes them particularly bad choices?

   _____

   _____

   _____

   _____

4. If you were Ron (the CEO), where would you draw the line? Which of the ten ideas would you actually authorize?

   _____

   _____

   _____

   _____

5. For this last question, knock two zeros off every figure in the first question. Imagine that you are signing a contract to build a home for your family with a "base price" of $150,000. The upgrades cost 1/100th of the office building prices. So a basic rainwater collection system for the home would cost $500, native landscaping would add $1,000, efficient windows are $4,000 extra, and so on. Which of the upgrades would you OK for your own home? Did you draw the line in a different place than you did in the previous question? If so, what is the difference between the office building construction and the home construction?

   _____

   _____

   _____

   _____

Animal Rights

There are essentially two big "law and ethics" issues where animals are concerned. The first involves general mistreatment of animals; the second relates to the Endangered Species Act.

Animal Cruelty Laws

Michael Vick had it all. He was the starting quarterback for a National Football League (NFL) team in the prime of his career, and he had a boatload of endorsements to boot. In short order, he found himself in prison after pleading guilty to felony animal cruelty charges related to dog fights between pit bulls at the Bad Newz Kennels on his property. At the time of this writing, Vick has served his time and has found new NFL employment with the Philadelphia Eagles. He seems to be rebuilding his playing career nicely, but it remains to be seen whether or not he will be able to fully rebuild his endorsement portfolio.

All states except for Idaho, Mississippi, and the Dakotas make some kinds of animal mistreatment a felony, and every one of them has at least high-level misdemeanor offenses on the books. But, usually, only certain activities are criminalized. The law commonly covers torture, failure to provide food and water, poisoning, and provoking fights. Frequently, only some kinds of animals are covered. "Livestock," like cattle, and "domestic animals," like dogs and cats, are covered much more commonly than other smaller creatures. Additionally, most states have exemptions if a potential wrongdoer was hunting or doing research.

People for the Ethical Treatment of Animals (PETA) and other organizations battle to expand the coverage of state laws and shrink exceptions. They seem to be making slow but steady progress.

Endangered Species Law

In 1973, President Nixon signed the Endangered Species Act. Under the law, the government has power to declare plant and animal species to be endangered and protect their habitats. Significant controversies sometimes arise when the protection of habitats places the government at odds with landowners who are not permitted to develop their land as they please. Questions like, "Are plants more important than private property rights?" and "Are bugs more important than jobs?" are sometimes asked. Debates seem particularly heated when the protected animal is not "cute and fuzzy."

In my neck of the woods (Austin, Texas), an interesting legal battle unfolded for more than 20 years. In 1983, an Austin man purchased a large number of acres, but he was not allowed to build a commercial development on the land because the Austin Cave Beetle and five other species of endangered insects were found on his property.

In the Austin man's lawsuit (*GDF Realty Investments* v. *Norton*), his lawyers presented a unique legal argument based on the Constitution. In theory, the U.S. Congress is not supposed to be able to pass any laws it wishes; it is supposed to pass only 18 specific types of laws that are listed in Article I, Section 8 of the Constitution. Most laws that regulate companies are passed under Congress' authority to regulate "interstate commerce."

The Austin man argued that the insects on his property did not impact interstate commerce because they were never bought and sold. A zoo animal, one desirable as a pet, or one needed for medical research, might be sold for a price and included as a part of "interstate commerce," but the bugs on his land were worthless in terms of having no cash value. Therefore, he argued, the government had gone beyond its authority in banning his development in the name of protecting the insects.

The Fifth Circuit disagreed. It found that products derived from animals are often commercial and that, by harming ecosystems, commercial interests might be affected if the "interdependent web" of all species were threatened. The judges also speculated that the Austin Cave Beetle might have unknown uses—for example, they might plausibly be used in the future to fight disease or in other unforeseeable ways.

The Austin man lost the case and the chance to start a development worth potentially tens of millions of dollars.

Ethics Issues

The law covers many situations where some species are concerned, but many others are not regulated. What if someone is mean to a "regular, unprotected" animal? What if someone is cruel to a larger animal but in a way that meets a legal exemption? What if someone acts "preemptively" in anticipation of future government action under the Endangered Species Act? The following scenarios look at these kinds of situations.

SCENARIOS

Jake the Boy

One Saturday morning, Jake, age 12, took a walk in the woods behind his house. He carried a backpack, and he wandered aimlessly, enjoying the rich smells, quiet sounds of wildlife, and his footsteps on the narrow dirt path. Sunlight and shadow battled for prominence in the thickening woods.

After two hours of walking, Jake came to a stop in a clearing. He perched atop a fallen tree and retrieved a bologna sandwich from the side pocket of his backpack. The sun was bright in the clearing, and Jake began to sweat.

He spied a large ant mound nearby, and he stirred it with a large branch. Then, to amuse himself, he removed his glasses and used the lenses to focus the sunlight into a white hot point. He guided the pinpoint of light slowly over the ant mound. A dozen unlucky ants were fried.

Tiring of the game, Jake replaced his glasses, packed his trash back into his backpack, and continued on his way.

Alice the Monkey

Alice, a nonendangered monkey, was born in a zoo. She lived in the zoo for many years and was treated reasonably well.

When she was five, a visitor to the zoo dropped a lit cigarette over a rail and into Alice's area. Alice picked it up and, mimicking what she had seen visitors do, Alice took a drag. She liked it and took another. A boy yelled, "Hey! A smoking monkey!" The zoo patrons cheered Alice on, and word spread.

As the days went on, many cigarettes were tossed over the rail, and Alice smoked a dozen or more most days to the delight of most of the visitors. The zookeepers were told to allow the smoking because the zoo began to sell many more tickets to new guests who wanted to see the smoking monkey.[1]

Eventually, when Alice was ten, the zoo fell on hard times. It went bankrupt, and Alice was sold to a medical research facility. For the next two years, she was part of an experiment on the effects of calorie restriction. Alice was fed an ultra-nutritious diet but was given 30 percent fewer calories than usual. The research team was seeking to determine whether eating an extremely low-calorie diet might extend human lifespan.

Alice ate little, but she was energetic and felt terrific. But, alas, the experiment ended when the research team failed to have its grant renewed, and Alice was placed in a different study.

In her next study, Alice was injected with large quantities of methamphetamines. The research team used Alice and other monkeys to study the effects of meth addiction. They also studied the effects of withdrawal. Alice was injected with meth daily for six weeks, then given none for four weeks. She felt horrible throughout the experiment, particularly in the first few days of each withdrawal cycle. After two years of cycles, Alice died.

The research was ultimately used to improve a prescription drug to help humans in drug treatment programs get clean after battling meth addiction. The drug became a highly successful form of therapy. Patients in rehab who received the drug had only a 50 percent relapse rate. Patients who did not receive the drug had an 80 percent relapse rate.

Larry the Landowner

Larry owned several thousand acres of forest. He made his living operating a company that employed lumberjacks and sold harvested trees to a local paper mill. One day, his logging chief dropped a small-town newspaper on his desk. "Seen this?" he asked Larry.

"No," Larry replied. "What is it?"

"Bad news, boss. Page five."

Larry turned to page five and saw an article entitled, "Endangered Owls Found Near Greendale."

"Aw, crap," Larry said.

"Yep."

"How far away is Greendale? Hundred miles?"

"More like 80. What are you going to do, boss?"

Larry sipped his coffee and pondered, but not for long. "I'm going to do what I always figured I'd do if those owls got too close. They like the older, taller trees for nesting, right?"

"Right."

"All right, well, we're not going to leave any older trees around for them to stake out as a protected habitat. Spread the word—any tree over 20 years old comes down. Start with the land closest to Rockdale and work backward."

---

[1] This is based on a real case at an Australian zoo. Search for the video on YouTube.

"That'll hurt you in the long run, boss. We've only been cutting trees 30 years and older. You'll make 20, maybe 30 percent lower profit off younger trees."

"Yep. But I'd rather make 30 percent less money than 100 percent less money. I'm not going to have my property made into an owl hotel."

DISCUSSION QUESTIONS

1. Did Jake do anything wrong? Would he have done anything wrong if he burned a frog? A squirrel?

2. Did the zoo act wrongfully by allowing Alice to smoke?

3. Did the research team act wrongfully in carrying out the calorie restriction experiment? What about carrying out the meth experiment, which killed Alice but generated a useable therapy for humans? Are you likely to avoid general products that are tested on animals?

4. Did Larry act wrongfully or reasonably?

5. Going back to the background and the Austin Cave Beetle case, what do you think of the court's application of "interstate commerce"? Is the distinction the plaintiffs proposed a reasonable one: Should insects without a commercial value be less protected than, say, the bald eagle? Or would such a rule, if followed, create an unacceptable slippery slope?

"Perfectly Good" Items: Wasteful Business Practices

BACKGROUND

My grandmother was a child during the Depression, and, to this day, she is very much against throwing away any potentially useful item. As an example, when her morning newspaper is delivered, she removes the rubber band that holds it together and hangs it over the inside doorknob in her laundry room. At times, supply exceeds demand, and several dozen rubber bands compete for space on the knob. "Why do you do it?" I once asked her. "Because they're perfectly good," she replied.

Companies of many types often face a dilemma with things that are "perfectly good" but that, because of market forces, have actually become a liability.

In early 2010, the state of Florida faced an unusual cold snap. Fruit farmers took drastic steps to save their crops, and they were largely successful. But a couple of months later, some of the farmers faced an unexpected problem. Because of the weather and methods of crop-saving, much more fruit than usual became ripe at the same time.

Strawberries, for example, are usually harvestable over a period of several weeks. In Florida in 2010, however, nearly all strawberry crops were ready to pick within the same two-week period. This created a tremendous oversupply of berries for those two weeks, and the usual price of $1.00 per pound dropped as low as $0.25 per pound. Most farmers pay that amount or more on labor and shipping costs to harvest a pound of strawberries, so some farmers found it "cheaper" to let the strawberries rot in their fields.

Many homeless advocates and leaders of food banks expressed outrage. "One in six Americans is at risk for hunger! Perfectly good food can't be allowed to go to waste," they argued. "If you won't harvest your crops, at least let us come harvest them and put them to use."

Although one might argue that there is a moral responsibility to make use of useful items, property law does not require it. First-year law students are all acquainted with the "bundle of sticks" example that describes property rights. "Sticks" (rights) in the bundle include the right to occupy property, and the right to use it, exclude others, transfer it, lease it, and so on.

A farmer is under no legal obligation to allow a food bank to visit his farm and harvest the crops he is allowing to go to waste. Some farmers who refuse such offers claim they fear legal liability if anyone were to be injured on their farms, but such a reason is not necessary. The farmers could simply say, "This is private property, and I don't feel like letting you stop by."

Although the legal standards change a bit when one discusses manufactured goods, the basic idea that an owner can do whatever is desired with property is essentially the same.

The Cash for Clunkers Program

Sometimes, the government gets in on the act. In 2009, Congress allocated a total of $3 billion to what came to be called the Cash for Clunkers program. The idea was to both stimulate the auto industry and replace heavy-polluting vehicles with newer models. About 700,000 Americans took advantage of the program by trading in their old cars on models with better fuel efficiency. Most received government rebates of $3,000–$4,000. On average, trade-ins got 16 miles per gallon, and the new cars got 25 miles per gallon.

Germany and other nations had experimented with similar programs and found that many clunkers were simply resold to new owners, eliminating any pollution benefit. So, as part of the Cash for Clunkers program, Congress required the destruction of the engines of traded-in clunkers.

The oil was drained from the trade-ins and replaced with a liquid that, when heated, fuses into a glasslike material. The clunkers' engines were run with the new liquid until they seized up, all moving parts effectively fused together and completely worthless.

Critics condemned the destruction of working engines as wasteful. Salvage yard owners in particular stressed the value of dismantling engines and selling components as spare parts. Supporters argued that the destruction of the clunkers was a practical way to ensure that environmental goals were met.

What Obligations Exist?

The scenarios that follow describe three fictional companies that all must confront the issues raised so far. What *should* companies do with useful but unprofitable items?

SCENARIOS

BigSoft Software Company

"I expected good things, but I never thought that WordSmith Prime would sell so well in the first month," said the community outreach officer.

"We're definitely raking it in," the vice president agreed. "We're doubling all expectations. I'm just giddy."

"I think everyone is. Congratulations all around."

"Thank you, thank you. And you wanted to see me about something with the old software?"

"Yes. We have about 20,000 'old version' WordSmith CD ROMs sitting in our warehouse."

"Yeah, I thought we were going to destroy those when we rolled out WordSmith Prime."

"That is the plan, but it hasn't been done yet. I'm wondering if you'd be willing to consider donating them to schools instead. I have four school districts lined up who need software for their classroom computers. These kids just need something to learn on—they don't need all the latest bells and whistles that a professional needs."

"I don't know...I mean, we already decided to scrap them. We figured, why sell WordSmith to someone at a discount when we can sell him WordSmith Prime for $229? I guess we're talking educational uses here, so the WordSmith Prime cost would be $79, but still—these schools have to buy a word processor from somebody. Why give them one for free when a lot of them might buy WordSmith Prime for $79?"

"We could claim a tax deduction, maybe a lot of goodwill. Maybe establish brand loyalty—a kid who learns on WordSmith would be more likely to stick with future versions of WordSmith when she's older."

"That's a lot of maybes."

"I think it's the right thing to do. It seems wasteful to just destroy 20,000 perfectly good versions of the program that was our bestseller until a month ago."

Alpha Pharmaceuticals

"Africa?" asked the drug company CEO.

"Yes, ma'am, that's my recommendation," said the consultant.

"Why Africa?"

"Several reasons. And just to be clear, I'm recommending only the batch of 500,000 last-generation vaccines that are in your refrigerated warehouse and are still unexpired."

"OK. Go ahead."

"So, basically, those vaccines are perfectly good. The 1 percent failure rate is substantially better than the 100 percent failure rate of not vaccinating at all."

"Try telling that to the FDA. Or the trial lawyers."

"I understand. But the doses will still stop the disease from forming 99 times out of 100, and, in any event, won't harm anyone. In the United States, the disease is rare, but in some parts of Sub-Saharan Africa, it strikes tens of thousands of children every year. The 500,000 unused vaccinations could plausibly save several thousand lives."

"And we would get it to them how?"

"Nurses International has offered to pick up the vaccines, ship them, and administer the doses at no charge. Sound good?"

"I guess. We've just had so much bad publicity over the vaccine already, and goodness knows how much the lawsuits will end up costing us. I think it might just be better to destroy the remaining doses."

"I understand your feelings, but this is a chance to do something good. This is not a defective vaccine—it's merely one that doesn't meet the 100 percent effectiveness expected by the U.S. market. It is substantially better than no vaccine at all. Several thousand lives."

"I'll consider it," the CEO said.

Smith and Jones Law Firm

"Thank you for meeting with me," the activist said.

"No problem. I should warn you, I only have ten minutes—a couple of our big clients are stopping by at noon, and I need to get set up for that meeting," said the office manager.

"This won't take long at all. Are you familiar with what we do?"

"I've heard of you, I think. Some kind of environmental work is all I can really say."

"That's OK. We're one of the largest facilitators of recycling in Pennsylvania. We specialize in partnering with large employers like Smith and Jones, and we helped recycle over three million plastic bottles, a million aluminum cans, and ten million pounds of paper last year."

"That's admirable."

"Thank you; we think so. We'd like to add you to our list of partners. We estimate that you have about 300 employees, correct?"

"In the neighborhood of 300, yes."

"Three hundred people drink a lot of soda and water in a year, not to mention the amount of paper that I imagine is used in a law firm."

"True enough."

"We can offer to help you recycle all of your waste at no charge to you. We would provide tasteful but large recycling bins clearly marked 'bottles,' 'cans,' and 'paper' throughout your building. Once every two weeks, or more often if you need it, our employees will come to empty the bins and take the recyclables away. The only thing your employees have to do is drop their trash in the right bin."

"Uh-huh. And what's your angle? If you don't charge us for this service, how do you make any money?"

"Well, we're a nonprofit, but, of course, we have salaries and other expenses. The legislature created a program two years ago that provides about half of the money we need to operate, and the amounts recyclers give us for the bottles, cans, and paper make up the other half. We get by nicely."

"Hmm…"

"So what do you say? Can I put you down as a green partner?"

"Maybe. I mean, I appreciate what you're trying to do. I recycle at my house, and I think it's all fine and noble and all that."

"And now your entire firm can do the same at work—at no cost."

"No cash outlay, true, but the problem is the IP."

"IP?"

"The intellectual property. This is a big firm. Our files are full of sensitive and confidential information about some of the biggest companies and the wealthiest people in the state. Someone could walk out of here with a fortune's worth of information in a single manila folder under his jacket, or on a flash drive."

"Sir, I assure you that none of our workers would ever…"

"Maybe, maybe not. But I don't know anything about any of your people."

"Surely you have a custodial staff?"

"Yeah, but they're screened by us. Actually, by me. I do a thorough background check on anybody who gets access to this building."

"We'd be glad to agree to any rules you set. Off-limits areas, supervision while we're here, anything you think is necessary."

"Maybe. Listen, I believe that you're sincere. I'm not saying no, I'm just saying I need to think it over."

DISCUSSION QUESTIONS

1. Evaluate the situation presented in the background material involving the strawberry farmers. If a food bank offers to come to a farm with laborers and harvest all unwanted fruit, is a farmer morally obligated to agree to the offer? Should it be a legal requirement when food is involved?

2. Evaluate the second situation in the background material—the Cash for Clunkers program. Set aside your feelings on the overall program and focus on the part of the law that required the destruction of engines. Was it right to disable "perfectly good" motors? Would you have preferred an alternative?

3. Moving to the scenarios, assume for the next three questions that the companies eventually chose *not* to go through with the proposals. Did the software company act wrongfully? Why or why not? Did the pharmaceutical company act wrongfully? Does the fact that the medicine might have saved lives make the situation different from that of the software company?

_____

_____

_____

_____

4. Did the last company act wrongfully in refusing the recycling program? Do you use such bins yourself? If yes, how far out of your way would you go to find one?

_____

_____

_____

_____

5. Now, instead of having a cost of "no money and slight inconvenience," suppose that in all of the fictional scenario cases, a small but identifiable cost had existed, say, 1/10 of 1 percent of the company's revenue. (So, for example, if the software company has revenue of $20,000,000, the costs of the software donation program would have amounted to $20,000.) With this fact changed, would your answers to any part of the previous two questions change?

_____

_____

_____

_____

UNIT 10

International Ethics

Unit Background

In today's global business environment, companies must consider stakeholders beyond their own borders like never before. When, if ever, do the needs of "far away" stakeholders take priority over the needs of those closer to home?

Module 52

Overseas Working Conditions. [Many types of manufacturing operations have been moved overseas in a quest for lower labor costs. Many other nations have few, if any, laws that protect workers from abuse. When is a U.S. company morally obligated to demand improved working conditions for its overseas contract workers?]

Module 53

Fair Trade Programs. [Many "fair trade" programs exist that claim to improve wages and living conditions for poorly paid international workers. Should companies give consumers more fair trade options? Do most consumers care about having such options?]

Module 54

The Foreign Corrupt Practices Act and Bribes. [The FCPA makes it illegal to bribe the decision makers in foreign governments for the purpose of securing contracts. Legalities aside, are companies ethically obligated to "play fair" when bidding for foreign government contracts?]

International Ethics

There appears to be less emphasis on international business ethics during the current recession. Arguments along the lines of "We have plenty of problems right here at home, so why should we pay attention to everyone else's problems?" seem to be politically popular. One reads fewer articles about overseas working conditions these days.

But the fact remains that countless millions of people who make goods for sale in the United States work in very poor conditions and for very low wages. Sometimes, American companies act swiftly when they are made aware of abusive practices by their overseas contractors. Other times, corporations don't seem to care, as long as labor costs are kept low.

The first module in this unit looks at a typical sweatshop and asks: Under what circumstances should an American company take action to require better working conditions for international workers?

The next module shifts from companies to consumers. It presents ideas related to fair trade programs and speculates about people's willingness to support them.

The last module looks at paying bribes to foreign governments in order to secure contracts.

MODULE 52

Overseas Working Conditions

In June of 2010, the media reported on ten suicides at a Foxconn factory in China. The story reignited debate on the use of sweatshop labor in developing nations.

Factory Workers in the United States

Factory workers have won substantial upgrades in the United States over the past century. They have, in most industries, won the right to form labor unions and bargain collectively with their employers. They have won a federal minimum wage that today stands at $7.25 per hour. This is not a large sum, but it generates about $15,000 per year in income for a full-time worker, which is enough to live above the poverty line in the wealthiest country in the world.

In the United States, most assembly-line workers must be paid 1.5 times their regular wages if they work more than 40 hours per week. The Occupational Safety and Health Act and similar laws place numerous workplace safety requirements on companies.

Factory Workers Outside the United States and the "Race to the Bottom"

Few, if any, of these protections exist in many nations that have become manufacturing hot spots. Free trade policies are beneficial in that they make the global economy work more efficiently, but they have the effect of creating a "race to the bottom." Manufacturers constantly seek the lowest labor cost in the world. Nations with millions of workers in desperate circumstances tend to win the battle.

I am working on a laptop that was made in China at a table that was made in Indonesia. I am wearing a shirt from India and a baseball cap that was stitched together in Bangladesh. The pen I am using to take notes bears a "Mexico" stamp on the bottom. My cat/research assistant here was made in America, but her collar and food dish are from China.

American workers can compete with anyone in the world if the issue is making good products. They are often completely uncompetitive when it comes to the wages for which they are willing to work. The $7.25 a U.S. worker expects per hour will buy 20 hours of labor somewhere else.

Foxconn Technology Group

You likely own more than one gadget that was assembled at a Foxconn factory in China. Intel, HP, and Dell all contract work out to Foxconn. Apple iPhones and iPads are made by Foxconn, as are Amazon's Kindle, Motorola cell phones, the PlayStation 3, Nintendo Wii, and Microsoft's Xbox360.

Foxconn may represent the natural endgame of free trade. The company wins big contracts with many of the world's largest technology companies because it offers, in its own words, the "Lowest Total Cost Solutions." Foxconn complies with Chinese law, but the company works its employees hard. A typical employee works 10- to 12-hour shifts, 6 days a week, and is paid about $130 per month. Discipline is strict, and mistakes seldom pass without criticism. Many of the ideas in this module's scenario are inspired by Foxconn practices.

The company defends itself by pointing out that it maintains a swimming pool for employees and holds chess tournaments for them. But critics dismiss such perks as trivial and point to the ten employees who, through the first half of 2010, decided that life was no longer worth living.

The Future

Foxconn is certainly not the worst employer in China. And it will improve. Its partners have too much to lose because bad publicity costs large companies millions of dollars. When Nike was a target of similar bad publicity in the 1980s, it established closer oversight of its overseas contractors, and the company minimized its problem. Today's companies will follow the Nike blueprint. Apple will lead the way by demanding that workers be treated better, and it will get results. Wages will be increased, and Foxconn workers will be treated less harshly. Nintendo, Dell, and the rest will do their part as well.

The interesting ethics question is whether more CEOs will choose to act *before* a crisis develops. Information control is tight in some nations, and few stories leak out. For every worker who works at a Nike supplier or a Foxconn operation, hundreds work at similar jobs in obscurity.

Large American companies have clout with their partners whether or not the media is paying any attention. They can demand better working conditions for workers, or seek partners that treat workers reasonably in the first place. The following scenario investigates whether or not U.S. companies should act.

SCENARIO

President's Office

"We need to cut ties with Quality Dragon Limited," the vice president said, summing up his argument. "The contract is up in six months, Al. I'd love to end it now, but I'm resigned that the best-case scenario is just that we go with somebody else in six months."

"I don't think that's necessary," the president replied.

"They abuse their employees. It's wrong to continue our relationship with them."

"Their workers are not prisoners!" the president said sharply. Calming down somewhat, he continued. "They are free to end their employment at any time. They are not beaten. In all the reports about them, there are no documented cases of physical abuse. They are paid on time. They work there because they want to work there. It is better than the alternatives. Just because you would not want to take those jobs doesn't mean that no one else does."

The vice president set his jaw. "You're wrong."

"Excuse me?"

"I said you're wrong, Al. Even if it costs me my job, you're wrong. You are…brilliant… when it comes to controlling costs. And that's almost always a good thing. It's why we're growing. We were nearly bankrupt when you came aboard. But it's not a good thing this time."

"Go on."

"We are morally required to use our negotiating power to insist on humane treatment of the people who make our products. Even if our labor costs increase. And I don't think they'll increase by much. I'm not talking about paying them a fortune, just..." he trailed off. "Look, you're going over there next month. Just talk to one of them. You'll see."

"Hmmph. Maybe I will—just so I can tell you that *you're* wrong." He smiled slightly.

One Month Later: China—Hotel Suite

"We have a worker downstairs in the conference room, boss," said the executive assistant.

"Excellent!" Al said. "No problems?"

"Not on Sunday. They're not on a fixed schedule, and surveillance is light. I found the guy wandering around the edge of the property by himself. I had the interpreter explain who I was and asked if he could leave the property. He said yes, that it was allowed. So we offered him $10 for his trouble and arranged to pick him up a mile down the road. Piece of cake."

"How does he seem?"

"Quiet. Thin. What can I say?"

"OK. I'm headed downstairs."

Hotel Conference Room

"Explain to him that I am the president of his employer's largest client," Al said to an interpreter. "That...I can make demands...if I am unhappy with how his factory is run."

The interpreter spoke at some length. The Quality Dragon worker nodded once when she finished and said a single syllable. He did not look up from the table. "He understands," the interpreter said.

"Good, good," Al said. "Ask him his name."

The interpreter relayed the question. "Ping," the worker said softly.

"Hello, Ping. I'm Al." Ping nodded once.

Al:	"Ping, will you help me understand? About how Quality Dragon treats workers?"
Ping:	"Yes, sir."
Al:	"I will not let them fire you, whatever you say. Do you believe me?"
Ping:	"Yes, I would like to believe you, sir."
Al:	"OK, then, the truth, please. Will you tell me what a workday is like for you?"

Ping did not answer, and a long silence stretched out.

Al:	"Ping? I want to help. I need to understand."
Ping:	(After another lengthy pause) "My mother lives alone. She is very poor."
Al:	"Ah." (*smiling*) "Very noble of you. Very. Alright, then. My company sponsors a school where American students learn Mandarin. It's about 100 miles from here. I will guarantee to find your mother a job there, doing anything she is able to do. Fair enough?"

The translator conveyed the message, and Ping absorbed it.

Ping: "That would be most kind, sir. She will work happily and well for your school. Thank you."

Al: "Consider it done. Now. Back to my question. What is a workday like for you?"

Ping collected his thoughts for a moment. He began to speak, slowly at first, and then with increasing pace and volume. Al listened to the interpreter, but kept his eyes on Ping.

Ping: "We are awakened at 5:00 AM. They shout at us and order us to hurry. We are fed a poor meal and are at our stations by 5:30, although work does not begin until 6:00. We work from 6:00 until 1:00 PM. We have one restroom break at 9:00 AM for ten minutes. I have time to smoke one cigarette. We are not permitted to talk to other workers. If we do, even quietly, we lose pay, and the supervisors scream at us. If we make an assembly error, we lose pay, and the supervisors scream at us. If we yawn, we lose pay, and the supervisors scream at us. If we fail to meet an hourly quota, we lose pay, and the supervisors scream at us.

"I drill holes into the outer casing of your phones. It is the place where a charger can be plugged in. I must process 120 per hour. And the holes must be perfectly located and perfectly straight. Every 30 seconds, a new one. It is difficult to keep focus. I try to make fewer than 10 errors per day. One day, I made only 4 errors. Another day, I made 18. On that day, my supervisor slapped me and docked me my entire day's pay.

"We have 30 minutes for lunch. The company provides a poor meal. We can pay for better food at the cafeteria, but it is very expensive. I only buy the good meal once a month. One time, I bought a pop." (*smiling*) "It was wonderful. We may speak quietly at lunch. I have a friend, but we are often too tired to speak. At 1:30, we go back to work until 8:30. We have another ten-minute break at 4:30. Work is more difficult in the afternoon. The sun warms the factory, especially in the summer. Water is not allowed on the assembly floor. Sometimes, water is available at the restroom break. The supervisors are angrier and less patient. They call us names that no one should be called, but I am numb to them. Most days.

"If we miss our quota, or if we have a heavy order from a client, we work late. This happens several times a month. Eventually, we are fed, and we are returned to our dorm. We have 12 men to a room, and we sleep in bunk beds that are three bunks high. The room smells bad, and there are ants. We usually fall asleep quickly.

"We work six days per week. On Sundays like today, we do not work. I spend much of the day sleeping. There are televisions in the recreation building, and there are chess sets. I like to play chess with my friend on Sunday. Sometimes, we share a pack of cigarettes and play all afternoon. It is pleasant to do something slowly and have time to think.

"I am supposed to be paid $150 per month. But the supervisors always look for reasons to dock your pay. No one gets his full pay. I usually get about $110 at the end of the month. I keep $50 for myself and send $60 to my mother. There are things you must buy here. They require you to shave but do not give you razor blades. You have to buy soap. They provide you a jumpsuit once a year, but you have to buy socks and underwear. And I have to buy cigarettes. What else do I have?

"That is what it is like for me, sir."

The translator trailed off. Al shook his head slightly, as if to emerge from a trance. Ping returned his gaze to the table in front of him and fell silent.

DISCUSSION QUESTIONS

1. To what degree do you agree with the vice president's statement: "We are morally required to use our negotiating power to insist on humane treatment of the people who make our products"?

Completely Disagree ← ─────────────── → Completely Agree
1 --- 2 --- 3 --- 4 --- 5 --- 6 --- 7

2. If you were the president of the company in this module, would you renew the contract with Quality Dragon Limited if no changes were made to its operation?

_____

_____

_____

_____

3. What parts of Ping's story indicate to you that he is being treated wrongfully? Or does he seem to be treated reasonably in your opinion?

_____

_____

_____

_____

4. Assume that correcting the following problems would each result in a 1 percent cost increase for the company profiled in the module. Assume that you are the president of the U.S. company. Place a checkmark by the items that you would insist on, keeping in mind that each increases your labor costs.

_____ Reducing employees' workdays to a maximum of 12 hours.

_____ Improving the quality of food served to employees

_____ Eliminating reduced pay for employees who exceed their quota for errors

_____ Building additional dorms so that workers sleep with no more than four to a room

_____ Prohibiting unpaid overtime

5. As a consumer, are you keenly aware of how much things cost? Would you notice if food prices rose by 5 percent? What about smart phones, computers, and TVs? Would a 5 percent increase in price to these items be noticeable? What if the increase were 2 percent?

_____

_____

_____

_____

Fair Trade Programs

To recap a key idea from Module 52: Globalization has created a particular kind of "race to the bottom." Manufacturers are constantly on the lookout for low labor costs, and they are often willing to seek workers anywhere in the world. This tendency has driven the wages paid to countless millions of the world's workers into the range of $0.25 to $0.50 an hour. If workers in one country are unwilling to work for such small wages, then operations often shift to countries in which people are more desperate and willing to work for what is offered.

Module 52 posed the question: Do American corporations have an obligation to raise the wages of overseas workers who produce their products? This module asks: If corporations won't act, are there circumstances in which *consumers* might act in a way that boosts international wages?

How Much Money Is Needed to Make a Sizeable Difference?

A recent study looked at the clothes sold at three American retailers—Sears, Walmart, and Target—and asked: If $100 is spent on clothing at the cash register, where does the money go? A lot of it goes to the retailer, and another significant percentage goes to the clothing company (like Hanes, Levi's, etc.). A lot of it goes to pay for the cost of the denim, cotton, or other fabric used to make the clothes. In the end, only $6 goes to the wages of the people who actually make the clothing.

Textile workers in many places are paid enough to afford rice and very basic shelter and clothing, but little else. A very modest boost in prices of 3 percent could lead to a 50 percent increase in their standard of living, if the money all "trickled down" to them.

Who (If Anyone) Would Drive a 3 Percent Price Increase?

If the wages of international workers are to be raised, companies are in the best position to raise them. Some have done just that, but many won't, at least not voluntarily.

So what happens then? The government could try to take action. Higher tariffs on goods imported from nations that lack reasonable minimum wage requirements might be useful. But verifying compliance is tricky in the international arena. And several treaties can make raising tariffs a difficult issue.

Those concerns aside, Congress probably lacks the political will to impose such programs. Lots of voters might react by saying, "We're in a recession—you need to focus on helping workers right here in America!"

So if the corporations and the government won't take action, what then?

Consumers

American consumers might ultimately have to be the driving force behind raising subsistence-level wages of overseas workers. Certainly, customers have acted in ways that have required individual companies to behave differently. Sometimes a news story breaks about a corporation that treats international workers miserably, and customers are so distressed that they stop buying the company's products for a time. But such cases tend to be few and far between.

Sometimes, consumers will agree to pay a premium for products that promise to help raise the standard of living for poorly paid workers. "Fair Trade" coffee beans have become reasonably popular in recent years, for example.

What if a "Fair Trade"–type program expanded significantly? What if an organization came into being that certified all kinds of products and promised that anything carrying its label was made by workers who were paid enough to guarantee a reasonable standard of living? Would consumers be willing, or not willing, to pay a small premium for many purchases?

One barrier would clearly have to do with trust. A certification organization that promised, "Yes, the products we certify cost about 3 percent more than 'regular' products, but nearly all of the extra money goes to support increased wages for poorly paid workers," would have to prove to be reliable and trustworthy over time. But what if that happened? What if a single organization emerged to be credible and well liked by a large percentage of the public? If it presented consumers with clear choices and the ability to directly help raise international wages, how would consumers behave?

SCENARIO

Living Wage Certification Corporation

Living Wage Certification Corporation (LWCC) has become something of a media darling. It has received extensive and very favorable coverage from television news programs, newspapers, and magazines.

LWCC's mission is to "substantially improve the basic living conditions for workers worldwide." When the corporation certifies a product, it is giving its guarantee that the low-level workers who most directly produce the item are paid at least 1.5 times the average wage paid by other companies for similar work in their home country. So if a typical worker in a clothing factory makes $0.30 an hour, a LWCC certification on, say, a hat assures that the worker who stitched the hat together was paid at least $0.45 an hour.

The number of products that carry an LWCC designation has increased dramatically in recent years.

At the Department Store

Carol stops at a department store and tries on several pairs of jeans. After trying on several styles, she settles on the one she likes best. The rack where she found the jeans she intends to buy lists the price as $70/$72. The small text on the price tag reads: "Price is $70 for Martin Smith Straight Leg Jeans, or $72 for LWCC–certified Martin Smith Straight Leg Jeans."

On closer examination, Carol sees that the jeans in her hand are marked at $70, but some pairs on the rack have a green tag with a familiar LWCC logo. The green-tagged pants are marked $72.

Carol flags down a clerk. "What's the difference in the jeans with and without the green tag?" she asks.

"No difference, really," the clerk answers. "Same jeans, same fit. The certified jeans are made at a different place—the boxes we get are from India and not Bangladesh, I think—but the denim is the same, and everything else is the same."

"Thanks," Carol says. As the clerk walks away, Carol sees that, on the rack, there is a pair of the jeans in her size that has the LWCC label.

At the Coffee Shop

After buying the jeans, Carol stops at a new coffee shop. She orders an extra tall, grande, mocha-frappa-cappa-chino with an extra helping of chemicals that taste vaguely like pumpkin, if you show a customer a picture of a pumpkin on a cardboard cutout at the counter, and that customer's thinking of pumpkins already.

"Living Wage Certified?" the smiling clerk asks as he prepares to make a drink that will contain enough caffeine to stun a medium-sized horse.

"Ah, what?" Carol asks.

"Your drink will be $7.25 if we use certified coffee beans; otherwise, it'll be $7."

"Oh. Ah, do most people get the certified beans?"

"Most people do," the smiling clerk says, nodding.

At the Grocery Store

After finishing her coffee, Carol stops at the grocery store. She is out of nearly everything, so she fills her shopping cart.

The Living Wage Certification Corporation has found it impracticable to offer "living wage" choices on the huge number of low-priced items at grocery stores, so it takes a different approach there. The company established relationships with chains of grocery stores and convinced the stores to put up LWCC displays at every cash register.

The displays have tear-off coupons in amounts of $1, $3, and $5 that the checkout clerk can scan. Above the coupons is this statement: "Help LWCC support agricultural workers throughout the world. Your donation will be used to ensure living wages for the people who grew, harvested, or made the items in your shopping cart. Suggested donation: 3 percent of your total bill."

Carol reads the display as the clerk scans her items. Her bill comes to $100. She eyes the $3 coupon as the clerk asks if there will be anything else.

DISCUSSION QUESTIONS

For all questions, assume that an organization like LWCC actually exists, you are aware of it, and trust it, and the organization has set up the kinds of programs described in the scenario.

1. If you were in Carol's position, which of the jeans would you buy: the $70 "standard" pair or the $72 certified pair? Why?

_____

_____

_____

_____

2. Would you pay the extra quarter for the coffee? Why or why not?

_____

_____

_____

_____

3. Would you make the $3 donation at the grocery store? If so, how consistently would you do so? If not, why not?

_____

_____

_____

_____

4. If an organization like LWCC came to prominence, how many people in general do you think would usually pay the extra 3 percent for purchases? Most? Half? A few?

_____

_____

_____

_____

5. Imagine that it is ten years from now. You are no longer a student, and you have been earning a steady salary (or an increased salary if you are employed now) for several years. Would you be more likely to spend the extra money in the three ways discussed in the scenario, or would increased personal income not be a factor in this kind of decision?

_____

_____

_____

_____

The Foreign Corrupt Practices Act and Bribes

BACKGROUND

For this unit to work, we must step into a time machine and travel back to the year 1976. Ah…1976. America celebrated its bicentennial with outrageous fireworks displays. The U.S. Mint produced quarters with cool reverse sides. Cars were very large and very, very ugly. Your humble author was four years old.

We will have to travel back in time because, since 1977, the business practice described in this unit has been illegal. It no longer presents an ethical dilemma because businesspeople are no longer able to freely choose a penalty-free course of action. Jail time now awaits if an unwise choice is made. However, in the past, many companies faced a difficult ethical decision, and we can use this decision to examine some broader ethical issues.

The Foreign Corrupt Practices Act of 1977

In 1976, the Securities and Exchange Commission (SEC) conducted a study and presented its findings to Congress. The study looked into a practice that was then common. At the time, many U.S. companies paid bribes—sometimes large bribes—to foreign government officials in order to secure contracts. For instance, say your company manufactures automobiles, and a foreign government is looking to buy 5,000 cars for government use. Would secret cash payments of $75,000 to two key members of the nation's parliament help to secure the votes necessary to get the contract? Quite possibly, yes.

The SEC's study identified 450 U.S. companies that had engaged in this practice. Some members of Congress expressed outrage. Many Americans viewed Washington unfavorably in the years after the Watergate scandal and the resignation of President Nixon. Representatives seized an opportunity to claim that they would "clean up corporate America" and show that they stood firm against "inside dealing."

In 1977, President Carter signed the Foreign Corrupt Practices Act (FCPA). The law made it illegal to bribe foreign officials. The maximum punishments for violators were set at $100,000 and five years in jail. Companies can be fined millions.

Legal and Illegal Bribes

The FCPA targets bribery to decision makers. U.S. companies (and U.S. citizens working for foreign companies) may not make payments to acquire new business or retain existing business. Bribes need not be large or monetary to violate the law. "Anything of value" offered to foreign officials for the purpose of acquiring or retaining business is illegal.

The law does allow for "grease" payments to be made after contracts have been awarded to move deals along. For example, small payments made to customs officials and issuers of permits for preferential speedy treatment are legal.

Controversy

Many nations do not have anything like the FCPA, so if a U.S. company competes overseas with a foreign company, the playing field can be uneven. Some argue, "Why should foreign corporations get the inside track? Regardless of who makes a better product, a company that is allowed to bribe the key decision makers will often be able to beat a company that can't pay off under the table."

Going beyond this general criticism of the FCPA, one can make a case that bribes to foreign officials are a good thing for many of a firm's immediate stakeholders. If large contracts are secured, the shareholders benefit, at least in the short term. Employees have more work to do and are less likely to be laid off. Suppliers receive larger orders, and communities benefit when companies operate at full capacity.

Bribes are detrimental, but in a way that is vague. Bribe payments distort free competition, and they interfere with the efficient workings of free markets. And corrupt government is bad for the people governed.

Also, illicit payments can be harmful to a company in a more direct way. If the media discovers and reports on such activities, the public's confidence in a company can be undermined. Customers sometimes turn away, and share prices occasionally plummet if U.S. consumers think that a company is behaving wrongfully.

This module examines issues surrounding the FCPA. Remember that we are going back to 1976. Televisions are not made in the United States these days, but they were back then.

SCENARIO

1976—At a Restaurant

"Here you go," said the cheerful waitress. She placed fresh margaritas in front of the two executives, and she collected the four empty glasses with salt-encrusted rims from the table.

"Thanks a lot," said Phil. He wore an orange suit with bell-bottom pants and had long sideburns.

"Great, thanks," said Dale. He wore a pale blue suit with bell-bottom pants and had even longer sideburns.

The waitress walked away.

"So anyway," Phil said as he sampled the new drink, "anyway, anyway…"

"You know what we have to do," Dale said.

"I know what you *think* we have to do."

"Phil," Dale paused for a moment. "We have to go to Berlin."

Phil had no reply for a long time. Eventually, he drained his glass and spoke quietly. "I don't think we should do that, Dale. I really…do not." The margaritas were starting to hit him.

"It's the only way."

"Maybe."

"Maybe, nothing. It's our last shot to keep everybody working. The Germans are buying 50,000 units, Phil. Fifty *thousand* televisions. That buys us six months, maybe a year, to get back on our feet."

"I don't know, Dale. I really don't."

"Look at it this way, my friend. We would be spending $250,000 to get a contract that nets us $2,500,000 profit. Why would any sensible person ever pass up a certain 10-to-1 return?"

"It just doesn't seem right to me."

"It's completely legal."

"Even so."

"It's how business is done on this committee. Herr Dietz and Herr Schultz vote to award the contracts to whoever has met their asking price. End of story. You don't get a contract out of this committee without paying Dietz and Schultz."

"It just seems wrong."

"It *is* wrong, but that's not our problem. Let the Germans clean up their system. Until they do, you have to pay Dietz and Schultz to get this kind of a deal signed. And they want $125,000 each for their votes this time."

"I don't want to be a part of it. What are we going to do, Dale? Are we going to literally stuff 2,500 hundred-dollar bills into a briefcase and pass it to them under a table somewhere?"

"Exactly."

"You're out of your mind."

Dale's mood turned from friendly to cold. "Someone is going to pay them what they want. If we don't, one of our competitors will. And then we will lose our last chance to avoid shutting down the California plant. And 500 of our employees will be out of a job. And our market share will continue to sink. And we will be a large step closer to ceasing operations altogether." Phil had no response to that, and Dale continued. "So," he said, ticking off his fingers as he made points. "If we don't do this...

"One. Our shareholders take a beating. You remember the shareholders? They own the company that pays us our tidy salaries.

"Two. Our employees get a pink slip. You remember them—they work their butts off for low wages on the factory floor producing the things that make our jobs possible, and all they ask is that we keep the operation going.

"Three. You and I are in even more trouble. How long do you suppose the board will stick with us if we don't pull out of this tailspin? How do your finances look, Phil? Because I bought a new house last year, and I'm cutting things pretty close with the old budget, myself.

"Four. Our suppliers get hurt. How many of the small firms that make switches, electric plugs, or antennas for us are going to get hurt?

"There are more, but I'm running out of fingers. So let me ask you a question. Who benefits if we play nicely and don't make the payment? The payment that, I repeat, *does not violate the law.*"

"I don't know, Dale." Phil didn't even look up from his glass.

"Yeah. And you know why you don't know? Because *no one* benefits. No one is better off from your, what, moral stand. Oh. Except for our competitors. They benefit quite a lot, actually. They get rewarded nicely for playing the game the way it's played. 'When in Rome...' and all that, you know?"

"I don't think I can do it."

"That's fine. Perfectly fine. Just authorize me to draw the $250,000, and I'll take care of everything. More bratwurst for me, right?"

Phil waved the waitress over and held up his glass. "Another round," he said. The waitress nodded and headed for the bar. "I'll think it over, Dale."

"Well, think fast, because we don't have a lot of time."

"I will. I'll let you know tomorrow."

"That's fair enough, Phil."

DISCUSSION QUESTIONS

1. Should Phil allow Dale to draw the money and make the bribe payment that is, in the era presented in this module, completely legal under U.S. law?

   _____

   _____

   _____

   _____

2. Is the Foreign Corrupt Practices Act a good law? Should the United States try to "clean up corruption" around the world, or does the law place U.S. companies at a competitive disadvantage?

   _____

   _____

   _____

   _____

3. Phil laid out several stakeholders who stand to lose if the bribe payment is not made. Are there any stakeholders that would benefit if the bribe is not made? If so, who are they?

   _____

   _____

   _____

   _____

4. Stakeholder ethics aside, is this one of those things that a company "just can't do"? If so, why?

   _____

   _____

   _____

   _____

5. Speaking generally now, should the U.S. government place restrictions on how U.S. companies may behave when they operate outside the United States? Should we stretch, for example, environmental laws to U.S. operations in other countries? Discrimination laws? Minimum wage laws?

   _____

   _____

   _____

   _____

UNIT 11

The "Great Recession"

Unit Background

Causes of the current economic downturn are complex, but many identifiable parties certainly played a role in destabilizing the economy. The recession has also created new ethical dilemmas.

Module 55

Mortgage-Backed Securities and Root Causes of the "Great Recession". [Although complicated investments are not inherently harmful, they did have the effect of spreading the damage of the collapse in the housing market far and wide.]

Module 56

The Mortgage Meltdown—Big Investors. [When the housing market collapsed, losses were often dramatic. This module asks: Who is to blame—companies that offered complex real estate investments, ratings agencies, or investors who failed to recognize an investment that was "too good to be true"?]

Module 57

"Outsourcing Yourself". [The recession has caused millions of people to rethink many basic parts of their lives, including the place where they live. Is there anything wrong with leaving a community in search of a more favorable economic environment?]

Module 58

The Making Home Affordable Program. [One of the Obama administration's early programs established a substantial government fund and created policies to help struggling homeowners make mortgage payments. This module looks at the role of government in addressing a sputtering economy.]

Module 59

"Strategic Defaults" and Foreclosures. [Some homeowners are playing a game of "chicken" with their lenders and are skipping mortgage payments in favor of paying off credit cards and other bills. Is this practice reasonable? Is it ethical?]

The "Great Recession"

No business textbook published in early 2011 would be complete without a look at the current economy. A number of modules in other sections of this book give some attention to the recession, but this unit addresses it exclusively. Many players share some blame for causing the economy to take a nosedive, starting in 2008. The first two modules look at several of them. One of the modules looks at a very expensive government program that was passed to try to decrease the recession's negative impact on American families. The remaining modules present difficult choices that many people face as their income falls and they struggle to make ends meet.

Mortgage-Backed Securities and Root Causes of the "Great Recession"

At the time of this writing, the economy is in bad shape. We are not in a period as dreadful as the Great Depression of the 1930s, but we are in an extremely deep recession. Unemployment, at 10 percent, is about twice the levels of recent decades. And, unfortunately, job losses may not be finished; a recent headline forecast at least one hundred thousand teacher layoffs next year.

In the 1930s, Congress sought to address the root causes of the Depression, and substantial new laws were passed. In 2002, the federal government again took action in response to the collapse of Enron and other firms and changed accounting regulations. The government is currently busy with yet another round of significant legal reforms. Some have been passed already, and many more are on the drawing board.

There is no single cause of the current "Great Recession," but the collapse of the housing market is without a doubt a mighty contributor. Many proposed reforms seek to change the rules surrounding one or more types of transactions that were central to creating the housing bubble.

In determining which of the proposed laws is passed, the *perceptions* of law-makers and the voters who elect them are critical. Ultimately, some actors will be blamed more than others, and they will bear heavier burdens when new laws are passed. It will matter a great deal whether companies are deemed to have acted wrongfully or unethically. "Bad guys" will end up facing more regulations than those who were "merely misled" or "merely naïve."

Collapse of the Housing Market—Chain of Events

This module focuses on the basic chain of events that led to the mortgage meltdown. Module 56 focuses on more subtle and complicated causes.

The road to recession started with some members of Congress wanting banks to increase opportunities for people to own their own homes. To advance this goal, banks were encouraged to make more mortgage loans to borrowers with borderline credit scores.

In the end, many more people were able to qualify for loans. A number of these new borrowers did, in fact, "just need a chance," and they reliably made their mortgage payments. But many borrowers bought homes that they simply could not afford. Some banks made defaults more likely by making loans to applicants with very low credit scores, far below the scores for approval that the government advocated.

A third part of the problem was the skyrocketing popularity of mortgage-backed securities. Investment banks purchased millions of mortgage loans and bundled them together into mortgage-backed securities. The investment banks then sold the bundled mortgages to investors all over the world, spreading the risks of the growing housing bubble far and wide.

Mortgage-backed securities (MBS) are essentially "buckets" of mortgages. If you invest in an MBS, you buy a small slice of every mortgage in the bucket, and you receive a small slice of all monthly payments home owners make on those mortgages. If every borrower who took out every mortgage in your bucket pays his or her mortgage on time, then you get a very nice return. If most pay on time but a few do not make their monthly mortgage payment, you receive a decent return. But if large numbers of mortgages in the bucket go into default, your losses may be substantial.

Often, many of the loans put into new mortgage-backed securities were made to borrowers with poor credit scores. In 2008, when many became delinquent at about the same time, the value of many mortgage-backed securities plummeted. Investors were hit hard, as was every investment bank that was a significant player in issuing MBSs. Eventually, banks wrote off nearly one trillion dollars in losses. Credit of all kinds—mortgage loans, car loans, credit cards—became harder to get as the banks switched to new and often very strict lending standards. Individuals who had lost half of their investment assets or more cut back on spending. And many businesses, faced with fewer customers and greater difficulty in borrowing money, scaled back their operations and laid off workers.

SCENARIO

U.S. Congress—Representative Smith's Office

"I've been committed to this cause for 20 years," said Representative Smith.

"I know, I know," Representative Jones replied.

"Home ownership is a key part of the American Dream, and the bottom line is that the American Dream is not being realized by everyone. We have to lean on the banks to make more loans if they won't do it themselves."

"But the banks have to make a profit. We can't force them to make loans to people who won't be able to pay them back."

"That's not what I'm talking about—not at all. But there are millions of hard-working people who could pay off a mortgage if they just had a chance to get one in the first place. And they shouldn't be doomed to renting property all their lives for lack of opportunity."

"Look, if a bank is . . . discriminating, or something like that . . . then of course the government should get involved. But if a bank is saying, 'based on our experience, you don't make enough money to be a good bet to pay off this loan,' then I think we should leave that call to the bank."

"Banks don't exist merely to make profits, and I'm going to push hard to encourage them to make more loans. I want everybody with even a decent FICO score—say 620—to have a chance to own a home."

Kitchen Table—Apartment #230

"We should do it," Harry said to his wife.

"I just don't know," Carol replied.

"I don't want to rent this place forever," Harry said as he spread his arms wide and gestured to the apartment. "The guy said we'd get the loan for sure. We should stop talking about it and get it."

"I want to, but I just don't think we can afford it."

"We can afford it. The bank wouldn't loan us the money if we couldn't."

"Maybe." Carol found a document on the table. "But look at these estimated costs. The mortgage payment is $400 more than our rent. Property taxes and the other escrow stuff will add another $400 a month. And our bills will be more—it costs more to air condition a house than a little apartment. We'll need at least an extra $1,000 a month."

"We have an extra $1,000 a month."

"Not really. We have, maybe, an extra $750 a month, and that's if we don't have any unexpected expenses."

"OK, true, but I'll get a raise in a couple of months, and you'll get one this summer."

"Probably."

"Probably. And we can cut back on expenses. We need a house. I'm tired of flushing our money down the drain to the landlord."

"I am, too. I just don't want to get a house and then lose it."

"We won't."

Bank President's Office

"We'll lose money if we drop the cutoff to 620. We know anybody with a credit score of less than 680 is a bad risk," the CEO said.

"What can I say? This is what the Feds want us to do," said the senior vice president.

"They can't force us to do it."

"Sure they can. Not with this," the VP waived a fax. "This is just a friendly request. But if we don't voluntarily comply, they'll step up the pressure—you know they will."

"We'll lose a fortune."

"No, we won't," said the junior vice president, speaking for the first time. All heads at the long conference table turned toward her.

"How's that?" the CEO asked.

"If the Feds want us to make more loans, we'll make more loans. In fact, we'll make a loan to everybody who walks in the door and asks for one, no matter what their credit score is. And we'll sell every one of them to an investment bank. We won't have any problem finding takers—those guys are going crazy putting together mortgage-backed securities. We make money off of every loan we make, and if the government is wrong, and people can't pay off the mortgages, somebody else will take the loss. We'll double our profit, and if anybody complains later, we'll say, quite accurately, that we were furthering the government's directive to make more loans."

"Hmm . . ." the bank president said.

Big State Bank—Break Room

"Hey, Brent," Mark said.

"Hey, man, what's up?" Brent replied as he filled his coffee cup.

Mark nodded toward the window. "Yours?" he asked, looking at the couple walking to their car in the parking lot. The couple was all smiles.

"Yep. Harry and Carol. Just took out a $120,000 mortgage."

"Nice."

"Yeah, that's three so far today."

"Ka-ching."

"Yep."

"Think they'll be able to pay it off?"

Brent laughed. "Not a chance."

Mark shrugged. "Not our problem."

"Nope."

A Phone Call in Middle America

"So what else is new?" the father asked his son.

"Not much," the son replied.

"Ah."

"Hey, I got my quarterly statements in the mail yesterday. The big fund was way up again—it's up 30 percent so far this year. At this rate, I'm going to retire when I'm about 40!"

"Thirty percent? What's it in?"

"Mostly mortgage-backed securities."

"Come on, why do you put your money in that junk?"

"Ah, because . . . it's up 30 percent for the year, Dad."

"And how long do you think that's going to last?"

"I don't know, but it's going pretty well so far."

"There's no free lunch, Danny. Stuff that grows that fast always comes crashing down."

"Maybe, maybe not."

"Maybe for sure."

"Maybe I don't want to always play it safe and make a few lousy percent every year like you do."

"That 'few lousy percent' adds up. I'm 60 years old, and I have enough money to last forever. You can't do better than that."

"I'm just playing it my way, Dad."

"You should cash out your lucky winnings on Monday and be glad to have them."

"No thanks, Dad."

DISCUSSION QUESTIONS

For questions 1 and 2, please circle the response you most agree with. If you disagree with the first three choices, circle the fourth option, and fill in the blank with your answer.

1. In encouraging lenders to make more mortgage loans, the government was:

   a. Advancing sound policy that was misapplied by the banks
   b. Advancing a well-intentioned but misguided policy
   c. Advancing an inappropriate policy
   d. _____

2. Focusing now on the bank that made loans to people who couldn't afford them and then sold the loans to investment banks, the institution:

   a. Did nothing wrong
   b. Acted unethically toward its own customers
   c. Acted unethically toward investors who ultimately bought questionable loans
   d. _____

3. Assume that Harry and Carol are unable to consistently make their mortgage payments and that they lose their home to foreclosure after two years. How much blame falls on them for taking out the loan when they knew they might have problems repaying it? One hundred percent? Some smaller figure? What if they had been less realistic about their finances and had completely believed that they would be able to repay the loan? Does any additional blame for the foreclosure go elsewhere?

   _____

   _____

   _____

   _____

4. Assume that Danny the investor sticks with the mortgage-backed securities. Over the next six months, he loses two-thirds of his money. What percentage of blame for his losses rests on his shoulders? One hundred percent? Some smaller figure?

_____

_____

_____

_____

5. Rank the groups described in this module. Place a #1 by the group who seems most to blame for the mortgage meltdown, a #2 by the second most blameworthy group, and so forth.

_____ Government officials who encouraged loans to borderline borrowers

_____ Banks that made loans to borrowers who could not afford them

_____ Borrowers who took out loans they eventually could not repay

_____ Investment banks that created mortgage-backed securities

_____ Investors who bought and held mortgage-backed securities

The Mortgage Meltdown—
Big Investors

BACKGROUND

Module 55 looked into the roles played by government policymakers, borrowers, lenders, and "small" investors in creating the housing bubble and the subsequent collapse of the housing market. This module will look at the large-scale investors.

Many currently proposed reforms seek to change the rules surrounding one or more types of transactions that were central to creating the housing bubble. In determining which of the proposed laws is passed, the *perceptions* of lawmakers and the voters who elect them are critical. Ultimately, some will be blamed more than others, and they will bear heavier burdens when new laws are passed. It will matter a great deal whether companies are deemed to have acted wrongfully or unethically. "Bad guys" will end up paying a higher price.

To recap, the government encouraged lenders to make more mortgage loans to applicants with mediocre credit scores. The goal was to give more people a chance to become homeowners. Millions of new loans were issued to home buyers, and the loans came to be called "subprime."

Investment houses like Goldman Sachs and Lehman Brothers purchased many subprime loans, mixed them together with "regular," non-subprime loans, and packaged them together into mortgage-backed securities. These were mixed even further with additional subprime loans and other kinds of assets and packaged together into "collateralized debt obligations" (CDOs). CDOs were mainly sold to institutional investors.

Ratings Hocus-Pocus

Investors rely on ratings agencies like Moody's and Standard & Poor's (S&P) to help them assess the relative risk of investments. Often, the firms are quite accurate in their assessments. But on investments built on subprime mortgages, both firms often made significant miscalculations in creating computer models and vastly underestimated risks.

A rating of "AAA" is supposed to indicate a chance of default over a ten-year period of far less than 1 percent. Just before the crash, the overwhelming majority of mortgage-related securities received AAA ratings.

But in 2007, 11 percent of adjustable rate subprime mortgages went into default. In that same year, both Moody's and S&P initially rated the Abacus fund described below as AAA, even though it was full of adjustable rate subprime mortgages. The fact that assets with a 1-in-9 risk of default in a one-year period were ever packaged into a form that received an AAA rating is utterly astonishing.

Many have called the role of ratings agencies into question, including some members of Congress. New regulations under consideration may seek to deemphasize the reliance of investors on ratings agencies, help to create more competition between established and startup ratings agencies, or both.

Goldman Sachs Lawsuit

At the time of this writing, the government has brought a civil case against Goldman Sachs (Goldman) alleging fraud. In 2007, Goldman created "Abacus 2007-AC1." Abacus was even more complex than a normal CDO. It was a *synthetic* CDO, which allows investors to make or lose money based on the performance of real assets. Abacus held no actual mortgages, but it referenced a pool of about 500,000 real mortgages.

The government's case centers on the fact that another of Goldman's clients, Paulson & Co. Inc. (Paulson), made one billion dollars when Abacus collapsed. Nearly anything can be insured against loss. This is true whether the loss comes in the form of a fire that burns a building down or in the form of homeowners who lose the ability to make their mortgage payments. And whenever insurance is sold, whether simple or complex, one side bets on "something good" and one side bets on "something bad" happening. Paulson bet mightily that many Abacus mortgages would go into default, and they were absolutely correct. Eventually, over *half* of the Abacus mortgages went into default.

The government will argue that Abacus was designed to fail, and that Paulson helped Goldman in selecting the Abacus mortgages. In the end, the government is accusing Goldman of wrongdoing in attracting investors to make a "something good will happen" bet to go against Paulson's "something bad will happen" bet.

SCENARIO

Cast of Characters

> Roger .... as *Institutional Investors*
> Tex .... as *the Ratings Agencies*
> and introducing **Big State Casino** .... as *the Investment Banks*

Smalltown

Roger lived a dull life in Smalltown, Illinois. He finished high school (barely) and took a job at a little bakery on the edge of town. Eight years later, he still worked there, and he still made minimum wage. For a while, he dated a girl who used way too much eye shadow and listened to The Cure a lot, but the relationship didn't really go anywhere. Roger paid his modest bills, grew a thin moustache, and lived day-to-day.

But then . . . one day, Roger inherited $25,000 from an uncle! He told the owner of the bakery what he really thought of him, threw down his apron, and quit. He bought a bus ticket to Las Vegas and told the bus driver, "I'm going to be rich!"

Big State Casino—Las Vegas

Roger took his $25,000 stack of chips and turned away from the window. He was nearly blinded by the casino's lights, and he walked around for some time. Eventually, he sat down next to a man in a white cowboy hat.

"Hi," Roger said to the man. "I'm Roger."

"Tex," the man replied, nodding once.

Roger became excited. A friend had once told him that men named after states were excellent gamblers. Roger decided to hit his new acquaintance up for advice. "So," he said, trying to sound casual, "what are you gonna play tonight?"

"Mmm . . . haven't decided yet," Tex replied nonchalantly. He offered nothing further.

Roger tried again. "Well, I'm looking to make a big score tonight." No response. "I've got a stake of $25,000 here," he added.

"Mmm," Tex replied.

Roger became increasingly sure that he was talking to a real expert. "If you were me, what would you play to, you know, really cash in?"

Tex thought for a moment. "Well," he said, "if you really want to win big . . . "

"Yeah?"

"I mean if you really want to rake it in . . . "

"Yeah?"

"You might try . . . "

"What? What?"

"Super Ultra Poker."

Roger savored the sound of that for a moment. "Super Ultra Poker."

"Yep. Super Ultra Poker."

"How do you play?"

"Well," Tex said, leaning closer, "up there, at the purple table, it goes like this." For several minutes, he described a game that incorporated the results of all other games in the casino. Roger's focus ebbed and flowed. He caught some phrases and lost others. "So you're betting that a preponderance of the slot machine winners exceed . . . of course, if the mean payout at the blackjack tables is diminished . . . derived by calculating . . . integrated against the results of matched primary numbers . . . " At some point, Tex stopped talking.

Roger was overloaded but remained enthusiastic at having inside information. "And . . . and you're sure this is a good bet?"

"As far as I know," Tex replied. "I've seen nothing but big winners walking away from that purple table all week."

"Wow. Hey . . . hey, thanks, man."

"No problem."

Fifteen Minutes Later

"House wins!" The dealer raked the last of Roger's chips off the purple felt and into a hole in the table in front of him.

"What?!" Roger shouted with his hands held wide.

"Sorry, mister. The median yield exceeded the premium spread by less than the product of the lesser of the zero point value and the standard accelerated lincecum."

"You're making all of that up!"

"I assure you that I am not."

"Tim Lincecum is a pitcher for the San Francisco Giants!"

"It's all in the player's agreement you signed when you sat down."

"Waarrgh!" Roger lunged for the dealer. He was intercepted by a pit boss who was approximately the size of a refrigerator. The large gentleman had no discernable neck. He dragged Roger roughly but efficiently toward the exit. On the way, Roger slid by Tex's table.

"And YOU!" he shouted at Tex. "You're next! I'll get you and teach you not to . . . " his voice faded rapidly as the pit boss rounded a corner. Tex shrugged and took a sip of his drink.

Five Minutes Later

Roger limped gingerly to a bench in the park across the street of the casino. Both of his eyes were blackened, but he was otherwise reasonably well put together in spite of everything. He sat down next to a girl who was wearing way too much eye makeup. "Hey," he said to her.

"Hey," she answered timidly.

"Do you like The Cure?" Roger ventured.

She did a double take. "They're . . . my favorite. How did you know?"

"Just a hunch."

"I'm Vanessa."

"I'm Roger."

And because someone in one of these "I lost all my money on a bet I didn't understand in the slightest" situations ought to find a silver lining, let's say that Roger and Vanessa lived happily ever after.

DISCUSSION QUESTIONS

1. Do you blame the investment banks that sold CDOs and other complex real estate investments for contributing to the current economic mess? Did they act any more or less wrongfully than the casino in the scenario that created the difficult-to-understand game of Super Ultra Poker?

   _____

   _____

   _____

   _____

2. Do you blame the ratings agencies that rated complex investments as AAA when in fact they often largely consisted of ultra-risky subprime mortgages? Did they act any more or less wrongfully than Tex, who declared Super Ultra Poker to be a good bet in the scenario?

   _____

   _____

   _____

   _____

3. Do you blame investors for being greedy and contributing to the recession by purchasing complex investments? Do you have any more or less sympathy for them than for Roger in the scenario?

   _____

   _____

   _____

   _____

4. For this question, ignore the overall economy and focus only on the losses on the CDOs and other complex real estate investments themselves. Assign a percentage of blame to each of the investment banks, ratings agencies, and investors so that the total equals 100 percent. (So, for example, you might say 50 percent to one group, 50 percent to another, and 0 percent to the third.) Now do the same thing for the casino, Tex, and Roger from the scenario.

   _____

   _____

   _____

   _____

5. Should the government create new regulations to address any of the three groups in this module? Should investment banks be more regulated and less able to offer complex investments? Should ratings agencies that miss the mark on their ratings face greater legal liability? Should investors be restricted in their ability to purchase complex investments until they show (perhaps through passing an exam) that they fully understand what they are investing in?

_____

_____

_____

_____

"Outsourcing Yourself"

Other modules in this collection have examined ethical dilemmas related to outsourcing, but they have focused on organizations. For the benefit of readers who are completing these modules individually and not in the form of a textbook, a brief recap of those issues follows.

If a company pays its U.S. workers $20 per hour, but the same work could be done overseas in exchange for $2 per hour, what should the company do? Are its leaders obligated to move the operation outside the United States so that its labor costs can be reduced and profits increased? Are any obligations owed to employees or the communities that have grown up around a business? And if a company is operating overseas, does it ever have an obligation to *insource* jobs back to America? Most manufacturing jobs have left the United States, but some companies are bucking the trend and building new plants here. Is this justifiable if the shareholders will make less money?

This module, though, examines a dilemma that has become more common with the advent of the recession. It focuses on whether a person can ethically outsource *him or herself*.

State and Local Taxes

The recession has laid waste to the budgets of almost all cities and states. People are spending less money, so less sales tax is collected. Property values have dropped and so have property tax collections. States with income taxes have taken a hit, because more unemployed workers means fewer incomes to tax.

The budget gaps are severe. California, for example, is facing a $26 billion deficit. This reality leaves state legislatures with difficult choices that essentially lie in two categories: raise taxes or cut spending. Many states seem to be pursuing the cut-spending option, but such cuts are difficult. They involve layoffs to state workers and reductions in services for residents of the state, among other problems.

Some states have made raising taxes a component of closing budget gaps. Taxes on the wealthy, "sin taxes" on alcohol and cigarettes, and gas taxes seem to be the most popular, but many states are poised to increase taxes more broadly.

Workforce Mobility and "Tax Shopping"

The Internal Revenue Service (IRS) released interesting data in June 2010. It reflected the average household income of people moving into and out of every county in the United States.

In Collier County, Florida, the average family moving into the county earned about $300,000, whereas the average family moving out of the county earned about $100,000. The majority of the counties with similar disparaging gaps were in Texas and Florida, two states with no state income taxes and low overall tax burdens.

It appears quite possible that some people, especially those who earn high incomes, are engaging in "tax shopping"—leaving states with high taxes and relocating to states with lower taxes. Not everyone can make such a migration conveniently, but a growing number of people can. Nearly 20 million Americans do most, or all, of their work at home.

To whatever degree tax shopping exists, it will likely accelerate as some states increase taxes to attempt to raise needed revenue.

Most media reports on tax increases focus on lawmakers and whether raising taxes is "fair" or "correct." But the *response* that people make to higher taxes raises interesting ethical issues.

SCENARIO

Wood Lawn Cemetery

The mourners parked their cars and walked by ones and twos to the gravesite. A light rain fell, and a cold wind blew from the north. The crowd grew to 100, then 200, and finally to 300 before the priest began to speak. Everything was a blur to Meg Nelson. She held her husband's hand and stared at her mother-in-law's casket.

Ashes to ashes, dust to dust.

Two Months Later

Meg Nelson woke up late and found her husband at the kitchen table. He was banging away on an old calculator and scribbling notes on a pad of paper next to his laptop. "Morning, Tom," she said to him.

"Good morning, dear," Tom said without looking up. "There's coffee."

"Excellent." Meg retrieved a cup and sat down at the table. "And what are we working on today?"

"Taxes. Texas. Taxes in Texas. Did you know they still don't have a state income tax in Texas?"

"Ah, no. I didn't know that."

"Well, they don't. Nothing. Nada. Zero state income tax. We've been paying 9 percent here for years, and it's going up to 11 percent next year. Eleven percent of everything, and for what?"

Meg knew that when Tom got on a roll, his questions were rhetorical. She waited a moment without answering, and, sure enough, he continued with his thought.

"I'll tell you what, Meg. Nothing. We pay $7,000 a year in property taxes here and 7 percent sales tax. In Texas, we'd pay $7,000 a year in property taxes on a house this size, and pay 7 percent sales tax. But no income tax. We'd have an extra $20,000 a year in our pockets if we moved to Texas."

Now Meg responded. "Whoa," she said.

"It's a new idea, I know that."

"You can say that again. Tom, we've lived here for 25 years."

"I know we have, but we're not tied to this place anymore. The kids are grown up. My mother, God rest her soul . . . I wish she were still with us, but . . . " Tom lowered his voice. "We don't have to be here to take care of her anymore. And I can write anywhere. It's not like we live next to my publisher now. And your company has a branch in Austin."

"Tom, I like it here."

"I like it here, too. What I don't like is paying $20,000 a year that I don't have to pay."

"We're a part of this community. We can't leave to . . . to save money."

"Of course we ca–"

Meg cut him off. "Tom! This town has meant a great deal to us. We have raised our children here. They received excellent educations, and they had a safe place to grow up. Everything we like to do has been funded by the town or the state: the parks, the jogging trail, the performing arts center, the nature conservatory. We've lived happily here. And now the state is short of cash and needs to raise more money for a while, and you want to leave? It seems . . . it just doesn't seem right, Tom."

"Our tax dollars have supported the schools and everything else for the 25 years we've lived here. I see no reason for us to feel obligated to pay for another 25 years. And I'll bet they have parks and schools and performing arts centers in Texas and that they manage to get by."

"Tom . . . "

"I won't make you move if you would just rather live here. But you like Texas. We have a great time whenever we go there. And we'd be closer to the kids than we are now. It seems like a sensible thing to consider."

"I don't know, Tom."

"And here's another thing. As we've seen up close this year, we won't live forever. And another little stink bomb in the governor's plan for next year will raise our state estate taxes to 12 percent."

"I know. I saw that on the news."

"So that's yet another pile of money that the kids won't get if we still live here when we pass."

"And Texas, of course . . . "

"No estate taxes go to Texas when Texas residents pass away. And, look, you know me—I like stability. I don't want to move for no reason. But look at this." Tom turned his notepad upside down and checked off figures as he described them.

"So let's say we work for another 15 years and live for another 30. If we live those years in Texas, we'll have something like 6 million dollars when we die. But if we live here and pay the higher state taxes, we'll only have about 4 million dollars. But then, the state estate tax would gobble up another half a million dollars if we are still here. And we can't assume that this will be the only year when taxes go up around here, so I'm estimating another half a million more that we'd lose. So our estimated "final score" in the bank is 3 million dollars. Half of what it could be in Texas. It's not a little bit of money, Meg. It's a mountain of money."

Meg looked over the figures. Eventually, she said, "It still doesn't seem right to jump ship. I mean, what would happen if everyone just moved like we did? How would the state keep going?"

"The state isn't a charity, and we don't 'owe it to them' to make donations. We do have an obligation to help the kids, even though they're grown. I'll feel better on my deathbed if they stand to inherit twice as much money. And we owe it to ourselves to keep what we earn and enjoy it. We'll only go around once, dear."

Meg sipped her coffee. "Well," she said. "So you've been busy this morning, then."

Tom left his serious expression behind and returned to his normal and friendly self. "That I have, my love."

"Usually you're just watching soccer at 8:30 AM on a Saturday."

"Ah, but the early game today was at Tottenham, and I am bored to bloody tears by Tottenham."

"My husband, the fake Englishman."

"That's me," Tom replied. "So what do you say we take a vacation down to Austin? No pressure. Just have a look around for a while. I know another writer down there from a couple of my conferences. His name's Bredeson. Goofy-looking fellow, but interesting. I'm sure he'd show us around. What do you say?"

"To a vacation, I say yes. To the other thing, I say we'll talk about it later."

"A vacation it is, then."

DISCUSSION QUESTIONS

1. Do Tom and Meg have any ethical obligation to stay put and not move to Texas? Why or why not?

   _____

   _____

   _____

   _____

2. Would taxes ever drive you to consider moving to another state, or would it be a nonissue in your own life?

   _____

   _____

   _____

   _____

3. If Tom and Meg owned a small business that employed ten people, would they have an obligation to stay put and not relocate the business to Texas?

   _____

   _____

   _____

   _____

4. Many states today are broke, or nearly so. If a state runs out of money from its usual sources, how much should it raise taxes, and how much should it cut spending? Allocate 100 percent between those two options. (In other words, fill in 50 percent and 50 percent if you think states should do both evenly, 100 percent and 0 percent if you think states should entirely focus on cutting spending, etc.)

   _____ Cut Spending   _____ Raise Taxes

5. Assume that you have a job offer from a large company that has branches all over America, and the company will assign you to the branch location of your choice. Rank the following from #1 (most important to you) to #7 (least important to you) in deciding where you will live.

   _____ Low taxes

   _____ Good weather

   _____ Close to family

   _____ Low crime rate

   _____ Good public schools

   _____ Pleasant scenery

   _____ Entertainment options/nightlife

The Making Home Affordable Program

We are currently in the depths of a severe economic downturn. It is much worse than a typical recession, but so far it is not nearly as severe as the Great Depression of the 1930s. Some have begun to call our current problems the "Great Recession."

Many things have contributed to the Great Recession, but this module will focus on the role real estate has played. A fundamental problem has been and continues to be that too many people are unable to consistently make mortgage payments on their homes. When loans are defaulted upon, losses are substantial for the lenders and investors who hold them, and borrowers lose their homes.

Within a month of taking office, President Obama announced a $75 billion federal program called the Homeowner Affordability and Stability Plan. The administration has since started referring to the plan as the **Making Home Affordable Program (MHAP)**. The two primary goals of the program are related to loan modifications and loan refinancing.

Many portions of the MHAP are currently set to expire between 2010 and 2012, but they might be extended. The government seems to want the largest possible number of people to be able to recognize the American Dream of homeownership.

"Underwater" Loans: Negative Equity

Negative equity refers to a loan balance that is larger than the value of the asset for which the loan was made in the first place. It is not a new or uncommon phenomenon. Borrowers who finance most of the purchase of a new car, for example, almost always find themselves "upside down" for a time because the value of a new car tends to drop about 25 percent as soon as buyers take possession.

The unusual occurrence in 2007 through 2010 was the large number of homeowners who came to have negative equity in their homes. In the early years of this century, many borrowers came to carry little home equity either because they put little money down on a new home or because they took out home equity loans to cash out the rising values of their properties. Then, when the housing market collapsed and values plummeted, many homes were left "underwater." Approximately one in four homeowners is currently in this situation.

Under the Making Home Affordable Program, most mortgages are eligible to be refinanced at the time of this writing as long as the outstanding balances are not more than 125 percent of the value of a home. Thus, homeowners who are less than 25 percent underwater are able to refinance their loans at lower rates. Through the first year of operation, the government reported that 3.8 million homeowners had refinanced their loans under the program, and that, in doing so, they had saved a total of nearly $7 billion.

Borrowers with Income Insufficient to Make Monthly Payments

The Obama administration has repeatedly expressed concerns over borrowers who have become unable to make their mortgage payments because of unemployment, underemployment, other loss of income, or medical expenses. In 2009, the president announced a target of assisting 3–4 million homeowners to make mortgage payments by 2012 with a goal of "preventing avoidable foreclosures and stabilizing neighborhoods." Fifty billion dollars, two-thirds of the overall money allocated to MHAP, was earmarked for this purpose. Most Americans who have had a sharp drop in income or in the value of their homes are eligible to apply for a "trial modification."

Under the new program, mortgage holders are paid $1,000 for each trial modification offered that is accepted by a borrower. If a borrower stays in the program, the lender can receive an additional $1,000 per year, up to three years, and the borrower can receive $1,000 per year, up to five years.

Trial modifications typically last for three months. If, at the end of that time, a borrower has been able to make the modified payments, the borrower can apply for a permanent modification.

Through the first year of operation, the government reported that over 900,000 borrowers had accepted trial modifications under the program to reduce monthly payments. But only 66,000 (7 percent) of the trial modifications had become permanent modifications by the end of 2009. Banks reported widespread misrepresentation of drops in income by borrowers and a widespread inability by borrowers to make even the reduced payments they had agreed to make.

Proponents of the plan hope to modify it in coming years to increase the number of trial modifications that become permanent. Critics argue that $50 billion is a hefty price tag for a program that usually only postpones the inevitable loss of a home.

In light of the large number of trial modifications that fail to become permanent, the MHAP may present an ethical dilemma for some lenders. The bank in the scenario that follows is fictional, but the statistics are accurate.

SCENARIO

Texas Bank

"Ron, come in, come in," said the CEO of Texas Bank.

"Afternoon, sir," Ron said. He took a seat opposite the CEO.

"So you want to talk about our mortgage portfolio?"

"I do," Ron said. "I think we're missing an opportunity."

"Tell me about it."

"All right. So we hold about 10,000 mortgages, right? And a lot of them are in trouble." The CEO nodded and rubbed his eyes, and Roger continued. "As we discussed last month, about 2,000 of them are more than 60 days behind. Another 1,000 of them are current, but they're underwater."

"It's a mess," the CEO agreed.

"Some of our competitors have signed 'participation agreements' with the government to modify some of their loans under the Making Home Affordable Program."

"Bailout money thing?"

"More or less."

"What do we have to do?"

"Mostly find people who could pay their mortgage if the payments were smaller. We have to adjust payments down to 38 percent of a borrower's income."

"So if somebody has a monthly gross income of $4,000, we have to knock the mortgage bill down from whatever it is to about $1,500?"

"Correct."

"What's our benefit?"

"We get $1,000 per person that we sign up."

"Really?"

"$1,500 per person if they're not behind on their payments when we sign them up."

"Hmm," the CEO punched some numbers into a calculator on his desk. "So if we sign up our 2,000 defaulters . . . and add our 1,000 underwater folks who aren't behind, we get . . . $3.5 million?"

"Exactly."

"Just like that?"

"Just like that."

"What if they still can't make the payments?"

"We keep the money anyway. And then we foreclose just like we would have done in the first place. And if they can make the new payments, we get $1,000 per year for up to three years. 'Pay for Success' payments, they're calling them."

"Really." It was more of a statement than a question.

"Yes, sir. We're taking heavy losses on our mortgages, but this is money on the table, ready to be snapped up."

"No catches?"

"No big ones. The loan balance can't be more than about $700,000, but only two of ours are that large. The mortgage has to have been taken out before 2009, but we've been much stricter in our lending standards for new loans, and there aren't many of the new ones in default. The program doesn't last forever, but we can sign people up until the start of 2012. It gives our customers a chance to keep their homes. It's good for us, too. It just looks good."

"Interesting. I'll talk this over with Jane later today."

"OK. She . . . ah . . . she's not as enthusiastic about this as I am."

"That's how it always is. If I talk to both of you and take an average, I usually know what's best for us." The CEO smiled.

Later that Day

"Ron really likes it," the CEO said.

"Ron doesn't care about our customers," Jane said.

"I'm not sure about that, but tell me what you mean anyway."

"Well, we can definitely sell our customers on this and get paid." Jane flipped through her notes. "More than 80 percent of borrowers in Texas take the deal when they are offered a loan modification under this program."

"Isn't that what we want?"

"Yes and no. I mean, if we're talking about a customer who really can make the new lower payment and get current on his loan, then, yes, we want him to take the deal, and I have no problem with us being paid for modifying his loan. But most loan modifications don't work out."

"No?"

"No. Under the program, if a borrower gets a 'trial modification' and can make the new payments for three months, then he can be offered a 'permanent modification.' But less than 10 percent of trial modifications have become permanent modifications."

"Why is that?"

"Lots of reasons, but the biggest one is that, even after their payments are reduced, people still don't have enough money to make their payments. The recession is tough. Even people with jobs have lost hours, taken pay cuts, that kind of thing. They overestimate what they can afford."

"But this program at least gives them a chance to stay afloat."

"Some of them, but not most of them. Most of the borrowers in the program are going to lose their homes no matter what. They just can't afford them. So, in my opinion, this program—for most borrowers—makes them throw good money after bad. They prolong the inevitable for a month, two months, maybe three months, but no more. They spend thousands on a hopeless cause, and that's money that they could use when they have to start over to pay rent on an apartment, or a smaller house, or whatever."

"But these are adults. Surely we can count on them to determine what's in their best interests?"

They're desperate adults who will try anything to stay in their homes, even for a little while longer."

"Hmm . . ."

"Look, I'm not saying this program is all bad. I think we should participate in it. But we should do an analysis before we offer a customer a loan modification and assess whether he's likely to really be able to make the new payments. I've got stats on our ten biggest competitors here." Jane flipped through her notes again. "At one end of the spectrum, one of them converts 85 percent of their trial modifications to permanent modifications. At the other end, one of them converted 3,000 out of 200,000. That's 1.5 percent. If we start participating in this program, I want us to be like the former and not the latter. I don't want us to offer a loan modification to everybody, just to our customers who are most likely to actually be able to keep their homes over the long term."

The CEO thought it over for a moment. Eventually, he said, "Ron told me, 'The government wants us to do this. It wants us to be a partner and sign people up who need help.'"

"I don't know what to say to that, exactly," Jane replied. "I do know that a lot of our customers would be worse off if they signed up for this program than if we left them alone."

DISCUSSION QUESTIONS

1. Should Texas Bank agree to participate in the Making Home Affordable Program at all?

_____

_____

_____

_____

2. If Texas Bank does sign up, should its policy be to modify as many loans as possible, or only those issued to people most likely to be able to make payments over the long term if their loans are modified?

_____

_____

_____

_____

3. Should borrowers be given prominently displayed statistics that indicate most loan modifications are unsuccessful in helping borrowers keep their homes over the long term before they sign any final loan modification paperwork?

_____

_____

_____

_____

4. Assume that you are a borrower and that you are behind on your mortgage. Assume further that you are offered a loan modification under the MHAP and that, three months later, still unable to make your payments, you lose your home. Would you personally feel that you had "thrown money away in a lost cause," or would you be glad to at least have had the chance to get current on your mortgage payments?

_____

_____

_____

_____

5. What do you think of the MHAP overall? Is it a reasonable idea, or is it, as some critics argue, a poor use of taxpayer money?

_____

_____

_____

_____

"Strategic Defaults" and Foreclosures

BACKGROUND

Foreclosure is the process by which the holder of a mortgage repossesses a borrower's property and seeks to have the *entire* debt repaid promptly. Foreclosure usually happens as a result of a borrower failing to make timely payments, and it usually results in a property being sold at an auction to the highest bidder.

If all goes well, the auction raises enough money to fully repay a loan. In occasional cases, the auction raises more than the mortgage balance, and the surplus is returned to the borrower who has lost his home. Generally, however, an auction raises far less money than is owed.

Why Foreclosures Are Bad for Borrowers

The most obvious downside to a foreclosure is that a borrower can no longer live in the home. At the time of this writing, some three thousand families a day face losing a home to foreclosure. In addition, a problem that many people fail to anticipate can arise later.

In the current housing market, a foreclosure auction usually generates less than the outstanding loan balance. In such a case, in the majority of states, the mortgagee can seek a **deficiency judgment** requiring the borrower to pay the remaining amount.

Mortgagees have become increasingly aggressive in recent years as their losses from mortgage defaults have increased, and many routinely pull credit reports on defaulting borrowers to assess whether the borrowers have enough assets to make a deficiency judgment worth pursuing.

Newspapers seem to commonly feature stories on former homeowners who "thought they were done" when their homes were sold at auction and who express distress and surprise that they have to come up with additional funds to pay a deficiency judgment.

Why Foreclosures Are Bad for Lenders

Foreclosures almost always lead to losses for lenders. The current housing market is depressed overall, and foreclosure properties tend to attract bids lower than the market value for similar houses in the area, often due to concerns that they have not been well cared for. A lender loses an average of $50,000 per foreclosure, according to the Mortgage Bankers Association.

A lender always loses money in the form of missed payments. Often, lenders also must continue to make tax payments on the property even if the occupier of the property is no longer making her mortgage payments. If a borrower has abandoned her home, the lender has to pay for lawn maintenance and repairs. Homeowners' association fees and fees to collection agents sometimes come into play.

Often, court fees must be paid. Auctioneers must be hired. In some states, laws require a sheriff to supervise a foreclosure auction, and sheriff's fees can be substantial.

Deficiency judgments can reduce losses, but, often, borrowers who default on their loans either seek formal bankruptcy protection or have so little in assets that most losses cannot be recaptured.

The Game: Borrowers and Strategic Defaults

The current recession has put substantial pressure on the finances of millions of households. For many, a breaking point eventually arrives and not all bills can be paid. If a person has only $2,000 available, but he has $3,000 in bills to pay, he must prioritize some bills over others. This kind of choice has been characterized as a "strategic default."

A 2010 *U.S. News & World Report* article, "Forget the Mortgage, I'm Paying My Credit Card Bill," discussed a recent study by TransUnion, one of the three major credit reporting agencies. The study found that, in 2009, the number of people who had fallen behind on their mortgage payments, but who were not behind on their credit card payments, had increased *over 50 percent* in a single year, from 4.3 percent to 6.6 percent of all Americans. The article offered several explanations for the shift, including the fact that credit cards are seen by some as more "basic" for their survival, and the fact that foreclosures, because of costs and legal regulations, often take many months to be completed. Credit card accounts, on the other hand, are often cancelled after a small number of missed payments.

An average U.S. household carries over $12,000 in credit card debt. Millions of families have sought bankruptcy protection in recent years, and, in most cases, the credit card companies receive next to nothing and have to write off the $12,000 as uncollectible debt.

But when credit card issuers write off bad debt, the losses are spread out across a vast ocean of shareholders. When a major bank has new credit card defaults amounting to one million dollars, no particular person feels a dramatic impact because the losses are heavily diluted.

When homes are foreclosed upon, communities feel significant effects. Property values drop for everyone in areas with a high concentration of foreclosures. The properties themselves tend to be neglected and are sometimes abandoned, which can lead to an increase in crime. Decreasing property values impact a community's tax base and hurt its ability to provide basic services and maintain schools. Losses are more concentrated when mortgage loans go into default.

The Game: Lenders and Foreclosures

Because of the likelihood of significant losses described earlier, lenders often must face difficult decisions about when to press forward with foreclosures. The right to foreclose often arises after a second missed payment, but many lenders do not exercise it right away. Similarly, many Americans must decide if and when to make mortgage payments if they do not have enough money to pay all of their bills.

In the following scenario, a bank and a couple independently work through many of these issues that have become all too common in recent years.

SCENARIO

Greentown Bank

"OK," Ann frowned and grimaced. "Let's move on to this month's foreclosures. How many this time?"

"Four possibles," Reggie reported.

"Let's hear it."

"First up—the house at 123 Oak Street is three months behind on payments. We've been in contact with them, and he's lost his job. She's still employed as a teacher."

"What kind of job did the husband lose?"

"Sales."

"OK, go on."

"He says he's looking, and I believe him. They hadn't missed any payments for the past six years, and we've held their mortgage for the last three."

"What would the house fetch at auction?"

"Maybe $30,000 less than what they owe us."

"They have any assets?"

"Nothing major as far as I can tell. We could try to garnish her wages for now, and put a lean on his income when he has another job. A default judgment might cut our losses over the long term."

Ann made some notes. "OK," she said, "moving on."

"House number two is 123 Pine Street. Single guy, laid-off autoworker."

"Ouch."

"Yep, those jobs aren't coming back, at least not here."

"How far behind is he?"

"Just two months. He's had some money from a severance package, but that appears to be just about dried up. No other assets to speak of."

"How much will we lose if we foreclose?"

"About $50,000."

"All right. Next."

"Next is 123 Birch Street. Way behind, ah . . . six months. The wife was in a one-car accident last year and has had a lot of problems—medical expenses, had to cut back on hours at work, that kind of thing."

"Any record of what happened with the accident?"

"No police record or anything—she wasn't ticketed. All I can verify is that it happened at ten o'clock at night and that an ambulance took her to the hospital."

"OK. Any signs of improvement?"

"The husband talks to me regularly, but he seems to make promises that don't end up happening."

"Yeah. Any assets?"

"Not really. We'll lose about $40,000 overall in the short term."

"OK," Ann said as she made more notes. "You have one more?"

"Yep. Last one is 123 Elm Street. This one is kind of scary."

Ann smiled for the first time in a while. "A 'Nightmare on Elm Street,' Reggie?"

Reggie smiled, too. "You might say that."

"Scary as in how?"

"Scary as in these people are both employed, and they have the money to pay their mortgage, but they're just not doing it."

"How far behind are they?"

"Two months."

"Are they aware of it?"

"I talked to them yesterday. 'We've had some problems, but we'll catch up real soon,' they told me."

"Hmm . . ."

"It's almost like they're daring us to foreclose."

"How much do you think we'd lose?"

"That loan is way underwater—maybe $70,000."

"Do you really think they're playing chicken with us?"

"I don't know, but if everybody who's behind on payments starts doing this . . ."

"I know. We can't afford to foreclose on everybody at once."

"Scary," said Reggie.

"Scary," agreed Ann.

123 Elm Street

Tom and Ellen Smith sat at their kitchen table. A large number of bills and bank statements lay spread out before them. Tom rubbed his hand through his hair. "Look," he said, "if we declare bankruptcy, we'll lose the house for sure. If we do it this way, we might not lose the house."

"We're already two payments behind," Ellen stated. "If we miss another payment, they'll foreclose on us anyway."

"Maybe not!" Tom said, a bit too loudly. "I'm sorry," he said, lowering his voice. "Look, we know people who have gotten a lot longer from the bank. Ed and Mary were *eight* months behind before they lost the house. They'll call and send letters and make threats, but everybody's in trouble, and they can't foreclose on the whole town at once."

"What'll we tell the kids if we have to go?"

"We won't have to tell the kids anything. I'm trying to save the house, and I think we will. Look here," he said, pointing to a legal pad. "Last month, we had $400 in checking at the end of the month and $12,000 on the credit cards. This month, we have $800 in checking and $11,800 on the cards. We came out $600 better this month by cutting back on everything."

"And by skipping the $1,000 mortgage payment again."

"Yes, but we're closer to being able to make it. If we can save that $600 every month, and if I can get just a little more overtime, we can make it work."

"But you said you wouldn't be able to get more overtime for another couple of months."

"Right, so we just have to hang on to everything until then."

"I'd still feel better if we made the mortgage payment."

"So would I, but that will make us $400 short on something else. We've cut our spending as much as we can—we don't even have cable anymore. Which $400 worth of other bills should we not pay?"

"I don't know, Tom."

"Look, we have to pay the utilities. We can't make do without electricity and water. The only other thing is the $400 minimum payments on the credit cards."

"We can't skip those?"

"Come on, Elly, you know those guys are ruthless. They'll close the accounts after two months, tops."

"But they can't take our house. And we can just pay cash for everything."

"But they can take our cushion. What happens if the cards get cancelled, and one of the kids gets sick? What about last month when my car broke down? We didn't have two grand in the bank. It would still be parked on the mechanic's back lot if I hadn't been able to put the repairs on a credit card."

"I don't know, Tom."

"Look, it'll get better. I'll get the overtime eventually, they owe me. And you'll get a raise in May."

"Maybe."

"Look, we just have to keep everything going for now. And banks just take longer to act than credit card companies. If it were the other way around, I'd say we should pay the mortgage this month."

"I guess so."

"This is the best way to keep everything together."

DISCUSSION QUESTIONS

1. If you were Ann, which of the four houses would you foreclose on, and which would you give more time? Why?

123 Oak Street	Foreclose // More Time
123 Pine Street	Foreclose // More Time
123 Birch Street	Foreclose // More Time
123 Elm Street	Foreclose // More Time

2. Would your answers to the first question change at all if the economy were significantly better than it is currently? What if it were significantly worse?

3. If you were in Tom and Ellen's position, would you give priority to making the mortgage payment or making the credit card payments? Why?

4. Debt trade-offs aside, could you survive without credit cards if necessary? What would be the biggest problems you would have if you no longer had credit cards?

5. During the recession, some lenders have "frozen" foreclosures for a time, which means that they have suspended all foreclosures for weeks or months. Some state governments have at least considered requiring statewide freezes. Are such policies reasonable during an economic downturn? Would policies like freezes be better or worse if they were required by the government?

UNIT 12

Government Actions and Corporate Influence

Unit Background

Congress, the President of the United States, and especially the Supreme Court play key roles in shaping the legal environment of business. This final unit examines several current issues.

Module 60

Politics and the Supreme Court. [The Supreme Court interprets the law, but the president acts as a "gatekeeper" and determines who is nominated to sit on the Court in the first place.]

Module 61

Citizens United Case: Free Speech, Corporations, and Participation in Elections. [Perhaps the most significant decision of 2010 involved the free speech rights of organizations.]

Module 62

Long-Term Unemployment. [The recession has created high rates of overall unemployment. In particular, it has caused millions of people to be unemployed for unusually lengthy periods of time.]

Module 63

Immigration Policy. [The State of Arizona touched off a political firestorm with a new 2010 law that attempted to crack down on illegal immigration. Many other states will likely debate similar measures in the years to come.]

Module 64

Health Care Legislation. [Proposed health care reforms in the opening years of the Obama administration created more Congressional debate than any in recent memory. The Supreme Court may soon weigh in on whether the reforms are acceptable under the Constitution.]

Government Actions and Corporate Influence

The U.S. government, by creating new laws, often shifts the boundary between law and ethics. The notions of right and wrong of presidents, representatives, and justices often take the law in new directions.

The first two modules in this unit look at the Supreme Court. The balance of power between liberal and conservative justices may be the most overlooked dynamic in law, and the first module describes it. The second module looks at a particular new dilemma that the Supreme Court presented companies in 2010.

Three recent political contentions round out the book. Immigration policy is a hot topic these days, as is the payment of long-term unemployment benefits to laid-off workers. Finally, there was no issue debated more during the first part of President Obama's time in the White House than health care, and that topic is addressed in the last module.

MODULE 60

Politics and the Supreme Court

BACKGROUND

This series of modules usually focuses squarely on business ethics ideas. But the borderline between ethics and law, between what is allowed and what is required, is constantly in motion. Ideas about right and wrong can drive law in new directions, and, often, the courts are at the forefront of changes. A look at the legal and ethical environment in which companies operate would be incomplete without a look at the Supreme Court and the process by which its justices are selected.

The Supreme Court

The Supreme Court is composed of nine justices. Although few Americans recognize them, they are among the most powerful people in the world. Among them, they decide what American laws *mean*. The power to interpret a law can be every bit as significant as the power to create a law in the first place. And different justices have very different ideas on how laws ought to be interpreted.

To simplify, "conservative" justices tend to apply the law literally, or exactly as written. They often apply laws narrowly and only to circumstances that seem to be obviously called for in the law itself. "Liberal" justices tend to ask big-picture questions like, "What is the purpose of this law? Why was it passed in the first place?" They will sometimes imply ideas and apply laws in ways that are not, at least directly, called for. To illustrate the difference, let's look at the right to privacy.

The Constitution describes many liberties. The rights to free speech, due process of law, and equal protection are very well known. They are also directly mentioned by name in the Constitution. But the right to privacy is not. It exists, but it was implied by a liberal-leaning Supreme Court in the 1960s and 1970s. Conservative justices tend to argue that the right to privacy should be applied weakly or not at all, because it is not literally mentioned in the text of the Constitution.

The balance of power between liberal and conservative justices is important. Dozens of significant legal issues come out in opposite ways when they are reviewed by liberal and conservative courts.

337

The focus of the government depends a great deal on whether the president is a Republican or a Democrat and on which political party controls Congress. In the same way, it matters whether the fifth (majority-forming) vote on the Supreme Court belongs to a conservative or liberal justice.

Replacing Justices

The justices have job security that most people can only dream of: They have lifetime appointments. Once they "get the job," they can keep it for as long as they like, and they never have to be reelected, reappointed, or answer to anyone.

As a consequence, vacancies on the Court are rare. On average, one justice retires or passes away about every three or four years. Sometimes, though, a decade or longer passes without any changes to the makeup of the Court.

When there is a death or retirement, replacement justices are nominated by the president. They must then be approved by a majority of the members of the Senate. Appointments can generate controversy, and presidents must take this into consideration.

Presidents are not required to follow any particular rules in making nominees. They often select experienced judges as well as someone who agrees with their point of view on key issues that blocks of voters follow, like abortion, affirmative action, and gun rights. They frequently, but not always, present candidates that the Senate will be likely to confirm. Other issues like the race, gender, and age of possible nominees can also come into play.

In recent years, President George W. Bush was 2-for-2 in getting conservative nominees through the Senate and onto the Court. President Obama, at the time of this writing, is also 2-for-2 in getting liberal nominees through the Senate.

In the following scenario, I have deliberately avoided labeling President Williams as a Republican or Democrat. Many people react quite strongly to political party affiliation, and I wanted answers to the questions that follow to be unaffected by whether the hypothetical president is a member of one party or the other.

SCENARIO

In the Oval Office

Larry Johnson, the White House Chief of Staff, entered the Oval Office and closed the door behind him. He found President Williams on the phone. The president saw Johnson, raised one finger, and continued with his call. After a minute, he hung up.

"Larry," he said.

"Mr. President," Larry replied. "I have a working list of Supreme Court nominees here," he said, raising a file. "The team has whittled it down to five names."

"Ah, excellent. How many of them do I know?"

"Personally—three, I think. You'll have heard of the other two. I knew you'd want to have a chance to add or delete names before we release a short list to the press."

"I do indeed. Let's hear them."

"Yes, sir. Evan Richard Atkinson is first on the list."

"I thought he might be," the president said.

"He's clearly the most experienced, most qualified candidate. Twenty-five years as a federal judge. Impeccable record and credentials. He'd pass the Senate easily."

"I agree."

"The only drawback as far as we're concerned is the, ah, the strength of his convictions. He seems to agree with you on most issues, but he's not as strongly aligned as some of the other candidates. Particularly on abortion."

"Can't overlook abortion."

"Right. His opinions are, ah, largely but not entirely in agreement with your own views."

"That's the sense I get." The president made a few notes.

The Chief of Staff continued. "Next is Professor Benson."

"My favorite law professor."

"Yes, Mr. President."

"Wouldn't that be something to put him on the Court? And it's not just that I think well of him—he's probably the sharpest legal mind in the country."

"Yes, sir, we agree. He hasn't been a judge, but we think that, with his name recognition, he'd pass the Senate easily. And he's strictly aligned with your point of view on all the key issues."

"He'd have to be—he taught me most of those ideas in the first place!" The president smiled.

"Yes, sir. Our only concern is his age."

"Let me guess," President Williams said. "Sixty...four?"

"Actually, he's 69."

"Ah."

"So he'd serve 20 years, tops, and probably more like 10 to 15."

"I see. But, you know, I saw him this fall at the Harvard–Yale game. He takes good care of himself."

"That he does."

"OK." The president made more notes. "Who else have you got for me?"

"Third is Mary Cavanaugh."

"Second Circuit?"

"Yes, Mr. President. Her opinions strongly reflect your point of view, and she has 17 years experience as a judge, 8 of them as a federal judge."

"OK."

"And she's only 42."

"Wow."

"She was first elected to the bench straight out of law school."

"That's outstanding."

"Her resumé is strong, and we think the Senate would go for her. And she could be influential for the next 40 years."

"That has a nice ring to it."

"Yes, sir, it does." Johnson waited while the president made more notes before he continued. "Our fourth candidate is Roger Dawson." Johnson cringed a bit.

"Dawson?" the president asked, surprised but not agitated.

"Yes. The, ah, committee thought he was worth putting on the short list. If you wanted to go this way, he'd pass the Senate 100–0. He's nearly as experienced as Atkinson. And the press would applaud you for appointing a moderate and 'reaching out to the other side.' That's, ah, not a bad thing in an election year."

"No, it's not a bad thing. But Dawson's...he really is a moderate, isn't he? From what I can remember, I agree with him about half the time and disagree with him about half the time."

"Yes, sir. That's about the size of it. At the very least, we thought he'd be a good person for the official short list we release to the press. Whether you nominate him or not, if we include him, it might make the process seem less driven by ideology."

"Yeah. Yeah, you're right." The president paused. "How many years on a federal court?"

"Thirty-three."

"Huh. Well, let's keep him on the list."

"Will do. And there's one more: Anna Lee."

"OK."

"She's a very well-regarded district court judge in Texas, and she's served for 20 years. She was a lawyer for a while before being appointed to the bench. She's very accomplished and well regarded, but she's unknown compared to someone like Judge Atkinson. Still, her opinions show she agrees with you on most issues. Not as strongly as Professor Benson or Cavanaugh, but strongly enough. And there's..."

"There's never been an Asian American on the Supreme Court," the president finished.

"There's never been an Asian American on the Supreme Court, " Johnson repeated. "LBJ was the first president to nominate an African American. President Reagan nominated the first female justice, and President Obama nominated the first Hispanic to the Court. You could nominate the first Asian American. She's highly qualified, and she sees things our way. We thought that Ms. Lee was a good addition to the list."

"You were right, and she is. How old is she?"

"Ah," Johnson checked his file. "She's 58."

The president made some final notes. "OK. That's all of them?"

"Yes, sir, unless you want to add anyone."

"I might. Sit on that for a couple of days and let me think about it. Let's shoot for a press release on Thursday."

"Will do. Thank you, Mr. President."

DISCUSSION QUESTIONS

1. If you were the president, how would you rate the five candidates? Rank them from 1 to 5, with #1 being your top choice, #2 as your second choice, etc.

_____ Atkinson (most experienced judge)

_____ Benson (extremely accomplished law professor)

_____ Cavanaugh (young judge, agrees with president on all issues)

_____ Dawson (judge with moderate values)

_____ Lee (experienced judge, could be first Asian-American justice)

2. Discuss your top two choices. Why were they at the top?

_____

_____

_____

_____

3. Which two candidates do you think *actual* presidents would be the most likely to nominate? If you think one of their top two choices would differ from yours, why do you think actual presidents would tend to dismiss one or both of your top choices?

_____

_____

_____

_____

4. Would a president's Supreme Court nomination ever be likely to influence your vote? Or would other issues always make a candidate appealing or unappealing? What are the two issues *most* likely to influence your support for politicians?

_____

_____

_____

_____

5. Should Supreme Court justices have lifetime appointments, or should they have to go through a nomination-and-confirmation process every so often?

_____

_____

_____

_____

Citizens United Case: Free Speech, Corporations, and Participation in Elections

BACKGROUND

In January 2010, the Supreme Court issued something of a bombshell. By a 5–4 vote, the Court overturned parts of a key law, which will have a significant impact on the degree to which U.S. corporations can influence political elections.

In *Citizens United* v. *Federal Election Commission*, a nonprofit organization made a documentary that was highly critical of Senator Hillary Clinton. At the proposed release date in early 2008, Clinton was the chief rival of then-Senator Obama for the Democratic presidential nomination. The lawsuit arose over the issue of whether the government could prohibit the movie or ads promoting it under the McCain–Feingold Act of 2002. In the end, the Supreme Court overturned a longstanding precedent that banned corporations from using their profits to seek to influence elections.

At the heart of the decision was the First Amendment and free speech rights. To repeat four points from other modules and include one more fact:

1. The Constitution sits atop the U.S. legal system. No kind of law can violate any part of the Constitution, and any law that does can be struck down by the courts.

2. The Supreme Court has the final say on what the Constitution means. Many important parts of the Constitution are vague. Many key liberties, for example, are described by a single sentence or a single phrase that was written more than 200 years ago. In the end, it is fair to say that the Constitution means whatever a majority of the current Supreme Court says that it means.

3. Although the media likes to call the nine Supreme Court justices "liberals" or "conservatives," a much more relevant distinction is between "literalist" and "nonliteralist" justices. Some justices tend to read and apply laws exactly as they are written, whereas others tend to be more flexible. Neither side is necessarily "right" or "wrong," but each does have a distinctly different way of interpreting and applying the law.

4. Of the nine justices as of fall 2010, four tend to be literalists (John G. Roberts, Samuel A. Alito, Clarence Thomas, and Antonin G. Scalia). Four tend to be nonliteralists (Elena Kagan, Ruth Bader Ginsburg, Sonia Sotomayor, and

Stephen G. Breyer). The last, Anthony M. Kennedy, is a moderate who tends to side with the literalists somewhat more often than not. On many issues, he is the "swing voter."

5.   Justice Kennedy sided with the literalists and wrote the opinion in the *Citizens United* case.

The actual text of the First Amendment, from which free speech rights are derived, is: "Congress shall make no law abridging the freedom of speech." The most literal interpretation of the statement is that any congressional statute that limits speech cannot stand.

In his opinion, Justice Kennedy wrote, "When Government seeks to use its full power, including the criminal law, to command where a person may get his or her information or what distrusted source he may or may not hear, it uses censorship to control thought. This is unlawful."

But the Supreme Court has long allowed for some laws to restrict speech that incites "imminent lawless action," is "obscene," or that places "reasonable time, place, and manner restrictions" on how, when, and where messages can be spread. Laws that allow for arrests of people trying to start a riot, ban child pornography, and place limits on rallies near schools during school hours have been upheld under such standards.

In the *Citizens United* case, the four dissenting justices opined that corporations should not enjoy the same free speech rights as people. The dissenting opinion said, among other things, "The fact that corporations are different from human beings might seem to need no elaboration, except that the majority opinion almost completely elides it."

Reaction to *Citizens United* began immediately and was intense. In the immediate aftermath of the decision, President Obama criticized the Supreme Court's decision during the State of the Union Address with most of the justices seated right in front of him. A video clip of Justice Alito seeming to mouth the words "not true" during the speech generated large numbers of views on the Internet.

Critics of the ruling argue that wealthy corporations will be able to spend so much money that they will drown out other voices during political campaigns. They lament the fact that the rules have been changed after nearly a century of precedent under McCain–Feingold and similar laws.

Not everyone is critical of the opinion. Some commentators hail the ruling as one that will help to unseat incumbents in Congress. Candidates who are already members of Congress and who are running for reelection tend to have more money available for campaigning than do their challengers. Those who support the *Citizens United* ruling argue that challengers will be able to mount more aggressive campaigns with corporate backing behind them. (Corporations are still banned from giving money directly to candidates or to political parties, but they can run ads in support of or in opposition to specific candidates.)

In the end, it seems likely that corporations will be free to run campaign ads for the immediately foreseeable future. Overriding a Supreme Court opinion requires either a constitutional amendment or a new Supreme Court with a different balance of power between literalist and nonliteralist justices. An amendment seems unlikely, if for no other reason than that it requires a two-thirds majority vote in Congress as a starting point, and it seems improbable that the current deeply divided Congress would reach a broad consensus on any issue whatsoever. As for the other possibility, justices have lifetime job appointments. A voluntary retirement by one of the literalists, and his replacement by a nonliteralist, is possible but not particularly likely in the near future.

For now, corporations will have to choose whether and how deeply to become involved in elections. This issue may create a minefield for corporate leaders, as the following scenario illustrates.

SCENARIO

Energy Company Boardroom

"Oh, I don't know about that." The political consultant made small talk with one of the directors before the board meeting. "The Mets have made some atrocious signings lately, I'll grant you, but this guy is the real deal. I was watching him warm up in the bullpen with my son last week, and he can still *throw*."

"Yeah, but will his arm break down again?"

"I'll tell you this: If it doesn't, we'll catch the Phillies by Labor Day."

"Well, good luck to you. You know, the last time…"

"Sorry I'm late! Sorry I'm late!" the chairman said. He burst into the boardroom, closed the door behind him, and took his seat at the head of the long table. "Ah!" he said, spotting the political consultant, who was seated to his right. He offered his hand. "I'm Jack Armstrong. Call me Jack."

"Pleasure to meet you, Jack," the consultant replied. "Richard McGee."

"And you're the guy who's going to tell us how to get the Greenies off our backs?"

"I hope so, yes."

"Excellent! Why don't you set up while we do a few preliminaries?"

"Can do."

Richard retrieved packets from his briefcase, set up an easel, and booted up his laptop. Ten minutes later, he started his presentation.

"So," he began. "I don't have to tell you that if the Smith–Jones bill ever passes Congress, it will be an utter disaster for your company. Some energy companies would be minimally impacted by it, but for a coal-dependent operation, well, let's just say your ability to compete would be quite diminished."

Grumbles and mutterings were heard around the table.

"The House already passed it. The president wants it. The only thing that has kept it from becoming law this summer is that the Senate has been too chicken to bring it up for a vote in an election year. If all of the incumbents win reelection in November, I count 60 senators who would vote for the bill, 38 who would vote against it, and 2 who are too close to call. The supporters won't be shy about it after the election—if they number 60 or more and can't be filibustered, then the bill will pass sometime next year.

"Here's the bottom line: To be comfortable, you need three candidates who see things your way to win in November and unseat current senators who don't see things your way." Richard flipped a page at his easel. The new sheet showed a large map of the United States with three states highlighted in red. "These are your best bets. There are 33 senators up for reelection, and these three races are particularly close.

"As far as I can tell, you generate a profit in the neighborhood of $1 billion per year, correct?"

"Correct," the chairman answered.

"And you have a fair amount of cash on hand for a project such as this?"

"We do," the chairman said, "within reasonable limits."

"Is $70 million 'within reasonable limits'?"

The chairman paused. "We'll have to discuss that. But perhaps." There were some nods and some startled faces around the conference table.

"Of course. And I can come up with a cheaper plan B, if necessary. But in my opinion, $70 million is the price that gives you the best chance of a favorable outcome." Richard clicked, and photos of three senators filled the boardroom's main screen.

"These are the three incumbents you have the best chance to get rid of. Forty-four of the seventy million would go to saturation advertising in their home states from Labor Day to Election Day. I want to buy TV ads during local news programs all day and during most prime-time shows. I want every viewer to see your ads at least a dozen times before they go to the polls.

"In state #1, the challenger—your candidate—is a squeaky-clean state representative, but no one knows much about her outside her own district. She had a cakewalk in the primary—her opponent dropped out after an embezzlement scandal surfaced. I want to run ads showing people what she's done at the state house. She carries herself well, has a nice family. People will like her if they see her. Your money makes *sure* people will see her.

"In state #2, your guy hasn't really done much. But his grandfather was a legitimate hero at Normandy, and his dad was a coal miner. Great-grandparents were immigrants who came through New York with nothing in their pockets—I can see the ad with the Statue of Liberty already. A lot of voters will appreciate his family's story. And we can make him a sympathetic figure. When his opponent correctly points out his lack of credentials, we'll have him respond in ads by saying his opponent 'won't focus on the issues' and 'won't stop the personal attacks.' The incumbent is unpopular. This strategy will work if we have the funds to tell the story our way often enough.

"In state #3, we go negative. Really negative. Our opponent has been in the Senate a long time, and he's had maybe one hundred thousand pictures taken. We have three of them that show him smiling with world leaders who have become... unpopular, of late. We're going to use them to tell a story about the senator putting foreign interests above U.S. jobs and national security. He's basically a free-trade guy, so it will be easy to focus on his votes in a way that backs up our implications. People are angry; they think America is losing its place in the world order. Our polling shows that this kind of campaign will be highly effective this year. Your company also employs about 20,000 people in state #3, so we might even put the focus on you in our ads there. 'We're working hard to keep you working, unlike your senator,' something along those lines.

"Now, if you pick up even one of these three seats, you might be safe from having the Smith–Jones bill pass. If you win all three, you'll definitely be safe, *if* you don't lose any current senators who are on your side. Thirteen of the races this fall are senators running for reelection who you want to be reelected. All of them are ahead in the polls by decent margins. I'm recommending that you put an average of $2 million toward ads in each of those states as insurance. We'll run generic 'Senator Blank, hard at work for you' ads with the candidates in front of an American flag.

"Now, some of you have had concerned expressions on your faces during my presentation." There were smiles, some genuine and some uncomfortable, around the table. "I'd like to point out a few things to those of you who might be...squeamish... about entering the political arena.

"First, all of your stakeholders benefit if the Smith–Jones bill never passes—your workers stay on the job, your shareholders make more money, and your customers pay lower prices.

"Second, you won't be the only ones doing this. Just because this kind of thing hasn't been allowed until recently doesn't mean that you'll be alone. Most big companies will be throwing money into the game from now on. And if you throw in more money than most, well, it's because you have more at stake.

"Third, corporations are nothing more or less than the people that work for them. A corporation with no employees is just a file of paperwork in a drawer in a Secretary of State's office somewhere. People have the right to express their political opinions, and these ads would be giving your workers the chance to exercise their right to free speech in an impactful way.

"So what questions do you have for me?"

DISCUSSION QUESTIONS

1. Is political advertising by for-profit corporations appropriate? Do you agree with the five members of the Supreme Court who voted to allow it, or with the four who dissented and would have drawn distinctions between free speech by individuals and organizations? Why?

_____

_____

_____

_____

2. Is political advertising by a nonprofit political organization like Citizens United any more or less appropriate than advertising by for-profit corporations like the one described in the scenario?

_____

_____

_____

_____

3. Rate the ads proposed by the political consultant on the following scale. Would it be unethical or reasonable for the energy company to finance them?

	Completely Unethical ←——→ Completely Reasonable						
State #1 (positive ad, good candidate)	1	2	3	4	5	6	7
State #2 (positive ad, poor candidate)	1	2	3	4	5	6	7
State #3 (negative attack ad)	1	2	3	4	5	6	7
Various States (generic positive ads)	1	2	3	4	5	6	7

4. Focusing on the price tag of the proposed ads, is it reasonable for this energy company to spend 7 percent of a year's profits toward this end? If so, would you authorize additional money if you thought it would benefit the company? If not, is there a smaller amount of money that you would find acceptable?

_____

_____

_____

_____

5. If you had a vote on this board, how many of the four proposals (state #1, state #2, state #3, and general ads spread among 13 states) would you vote to accept? Which ones would you authorize?

_____

_____

_____

_____

Long-Term Unemployment

At the time of this writing, the unemployment rate has been hovering at around 10 percent for quite a while. A substantially higher than usual number of Americans are out of work. Particularly troubling is this: Nearly five million Americans have been looking for a job for longer than six months. Long-term unemployment is a widespread problem during this recession.

Unemployment Insurance

For decades, the federal government has been involved in providing unemployment benefits to unemployed workers. Most companies pay about $60 per year to the Internal Revenue Service (IRS) to cover the costs of unemployment insurance. The IRS then uses this money to fund agencies in individual states that directly pay benefits to laid-off workers.

About twelve million people are currently collecting benefits. On average, each receives about $800–$1,200 per month of unemployment, or about $10,000–$15,000 per year.

Traditionally, benefits have expired after six months. But during the recession, Congress has passed a series of extensions, and workers can now collect benefits for as long as 99 weeks, which is about four times longer than usual.

Controversy #1

Critics of extended unemployment benefits argue that the benefits actually make the unemployment problem worse by discouraging people from seeking jobs and accepting job offers. "If a guy is collecting $15,000 in unemployment benefits and has a job offer at $23,000, why would he take the job? He'd be working all year for only $8,000 more than he's got now. He'll pass on the job and wait until he gets a better offer somewhere else. With 99 weeks of benefits—and maybe more if Congress keeps extending the maximum length of time—he'll feel like he's got all the time in the world."

Advocates of extended benefits scoff at the notion that people won't look for work as diligently as they can. "No one wants to be unemployed," they'll argue. "Millions have been laid off through no fault of their own, and they are eager to reenter the job market. We must not turn our backs on them in their time of need. It is wrong to leave them without any source of income, and the reality is that, with a tight job market, it just takes longer to find a job these days."

The media has covered this first controversy thoroughly. But a second debate, which is usually held within companies and behind closed doors, has received less attention.

Controversy #2

Since the invention of the help wanted ad, many job postings have carried requirements like "Experience Required," "Must be a High School Graduate," or "Must be Willing to Work Weekends." But some ads now bear the statement "Must not be Unemployed."

Some companies have made the decision to let applicants know up front that they have no chance of getting the job if they are not currently working. This is infuriating for job-seekers who are already facing an uphill battle to find a new job. And for every company bold enough to post this requirement in an actual job posting, many more privately follow the practice of eliminating unemployed applicants immediately.

This practice amounts to discrimination, but it is completely legal. Federal law bans just seven types of discrimination. A company cannot exclude workers based on race, gender, religious faith, national origin, age, disability, or genetic test results. A few states go further than the national government does and ban, for example, discrimination based on sexual orientation. But excluding applicants based on whether they are currently employed is not illegal anywhere.

So the practice becomes a question of ethics. The following scenario examines the issues that cause many corporate leaders to at least consider current employment status.

SCENARIO

Executive Manager's Office

"So that's the good news," said Gene's manager, Linda. "We have a green light to hire 50 people. Things are finally turning around for us."

"Excellent. It will be nice to be actually hiring again," said Gene, the head of the human resources department.

"So before we post anything, I want to run some things by you that came up at our meeting."

"OK."

"Some people were concerned at the…number of applications we would get for these 50 positions. Specifically, there were concerns about your office's ability to process all of them."

"We'll handle whatever comes our way, no problem."

"I know you will. I think I put it poorly—no one is questioning your efforts. We just want to make it easier on you. You do expect a lot more applications than usual because of the recession, right?"

"Well, sure. Lately, we get two or three times the usual number of resumés for the small number of openings we have. Lots of people are out of work."

"Yeah. And with the extra resumés—are you getting any more high-quality applicants than usual?"

"Mmm…depends. Sometimes. Not always."

"Look, here's the bottom line. A lot of our competitors have started including the line 'Currently Employed Applicants Only, Please,' or something to that effect," Linda said. "Some of the execs here want to do the same thing when we post ads for the new openings."

"Oh," Gene said. "Well, I mean, is that necessary? Or, ah...fair?"

"The feeling is that we ought to focus our efforts on people who have not been cut at their last job."

"But, Linda, you know how things are. A lot of people have been 'cut' in the last few years who are excellent workers. And, besides, this will make us look...cold and heartless."

"Well, if you don't mind sifting through a larger pile of resumés, we don't have to *actually* post it in the ads. We can just have a policy of shredding any resumé from an applicant who is unemployed."

"Wow. Is this a done deal?"

"No. Several of us wanted to think it over, and I wanted your input first. We're going to discuss it again on Monday."

"I tell you, it doesn't sit right with me."

"Tell me why."

"Well, look, my job has always been to find the best person for every open position we have. And to do that, I want as many applicants as possible. I'm more likely to find a perfect match for a job if I have 20 candidates than if I have 10 candidates. I don't see that anything should change just because more people are out of work than usual."

"But this is 50 positions. Wouldn't you like to have fewer applications to deal with? I mean, it's not like we don't do this kind of thing already—excluding some people up front. When we interview college seniors on campuses, we require a minimum grade point average to get an interview, correct?"

"True, but that's not the same thing. GPAs are...earned. They directly reflect on the work someone has done. But a rule excluding people based on current employment status...that might or might not have anything at all to do with the quality of the work that they do. I don't like it."

"Come on, Gene. Maybe for some people, but haven't a lot of people been laid off specifically because they were mediocre employees?"

"Some of them, yes. But I don't like to generalize. I like to look at every person on his own merits. And besides," Gene paused. "I think we have an obligation to at least take a look at unemployed workers."

"Why?"

"Because *someone* has to rehire them. We can't have 10 percent unemployment forever—it'll sink us. Someone has to put them back to work. And if we're in a position to turn the corner and expand, we should do our part."

"That's a little abstract, Gene."

"I don't think that it is. If every company leaves the task of putting everyone back to work to other companies, nothing will improve. Real people in my neighborhood are struggling to hang on until they can find work. I'm sure it's the same in your neighborhood. Someone has to help."

"We need these new jobs done well. We're not a charity."

"And we can find people to do them well from applicants who have jobs *and* from applicants who don't have jobs. I'm not saying that someone gets a free job just because she's unemployed. But everyone should get a fair chance."

"Yeah. Maybe so. I have to think some more about this before Monday. Thanks for coming–"

Gene interrupted her. "Did anyone bring up the tax credit?"

"Which tax credit?"

"The new one for hiring unemployed workers."

"Ah, no. What is it?"

"Congress just passed it. If we hire an unemployed worker, we don't have to pay our half of that worker's Social Security taxes for a year."

"Really?"

"Really. That makes hiring an unemployed applicant 6.2 percent cheaper for a year."

"I hadn't heard of that."

"I'll email you the law."

"Huh. That's...interesting."

"I thought you'd think so."

"I'll definitely bring it up Monday. And it's for a year?"

"Actually, it's for the rest of this year. But Congress has been known to extend programs like this one. I wouldn't be at all surprised to see it stretched beyond New Year's."

"Yeah. Well...it might change some people's minds."

"Including yours?"

"Maybe. Maybe so," Linda said.

DISCUSSION QUESTIONS

1. Should a company give added consideration to applicants who are unemployed, less consideration, or the same amount of consideration as currently employed workers? Is this obligation different during a recession than it is during normal economic times?

_____

_____

_____

_____

2. Are workers ethically obligated to take a job if it pays substantially less than they usually earn? Are workers obligated to take a job if it fails to make use of their skills and training?

_____

_____

_____

_____

3. Rate your agreement with the statement: "Extended unemployment benefits discourage unemployed workers from taking job offers and seeking jobs in the first place."

Completely Disagree ◄—————————————► Completely Agree
1 --- 2 --- 3 --- 4 --- 5 --- 6 --- 7

4. Should the government continue to offer extended benefits for as long as 99 weeks to unemployed workers during the recession? If not, what maximum number of weeks would you set?

_____

_____

_____

_____

5. Should the government make it illegal to discriminate against unemployed workers in the same way that it is already illegal to discriminate based on race, gender, and other factors? Or would this lead to an unreasonable number of lawsuits brought by unemployed workers against companies that had different reasons for hiring other candidates for positions?

_____

_____

_____

_____

MODULE **63**

Immigration Policy

BACKGROUND

In April 2010, the state of Arizona passed a new law aimed at curbing illegal immigration. It touched off an immediate firestorm, and it placed immigration policy squarely in the national spotlight.

Because the legal outlook is so murky, and people's opinions of right and wrong will be so critical in resolving the issue, it is essentially, at this point, an ethics question. And because countless employers rely on illegal immigrants as a source of labor, it is a business ethics issue.

Immigration Policy Around the World

Countless nations have struggled with immigration policy, and each has come to its own conclusion. In Germany, immigration is more restricted than average. Immigrants from non-EU nations may come to the country only if they qualify as "skilled laborers" or students. Some immediate family members (such as spouses) of these categories of immigrants are permitted, but only if they can pass an exam showing fluency in German.

Canada has less restrictive immigration laws. It allows for entrepreneurs and immigrants nominated by a provincial government to apply for permanent status. Extended family members are sometimes granted residency as are the skilled laborers and students that German law permits.

In the United States, the debate in recent years has often centered on undocumented workers. An estimated twelve to fifteen million illegal immigrants currently reside in the United States. In the 1980s, Congress passed an "amnesty" law that gave many undocumented workers a path to become U.S. citizens. Some have called for a similar bill to be passed and grant a second wave of amnesty. Others have argued for a crackdown on illegal immigration, which leads us to the recent Arizona statute.

The Arizona Law

The recently instituted Arizona law makes it a state crime—a misdemeanor—to be in the United States illegally. It requires Arizona police to ask for identification if officers have "reasonable suspicion" that the person is in the country illegally.

351

It is worth stating that the officer must have lawfully detained a person for an independent reason before seeking to determine residency. So if an officer sees someone just walking down the street, he may not inquire about that person's residency status. If an officer has pulled someone over for speeding, however, and if he then has reasonable suspicion about whether the speeder is a legal resident, he may demand identification.

Critics argue that the law will lead to racial profiling and that U.S. citizens of Hispanic descent will be harassed by police. President Obama called the law "misguided." Several legal challenges were filed almost immediately.

Lawsuits

Polls show that about 64 percent of Arizonans support the law. But the Constitution lays out many principles that must be adhered to regardless of whether or not they are supported by a majority.

Multiple legal theories for attacking the new law will likely arise, but the argument most likely to succeed is that the law violates the Supremacy Clause of Article VI of the U.S. Constitution. No law may conflict with any part of the Constitution, so if the courts accept the Supremacy Clause argument, the Arizona statute will be voided.

In short, Article VI makes statutes passed by the U.S. Congress "the Supreme Law of the Land." State laws that conflict with Article VI cannot stand. However, the Arizona law doesn't seem to directly conflict with federal law, because Congress has already defined certain types of entry into the United States as illegal.

Courts have also found that laws violate Article VI if they create an "obstacle" to executing a "congressional objective." There is no clear answer as to whether the Arizona law may actually create obstacles to any congressional objectives.

In the end, it is difficult to forecast how the courts will rule on the immigration law.

Boycotts

Beyond legal challenges, many groups have organized boycotts that may, in the end, prove to be the most effective way to repeal the Arizona law. Consider that, in the 1990s, Arizona stopped recognizing the birthday of Dr. Martin Luther King, Jr., as a holiday. Threatened boycotts led the National Football League to cancel plans to hold the Super Bowl in Phoenix. Eventually, Arizona changed its mind on MLK's birthday, and Phoenix was eventually awarded another Super Bowl.

Shifting back to the present, Major League Baseball is now falling under pressure to move the 2011 All Star Game out of Phoenix. The league has not changed its plans at the time of this writing.

Sports aside, groups have begun to cancel conventions in Arizona and call for tourism boycotts. I live in Austin, Texas, and the Austin City Council has voted to end both travel to Arizona as well as business with the state. In a time of economic downturn, any action that places additional strains on businesses may be an effective tactic for changing minds.

Other States

Of course, it may be that the courts uphold the law, the boycotts fail, and additional states pass similar laws. Two members of the Texas legislature have already announced plans to introduce immigration bills during the state's next legislative session in 2011, and many states may follow suit with debates on this issue in the coming years. The following scenario looks at arguments that would likely be presented during such deliberations at various state capitols around the United States.

SCENARIO

Following are excerpts from speeches given on the Senate floor.

Senator 1

"Our policy should be to welcome anyone willing to endure great hardships and come to our state to work and build a better life. Immigrants do the work that otherwise would go undone. Even Ronald Reagan, who is idolized by many of the same people who will speak after me today, recognized this. He signed a law that placed millions of undocumented workers on a path to citizenship.

"Everyone in our great state today who is not of Native American descent had ancestors who immigrated from somewhere else. Immigration has always kept America, and this state, strong. Any law that seeks to 'crack down' on immigration is a law against the principles on which we are founded.

"Furthermore, the proposal you will hear from the next speaker will result in the endless harassment of American citizens in the hopes of finding a few undocumented workers.

"We should pass no new immigration law."

Senator 2

"It is imperative that we regain control of who enters our state. Our resources can only be stretched so far, especially during these difficult economic times. We simply cannot afford to provide social services for everyone who would like to live here.

"I am not anti-immigration. I agree with my colleague who just spoke that immigration made this state strong and helps to keep this state strong. But it must be done through legal channels. It is not fair to allow the millions who wait patiently for an opportunity to come to America legally to be passed over. Less illegal immigration means we can allow for more legal immigration.

"This proposed law will not lead to racial profiling. Officers cannot ask anyone for identification without probable cause, and it will not allow for officers to ask anyone for identification who has not already been detained for a valid reason. We trust officers to be sensible and reasonable. They will be sensible and reasonable in carrying out this policy, just as they are in carrying out others.

"This state should pass a law that mirrors Arizona's immigration policies."

Senator 3

"I see valid points in both positions presented so far. I agree that illegal immigration is a significant issue that needs to be addressed. But I also believe that, at times, an Arizona-style law may lead to racial profiling and the harassment of citizens, at least in some cases.

"I believe that the best way to discourage illegal immigration is to focus on employers. We simply must punish employers who knowingly give jobs to undocumented workers. If the jobs dry up, so will a large part of illegal immigration.

"Companies must face strict, no-nonsense requirements for verifying workers' legal status. If they fail to meet the standards, they must face criminal punishments. First offenses should be misdemeanors with large fines but no jail time, and second offenses should be felonies with mandatory jail time.

"We must crack down on those who knowingly hire undocumented workers."

DISCUSSION QUESTIONS

1. Which of the three proposals do you like the most? Why?

_____

_____

_____

_____

2. Which of the three proposals do you like the least? Why?

_____

_____

_____

_____

3. Would you be less likely to go to Arizona on vacation as a result of the immigration law? Would you be less likely to do business with companies from Arizona?

_____

_____

_____

_____

4. Should a state like Arizona be free to set its own immigration policy, or should the courts require such laws to be set exclusively by the national government?

_____

_____

_____

_____

5. In the end, if a state adopts an Arizona-style law, it will be actual police who will implement the law when encountering actual people. If a law uses the "reasonable suspicion of illegal immigration" language, to what degree are you concerned that police officers would engage in racial profiling? Not concerned? Somewhat concerned? Quite concerned? Please explain your answer.

_____

_____

_____

_____

Health Care Legislation

BACKGROUND

Opening Point #1: This text has often used the point where law ends as a starting point for a discussion of ethics. But, of course, the law changes, and the judges and justices who interpret the law change.

Opening Point #2: The Constitution of the United States sits atop the legal system. No other type of law can conflict with any constitutional principle. So if Congress passes a statute, for example, and if the courts find that the new law violates some part of the Constitution, the law can be struck down.

Opening Point #3: Many important parts of the Constitution are extremely vague. Sometimes, a law is so unclear that interpreting it nearly becomes a question of ethics. The central questions of ethics are: What is *right*? What *should* be done? To a Supreme Court justice interpreting the Constitution, these are often questions as important or more important than any others.

Health Care

On March 23, 2010, President Obama signed a massive health care reform bill into law. The bill was debated passionately in Congress for nearly a year. Democrats and Republicans were deeply divided; in the end, every Republican in Congress voted against the bill, and nearly every Democrat voted for it.

The sweeping legislation carried a price tag in the neighborhood of $1 trillion. (Bill Gates couldn't even pay for 5 percent of it, were he so inclined.) Among many other provisions, the law substantially altered the ability of insurance companies to deny health care policies to Americans with "preexisting conditions," making it more difficult to cancel policies after policyholders become ill and requiring that parents be allowed to keep their children on health plans until age 26. In the end, 32 million uninsured Americans were estimated to end up with health insurance.

Literally within minutes of the bill being signed into law, the attorneys general of 13 states filed a lawsuit in Florida, arguing that it was unconstitutional.

The 10th Amendment and the Commerce Clause

The 10th Amendment to the Constitution reads "The Powers not delegated to the United States by the Constitution...are reserved to the States." Interpreted literally, it seems to indicate that only certain powers are given to the national government in Washington and that states retain the ability to create many kinds of laws within their own borders.

The question that naturally follows is: What powers are specifically granted to the national government by the Constitution? There are 18 specific lawmaking powers, and, conveniently, they are all located together in Article I, Section 8. Many of the 18 items are fairly specific. Article I, Section 8, gives Congress the authority to establish post offices and coin money, for example. But one of the 18 items is not so specific.

Partway through Article I, Section 8, Congress is given the power to "Regulate Commerce...among the several States." This is generally known as the commerce clause. Read broadly, it can allow Congress to pass laws on anything that impacts the economy. Read narrowly, it can be interpreted to allow for much less regulation of businesses from Washington.

In theory, any law that is unrelated to everything in Article I, Section 8, cannot stand because Congress lacks the power to pass laws that cover anything else.

Although the attorneys' general lawsuit may evolve in any number of ways, at the time of this writing, it seems likely that these two parts of the Constitution will dominate their arguments. They especially seem to be indicating that they will attack the provisions of the new health care law that require most people who can afford to do so to buy health insurance.

The argument will likely be that forcing citizens to spend money on something should not be counted as "commerce," and that Congress therefore lacked the power to pass the health care law under the 10th Amendment in the first place. They will likely try to draw a fundamental distinction between a person who chooses to buy or sell something and a person who is required to buy something.

The case will probably end up being decided by the Supreme Court at some point in 2011 or 2012.

Justice Kennedy

Senate Majority Leader Reid, former Speaker of the House Pelosi, a small number of undecided congressional Democrats, and President Obama were the key players in bringing health care reform into being. And now, perhaps, Justice Anthony Kennedy will decide whether the new law can stay on the books.

Of the current nine Supreme Court justices, four of them (John G. Roberts, Samuel A. Alito, Clarence Thomas, and Antonin G. Scalia) have a tendency to interpret laws narrowly and literally. These four may find the attorneys' general argument appealing. They may opine that requiring the purchase of health insurance is not the kind of thing that the writers of the commerce clause had in mind and that Congress went beyond the powers granted to it by the Constitution.

Four other justices (Ruth Bader Ginsburg, Elena Kagan, Sonia Sotomayor, and Stephen G. Breyer) have a tendency to interpret laws broadly. They will almost certainly think that the Constitution allows for a law like the one on health care.

That leaves Justice Kennedy, who is a moderate justice and who is the "swing voter" in many Supreme Court cases that are decided by a 5–4 vote. Might Kennedy be persuaded? It is fair to say that his opinion of what is right, and, more specifically, his opinion of what kinds of things count as "commerce," might be the key to the case.

As always, the following scenario is fictional. The Supreme Court gym does exist, though, and is directly above the main chambers.

SCENARIO

The Supreme Court

Justice Kennedy rubbed his eyes and looked at his clock. *9:00 PM already,* he thought. He took note of the quiet in his office. He tapped his pen on a legal pad several times, then tore off the top sheet, wadded it into a ball, and threw it in the garbage. Waiting for a moment, he threw the entire notepad after it. *Time for a break,* he thought. He left his second floor office, closed the door behind him, and made his way to the elevator.

When it arrived, he entered and pushed "5." He watched the numbers change as the elevator rose past the clerks' offices and dining room on the third floor, the library on the fourth floor, and arrived at the fifth floor with a soft *ding!* "Fifth floor, highest court in the land," Kennedy said quietly to himself, smiling. He emerged from the elevator and headed for a door that had a sign reading:

**Playing Basketball and Weightlifting are PROHIBITED While Court is in Session
DO NOT ASSUME THAT COURT IS OVER!**

As Kennedy had hoped, the gym was empty. He flipped a light switch and took a basketball from a rack near the door. He dribbled to the foul line and started to shoot free throws. As he shot, he thought about the oral arguments in the health care case.

Bounce, bounce, bounce…

"Wealthy nations have an obligation to care for citizens, and health care is a fundamental human right," an attorney representing the federal government and arguing in favor of allowing the health care law had argued earlier that day. "The federal government has long provided or subsidized health coverage for millions of seniors through the Medicare program and millions of low-income Americans and children through the Medicaid program. The law currently under attack is no different in its fundamentals than those that have been allowed by this Court for decades."

Swish!

"While caring for all is a noble goal, the government neither has the ability to pay for all things for all people, nor does it have the authority under the Constitution to make the attempt," a state attorney general, arguing against the law, had argued earlier that day. "Overly broad interpretations of the powers of the federal government have created a fifteen trillion dollar national deficit. We owe fifteen trillion dollars already! This law only adds to our debt, and that crushing debt will eventually bankrupt the nation. The United States is in desperate need of a more sensible approach to lawmaking and spending. The Constitution, if interpreted in the way the Founding Fathers intended, lays out just such an approach."

Bounce, bounce, bounce…

"This Court has for decades given broad authority to the Congress to regulate commerce. Health care amounts to one-sixth of the overall U.S. economy. How can it be reasonably said that health care does not fall under the explicit power given to Congress to regulate commerce?"

Clang!

"The Founding Fathers envisioned a limited government. Congress can't pass just any laws that it comes up with. The 10th Amendment is clear: Powers not specifically granted to the Congress are reserved to the individual states. It should be up to Texas to set health care laws for Texans."

Bounce, bounce, bounce…

"It is in the nation's best interests for as many people as possible to have health insurance. If people cannot access doctors, their health conditions become more severe and more expensive to treat. Benjamin Franklin said, 'A stitch in time saves nine,' and his statement has never had a better application than to health care. People need to be able to visit doctors as illnesses arise and not have to wait until illnesses are so severe as to require a visit to the emergency room."

Swish!

"If the government is allowed to require the purchase of health care, what's next? The government has a large stake in General Motors. Perhaps some would deem it in the 'nation's best interests' if everyone bought a GM car. Should the government be able to require citizens to do so? Allowing this health care law to stand sets a dangerous precedent and a treacherously slippery slope. If it is allowed to stand, where will Washington's ability to interfere with people's lives end?"

Kennedy continued to shoot and turn the case over in his mind. Eventually, the Sacramento native approached the free throw line for his last shot of the night. He thought of going to Kings games long ago with his father. He smiled and began talking quietly to himself.

"The crowd at ARCO Arena goes quiet as Kennedy approaches the line for his second shot. No time left on the clock. Kings 99, Celtics 99; this one is for the title." Kennedy dribbled deliberately three times, and the sound echoed softly in the empty gym.

Bounce…bounce…bounce…

He brought the ball to his waist, paused, brought it over his head, and released. The ball described a perfect arc and dropped through the center of the hoop.

Swish!

Justice Kennedy raised two fists over his head. "Nothing but net," he said.

He knew how he was going to vote in the health care case.

DISCUSSION QUESTIONS

1. In general, are you for or against the government being involved in health care reform?

Strongly in Favor ←——→ Neutral/No Opinion ←——→ Strongly Opposed
1 --- 2 --- 3 --- 4 --- 5 --- 6 --- 7

2. Are you for or against the portion of the law that passed in March 2010 that requires most people to purchase health insurance or face fines?

Strongly in Favor ←——→ Neutral/No Opinion ←——→ Strongly Opposed
1 --- 2 --- 3 --- 4 --- 5 --- 6 --- 7

3. Focusing now on Justice Kennedy, what role should precedent play in his decision making? Should a justice tend to decide cases in the same way that previous Supreme Courts have decided them, or should justices take a completely fresh look at legal issues each time they arise?

4. Which of the arguments presented did you find most persuasive? Which did you find least persuasive?

5. If you had the deciding vote on the Supreme Court, would you vote to uphold or overturn the health care bill based on the arguments presented in this scenario?

Turn Your Notes into Knowledge

You've reached a crossroads. Now that you've conscientiously taken notes, you can let all that hard work go out the window and surrender to the unforgiving power of forgetting. Or you can put in extra effort to retain all that valuable information and transform what you've read and heard into a permanent part of your knowledge. Congratulations. You've made the right choice. This chapter tells you how to:

- **Review to Cement Understanding**
- **Recite to Strengthen Memories**
- **Reflect to Add Wisdom**

How do you master your notes?

If you've taken notes thoroughly and conscientiously, you have every right to feel good about your efforts. But taking notes is not an end in itself. In fact, it is only the beginning. Far too many students jot down their notes and then forget about them until exam time rolls around. They leave them neglected in a desk drawer or repeatedly pass over their detailed textbook markings as they move on to subsequent chapters. This is a tragic mistake and a great waste of time and effort. The only way to take advantage of all the information you've jotted down or marked up and highlighted—to master information that you've worked so hard to understand—is to review it carefully, recite it regularly, and reflect on it deeply until it becomes a permanent part of your knowledge.

Review to Cement Understanding

What's wrong with reviewing notes just by looking them over?

What do you gain by conducting an immediate review?

Most students review their notes by reading them over and perhaps by asking themselves a question or two to see what they remember. This spot-check approach may be common, but it's also haphazard. A systematic approach not only makes your review worthwhile, but also enables you to gain a clear sense of how you're doing.

The purpose of the immediate review is to cement your understanding of what you've just read or heard. As you learned in Chapter 9, memory can be fleeting. Chances are that when you were taking notes, especially in a lecture, you were taking in information an idea at a time. You probably didn't have the opportunity to make sure you truly understood everything you'd marked or written down, and you almost certainly didn't have the chance to step back and see how things all fit together. That's where the immediate review comes in. By targeting key ideas with the Q System, you are able to verify that you understand your notes. And by pulling things together in summaries, you gain a valuable big-picture perspective.

Target Key Ideas with the Q System

QUESTIONING — SUMMARIZING — PLANNING

What is the Q System?

The left-hand margins of your Cornell System paper or the outside margins of your text should have remained blank up to this point. Here's your chance to put them to good use. At your earliest opportunity, move systematically through the notes you've just taken or the assignment you've just marked up, and come up with a question for each important idea. This is known as the Q System. Each question you write will provide a cue for the answer it addresses. Figure 11.1 provides a diagram of the Q System process.

How do you arrive at Q System questions for each important idea?

When using the Q System, try to avoid formulating a question that can be answered with a simple yes or no. Aim instead for questions that prompt you to recall key information. Arriving at a suitable question is a little like playing the popular TV game show in which contestants are given the answers and asked to supply the questions. And it's

Figure 11.1

Using the Q System to Review Your Notes

Whether you're reviewing textbook notes, lecture notes, or markings you've made directly in your textbook, the Q System is your best bet.

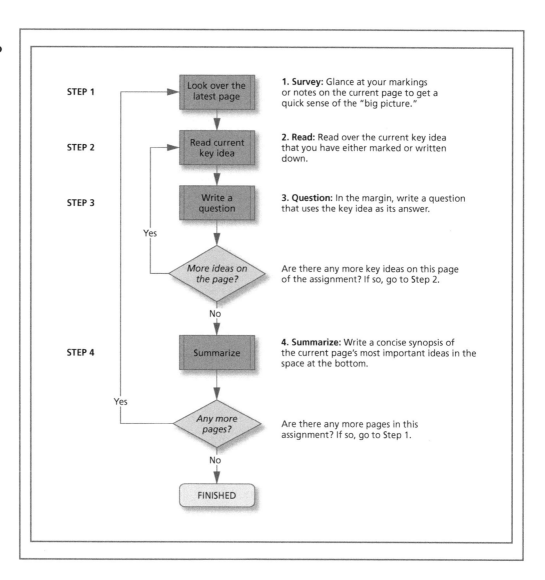

STEP 1 — Look over the latest page

1. Survey: Glance at your markings or notes on the current page to get a quick sense of the "big picture."

STEP 2 — Read current key idea

2. Read: Read over the current key idea that you have either marked or written down.

STEP 3 — Write a question

3. Question: In the margin, write a question that uses the key idea as its answer.

More ideas on the page? — Yes

Are there any more key ideas on this page of the assignment? If so, go to Step 2.

No

STEP 4 — Summarize

4. Summarize: Write a concise synopsis of the current page's most important ideas in the space at the bottom.

Any more pages? — Yes

Are there any more pages in this assignment? If so, go to Step 1.

No

FINISHED

almost identical to the process you went through as you were reading an assignment and converting the headings into questions. The only real difference is that this time you're using ideas from your notes or the lines you underlined in your textbook as the starting point. The goal is to pose a question whose answer most effectively sums up the entire key idea or paragraph. Jot (or type) the question down in the margin alongside the information it refers to. Figure 11.2 shows some marginal questions for a textbook passage.

www.cengage.com/success/Pauk/HowTOStudy10e

Figure 11.2
**Using the Q System
with a Textbook
Assignment**

WRITING GOOD PAPERS IN COLLEGE

What 2
aspects lead
to success?

    The techniques of writing a good paper are easy to follow. You should remember two important aspects that lead to success. First, start work early on the paper. Second, if you have a choice, choose a subject that you are interested in or that you can develop an interest in.

What 3
elements
might make
up a paper?

    Much of your work in college involves absorbing knowledge; when it comes to writing papers, you have the opportunity to put down on paper what you've learned about a subject, and perhaps your opinions and conclusions on the subject.

What's the
key in choosing
a topic?

    Writing is an important form of communication. To communicate well you must have something you really want to say. So if you have a choice of topics, choose one that intrigues you. If it isn't one that everyone else is writing on, all the better.

If not sure
of a topic,
do what?

    If you're not sure about your choice of topic, do a little preliminary research to see what's involved in several topics before you make a final decision. Remember the caution about allowing yourself enough time? Here's where it comes into play. Take enough time to choose a topic carefully.

What form should
your marginal
questions take?

    Repeat the process of formulating questions and putting them in the margin as you systematically move through all the paragraphs in your text or notes from your note paper. It's OK to abbreviate your question, especially if you are short on space. (Figure 11.3 shows an excerpt from some classroom notes with abbreviated questions in the margins.) But be certain there's nothing ambiguous about what you've written down. After all, you'll want to be able to read these questions throughout the semester. A badly abbreviated question may make sense to you now, but it could leave you scratching your head later on. The same applies to your handwriting. Make sure you can read it. You may want to use the modified printing style (explained in Chapter 10) to help you write quickly and legibly.

What should you do
if there's no space for
your questions?

    Properly ruled Cornell System note paper should provide plenty of room for your Q System questions. But if you've marked up your textbook and it has skinny margins, you have a handful of options to adjust for the limited space.

Try the Sticky Note Method

How does the sticky
note method work?

Jot down the same sort of question that you would have written in the margin, but put it on a "sticky note" instead (using one sticky note per question). When you've fin-

Figure 11.3
**Using the Q System
with Classroom Notes**

Sept. 10 (Mon.) – History 101 –
Prof. A. Newhall

A. Some facts about Alaska

Who purchased Alaska?	William H. Seward, Sec. of State –
When? Cost?	fr. Russia in 1867 – $7,200,000.
Rough dimensions of	Size – mainland: length = 1,500 mi. –
mainland?	width = 1,200 mi.
How long is the Yukon River?	Yukon River – 1,979 mi. long
Name kinds of minerals?	Minerals – oil, gold, silver, coal,
	chrome, iron, etc.
How are the forests?	Forests – commercial timber =
	85 billion board feet
Two most numerous fish?	Fish – world's richest in salmon
	and halibut
Name several kinds of fur?	Furs – seal, mink, otter, beaver,
	fox, etc.
What's the highest mt. in	Mt. McKinley – 20,320 ft. –
No. America?	highest in No. America
When admitted as state?	Statehood – Jan. 3, 1959 –
	49th State
Who designed the state flag?	State flag – designed by 13-year-old
	Benjamin Benson

---

ished writing the question, affix it near the paragraph it refers to. Because your sticky notes may come unstuck, it's often a good idea to put a circled number in the margin of your textbook next to the paragraph your question is intended for and to number your sticky note to match, adding the page number as well in case you renumber with each new page.

Use the Bookmark Method

What does the bookmark method involve?

One method that many students swear by is to jot their questions on slips of scrap paper that resemble extra-wide bookmarks (about two-and-a-half inches wide, the same dimension as the margin in Cornell System paper). Use one bookmark for each pair of facing pages, keeping a running list of the questions for the left-hand page on one side and putting the questions for the right-hand page on the other. Just as you did with the sticky note system, number each question and put a corresponding number in the

www.cengage.com/success/Pauk/HowTOStudy10e

margin alongside the paragraph it refers to. When you've written all of the questions for the two pages, you can lodge the slip in the book at just the right spot, the same way you would an ordinary bookmark.

Take Separate Notes

What is the advantage of using separate notes?

Of course, if your textbook doesn't offer an accommodating set of margins, it might be simpler to take separate notes. You'll miss some of the advantages of taking notes directly in your book (see Chapter 10), but you'll be able to carry the notes for your assignment (even stash them in a pocket or purse) without having to lug around the book.

What do you accomplish by writing marginal questions?

Regardless of the method you choose when using the Q System, you will be accomplishing something vital. The straightforward process of formulating questions should provide you with a thorough and immediate review of your material. Although it's possible to do so, it's unnecessarily difficult (not to mention pointless) to "fake" questions for each idea. Ask questions that truly get to the heart of the information. To be able to turn an idea into a meaningful question, you need to have a genuine grasp of that idea.

See the Big Picture with Summaries

SUMMARIZING — PLANNING

IT'S YOUR Q

In the same way that questions from the Q System provide you with a better grasp of the important ideas from your notes, summaries help supply the context. It's surprisingly easy to get caught up in the details of your notes and lose the grand scheme of things in the process. Writing a summary is a sure-fire way to force yourself to think about and come to grips with the broader ideas, trends, lessons, and themes that run through notes like a thread. Summaries supply a straightforward answer to the question, "What is this page about?" This cut-to-the-chase aspect of summaries should be especially handy when you're studying for an exam or doing research for a paper and want to go straight to the key information in your notes without having to read through every note on every page to find it.

The Standard Summary

What is the standard system for writing summaries?

The standard system for summaries is to write one at the bottom of every page. Figure 11.4 shows an example. If you're taking notes directly in your textbook, you may find that there's more room to write at the top of each page than at the bottom. Either place is fine. Regardless of whether you're taking notes in your textbook or on separate sheets, don't pen an epic; you probably don't have the time, and you definitely don't have the room. Just come up with a concentrated sentence or two that efficiently pulls together the key information on the page. If space permits, it's a good idea to use complete sentences for your summaries. This reinforces your goal of articulately expressing what's important on the page. It can be a little too easy to disguise your confusion in an abbreviated sentence. Now is the time to make sure you grasp what you've written down

Figure 11.4
Summarizing a Page of Lecture Notes in Two Sentences

Psych. 105 – Prof. Martin – Sept. 14 (Mon.)

<u>MEMORY</u>

Memory tricky – Can recall instantly many trivial things of childhood, yet forget things recently worked hard to learn & retain.

Memory Trace
— Fact that we retain information means that some change was made in the brain.
— Change called "memory trace."
— "Trace" probably a molecular arrangement similar to molecular changes in a magnetic recording tape.

Three memory systems: sensory, short term, long term.
— <u>Sensory</u> (lasts one second)
   Ex. Words or numbers sent to brain by sight (visual image) start to disintegrate within a few tenths of a second & gone in one full second, unless quickly transferred to S-T memory by verbal repetition.
— Short-term memory [STM] (lasts 30 seconds)
   • Experiments show: a syllable of 3 letters remembered 50% of the time after 3 seconds. Totally forgotten end of 30 seconds.
   • S-T memory — limited capacity — holds average of 7 items.
   • More than 7 items — jettisons some to make room.
   • To hold items in STM, must rehearse — must hear <u>sound</u> of words internally or externally.
— Long-term memory [LTM] (lasts a lifetime or short time).
   • Transfer fact or idea by
     (1) <u>Associating</u> w/information already in LTM.
     (2) <u>Organizing</u> information into meaningful units.
     (3) <u>Understanding</u> by comparing & making relationships.
     (4) <u>Frameworking</u> – fit pieces in like in a jigsaw puzzle.
     (5) <u>Reorganizing</u> – combining new & old into a new unit.
     (6) <u>Rehearsing</u> – aloud to keep memory trace strong.

How do psychologists account for remembering?

What's a "memory trace"?

What are the three memory systems?

How long does sensory memory retain information?

How is information transferred to STM?

What are the retention times of STM?

What's the capacity of the STM?

How to hold information in STM?

What are the retention times of LTM?

What are the six ways to transfer information from STM to LTM?

Three kinds of memory systems are sensory, which retains information for about 1 second; short-term, which retains for a maximum of 30 seconds; and long-term, which varies from a lifetime of retention to a relatively short time.
   The six ways (activities) to transfer information to the long-term memory are associating, organizing, understanding, frameworking, reorganizing, and rehearsing.

or read. If you don't understand things at this stage, there's a good chance that they will grow murkier with time. Make the effort right now to see clearly. If you still don't understand, you have time to get help from a tutor or instructor. If you wait, it may be too late.

The Wrap-Up Summary

What is the approach for the wrap-up summary?

Rather than summarizing each page, you may choose to write a longer summary at the very end of your lecture notes or textbook assignment. Depending on the length or importance of the assignment, this method may be enough, but in general it's not recommended, at least not in isolation. Even if you write several paragraphs for your wrap-up summary, you probably can't expect to approach the level of insight and detail that you gain from summarizing each page. However, if the lecture is especially brief or the reading assignment is a supplemental one that doesn't require a great deal of attention (see Chapter 10), a wrap-up summary may suffice.

The Split-Level Summary

Why is the split-level approach best for summarizing your notes?

The best way to review and summarize your notes is to combine the standard summaries with the wrap-up summary. Start with the standard summary, summarizing each page with a sentence or two. Then, rather than rereading all of your notes to arrive at a wrap-up summary, simply reread the summaries you've written for each page and come up with a summary of your summaries. This two-level approach makes your notes extremely useful and flexible. If you just need a reminder of what a single assignment or lecture was about, you can read the wrap-up summary. If you need more detail, you can go to the next level and read the summary on a particular page.

What else do questions and summaries provide besides an immediate review?

Formulating questions for each important idea in your notes and then coming up with summaries not only provides an extremely directed and effective means of review, but it also sets the stage for recitation, the most valuable technique you can use to help commit your notes to memory.

Recite to Strengthen Memories

What is the role of reciting?

Now that you've added Q System questions (and brief summaries) to each page and conducted a thorough review in the process, how are you going to hold on to all that valuable information? After all, forgetting never lets up. It works continuously to expel from memory what you worked so hard to put there. Luckily, you can bring forgetting almost to a standstill by using the power of recitation.

How does reciting work?

Reciting forces you to think, and this thinking leaves a neural trace in your memory. Reciting promotes concentration, forms a sound basis for understanding the next paragraph or the next chapter, provides time for consolidation, ensures that facts and ideas are remembered accurately, and supplies immediate feedback on how you're doing. Moreover, experiments have shown that the greater the proportion of reciting time to reading time, the greater the learning. Students who spent 20 percent of their time reading and 80 percent reciting did much better than students who spent less time reciting and more time reading.

What is the process for reciting?

The process of reciting is relatively straightforward. Go back to the first page and cover it with a blank sheet of paper, exposing only your Q System questions. (If you used the sticky note method, you should still be able to obscure the text while reading your questions. If you chose the bookmark method, you can use your marker to cover the text. If your notes and Q System questions are in a computer file, open the file and then open another empty file and use it as an electronic version of a blank sheet of paper to cover your text.) Read the first question, and answer it in your own words. Slide the blank sheet down to check your answer. If your answer is wrong or incomplete, try again. Do this until you get the answer right. Go through the entire assignment this way. (See Figure 11.5 for a diagram of the entire process.) Your aim is to establish an accurate, crystal-clear impression in your memory, because that's what you want to return to during an exam. If the impression in your memory is fuzzy at this time, it will be even fuzzier three or four weeks later (see Chapter 9).

Recite Out Loud

SUMMARIZING

IT'S YOUR Q

The traditional way to recite is out loud and in your own words. When you recite aloud, speak clearly so there's no mistake about what you are saying. Express the ideas in complete sentences, using the proper signal words. For example, when you are reciting a list of ideas or facts, enumerate them by saying *first, second,* and so on. Insert words such as *furthermore, however,* and *finally.* When you do so in oral practice, you will do so more naturally in writing during an exam. One of the best ways to recite out loud is in a group study or discussion (see Chapter 13), where there are people who can alert you right away should you answer your question incorrectly.

Recite by Writing

SUMMARIZING

How do you recite by writing?

If you are reluctant or unable to recite aloud, you can recite by writing out (or typing) your answers instead. This method is slower than traditional reciting, but it provides added benefits. Even more than reciting aloud, reciting by writing supplies solid proof that you can answer your questions. After all, you have a written record. And it provides excellent practice for essay and short-answer tests. To recite by writing, move through your notes a question at a time just as you would normally. But instead of speaking your answers, write them down on a separate sheet of paper. Then uncover the page and compare each answer you've just written with the one in your notes.

www.cengage.com/success/Pauk/HowTOStudy10e

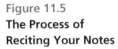

Figure 11.5
**The Process of
Reciting Your Notes**

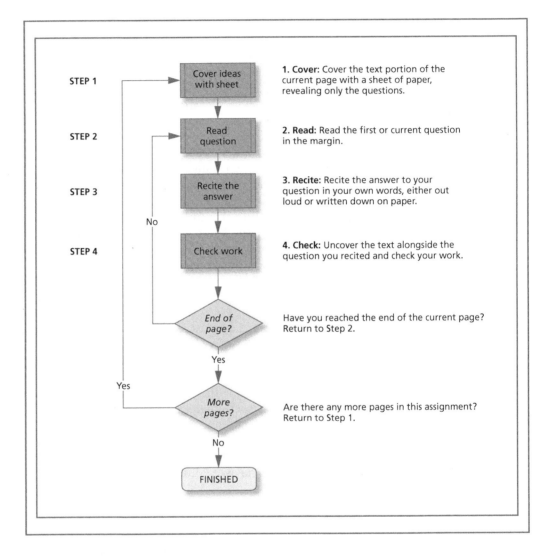

STEP 1 → Cover ideas with sheet

1. Cover: Cover the text portion of the current page with a sheet of paper, revealing only the questions.

STEP 2 → Read question

2. Read: Read the first or current question in the margin.

STEP 3 → Recite the answer

3. Recite: Recite the answer to your question in your own words, either out loud or written down on paper.

STEP 4 → Check work

4. Check: Uncover the text alongside the question you recited and check your work.

End of page?

Have you reached the end of the current page? Return to Step 2.

No

Yes

More pages?

Are there any more pages in this assignment? Return to Step 1.

Yes

No

FINISHED

ect to Add Wisdom

What is reflection?

After you learn facts and ideas through reviewing and reciting, take some time to mull them over. Use your innate sense of curiosity to speculate or play with the knowledge you've acquired. This is called *reflection*. To engage in reflection is to bring creativity to your learning. Ask yourself such questions as these: What is the significance of these facts and ideas? What principle or principles are they based on? What else could they be applied to? How do they fit in with what I already know? From these facts and ideas, what else can I learn? When you reflect, you weave new facts and ideas into your existing knowledge and create a fabric of genuine wisdom. History's greatest thinkers have relied on reflection for their breakthroughs. They make a strong case for reflection as a vital skill. With a technique or two to get you started, you can begin using reflection on your own to master your notes and gain lasting learning and genuine insight.

Learn Why Reflection Is Vital

REFRAMING

What did Bethe say about reflection?

Professor Hans Bethe, Cornell University's famous nuclear physicist and Nobel Prize winner, talked about reflection as used by a scientist:

> To become a good scientist one must live with the problem he's working on. The problem must follow the scientist wherever he goes. You can't be a good scientist working only eight hours a day. Science must be the consuming interest of your life. You must want to know. Nothing matters more than finding the answer to the question or the problem you are engaged in.[1]

What is the connection between reflection and creativity?

Professor Bethe went on to say that students who go only as far as their textbooks and lectures take them can become proficient, but never creative. Creativity comes only with reflection. That is, seeing new material in the light of what you already know is the only road to original ideas, for having an idea is nothing more than discovering a relationship not seen before. And it is impossible to have ideas without reflecting.

What was Whitehead's position on reflection?

Alfred North Whitehead, famous British philosopher and mathematician, strongly advocated reflection. He, too, spoke about the knowledge that grows out of throwing ideas "into fresh combinations." He viewed reflection as taking what one already knows and projecting one's thought beyond familiar experience—considering new knowledge and ideas in the light of the old, and the old in the light of the new.

What was Schopenhauer's point about reflection?

The famous German philosopher Arthur Schopenhauer had exceptionally strong views on the importance of reflection.

> A library may be very large, but if it is in disorder, it is not so useful as one that is small but well arranged. In the same way, a man may have a great mass of knowledge, but if he has not worked it up by thinking it over for himself, it has much less value than a far smaller amount which he has thoroughly pondered. For it is only when a man looks at his knowledge from all sides, and combines the things he knows by comparing truth with truth, that he obtains a complete hold over it and gets it into his power.

[1]Interview with Professor Hans Bethe, May 19, 1960.

www.cengage.com/success/Pauk/HowTOStudy10e

Reflections should not be left vague. Pursue the problem until ideas take definite shape. If you need more information, an encyclopedia or a standard book on the subject will often give you what you need to bring fuzzy ideas into focus.[2]

What is the connection between reflection and the subconscious?

The subconscious plays an important role in creative thinking and discovery. We have all had an exciting idea or even the solution to a problem suddenly flash upon us when we weren't consciously thinking about it. The great Hungarian physicist Leo Szilard came up with the solution to the nuclear chain reaction while crossing a London street. Archimedes arrived at the principle of displacement while sitting in his bathtub. The mind continues to work on concepts even when you aren't aware of it. The process that initiates much of this deep thinking is reflection.

Use Techniques to Help You Reflect

REFRAMING —— PLANNING

What is a big advantage of reflection?

A great advantage of reflection is its flexibility. It can be molded to fit your imagination. You can take it with you wherever you go and make use of it in spare moments. You can reflect while walking from one building to another, standing in line, waiting for a friend, or riding a bus.

What is a drawback of reflection?

But reflection's flexibility can also be a disadvantage if you're unsure of how to get started. This uncertainty prompts some students to skip over the reflection step completely. Although there are no specific reflection steps like those you might find for reviewing or reciting, there are a number of strategies you can use to ease into a reflective mindset.

Use the Silver Dollar System

How does the Silver Dollar System work?

You can reflect on the information from your notes and make it more manageable by using the Silver Dollar System:

1. Read through your notes and make an *S* in the margin next to any idea that seems important. Depending on the number of pages of notes you read, you'll probably wind up with several dozen *S*'s.
2. Now read only the notes you have flagged with an *S*. As you go through these flagged notes for a second time, select the ideas that seem particularly important, and draw a vertical line through the *S*'s that are next to them. Your symbol will look like this: $.
3. Make a third and final pass through your notes, reading only those ideas that have been marked $. Out of these notes, mark the truly outstanding ideas—there will be only a handful of them—with another vertical line so your markings look like dollar signs: $.

[2]Essays of Arthur Schopenhauer, selected and translated by T. Bailey Saunders (New York: A. L. Burt, 1892), p. 321.

The Silver Dollar System stimulates reflection by helping you compare the relative weights of the ideas you have noted. It shows you at a glance which ideas are crucial to remember and which are not. The **$** sign alerts you to the truly important ideas, the "Silver Dollar" ideas that should receive most of your attention. Next come the $ ideas; they are worthy but shouldn't clutter up your memory if you have a lot to remember in a limited amount of time. Finally, the *S* ideas can be ignored. Although you flagged these as potentially important ideas, since then you've twice marked ideas that were even more important.

Rearrange Your Information

How is rearranging your information helpful?

You almost always gain insight when you *reframe* information, that is when you look at it from a different framework or perspective. If, for example, you've been studying countries geographically, you might want to consider grouping them by their systems of government or comparing them chronologically. You may want to group existing information under categories such as "pros" and "cons" or "before" and "after," depending on the nature of the information you are mastering.

Use Software

How can software be used to aid reflection?

Computer software can provide most of the benefits of manual rearranging but without the drudgery and time expense. Some computer programs can take a split second to reconfigure information that would take hours to rearrange by hand. Most word processor and spreadsheet programs allow you to sort a table of information by one or more of its columns. More sophisticated tools found in many spreadsheet programs allow you to take an existing table and turn it into a brand-new table that clusters the information in any number of ways of your choosing. Thus, if you had a table that listed all the presidents of the United States, the years they took office, their political parties, and their states of birth, you would be able to see, for example, all the presidents from Ohio, all the presidents who were members of the Whig Party, or all the presidents who took office between 1800 and 1850. These clusters could trigger any number of reflective questions: What happened to the Whig Party? What other political parties no longer exist? Why are so many presidents from Ohio? Who was the first president from Ohio? Who is the most recent president from Ohio? Which state has produced the most presidents? How does the number of presidents between 1800 and 1850 compare with the number of presidents between 1900 and 1950? And so on. Because a computer performs it, the actual rearranging teaches you nothing. But the questions you ask as a result will stimulate reflection and strengthen your memories by allowing you to remember things in a variety of ways. In a similar fashion, the increasingly popular use of tagging on blogs and other Internet sites provides an extremely helpful means of quickly and dynamically grouping information in different ways to add context, broaden understanding, and aid reflection.

www.cengage.com/success/Pauk/HowTOStudy10e

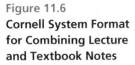

Figure 11.6
**Cornell System Format
for Combining Lecture
and Textbook Notes**

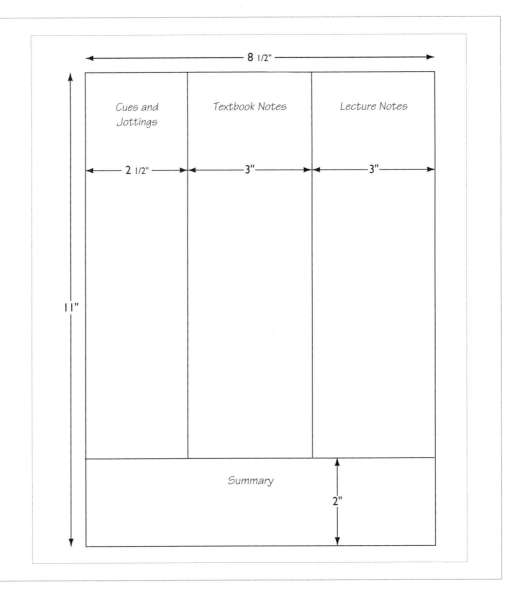

Put It in Context

*Why is context an
important factor in
reflection?*

Few ideas are meaningful when viewed in isolation. They need context to establish them in
a realm that you can truly understand. For example, if you read about a scientific discovery
from a certain time period, consider examining other events from the year the discovery
was made or the place where the discovery occurred. Was this before or after the Civil War,
the Second World War, the Vietnam War? Had the telephone, the radio, or the computer

been invented? Were people traveling by horse, by car, or by jet? These investigations supply a basic background (see Chapter 9) that will often yield a deeper understanding.

Ask More Questions

Why is it helpful to ask additional questions?

In press conferences, the follow-up question is sometimes more insightful than the original question. If you've been using the Q System, each idea in your notes or paragraph in your reading assignment has an accompanying question. Come up with a follow-up to the original question and see if your notes or your text can provide the answer. If not, you might want to dig deeper for clues.

Think Visually

How can concept maps be used as a reflection tool?

Chapter 8 explains how concept maps can be used to work out problems, explore possibilities, and establish connections. These are exactly the sorts of issues that reflection addresses. Take the key concepts from your notes or from a chapter assignment, put them in ovals on a plain sheet of paper, and try numerous ways of arranging and connecting them. If you do, you will almost certainly learn something that wasn't clear to you when those concepts were merely isolated words on a page.

Combine Textbook and Lecture Notes

How do you combine textbook and lecture notes?

Although the classroom lectures you attend should presumably relate to your reading assignments, you won't always see the connections clearly until you can actually place notes from both side by side. Using the format shown in Figure 11.6, jot down the most important information from a textbook assignment in the middle column of the three-column note sheet. Then add any lecture notes that deal with the same topic in the right column, alongside the textbook notes they pertain to. Finally, just as you did with your original notes, use the Q System to arrive at a question for which the textbook note *and* any related information from the lecture is the answer. It's impossible to predict in advance what you'll learn from this experience, but by combining two sets of notes you'll almost certainly arrive at an answer that is greater than the sum of the parts. This is the essence of reflection.

FINAL WORDS

How do a scholar and a student differ?

There's a huge difference between proficiency and creativity. You can become proficient by studying your textbooks and lecture notes, but you will never be creative until you try to see beyond the facts, to leap mentally beyond the given. If your object is simply to tackle tests, pass your courses, and emerge from college with a degree and reasonably good prospects for employment, this book should serve you well. But if your aspirations aim higher, this book will serve you even better. The things that distinguish a scholar from a mere student are perpetual curiosity and an unquenchable thirst for learning. Reviewing and reciting should help you reach your modest goals. Reflection will enable you to reach for the stars.

www.cengage.com/success/Pauk/HowTOStudy10e

CHAPTER CHECKUP

SENTENCE COMPLETION

Complete the following sentences with one of the three words listed below each sentence.

1. You can bring forgetting almost to a standstill with _____.

   summaries   recitation   questions

2. Creativity comes only with _____.

   practice   reflection   summaries

3. Ideas in your notes that you have marked with an *S* can be _____.

   saved   difficult   ignored

MATCHING

In each blank space in the left column, write the letter preceding the phrase in the right column that matches the left item best.

_____ 1. Reflecting   a. Method that summarizes an entire assignment as well as each page

_____ 2. Recitating   b. System that allows you to reduce and reflect on your note sheets

_____ 3. Split-level   c. Used as an alternative to the traditional method of reciting your notes

_____ 4. Bookmark   d. Using your innate curiosity to mull over ideas

_____ 5. Rereading   e. Alternate Q System method when your textbook margins are too narrow

_____ 6. Silver Dollar   f. Provided when you add questions and summaries to your notes

_____ 7. Reviewing   g. Mistakenly thought to be an effective method of reviewing

_____ 8. Writing   h. Repeating key information from memory and in your own words

TRUE-FALSE

Circle T *beside the* true *statements and* F *beside the* false *statements.*

1. T F Most students review their notes by reading them over.
2. T F When using the Q System, try to come up with yes-or-no questions.
3. T F It's OK to abbreviate your Q System questions.
4. T F If your notes are in a computer file, you will be unable to recite them.
5. T F Although reciting by writing is slower than traditional reciting, it provides added benefits.

Choose the word or phrase that completes each sentence most accurately, and circle the letter that precedes it.

1. The primary purpose of an immediate review is to
    a. cement your understanding.
    b. spot-check your notes.
    c. look up words or terms you don't know.
    d. make sure your notes are legible.

2. If your textbook's margins are too narrow for Q System questions, you can use
    a. the sticky note method.
    b. the bookmark method.
    c. separate notes.
    d. all of the above.

3. Adding summaries to your notes helps you
    a. zero in on key ideas.
    b. gain a broader perspective.
    c. anticipate multiple-choice questions.
    d. include questions you couldn't fit in the margins.

4. The traditional way to recite is
    a. out loud.
    b. in your own words.
    c. from memory.
    d. all of the above.

5. One strength and weakness of reflection is its
    a. cost.
    b. repetitiveness.
    c. flexibility.
    d. imagination

Think about the ideas outlined in this chapter and then draw upon your own opinions and experiences to answer each question fully.

1. Both the Q System and summaries help you master your notes but from two different perspectives. Which approach do you think will be easiest for you to adopt? Which approach will be the most valuable for you? Explain why in each case.

www.cengage.com/success/Pauk/HowTOStudy10e

2. Are you already in the habit of reciting your notes? If so, do you recite out loud or in writing? Explain your choice. If you haven't been reciting your notes up until now, why not? Has this chapter convinced you about the value of reciting?

3. Can you think of some specific examples where you already use the technique of reflection? If so, please explain. If not, suggest situations where you could use reflection in the future and mention a method of reflection that seems to best suit the way you learn and understand things.

IT'S YOUR Q

The Q System uses marginal questions to encourage active reading. You'll notice that most but not all paragraphs in this chapter are accompanied by marginal questions. Now it's your Q. Scan the chapter for any paragraph that is missing a question, reread the paragraph, establish the main idea, and then arrive at a question that elicits it. Use the questions in the surrounding paragraphs as models for your own marginal questions.

VOCABULARY IN ACTION

To expand the horizons of your understanding and to refine the precision of your thought, the three exercises that follow are designed to help you grow, strengthen, and maintain your own vocabulary.

SAY WHAT?

From the three choices beside each numbered item, select the one that most nearly expresses the meaning of the italicized word in the quote. Make a light check mark (√) next to your choice.

There are many examples of old, incorrect theories that stubbornly persisted, *sustained* only by the *prestige* of foolish but well-connected scientists. Many of these theories have been killed off only when some *decisive* experiment exposed their incorrectness.
—Michio Kaku (1947—) American theoretical physicist

1. *sustained*	suffered	prolonged	confirmed
2. *prestige*	reputation	charm	greatness
3. *decisive*	unmistakable	confident	conclusive

Voting is the most precious right of every citizen, and we have a moral obligation to *ensure* the *integrity* of our voting process.

—Hillary Clinton (1947—), U.S. Secretary of State

4. *ensure*   underwrite   guarantee   pacify

5. *integrity*   reliability   honesty   morality

VOCAB-U-LADDER

Use your knowledge of word synonyms and roots to connect the word at the top rung to the word at the bottom rung, using the words listed below.

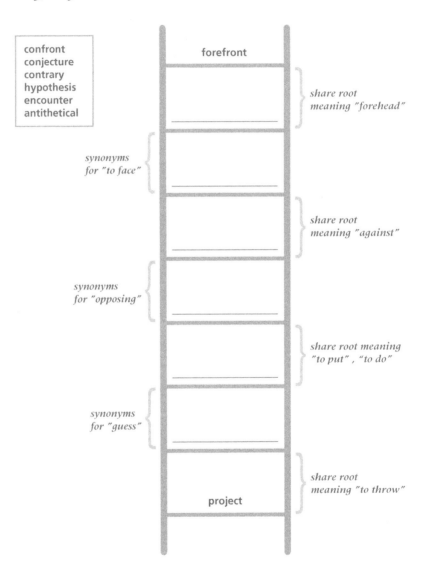

confront
conjecture
contrary
hypothesis
encounter
antithetical

forefront

*share root
meaning "forehead"*

*synonyms
for "to face"*

*share root
meaning "against"*

*synonyms
for "opposing"*

*share root meaning
"to put" , "to do"*

*synonyms
for "guess"*

*share root
meaning "to throw"*

project

backstory.

Here's the story behind a word that figures prominently in the chapter you've just read.

Cue Finding clues for cue leads to Q

cue kyōō *n.* 1. A signal, such as a word or action, used to prompt another event in a performance, such as an actor's speech or entrance, a change in lighting, or a sound effect. 2. a. A reminder or prompting. b. A hint or suggestion.*

Tracking down the story of a word isn't always easy. In fact, it can sometimes require quite a bit of detective work. Some words evolve naturally and often imperceptibly over time. As a result, when somebody finally steps back and asks "Hey, where did that word come from?" the answer may not be readily available. What's more, well-intentioned efforts to explain a word's origins can sometimes lead down the wrong path. For example, the word *queue*, which describes both a line of people and a pigtail, comes from the Old French word cue meaning "tail", the same source that gave us the word *curlicue*. So are the Q System cues you write in your Cornell-style columns related somehow to the French word for tail? That's doubtful, although some word experts have tried hard to make the connection. A more likely explanation comes from sixteenth century theater where actors would mark the margins of their scripts to indicate the places in the play where they were supposed to deliver their lines. Instead of drawing a line or an arrow, they would add the letter Q (or sometimes "qu") to the spots when it was their time to do the talking. Why a Q? Word detectives suggest that these marginal Qs were abbreviations for the Latin word *quando* meaning "when." And when the time came to refer to this Q mark in print, writers as well known as William Shakespeare and Henry Fielding started spelling it *cue*.**

* Adapted from "cue." *The American Heritage Dictionary of the English Language*, 4th ed. Boston: Houghton Mifflin, 2000. http://dictionary.reference.com/browse/cue (accessed June 4, 2009).
** Based on information from "cue." *The American Heritage Dictionary of the English Language*, 4th ed. Boston: Houghton Mifflin, 2000. http://dictionary.reference.com/browse/cue (accessed June 4, 2009).;"cue." *Online Etymology Dictionary*. Douglas Harper, Historian. http://www.etymonline.com/index.php?search=cue (accessed June 4, 2009).; "cue, n" *Oxford English Dictionary*, 2nd ed. 20 vols. Oxford: Oxford University Press, 1989.; "cue, n²" *OED Online*. Oxford University Press. http://sc-www2.santacruzpl.org:2062/cgi/entry/50055417 (accessed Jun 4, 2009).